The Financial Times Guide to Business Start Up 2012

FT Prentice Hall

FINANCIAL TIMES

In an increasingly competitive world, we believe it's quality of thinking that will give you the edge – an idea that opens new doors, a technique that solves a problem, or an insight that simply makes sense of it all. The more you know, the smarter and faster you can go.

That's why we work with the best minds in business and finance to bring cutting-edge thinking and best learning practice to a global market.

Under a range of leading imprints, including *Financial Times Prentice Hall*, we create world-class print publications and electronic products bringing our readers knowledge, skills and understanding, which can be applied whether studying or at work.

To find out more about Pearson Education publications, or tell us about the books you'd like to find, you can visit us at **www.pearson.com/uk**

The Financial Times Guide to Business Start Up 2012

Sara Williams

25th edition

Financial Times
Prentice Hall
is an imprint of

Harlow, England • London • New York • Boston • San Francisco • Toronto • Sydney • Singapore • Hong Kong
Tokyo • Seoul • Taipei • New Delhi • Cape Town • Madrid • Mexico City • Amsterdam • Munich • Paris • Milan

PEARSON EDUCATION LIMITED

Edinburgh Gate
Harlow CM20 2JE
Tel: +44 (0)1279 623623
Fax: +44 (0)1279 431059
Website: www.pearson.com/uk

The Financial Times Guide to Business Start Up was previously published as the *Lloyds TSB Small Business Guide*

First published by Penguin Books 1987–2000
Fifteenth to eighteenth editions published by Vitesse Media plc 2001–2004
Nineteenth to twenty-fourth editions published by Pearson Education 2006–2010
Twenty-fifth edition published by Pearson Education 2011

© Sara Williams 1987–2002
© Vitesse Media plc 2003–2011

ISBN: 978-0-273-76199-0

British Library Cataloguing-in-Publication Data
A catalogue record for this book can be obtained from the British Library

Library of Congress Cataloging-in-Publication Data
A catalog record for this book is available from the Library of Congress

10 9 8 7 6 5 4 3 2 1
15 14 13 12 11

Typeset in 9pt Stone Serif by 3
Printed and bound in Great Britain by Ashford Colour Press Ltd, Gosport

Contents

* An asterisk after the name of an organization or source in the text indicates that contact details are given in the References section.

Acknowledgements

The number of people who have helped me produce this comprehensive guide continues to grow. My debt to those who commented and supplied information for the original edition remains enormous; they helped me to improve the quality and content of the advice it contains to help you get new enterprises up and running, and keep them that way. For the current edition, the seventh published by Pearson as *The Financial Times Guide to Business Start Up* but the twenty-fifth since it was first published as the *Lloyds TSB Small Business Guide*, the checking and updating was carried out with remarkable efficiency by Jonquil Lowe. I'd also like to thank all the team at Pearson Education for the work they have done in publishing the guide so successfully under its new title.

If you have any comments on the guide, please e-mail smallbusiness @vitessemedia.co.uk.

Note

I have taken every care and effort to check the information and advice in this guide. Nevertheless, with a book as comprehensive as this one the odd slip may occur. Unfortunately, I regret that I cannot be responsible for any loss that you may suffer as a result of any omission or inaccuracy.

Updates and further information

Free updates throughout the year!

The Financial Times Guide to Business Start Up went to press in September, but you can keep up to date with the latest news, economic trends and regulatory developments affecting new and established small businesses by regularly logging on to the web site *www.smallbusiness.co.uk*.

The site also includes a huge range of tips, ideas and links to useful services across the following channels:

- Start a business
- Small business finance
- Employing staff
- Business banking
- Technology in business
- Legal advice
- Office and homeworking
- Sales and marketing
- Franchise directory
- Women in business
- Business insights

Log on to *www.smallbusiness.co.uk* – the resource for *your* business's success.

1

You and your ideas

As a way of earning a living, running your own business has two distinctive features. The first is that you do not submit yourself to a selection process; there is not, as there is with a job as an employee, a sifting carried out of possible applicants for a vacancy. There is no personnel manager wielding a battery of psychological tests or cunning interview questions to test your suitability for the job or the level of skills you have acquired.

You are the sole arbiter of your fitness to start and run your own business. This puts a very heavy responsibility on your self-knowledge, because without a doubt not everyone is suited to being an entrepreneur or being self-employed. The only external check on your fitness to found a business might occur if you need to raise money; in this case, a bank manager or other lender or investor judges you. But by the time you reach this stage, you may already have committed time and money to your project.

The answer to the dilemma of this self-selection process is self-analysis: know thyself. Additional insight can be provided by the opinion of colleagues, friends or family. But this can be fraught with emotional problems. Those you ask for an opinion may feel under pressure to give a favourable view for fear of offending. If an unbiased view cannot be expected, do not seek an opinion at all. Later in this book (p. 56), there is a checklist that you (and others) can use to carry out an assessment of your character and abilities. This should provide some assistance in answering the question 'Am I the right sort of person to succeed in my own business?' This chapter describes the type of person who makes the break. Some people talk over a number of years of running their own show but never take the ultimate step. Why do some people break the mould, while others only dream of it?

The second unusual characteristic of starting your own business to create your own income is that you decide what type of business it is and what market you will be selling to.

While you can select a salaried job in a firm of a particular size or selling to a particular market, you are restricted by the vacancies that are available. When it comes to establishing a business, in theory, the world is your oyster. A well-run business should succeed in any market. In practice, however, you can make success more likely by choosing your product and market carefully.

What is in this chapter?

The first section – **you** – focuses on individual characteristics and tries to answer these questions:

- who are you? (p. 3).
- what do you want? (p. 4).
- what will it be like? (p. 5).
- why will you succeed? (p. 7).
- why will you fail? (p. 8).
- how big a business? (p. 8).

The second section – **your ideas** – focuses on the business and your choice of business idea:

- what are your skills? (p. 10).
- which is the best market? (p. 10).
- no ideas at all? (p. 11).
- defining your ideas (p. 11).

You

The greatest determinant of the success of your business is you, your character and skills. This you must believe if your business is to have any chance of prospering. The type of person who blames external factors for failure and believes that their own decisions have little impact on the course of future events is not suited to building a business.

Who are you?

How frequently do you overhear, or partake in, conversations that run along the following lines: 'In a couple of years I would like to start off on my own if I can', 'I would love to have my own business but my financial commitments mean that I can't take the risk', or some other variant? Quite a number of people dream of running their own show, but not all take the plunge.

In some ways, it is hardly surprising that entrepreneurial dreamers are slow to take concrete steps towards making their business a reality. Lying ahead of them, maybe for a number of years, is the unknown: financial insecurity, long working hours, long-term financial obligations and, at the end of it all, possible failure. What is different about those who jump and those who only talk?

The conventional image of an entrepreneur is of a strong-minded, positive risk-taker with a sense of destiny, seizing the ever-present opportunities. Well, this may be a reasonably close approximation of some successful entrepreneurs and you may be that sort of person, but this still does not explain why you are starting your own business and why now. There are many people like this who stay employees for the rest of their lives; and many more who start a business 'accidentally' but make a great success of it.

One plausible explanation for why some start a business and others do not is that those who go solo have received a rude shock to their lives. Their previously cosy existence has been disrupted. In 2010, a survey for the firm Opal found that only 12 per cent of new entrepreneurs had planned to go into business. Thirty-six per cent had started up because of redundancy, a fifth due to a cut in hours and 15 per cent because of a pay cut. There are plenty of other reasons that may sway you towards starting a business, for example: being sacked, not being promoted as expected, having your ideas at work rejected, feeling undermined, having a new boss foisted on you, being transferred to a different job or location, retiring but finding you need extra money, reaching a milestone age and feeling you have yet to achieve anything worthwhile, or realizing that corporate life does not provide the security or sense of worth that perhaps it did 30 or so years ago. Another catalyst could be seeing a friend or colleague in similar circumstances to you successfully making the break into self-employment.

If you have experienced one of these shocks, the comfortable niche in life that you have created for yourself may suddenly feel restrictive and unsatisfactory. Your response may be to try to seize control of your own life by creating your own job.

Obviously, this shock theory does not explain everyone's decision. There are those for whom starting on their own is a positive, not a negative, move. Some have mapped out their lives to include starting their own business. There are others for whom being an entrepreneur seems commonplace, because most of their family are either self-employed or have started a business. But there is no doubt that the proverbial kick up the backside is the starting point for many a new venture.

Government statistics show that there were 2.3 million active businesses in the UK in 2009, which is 16,000 more than in the previous year. It's easy to see why running your own business is popular: the threat to job security following the 'credit crunch' and fragile economy; the need for many older people to supplement their pensions; the opportunities created by the Internet for online businesses; the attractions of working from home or flexible (even if long) hours as a way of achieving work–life balance; enterprise education in schools; and the popularity of business-reality TV shows. Starting your own business may become normal, not abnormal.

But, for now, the conclusions are that:

- not everyone has the necessary ingredients for success.
- there may be many people who live out their working lives as employees who possess the vital skills and characteristics in full, but fail to take advantage of them.

What do you want?

An important part of your self-analysis should include what it is you hope to achieve by starting a business. Motives may range from achieving monetary gain to enhancing status, to establishing a comfortable working environment, to combining work and home responsibilities. You could have a combination of business and personal objectives. It may be a helpful exercise to note what your objectives are under the following headings, which are not exhaustive:

- *money*: how much? when? in what form? as much as possible? enough to live on?
- *working hours*: number of hours? amount of holiday? flexibility?
- *risks*: like a gamble? only low risk acceptable? prefer calculated risks?
- *stress*: looking for lower levels of stress? can cope with stress?
- *type of work*: want to be able to do the work you like? want to choose which work to do and which work to leave for others? want to

concentrate on what you are good at? feel your skills are being wasted? want to achieve your full potential?

■ *independence*: fed up with being told what to do? no longer wish to explain your actions to your superiors? think you can do better?

■ *achievement*: want to have the feeling of satisfaction that building your own business can bring? like to set yourself standards to achieve? to see if you can do it where others fail?

■ *power*: looking for the sense of power that being the boss can give? want to enhance your reputation or status? want to do better than someone else?

■ *personal relations*: want to get away from the problems of having to coexist amicably with others? prefer the feeling of isolation? happier on your own, away from irritating workmates?

■ *any other objectives*?

Once you have drawn up a list of objectives that you hope to achieve from being your own boss, you need to assess how realistic these are. A number you will find fit ideally with the notion of being self-employed; others will be quite contradictory. Part of your self-analysis should be to see how good or how bad a match your objectives are to the reality.

What will it be like?

Most probably the answer is much worse than you can imagine. There are a few people who start out and find the whole operation flows smoothly from the beginning; there are others who pretend everything is going well, while the reality is quite different; and there are others who openly admit how hard it is. One of the more dispiriting aspects is that while you may expect hard work for one or two years, it could continue for several.

The government publishes survival rates for new businesses in the UK. The data show that, after two years, around one in five new businesses has failed. After three years, three out of ten have ceased trading and fewer than half are still in business after five years. Taking advice, such as counselling or training, is likely to improve your chance of success – research suggests you are 20 per cent more likely to still be in business after 2½ years if you have taken advice at the outset.

If you manage to survive, life will not always be easy. Your business life may follow this pattern:

■ *money*: your income can prove to be a problem. At the outset, if not later on, you may find you cannot draw as much income from your business as you would like. Initially, you will need extra funds to fall back on; it can be very helpful if you have a spouse or partner who is earning.

- *working hours*: surveys show that nearly two-thirds of self-employed entrepreneurs and bosses running their own companies regularly use weekends to catch up on the paperwork and admin tasks that inevitably go with running a business. On average they work 55 hours a week, and three-quarters say they have to work even when ill. Dealing with 'red tape' averages about five hours a week. While, in theory, you can choose your working hours and be flexible, in practice you may find that you work all the hours possible. If your business is not going well, you will need dedication, drive and energy to overcome problems; even if the business starts off well, you may still find you cannot turn your back on it, because you want to make as much money as possible in case things start going wrong! You cannot win: until your business is well established you need to work long hours.

- *risks*: a gamble is an unlikely basis for a successful business; but if you only want to pursue low-risk ventures, you may be short of ideas to follow up. You stand the best chance if you are prepared to take calculated risks that allow you to make a sound estimate of the chances of success.

- *stress*: come what may, running your own business is a very stressful experience. You need to be able to cope with it or to seek advice on ways of overcoming it. Stress is not only caused by business problems; it may also occur in your domestic life as a result of allowing the business to overwhelm you. Your spouse/partner and close members of your family need to be very supportive and be prepared for what is to come.

- *type of work*: you need to be a jack of all trades. Unless you are forming a partnership or hope to raise sufficient funds to allow you to employ someone who can complement your own skills, you will find you act as salesperson, technical expert, accountant, administrator or whatever. The wider the range of skills you possess, the greater your chance of success. Be honest about what you can do well and what you do badly. If there are gaps, consider being trained in the area of inadequacy (see Chapter 3, 'A spot of coaching') or try to make sure you can afford expert assistance.

- *independence*: you remain totally independent in your business decisions only if you never borrow or raise money. Once you have done that, you may find that you have to explain your actions, although not usually on a day-to-day basis.

■ *achievement*: founding and controlling a successful business can yield a tremendous sense of achievement, but what happens if there are failures? What would be your reaction? To be a successful business manager, you need to be able to deal with failure. You must be able to accept failure without finding the effect devastating and yet to draw all the lessons possible from it, so that in future you will not make a similar mistake and your performance will be improved.

■ *power*: power can be a destructive influence in a business. There is no problem if you are a sole trader, but once you begin employing staff, you are trying to operate your business through others. Should the desire for power lead you to try to control employees in a way that is counterproductive for their work performance, your power will be a negative influence on the success of your business. Managing people properly is more important.

■ *personal relations*: one of the advantages of running your own show is that you select the people who work for you, and (provided you do not discriminate unlawfully – see Chapter 21, 'Your rights and duties as an employer') if you do not like them you do not need to employ them. But if you find it difficult to associate in a friendly manner with most people, you are unlikely to be a successful owner-manager. You need to be able to establish good relations with suppliers and customers, as well as with those you employ.

Why will you succeed?

The conventional view is that your business is more likely to be successful if it fulfils three criteria:

1 The people involved realistically assess their strengths and weaknesses and try to overcome shortcomings. This could apply to you alone if your business is as a sole trader. Or, if it is on a larger scale, it means you as the leading figure plus the rest of your management team should be balanced and with no obvious lack of skills. The quality of the management (you and others) is the most important criterion.
2 The idea and the market for it has the necessary growth potential and you have experience in that market.
3 Financing is sufficient to cover the shortfall of working capital (p. 319), especially in the early days.

If you cannot fulfil these criteria at the moment, do not accept defeat; you may be able to do so in the future. Most of the processes can be learned and acquired if your personality allows for realistic self-assessment. At this stage in the chapter, you should already have some self-knowledge about your strengths and weaknesses as an owner-manager. In Chapter 5, 'Are you sure?', the information is drawn together in a checklist (p. 56), which you can use as a quick test of where you stand.

Why will you fail?

You will fail if your operation does not match up well to the three criteria mentioned above. But some more specific problems are:

- overestimating sales and underestimating how long to achieve them.
- underestimating costs.
- failing to control costs ruthlessly.
- losing control over cash, that is, carrying too much stock, allowing customers too long to pay, paying suppliers too promptly.
- failing to identify your market because of inadequate market research.
- failing to adapt your product to meet customer needs and wants and failing to retain customers.
- lacking sufficient skills in one of the following areas: selling and marketing, financial, production, technical.
- failing to build a team that is compatible and complementary, if your business is on a larger scale.
- taking unnecessary risks.
- underpricing.

Many of these causes of failure are a result of lack of skills. Running your own business does not mean you have to be an expert at everything, but you do have to appreciate the importance of all these aspects so that you can control your business properly. Try to acquire an appreciation of the crucial factors to watch out for by seeking training or advice from others in those areas in which you are weak. Use this book as a starting point. If more help is needed, there are training courses and advice agencies (pp. 29, 32).

How big a business?

One factor to consider at an early stage is which track you are in – the fast-growth, medium-growth or slow-growth lane. You may know, from the assessment of your skills and character, that the most you aspire to is being a one-person business, pottering along steadily, making a good income for yourself. Or your analysis may convince you that, with the right funds and the right management team, you have the potential to look for swift growth. Your plans about raising money are determined by this consideration.

Your ideas

Frequently, the reason given for failing to take the step and start on your own is that you lack an idea of what you can produce and sell. This may be because there is a misconception about what is needed for a business to be successful. Your idea does not have to be novel, original or revolutionary. If it is, it may be helpful but, equally, it could be a hindrance. Trying to sell a product or service that has not been available previously can be an uphill struggle. Being first is not always best. The first to offer such a product has to educate a market and possibly establish a distribution structure. The second or third into a market can capitalize on all the effort and investment made by their predecessors. The moral is that you should not veer away from an idea because it is not original.

However, it does not follow that you can offer something identical to another business. If you do, how can the potential customer choose? It could only be on the basis of price (p. 180), which suggests that you will struggle to make a profit unless you can sell in volume. The ideal product or service to choose as a basis for your business is one that you can distinguish from the competition by including some additional feature or benefit that is not available in other products.

If you are starting from scratch, how do you come up with a business idea? The first stage is to draw up a shortlist of two, three or four ideas that you can define and research before selecting the one to run with.

There are two possible ways of choosing an idea:

1 Using an established skill, product or knowledge; in general, this gives you the greatest chance of success.
2 Identifying a market that looks ripe for development by your business and acquiring the necessary technique and knowledge.

In reality, the approaches must be closely interlinked; your business will not succeed if you have the skill or product but not the market, and vice versa.

What are your skills?

The logical business idea for most people is to choose an area in which they already have considerable expertise. Many self-employed people are simply practising their own acquired knowledge, such as engineers, solicitors, design consultants. Your expertise may be acquired as a result of your education or training on the job. If you have been employed as a manager of a supermarket, one obvious idea is to do the same but on your own. Or you may have worked in the computer industry and so possess considerable knowledge about products, the market and distribution.

Many people also opt to begin a business using a skill that they have acquired in their spare time as a hobby. Obvious examples are the craft-type businesses, such as jewellery making and pottery. The disadvantage with these is that you have not acquired any of the business knowledge needed to turn hobbies into a living. You will not know the suppliers or the distribution network, for example. However, given determination, this disadvantage should not be insuperable. A more serious problem may emerge later: you may have decided to base your business on a pastime because you found it enjoyable, but a few months of struggling to keep your head above water can soon turn a pleasure into a chore.

Which is the best market?

An alternative to choosing an idea based on your existing skills and knowledge would be to research some markets in which you believe there are profitable opportunities. The ideal market to base your business in is one that:

- is growing or is large.
- is supplied by businesses that are not efficient or are outdated.
- has a niche or sector (p. 14) that you can exploit.
- is not heavily dependent on price to help consumers select one product rather than another.
- is not already supplied by products that are heavily branded; that is, there is not considerable customer loyalty to products from one or more businesses.
- is not dominated by two or three very large suppliers but instead has a number of smaller would-be competitors.

In practice, there is only a remote chance of finding such a market; and, if you did, so would many other businesses, which would make it very competitive. But it would be unwise to base your business in a market that does not come up with some of these positive indicators. The moral is, do not be afraid of competitors; they prove that there is business there to get.

A tough economic climate might seem the worst time to start a business but, even when the economy as a whole is under pressure, there are still individual markets that present opportunities. For example, if households' disposable income is falling: people still eat but may turn to 'value' food products; they may cut back on big-ticket items but still buy smaller, afford-able luxuries, such as chocolate and mini-break holidays; and they may go out less so that home and garden become more important spending areas. Firms may cut back on expensive permanent staff but this may increase demand for freelancers and consultants; for some industries, such as debt collection, economic problems represent a boom time. Similarly, when the pound is low against other currencies, this can give a big boost to busi-nesses with a high proportion of overseas customers.

It is difficult to enter a market if you have none of the technical skills or industry knowledge necessary. In particular, if you need to raise money, the decision-makers will want to see some, if not considerable, knowledge and experience in that market. If you do not have it, you have to concentrate instead on demonstrating your all-round business skills and experience, the strength offered by your character and abilities, and the research you have undertaken into your chosen market.

No ideas at all?

If you cannot come up with an idea on your own, do not despair. Try organizing what is called a brainstorming session. Ask two or three col-leagues, friends or relations to join a discussion. Hold it as a proper meeting in peace and quiet, with paper and pencil in front of you. Spend a couple of minutes outlining the sort of idea you are after and what you have already considered but dismissed and why. Ask for their reactions and cross your fingers that some ideas will emerge. A brainstorming session need not last a long time. Probably a quarter or half an hour will be sufficient.

Defining your ideas

At this stage, you may not have focused on just one idea but still be con-sidering two or more. Whether it is only one or several, your next step is to draw up a pen portrait of each idea. Clearly, some of the aspects will be nothing more than wild guesses; you will need to carry out research before encapsulating your final choice in a detailed business plan with realistic forecasts. The brief sketch should define the following points:

- a description of the product or service.

- an indication of why it will sell.

- a description of the intended market: UK, Europe or global.

- your estimate of the approximate price.

- how you think it will be sold.

- a first stab at the amount of sales you can make.

- how it will be made, if it is a product.

- its approximate cost.

- whether revenues are likely to be more than costs.

Having drawn up these broad-brush definitions of a couple of the most promising ideas, you will find that during the detailed estimation and calculation stage, one idea will emerge as the favourite. You can concentrate on developing this one into your business plan.

Summary

1 An unusual aspect of starting your own business is that you make the decision yourself that you have the necessary qualities and abilities to make a success of it.

2 Analyse what you expect and hope to achieve from your own business.

3 Do not underestimate the problems and difficulties that emerge for business owners.

4 Use the checklists in Chapter 5, 'Are you sure?' (pp. 56, 58, 60, 63), to identify your weaknesses and strengths.

5 Use the many training courses and advice agencies listed in Chapter 3, 'A spot of coaching' (p. 28), to help to improve those weaknesses.

6 Do not be dissuaded from launching a business because you do not have an original idea. With the right management and a promising marketplace, a well-worn idea can be successful.

7 The market can be crucial in determining success or failure (rated second most important factor after management by providers of finance). Carry out detailed market research following the advice in Chapter 2, 'Who will buy?' (p. 13).

8 Develop brief descriptions of a couple of ideas before researching more thoroughly. Select the favourite and make up a detailed business plan before setting up the business.

Other chapters to read

2 Who will buy? (p. 13); 5 Are you sure? (p. 56); 7 Timing the jump (p. 72).

2

Who will buy?

By now you have probably narrowed down your shortlist of ideas. You may know which market you want to enter; you may have got your eye on a product that you think has potential. What you must do next is to study your prospective marketplace in detail. Researching the marketplace comes before raising money, making profit and cash flow forecasts, finding premises or any of the other steps you have to take to form your business.

This is especially true if you need to raise money for your proposed business and have to produce a business plan. You will not obtain financial backing unless you can show with confidence that you understand the structure of your market and have a clear idea of where your product will be positioned compared with the competition. The crucial questions are who will be your customers, why will they buy from you and how much can you sell.

Knowing the number of customers is not the only information yielded by studying the marketplace. More importantly, you should be able to obtain information about what your potential customer needs. This, in turn, should aid you to angle your product or service to satisfy the greatest demand.

It is much easier to persuade people to purchase something they already want; educating a market to buy your product if the market has expressed no great desire for it can be a long haul.

What is in this chapter?

This chapter is about market research and how you can proceed to find out about your particular market. But the first part of the chapter concentrates on what it is you need to know, rather than how to carry out the research.

First, the chapter helps you to define the bit (or segment) of the market you are specifically going for, *who will buy?* (p. 14): which are your customers and what are their common characteristics?

The next section, *why will they buy?* (p. 17), helps you to form your sales proposition to your target market. What are the main features and benefits that your potential customers are looking for? Can your product supply them? This process helps you to define your service or product specifically, and in relation to the competition, so that your product is differentiated from the run-of-the-mill.

The third section, *how much will they buy?* (p. 19), leads into how you can utilize the information to make realistic sales forecasts.

The final section, *how to do the research* (p. 22), looks at the nitty-gritty of carrying out the market research needed. How is it done? What sources do you use? Are some more important than others?

Who will buy?

Knowing which market and which product is only the start of the work you need to do before you will be able to begin selling. First, you have to research the market. You are not simply looking for lots of statistics to blind potential backers. You need the details to help you to plan your business strategy.

It would be a mistake to assume that you have an equal chance of selling to every customer in your market. If it is that sort of market, it implies that you are looking for volume sales. In turn, this suggests a market that is very sensitive to price levels and in which it is difficult to sort out one product from another. If this is the sort of business you are planning, think carefully. Few small businesses have the resources to make a success of this.

Basically, you should be looking for a niche in your proposed market that allows you to charge a reasonable price and so maintain reasonable profit margins. To achieve this, your product needs to be clearly distinguishable from the competition (called product differentiation).

The purpose of your research at this stage is to look for that niche. This process is called market segmentation. In everyday language, it means looking for a group of customers within your target market that has common characteristics, tastes and features. If you can find such a group, it allows you to tailor your product to meet its particular needs. Your search for a market segment need not be confined to the UK – extend your horizons and see if you can identify a market segment running across Europe or even the world. With the development of the Internet as a sales distribution channel, the world has shrunk and even small businesses can sell worldwide. Moreover, an international customer base can be a big advantage if UK growth is depressed and can benefit if sterling is low against other currencies.

Once you have sorted out the groups, you must look at the competitive position. Are there already suppliers to that group of people? The existence of competition does not mean that you should not try to enter the market, but it does mean that you need to be able to offer customers some additional benefit in your service or product, and it must be a benefit they want.

For a small firm, a strong attraction of using this market segment approach to sales is that you may be able to achieve a dominant position in that segment. This could mean becoming the market leader, with its attendant advantages of selling more at a higher price (p. 187).

If your business is on a smaller scale (perhaps only yourself or a couple of employees), it still makes sense to look for a niche, because of the advantages of being able to keep your prices above rock-bottom.

There are several different ways of grouping people. You could group people according to where they live, what kind of work they do or what their hobbies are. Other interesting characteristics to identify include behaviour in purchasing. Is price the key factor, for example?

What makes a useful market grouping?

The fact that you can identify a group of people with similar tastes in your target market does not necessarily mean that you have unlocked a source of sales. To be useful, a market grouping needs to have certain characteristics. First, the segment needs to be big enough to give you the living you require. You must also be able to differentiate it from other groups, so that its size can be measured. Another necessary characteristic is that the segment must be easy to reach. If not, you will experience problems getting your message across or supplying the product because of location. Finally, the group must have common features that actually lead to similar buying decisions.

A step-by-step analysis to identifying market groupings

1 Is your target market a consumer market? Or is it an industrial or professional market? If it is consumer, go to 2; if it is industrial or professional, go to 9.

2 Look at family and personal factors. Would age, sex, family size or marital status form the basis of different groups?

3 Is your product the sort that relies on supplying a local area? Location may be an important feature of a group.

4 Look at social class. Could this be important for your product?

5 Can you distinguish groups of potential customers on the basis of how much or how little they use or buy your product? Could your product be tailored to appeal to heavy or light users?

6 Are there psychological or social factors at work? Could the product appeal to those wishing to 'better themselves'? Is lifestyle important? Would prospective customers be likely to 'follow the crowd' or want to be seen as stylish? Could there be snob or prestige appeal? Would the product appeal to consumers concerned about the environment and climate change?

7 Price could be a feature that distinguishes one group from another. Is there an element of value for money in a target group's make-up? Some people go for the cheapest, no matter what. Most customers would say that they want good value for the money they spend.

8 How do the potential customers buy? Local shop, large supermarket or store? Mail order? The Web? Can you create a niche out of distribution methods? Now go to 14.

9 What type of industry will you be selling into? You could specialize in one industry or profession (called vertical marketing).

10 How big are the companies or businesses you are likely to sell to? Would you be interested in government contracts (see box below)? Size can mean different procedures in buying and frequency of purchasing. Can you create a distinguishing product benefit from the need to satisfy large, medium or small businesses?

11 Will one group of potential customers require quicker or more frequent deliveries than others?

12 Price could well create different market segments in industrial or professional users.

13 Will one group of customers be looking for a higher level of after-sales care or maintenance? Could this be your distinguishing product feature?

14 Consider what other categories might apply to your market. Each

market will have its own specialized characteristics apart from the general ones listed above.

15 Now look to see if there is a group with more than one of the characteristics listed above. This could define your target group.

Government contracts

The government has a special initiative to encourage small businesses to bid for government contracts. It has set up a web portal at *www.contractsfinder.businesslink. gov.uk* as a single, centralized source of information about public sector contracts. You can search available contracts and receive free e-mail alerts of new opportunities. Advantages of working with the government include: even with public sector spending cuts, the government is still a major purchaser of goods and services; and the government is committed to paying invoices promptly.

In a separate initiative, the coalition government has announced a new 'right to provide' initiative. This encourages workers to leave their public sector jobs and instead set up their own mutual businesses to provide the same services under contracts with the government department or organization that they used to work for. These businesses could range in size from just a handful of people working together to many hundreds. If you are interested in looking into this possibility, contact the Mutuals Information Service*.

What do you know about your likely customers?

To help you to understand your potential customers, and to help you sell to them, you need to know a range of information about them. If it is a business you are selling to, you need to have information on the organization and buying policies. Investigate the other suppliers to your customers and acquire and analyse information on the products bought by them.

Databases are the key. Set up a database for information about your potential customers and gather and collate as much as you can within the legal limits allowed (p. 175). Interrogating databases will help you to target potential customers more effectively.

Why will they buy?

Before you can answer this question, you have to find out what your customer wants. What are the benefits and features of a service or product that your target group rates most highly? Research is essential (p. 22).

An asterisk (*) after the name of an organization or source indicates that contact details are given in the References section.

Once you have the framework of your customer needs, you can begin to vary your service or product with the aim of meeting those customer wants and needs more successfully than any other supplier. There are a number of ways in which your sales package (that is, your product/service plus a range of other sales features of your business) can be altered to achieve the desired objective. These include:

- *appearance*: what material is the product made of? Does it look stylish? How about the colour? How is it packaged or presented? All these can be changed to match your target customer profile. If appearance is an important feature for your target group, it may be worth using a designer to help you to achieve this (p. 218).

- *delivery time*: if speed or reliability of delivery is important to your potential customers, concentrate on how you can improve or stabilize your delivery times.

- *maintenance*: does your target market look for prompt attention to faults? Or frequent maintenance visits? Adjust your strategy to allow for this.

- *performance*: identify the main requirement – for example, it may be speed, reliability or a low level of noise. This sort of consideration should be taken into account when you specify your product. If it is already past the specification stage, can it be altered?

- *quality*: this is rather an ethereal topic, as quality can be subjective, existing in the eye of the beholder. Or it can be objective, for example the evenness of the stitching. You can create an impression of quality by building up the image or reputation of the product to suggest this (p. 133). The appearance of quality tends to depend on all the variables of a product: appearance, service, packaging, reliability, performance and so on. You might opt to comply with recognized quality standards, such as those developed by the International Organization for Standardization*.

By adjusting your service/product in this way to meet the wants and needs of your target market, you are trying to establish that you have at least one unique feature that your competitors don't. Use this as the basis of your selling message to persuade people to buy. Your target market will buy if you convince them that it meets a need, conscious or unconscious. If your competitors already meet these needs, it is difficult to see what additional benefit your product can offer, but usually there is something.

It would be a mistake to believe that buyers act in a rational way, comparing products and choosing their purchase on the basis of some organized assessment. Even in an industrial market, buyers are affected by a number of emotional factors, sometimes not openly admitted. These can include wanting to be like someone else, to be considered stylish or a leader, or to be liked. Your potential customers may also want the best, a change, or to improve their personal standing. They may be trying to outdo the competition or to gain revenge on another person or business. So, if your product can't be differentiated in practical benefits, can it be distinguished in emotional ways?

One possible way you could think about your target market is to consider how it would match up to the range of cars available. Each car model has tried to establish its own niche, and it is possible to categorize your target buyers by the car you imagine they might buy. For example, if your market is likely to buy a Ford Fiesta, you can picture them as young, wanting something cheap and cheerful and not minding the lack of comfort. If it is a Rolls-Royce, your customers are looking for the ultimate in prestige, comfort and specification. A BMW is an executive car, indicating business success and achievement; the car is stylish and luxurious. And so on.

Once you have a mental picture of what your target group is looking for in a car, you might be able to use this picture to adapt your service or product to meet those same needs.

How much will they buy?

This is the third question that market research should help you to answer. You cannot plan your business unless you have some estimate of how much you are going to sell and when that is likely to happen. You need these data to help you to formulate your sales and cash forecasts.

The level of sales you can make over the years depends on:

■ the market size.

■ the market structure.

■ the market share you can establish (and the competition you face).

■ the market trends; that is, whether it is growing, static or declining.

■ the investment in time and money to sell your product.

You need to be able to forecast how much you need to put in to get sales established and how long this will take. Many business failures occur because this is underestimated. And many businesses would not start at all if the development period was accurately forecast at the outset.

Market size

The first step is knowing the market size. This could be either its monetary value or the number of units sold. Beyond this you need an estimate of the market potential, which is unlikely to be the same figure as market size because it is unlikely that everyone in the market will buy your, or an equivalent, product. Obviously, if you have the figure for the overall market but have decided to concentrate your business resources on a particular market segment, your next step is to assess the size of that particular segment. Even then, this may not give you your estimated market potential (the amount of sales you stand some chance of being able to make over a period of years).

Market structure

This is the process by which a product is sold to the end-consumer. Market structures constantly evolve, and the world economy has undergone a rapid restructuring with the development of the Internet and mobile devices as tools to sell products on a global basis direct to end-consumers. Over the past 20 years, distribution has moved away from face-to-face selling to selling by direct mail, telephone, Internet, mobile phones and, most recently, tablets such as the iPad. A key stage in selling used to be the role of intermediaries, businesses were placed somewhere between the end-consumer and the end-producer. Intermediaries include agents, distributors and brokers. But the restructuring of the global economy has squeezed this sector as a distribution channel. Nowadays intermediaries need to offer more than just a range of products: service is crucial.

The routes for direct selling include direct mail, telephone, e-mail, Internet, through your own web site, face-to-face, in person and retail outlets.

But not all markets can be reached by direct selling and, although a web site is fairly cheap to set up and easy for customers to use, do not underestimate the work involved in generating traffic to your site and then monitoring and fulfilling orders you receive this way. Small businesses may find that selling through others, or a chain of others, is still a lower-cost alternative. These can include distributors, agents, brokers, through an Internet portal or someone else's web site.

If you sell through others, you have to pay them a royalty or commission or sell to them at a lower price than you would sell to the end-consumer.

Market share

Unless you are supplying a completely new product or service, you are going to share the market with other businesses. To be in a dominant position (that is, the supplier of 25 per cent or more of the market) would be very rare for a small business.

To be able to forecast your sales you are going to need some idea of what share of the market your competitors have. You also need information about your competitors' businesses and products to enable you to position and price your own offering. Knowing the market shares gives you a measure of how successful the other businesses have been.

Monopolies are unusual, but there may be a duopoly (two businesses supplying 25 per cent or more of the market each) or an oligopoly (three, four or five businesses dominating it). However, many small businesses are likely to face a fragmented supply position, where there are lots of suppliers and one business is unlikely to achieve more than 5 per cent of the market. This is particularly true if it is a new industry or market.

Measuring market share is one thing, achieving it another. But there are some ways of influencing the share you can seize. On the whole, it is helpful to build a reputation for good, consistent quality. For this to be translated into market share, a second influence is maintaining a reasonable level of marketing activity: PR, advertising, search engine optimization (SEO) if you have a web site, and sales activity. A third influence is if your product is recognized as being ahead of the competition in performance, design or whatever.

Look at your competitors in a detailed fashion. The data it would be helpful to have include:

■ what are the competing products and how much do they sell?

■ how well have they done in the last few years?

■ how is the company organized?

■ how is its selling carried out?

■ if it produces goods, how is it done and what are the facilities?

■ who are the main customers?

■ what is the pricing policy and what sort of delivery is offered?

Market trends

Market size, market structure and market shares do not remain the same. What happens today may be totally irrelevant to what is happening in one, two or three years' time. The usual method of deciding what is going to happen in the future is to look at what has happened in the past and project it forwards. This approach is fraught with dangers. At the very least, you need to adjust the figures for changes that may occur or are forecast to occur.

On a general level, anticipated changes in the economy can affect the buying patterns of individual markets. There may be changes forecast in tax or other laws that will influence purchasing decisions. New information may emerge on the effect of certain items (for example, health hazards).

On a more specific level, there may be changes caused by government or local authority policy. And so on. You need to look closely at your market to guess what changes will occur that might affect the market trends. In any conversations with people already operating in the market, remember to ask what likely changes they think are on the cards. You may be better able to take advantage of them as a new entrant with no constraints from existing products, methods of operating or overheads.

Investment needed in sales

You need to make realistic forecasts of how much you will sell, when you will be able to do it and what you need to spend on selling and promotion to achieve it. Inevitably, if you are starting your own business, you are optimistic, but do not let optimism blind you to the uncertainty of making sales.

If you are in any doubt, a rule of thumb is to double the length of time you expect it will take you to achieve a certain level of sales. In this way, you will organize sufficient funds to keep the business going until you reach break-even. The danger of this rule of thumb is that your business may not seem sufficiently attractive to lenders and investors. Keep a balance.

It might be possible to obtain a more reliable estimate of sales by carrying out tests (p. 26) on a limited basis, though this is tricky for a small business.

How to do the research

There are a number of techniques for researching a market. The ways open to a small business are likely to be fewer than to a larger organization, simply because of money. In many cases, it will be you, the owner, who does the research. The basic research methods for small businesses include:

■ web research, studying competitors' web sites and looking for market and industry information.

■ desk research, studying directories and other literature.

■ interviews with customers, suppliers, competitors, distributors and ex-employees of competitors.

■ tests.

Web research

With a computer and a broadband connection, you have an enormous treasury of information at your fingertips in the Internet. If you do not have your own Internet access, bear in mind that you can now log on at most public libraries, through many community facilities, such as adult learning centres, and at cybercafés. But be aware that government and businesses increasingly expect – or require – you to interact with them online, so investing in your own Internet access now could be a good move. The World Wide Web lets you tap into computers around the world to gather a diverse range of data and ideas. However, there is so much information out there that it is easy to get bogged down. You need to use a good 'search engine' to help you find your way around. A search engine is a piece of software within the Internet that searches for items on the Web by keyword or key phrase. Different search engines are better suited to different tasks, for example:

■ *Google* is rapid and comprehensive. Hone down the very large number of entries you'll probably get by using precise, multiple keywords. While Google is dominant, *Yahoo!* and *Bing* offer a similar service.

■ *alltheweb.com*, owned by Yahoo!, includes advanced search tools to help you to hone your search.

■ *webcrawler.com* aims to improve coverage by combining the best results from several search engines, including Google, Yahoo! and Ask.

■ *www.yell.com* is the Internet version of *Yellow Pages* and lets you search by business type and location.

For a detailed guide to most of the search engines available, including those with a business specialism, see *www.thesearchenginelist.com*.

Depending on your area of business, you may find useful information on government web sites, such as HM Revenue & Customs* or the Department for Environment, Food and Rural Affairs*. You can find links to all government departments from the Number10* web site. Increasingly government statistical data are being centrally produced by the Office for National Statistics* and many previously unpublished government data sets are now available through a new web site, *www.data.gov.uk*. Government information for citizens and consumers tends to be channelled through the DirectGov* web site and information for businesses through Business Link* or its regional equivalents*. However, the government is testing a new single portal for government information and services, *www.alpha.gov.uk*, which could eventually replace DirectGov.

Desk research

The main sources of information are:

- directories.
- central and local government information.
- information from within your own business, if already up and running – keep good sales records and encourage your employees to be on the look-out for market information.
- trade associations.
- the trade press and special features in the quality papers.
- competitors' literature.
- published statistics and reports.
- former colleagues.

Your starting point for a lot of information can be your local public reference library. You will need to organize your research in a systematic way, because the danger is that you may end up with too much information, a lot of it irrelevant, and with no way of being able to gain quick and easy access to the data that matter.

If you plan to sell locally, your local authority might be a source of useful reports and survey statistics. You could also try your local chamber of trade or commerce, although these vary greatly in size and resources.

There are also the trade sources of information. Find out which are the trade magazines and, if they are not free, take out subscriptions. Organize cuttings' files. Contact the relevant trade association and obtain information about its members. Check out their web sites. Use trade exhibitions as an opportunity to pick up literature about your competitors and talk to potential customers about the market, the suppliers, the products and the gaps.

Interviews

The term 'interview' can cover anything from a chat at an exhibition to a brief telephone call, to a long face-to-face discussion in private. The main point is that you can pick up a lot of information simply by talking.

Whether you have started your business or not, good sources of information are customers, potential or actual. If you have access to a list, properly gathered and complying with the Data Protection Act (p. 176), you could carry out a telephone survey, limiting each interview to ten minutes, say. It would help you to analyse the information if you had prepared a questionnaire sheet. On the whole, you will find that most customers are usually ready to cooperate, as it may mean you develop a product more suited to their needs. Carry on with telephone interviews until you begin to feel that you are learning nothing new, because the same points are being repeated.

If you want detailed information, you will find that the telephone is not the best method of acquiring it. Instead, try to carry out a number of in-depth interviews.

If you are researching a consumer market, you should try to talk to the distributors and retailers as well as to the end-users. Most people are flattered to be asked their 'professional' opinion. Talking to the final consumers can be a bit of a problem because you may not know who these are. Perhaps a retailer will allow you to spend a day in the shop talking to customers? Asking people in the street outside the store is another possibility.

If your product is likely to be exhibited at trade fairs for the consumer, spend some time there asking about the market and product. Use a brief questionnaire to ensure that you ask the same questions so that the information can be analysed.

Interviewing competitors may sound an odd idea, but there is no harm in it and it can help you to understand what are common problems. If you come across any ex-employees of competitors, it is always worth a discussion, although you have to bear in mind that their view may not be entirely objective if they did not part with the business on good terms. And the information may be out of date.

Before you start your business, you could carry out some discreet research into how competitors organize their businesses by pretending to be a prospective customer. In this way you can gain some idea of the literature, prices, the way telephone queries are dealt with, selling methods or even how your potential competitors quote. It may seem unfair, but it is an unrivalled source of information and you may rest assured that once you are in business others will do it to you.

Tests

It would be a great help to you if you could test-market your product, especially if you will be setting up production facilities or ordering very large quantities. If you can try out a few before you make the substantial investment needed, you would be able to refine the product, satisfy yourself that the demand does exist and define the likely sales cycle (the length of time from first contact to purchase). To test this, buyers of the trial product need to be followed up and interviewed.

If you are selling by telephone or direct mail, you can test your product and your offer before launching into selling in volume. A pilot mailshot to say 5,000 potential customers can give you a huge amount of information about the likely response and sales.

If you are growing or producing local foods or drinks, you might be able to test on a small scale by selling at farmers' markets or in farm shops. For information on selling direct through these routes, contact the National Farmers' Retail & Markets Association (FARMA)*.

Summary

1 Market research that is undirected is not very useful; it needs to concentrate on who will buy, why they will buy and how much they will buy.

2 It is much easier to sell a product that meets some already perceived need rather than to try to educate a market to buy a new, perhaps revolutionary, product or service.

3 Look for groups within your target market that you think you can sell to, either because no one is currently selling to them or because you can adapt your product to meet their needs.

4 Use the step-by-step analysis (p. 16) to identify a suitable market group.

5 Rational and emotional factors affect your target group's willingness to buy. Research these and alter your product or sales approach to match.

6 Knowing how much customers will buy is crucial to your business

planning. You need to research market size, market structure, market share, the competition and market trends.

7 Try to carry out your research in a systematic way so that it can be properly analysed. Use desk research, interviews and test trials, if possible.

Other chapters to read

12 The right name (p. 132); **13** Getting the message across (p. 141); **14** Getting new customers (p. 157); **15** Building customer relationships (p. 172); **16** How to set a price (p. 180).

3

A spot of coaching

'I don't have the time' might be the instant reaction of a budding entrepreneur if it is suggested that training or asking for advice would be beneficial. At the other end of the spectrum, there may be people who could make a success of self-employment but 'don't know how to start'.

Training, counselling and seeking advice can all improve your chances of success, so do not dismiss the idea. If you have not yet started on your own, try to fit in some sort of training before you do so. If you are already under way, look around to see what training or help is available to fit in with your schedule – and don't wait until things are going wrong. Give yourself the greatest chance of success and consider it now.

There are an extraordinary number of organizations offering training or help for new or small businesses, including local enterprise agencies*, private training companies, online providers, local colleges, chambers of commerce*, local authorities* and banks. However, the simplest way to tap into the vast majority of these sources is through Business Link* in England, Business Gateway* in Scotland, Business Wales*, or Invest NI* in Northern Ireland. These are government-sponsored organizations that offer you a one-stop shop for finding out about all types of support and information relevant to business. All deliver their information and services through a web site and traditionally have offered local, face-to-face networks too. However, as part of the government's spending cuts, the Business Link regional network in England is to be abolished by November 2011. But the Business Link web site is being expanded and enhanced. There will also continue to be a telephone-based national business support centre.

An important source of local advice, training and mentoring is the network of local enterprise agencies* (LEAs). These are independent, not-for-profit bodies that are dissimilar in name, size, how they are funded and what they can do for you, but share the common aim of supporting small and growing businesses. You can locate your nearest LEA through the National Federation of Enterprise Agencies (NFEA)*.

Training courses

Obviously, the main purpose of attending a training course is to learn new skills and techniques. But a secondary purpose is that it gives you an opportunity to meet people with similar problems and possibly meet potential partners, suppliers and customers.

The diversity of courses available makes it difficult to describe an average course. On the other hand, this very diversity should ensure that you will find a course run somewhere that meets your needs and suits your personality, although obviously you do not want to travel too far.

How long is a course?

The length of courses available varies. There may be a one- or two-day taster. Or there could be a series of short modular courses, attended part-time (say, at weekends, in the evenings or spread over several weeks or months). Learndirect* offers a wide array of courses which you can complete over the Internet at your own pace.

What topics are covered?

The content of most of the general self-employment or small business courses leans heavily on the financial side. Topics such as cash flows, business plans and sources of finance, financial control, tax and book-keeping are covered. There should also be a substantial content on selling and marketing. Apart from these key areas, other topics that may be covered include premises, information technology, employment law, recruiting, time management, exporting, and other legal aspects of business and insurance. HM Revenue & Customs* run workshops around the country on tax-related topics, such as becoming self-employed and taking on your first employee.

As well as general courses, some organizations run more specialized ones, for example a two-day course concentrating on finance or marketing. If you feel fairly confident in general about your business expertise, this sort of course could help you to brush up your knowledge in your weakest area.

What sort of training?

Inevitably, with a fair number of courses, quite a lot of the information and training is given in a fairly traditional classroom format. However, in all courses there should be discussion and questions. The success of the course can depend as much on the quality and interest of the participants as on the trainers. Before you choose a course, try to find out a bit about the type of participants attending the course to gauge if it is the right level for you.

An increasing number of courses are trying to introduce a 'hands-on' approach. Your business plan will be presented to a trainer and the other course participants for discussion, suggestion and improvement. On a few courses, there may be an opportunity to present your plan to someone from a bank or other source of funds. This could simply be a training exercise. However, if you present your case well, the bank may want to discuss your business idea in more detail.

Attending a course in person is often the best route because of the chance to network with other people. But if this would be difficult – for example, you can't take time away from business during the day – an alternative is online learning. You study over the Internet at times convenient to you and at a pace of your own choosing. One of the biggest providers of courses over the Internet is the government through its learndirect* initiative, which offers a large range of courses designed for small businesses. If you don't have access to a computer at home, you can study from a learning centre, typically based in local schools, colleges and community centres.

Who runs the courses?

Courses are run by a wide variety of organizations, including training and enterprise councils, local enterprise agencies or colleges of further education or technology. The ideal trainer for a small business course is someone who has had experience of running a business and is a trained tutor. Before you choose a course, look at the backgrounds of the people running it.

A newly launched organization that has government backing is Start-Up Britain*. Based on a successful US format, this is a web-based resource set up by business organizations to provide a wide range of support for new and growing businesses. One of its initiatives is StartUp Saturday*, a series of courses for people new to business or wanting to brush up their skills. The courses are held on Saturdays in the stores of Staples, the business supplies retailer, initially in seven locations but going nationwide from September 2011. Each session lasts an hour and can either be taken separately or as part of a full 12-week course, and participants receive a workbook with information and case studies. Topics covered include, for example, researching the market, drawing up a business plan, financial aspects, marketing and selling. Individual sessions cost £10.90 or the whole 12-week course costs £103.15.

One ingredient for successful business training can be the support that you can get before and after the training course itself. To maximize the benefit from the time you spend, look for an organization running the course that can provide mentoring or counselling or has close links with one that does.

How to find a course

A good starting point for locating courses in your area is to contact the following organizations or use the searchable training directories on their web sites: Business Link*, Business Gateway*, Business Wales*, www.nibusiness-info.co.uk (part of Invest NI*) or learndirect*. Alternatively you can contact providers, such as local colleges, direct. To find out about colleges in your area, contact the Association of Colleges*. For information about StartUp Saturday*, visit its web site.

How to choose a course

1 If you don't know whether training will meet your needs, ask for advice from Business Link, Business Gateway, Business Wales or Invest NI. Alternatively contact the careers advice helpline at learndirect.
2 Decide whether you want a general or specialized course.
3 Try to find out about the trainers. Is there a good mix of practical business knowledge and teaching experience?
4 Find out about the kind of participants for whom the course is designed and, if possible, the individuals who will be on the course with you.
5 Ask if the training is mainly classroom-based. Go for courses with practical emphasis on business plans, especially if there can be a mock presentation for raising finance.
6 See if pre- and post-course counselling is provided or easily arranged.
7 Check the cost – there may be training allowances available.
8 Check whether you can get tax relief on the cost. If the course is connected

to your business and involves updating your skills, you should be able to deduct the cost as an allowable trading expense (see p. 388). If you are acquiring new skills, claim the annual investment allowance (see p. 394).

9 Check the hours of the course and, if applicable, find out the childcare facilities. If you cannot get to a course, check out learndirect.

Mentoring, counselling and consultancy

A mentor can give you *ad hoc*, informal advice on any aspect of setting up and running your business. Mentors are people who have been there themselves, having set up their own businesses, and so have a good understanding of the issues you are facing and the options available. Increasingly, you are likely to contact mentors online and may have access to more than one.

Help and advice on a one-to-one basis is given by counsellors. You could approach a variety of advice agencies at any stage of starting a business. Initially, counsellors can help by discussing your idea, and its strengths and weaknesses, and suggesting ways of carrying out market research.

At a later stage, counsellors can help you to prepare a business plan, including cash flows; you may even find a counsellor prepared to approach a bank manager with you. And counsellors will spend time with you if your business is hitting a sticky patch or if you feel you have a weakness in a particular area of your business and need fresh ideas or guidance.

The background of counsellors can vary a lot. All of them should be able to help in discussing your business idea, finding out about markets, preparing plans and budgets, advising on finance and helping you to find your way around the business world. If you need specialist advice or have more detailed problems, your counsellor will be able to help or will know who can.

For established businesses, there may be a need for consultancy on specific topics: design, marketing, quality systems, manufacturing processes and so on. Agencies can signpost you to consultants and may be able to offer help at a 'fair' rate.

Who provides mentoring, counselling or consultancy?

There are several sources:

1 *Business Link*, Business Gateway*, Business Wales** or *www.nibusinessinfo. co.uk (Invest NI*)*. If you want to talk to someone face-to-face about your needs, contact the organization's helpline or use the web site resources. For example, on the Business Link web site, find the Directories section and choose Business Support Finder. You are asked to specify the type of support you need from a list and could choose, say, 'Exchanging ideas and sharing expertise'.

2 From June 2011, the government plans to have added a new online service, The Mentoring Gateway, which is to provide access to a network of 40,000 experienced business mentors. At the time of writing, further details had not been announced. Check the Department for Business, Innovation and Skills* web site for updates. Start-Up Britain* has also announced plans to launch an online Mentor Marketplace.

3 *Local enterprise agencies* (LEAs). These vary in the services they offer, so it is worth checking whether your local one offers any consultancy services. LEAs operate throughout England and Wales. To find your local agency, contact Business Link* or Business Wales*. You can also find your local LEA in England through the National Federation of Enterprise Agencies (NFEA)*.

4 *Chambers of commerce*. Local chambers vary greatly in size and the resources they can offer. To find your local branch, see *The Phone Book* or contact the British Chambers of Commerce (BCC)*.

5 Other *ad hoc* agencies that may provide support for small businesses, such as Natural England*, English Heritage* and local authorities*, which offer advice and sometimes grants to businesses where this helps also to achieve the particular aims of the agency.

6 *Banks*. Many banks offer specialist services for small businesses and have a network of small business centres or advisers. They can direct you to appropriate counselling organizations and information services.

7 If you are unemployed and have been claiming Jobseeker's Allowance for more than six months, you may be eligible for the New Enterprise Allowance (NEA). This is a package to help you start up your own business and includes access to a business mentor during the planning phase of your business and the early days of trading. For information, contact Jobcentre Plus*.

Sharing problems with others

The business problem you are currently struggling with is unlikely to be unique; other businesses may have faced similar dilemmas. Picking someone else's brains can be a useful source of ideas and advice – if you can find the right brains, that is. One way of meeting other business people is to find out if there is a chamber of trade or commerce or a small business club operating in your area. Try asking your local library or LEA* (some enterprise agencies also run small business clubs).

The aims of clubs such as these are variously to promote the growth of small business in a particular area or field, to keep small businesses informed of relevant information and legislation, to provide a social situation in which business can be discussed, to act as a voice for small businesses both locally and nationally and, possibly, to promote trade between members.

You may also find that there are web sites with chat forums, where you may find useful suggestions if you raise a problem. Social networking sites, such as Facebook* and LinkedIn*, are becoming increasingly important as a way of discovering and exchanging ideas with people operating in the same field as you.

If one of your problems is being too small to undertake effective marketing of your products, you could consider working with other businesses by forming a joint venture or consortium. This is sometimes called a purchasing or marketing cooperative. Contact your local Business Link*, Business Gateway*, Business Wales* or Invest NI* to see if they can provide further information and assistance.

The media, books and exhibitions

Some of the national newspapers devote some space specifically to the small business sector. The *Financial Times* (Saturday edition), the *Daily Express*, the *Guardian* and *The Times*, for example, have pages which include business-to-business ads for businesses offering or wanting services, products or money, or businesses to buy and sell or franchises available – but see p. 85 for how to find a business to buy. The pages also have some editorial. There may be an article on the experience of one small business, but there are also usually up-to-date bits of information, for example about training courses, exhibitions, books and new finance packages.

There are quite a number of books written for small businesses. Some of them aim to be comprehensive, such as this one; others are more selective in particular areas. You could contact your local library, whose staff can be very helpful on suggesting sources of information. The Internet contains numerous sites offering general business advice, including Business Link*, Start-Up Britain* and *www.smallbusiness.co.uk* sites. Use search engines (see p. 23) to track down other sites covering areas in which you are particularly interested.

At an early stage of your business planning, wandering around business exhibitions can give you some ideas and useful literature. These are also an opportunity to speak to some potential customers and competitors. Ask your Local Enterprise Agency* if there is soon to be a local exhibition or check out the directory of events on the web site of Business Link* or your equivalent organization.

Other organizations

There are many trade associations covering different sectors – and you may gain information or support by joining one of them. There are also three well-known small business organizations that can lobby at a national level.

1. The Federation of Small Businesses*

This is the largest small business organization in the UK, representing over 205,000 small and medium-sized businesses. Its primary role is to act as a lobbying group promoting and protecting the interests of its members. But there are direct membership benefits too, including legal and tax advice, information on employment law and an employment disputes service. Members also get a range of special offers for insurance, factoring and so on. The yearly membership is £120 for a sole trader working alone and £170 for businesses with one to four employees, increasing after that on a sliding scale according to the number of employees. There is also a £30 registration fee in the first year.

2. The Forum of Private Business*

This Forum offers members a range of benefits including, for example, employment law guidance, a credit management service, marketing advice, help finding finance and a general advice helpline. The Forum offers four levels of membership. Introductory membership is free and offers web site and e-mail information; intermediate membership starts at £175 if you work alone, £250 for up to ten people, and includes extra services such as HR and finance templates, business advice and money-saving deals; advanced membership starts at £425 for a sole trader, £500 for up to ten people, and adds in networking events; expert membership is a more expensive package tailored to your business.

3. Professional Contractors' Group*

PCG represents the freelance small business community. Its members include professional freelancers, contractors and consultants in, for example, IT, management, finance, engineering, oil and gas, telecoms and accounting. PCG campaigns on issues such as taxation, agency regulations and e-commerce regulations. Membership benefits include professional expenses insurance (to cover the fees of professionals employed during tax enquiries, VAT disputes and so on), access to free tax and legal helplines, contract templates and preferential rates from a range of suppliers. It also maintains a fighting fund to back suitable legal cases to establish important principles in tax and employment law. Standard membership starts at £120 + VAT for a sole trader or company with one fee-earner.

Advice aimed at specific groups

If you are relatively young and thinking of starting a business, or if you are unemployed with little prospect of obtaining employment, or a woman or from an ethnic minority, or an older person, you are often able to choose more specialized counselling or advice.

If you are from an ethnic minority, you may find that there is a local agency in your area especially to help members of ethnic minorities who start small businesses. Many other agencies now recognize that you may prefer to see a counsellor from an ethnic minority.

Here is some information on three specialist national organizations:

1. Shell *Live*WIRE*

Shell *Live*WIRE is a UK-wide community investment programme funded by Shell UK Limited to stimulate young people (usually meaning 16 to 30) to explore the option of starting or developing their own business. As well as being active throughout the UK, *Live*WIRE programmes are now established worldwide.

Through the web site, young people can get free information on all aspects of starting and running a business, for example through an online Business Kit and Library, networking with other entrepreneurs, putting questions to online mentors and finding out where to get further business advice in their local area. Shell *Live*WIRE encourages sound business planning and continual monitoring of the business. It also runs an annual young entrepreneur competition with a £10,000 prize and monthly 'grand idea' awards of £1,000 for businesses in their first year of trading.

2. The Prince's Trust*

The Prince's Trust helps unemployed (or working less than 16 hours a week) 18- to 30-year-olds in England, Wales and Northern Ireland to set up and run their own business. It provides advice on employment options, business skills training, planning support, start-up funding and ongoing support from a mentor. Its web site includes a range of useful guides and a business planning pack. Young people on the programme also have access to a range of free or discounted offers, including, for example, online accounting systems, a legal helpline and office rental.

3. The Prince's Initiative for Mature Enterprise (PRIME)*

PRIME is a not-for-profit organization that helps people over 50 start up in business. On joining its free business club, you'll receive a starter pack of information, a list of organizations near you that can help new businesses, and details of training, workshops and other events coming up. PRIME runs taster sessions to help you decide whether self-employment is for you, its own training events and a mentoring service, all of which are free. It publicizes useful events arranged by other organizations, some of which are free and others low-cost. PRIME also lobbies government to remove barriers to older people's employment.

Summary

1 A great deal of help and assistance is available to businesses in the UK, much of it free. Please make use of it, as it can help you to avoid mistakes.
2 Business Link provides a centralized source of information about what help is available. It is often your best starting point.
3 Choose your training course carefully. Check that it is a practical course with emphasis on your own business plans.
4 Counselling can be a useful source of advice, not just when you start but also when you have been in business for some time.
5 Other business people can provide help and contacts – see if there is a small business club in your area.

4

Your business identity

An important decision to make early on is to decide what legal form your business will take. Whatever you decide is not irrevocable, but it will take time and money to undo mistakes. You can choose between:

- sole trader.
- limited company.
- partnership (or limited liability partnership).
- cooperative (mutual organization).

If you want to work on your own, your choice is either sole trader or limited company. If you want to work with others, your choice is between partnership, limited liability partnership, limited company or cooperative (or a sole trader if you intend to employ others, rather than work with them).

The form you choose can hinge on emotional factors, as well as objective ones. If you choose a cooperative as your form, this may be because of political, social or ethical reasons. If you choose a partnership, this may be because you have a close colleague with whom you work well. However, the choice between a sole trader and limited company will probably be made for monetary reasons.

What is in this chapter?

This chapter compares the pros and cons of becoming a sole trader, a partnership, a limited liability partnership or a limited company (pp. 39–48). Next, the chapter shows you how to set up each of these legal forms (pp. 48–53). Finally, it looks at forming a cooperative (p. 53).

Which type of business form

There are 12 elements you have to look at so that you can weigh up the pros and cons of each legal form.

1. The credibility of the business

There is probably very little to choose between a sole trader and a conventional partnership when it comes to credibility. On the whole, it is thought that a limited company may give your business added credibility, but this may not work if a customer researches your company and finds, for example, that it has a paid-up capital of £100, which is typical for a very small business. An LLP (limited liability partnership) may also give an air of credibility to your venture, as it means you have to meet certain commitments at Companies House*.

If you want to acquire a greater air of credibility, you could set your company up as a PLC (a public company), but this is much more expensive (see p. 50) and more onerous in legal requirements.

Summary

On balance, if you are going to be selling to large companies, forming a company or LLP will probably have the edge on credibility.

2. What happens with money you owe

If you are a sole trader, you are liable for all the money your business owes (your liability is unlimited). Your own personal assets, such as your house, furniture and car, can be seized to pay your business debts; in the final breakdown, you can be made bankrupt.

This unlimited liability also applies to a conventional partnership, with a further drawback: you are liable for your partner's share of the debts.

By contrast, the concept of limited liability appears very attractive and applies to both an LLP and a limited company. Shareholders' liability for debt is, in most cases, limited to the amount they paid for their shares. The personal assets of directors can be touched only if that company has been trading fraudulently or when the directors knew it was insolvent. But this protection for your personal assets may be illusory. When you are starting in business, it is common for you as a director to be asked for personal guarantees for a bank overdraft, leasing agreements, rent or credit from suppliers.

However, once you have become established you may be able to shed your personal guarantees; a sole trader or partner cannot shed unlimited liability.

An LLP is a separate legal identity, like a limited company. The firm itself and negligent members of the LLP will be liable for debts with all their assets, but other members of the partnership will not.

Summary

If yours is the sort of business that buys materials or services from other businesses, needs a small overdraft or has to operate from rented premises, forming yourself as a limited company or LLP has the edge. You may be able to get away with not guaranteeing all of these debts; it is certainly worth negotiating to avoid doing so.

3. What you do to start up

It is very easy to start up as a sole trader. Simply register with HM Revenue & Customs (HMRC)* as soon as possible after you start up. They will also then send you the details you need if you decide to register for VAT (see Chapter 31, 'VAT' p. 419). By November 2011, the Business Link* web site is due to include a new Start Up Hub from which you will be able to register a new company as well as registering for tax if you are a sole trader or partnership.

In theory, it is equally simple to start a conventional partnership, as you do not have to get a written partnership agreement. But this would not be a sensible or business-like approach. Partners argue, including members of the same family; you should accept that this may be so, no matter how unlikely it appears at the start. Get a solicitor to draw up a written agreement that covers things like profits split, work split, tax split and partner changes. See p. 49 for more on what should be in the partnership agreement.

An LLP can be formed by registering a name at Companies House* for a fee of £40, or £100 if you opt for same-day registration. (These fees are reduced to £14 and £30, respectively, if instead of doing the registration yourself, you go through a firm that operates software filing.) You need two or more people (a minimum of two people must be designated members and responsible for getting the accounts audited, sending an annual return to Companies House and so on).

You can set up a limited company yourself. This involves filling in various forms and drawing up certain documents (which can be adapted from standard formats). The company must be registered with Companies House. For a new company, this costs £40 (or £18 if you register online through Business Link) or £100 for a same-day service. (Again, the fees are lower if you go through a firm that operates software filing. In that case, the fee for standard registration is £14 and, for same-day incorporation, £30.) Alternatively, you can enlist the help of a solicitor*, accountant* or specialist company formation agent either to form your company from scratch or to supply an 'off-the-peg' company (i.e. one that already has a name and has already been registered). For a standard company, expect to pay between £50 and £200, including the Companies House fee. You can change the name of an off-the-peg company. There are some brief formalities and the change must be registered with Companies House for a fee of £10, or £50 for a same-day service, reduced to £8 (standard) or £30 (same-day) for online or software filing. If you use an agent to change the name, £25 to £30 is a normal charge. A private company must have a minimum of one person as director and all directors must be aged at least 16.

It used to be obligatory for every company to appoint a company secretary, who is responsible for ensuring the company meets certain legal requirements, such as maintaining records and filing information and reports with Companies House. The secretary cannot also be the sole director, which means that in general you need at least two people involved in running a company. However, since 6 April 2008, private companies may opt not to have a company secretary (although the director(s) must still make sure the various legal obligations are met) and this makes it possible for one director alone to set up and run a private company. If you opt out of having a company secretary, you need to notify Companies House. And, if your company's articles of association refer specifically to a company secretary, you need to amend the articles and file the amended version with Companies House. This change was brought about by the Companies Act 2005, which contains a number of other measures aimed at making it simpler to run a small-scale company, for example:

- since 1 October 2007, private companies no longer need to hold an annual general meeting.
- since 6 April 2008, many small companies do not have to have their accounts audited (see element 5 below).

You must meet the disclosure requirements set out in the Companies Acts if you form a limited company. This includes sending in an annual return, accounts and changes in the company's directors and secretary (if you have one) plus other information. Companies House publishes free online guidance, including GP1 *Incorporation and names*, GP2 *Life of a company – Part 1 Annual requirements*, GPLLP1 *Limited liability partnerships, incorporation and names* and GPLLP2 *Life of a limited liability partnership*. These can be viewed and downloaded from its web site, *www.companieshouse.gov.uk*. Companies House also holds regional seminars to help companies to understand their legal obligations.

Summary

Setting up as a sole trader involves the least work and fewest formalities.

4. Your accounts

As a sole trader and a conventional partnership, your accounts must follow accepted accounting practice to give a true and fair picture. But the exact form of the accounts is not laid down by law. In practice, this means you do not have to produce a balance sheet. It would, however, be advisable to do so to impress your tax office or bank manager and to help you to keep a proper check on the financial position of your business. (See p. 306 for what a balance sheet is.) It is possible to do your own accounts rather than employ an accountant. If your business is very simple, you could set up your own accounting system using a spreadsheet, but generally it is better to use an off-the-shelf software package or paper-based accounting system – computer and book shops offer a wide range. (On tax returns, some self-employed people have to provide only a three-line summary of their accounts, but they must still keep full and proper accounts to back up the summary.)

In contrast, the form of accounts for a limited company and limited liability partnership is laid down by law and must comply with detailed accounting standards. The accounts have to be filed at Companies House*: any member of the public can inspect them. A small company or small LLP can file a shortened balance sheet and special auditors' report if it chooses. The definition of 'small' is having two of the following: sales of £6.5 million or less, balance sheet total of £3.26 million or less, 50 or fewer employees on average.

There are penalties if you file your accounts late, even one day late. For private companies and LLPs, the potential fine ranges from £150 to £1,500.

Summary

The rules about your accounts are more onerous if you set up as a limited company or LLP.

5. Getting your accounts audited

As a sole trader or conventional partnership, you do not have to get your accounts audited if you do not want to. You may want to consider doing so, if the cost would not be too exorbitant, as it can help in dealings with your tax office. It may also help you if you need confirmation of income from your business – for example, to get a mortgage to buy a house or to help teenage offspring claim student loans.

If your business form is a limited company or LLP, you may have to get your accounts audited by an accountant. If your company has sales of less than £6.5 million and a balance sheet total of no more than £3.26 million, you will not normally need to do so.

Summary

Small private companies and small LLPs have similar audit requirements to sole traders. Rules for other companies and LLPs are more onerous.

6. Paying tax and National Insurance

As a sole trader or partner (including in an LLP) you pay two types of National Insurance contribution (NIC). If your earnings are above a lower threshold, you pay flat-rate Class 2 contributions of £2.50 a week in 2011–12. In addition, you pay Class 4 contributions as a percentage of profits. In 2011–12, Class 4 NICs are 9 per cent of profits between £7,225 and £42,475 and an additional contribution of 2 per cent of profits above the upper profit limit.

The business of a sole trader or partner does not have a separate identity from the individual concerned. So your profits are added to any other taxable income you have and subject to income tax if the total comes to more than your personal allowance (£7,475 in 2011–12 if you are under 65).

A company does have a separate identity from its owners (the shareholders) and directors (who are employees of the company). Corporation tax is charged on the profits of the company. Companies with profits under a set limit (£300,000 in 2011–12) pay tax at the small profits rate (also called the small companies rate) of 20 per cent.

Profits are worked out after deducting any salary you pay yourself. On earnings above a certain limit, Class 1 NICs are paid by both you as employee and by the company as your employer. You normally pay at a rate of 12 per cent of your pay above £7,225 up to £42,475 in 2011–12 and 2 per cent on earnings above the upper earnings limit. Your employer pays 13.8 per cent on all your earnings above £7,072 (without any upper earnings limit). Provided your salary is no more than £7,225, there is neither employee nor employer NICs to pay.

New businesses (whether companies, sole traders or partnerships) that start up outside London, the South-East and Southern England between 22 June 2010 and 5 September 2013 can qualify for a Regional Employer National Insurance Contribution Holiday. This applies in respect of the first ten employees you take on and lasts for the first year of each person's employment with you (but only until 5 September 2013 if that date falls within the employee's first year with you). The maximum saving per employee is £5,000 of contributions. The scheme is not automatic – you must apply to join it. See Business Link* for more information and how to apply.

Instead of or as well as paying you a salary, your company may pay out some or all of the profits in the form of dividends to the shareholder(s) – i.e. you. There are no NICs to pay on dividends. The dividend is paid with an income tax credit of 10 per cent (reflecting the corporation tax already paid on the underlying profits), which satisfies any liability for income tax at less than the higher rate. There is only extra tax to pay if, when added to any other income you have, you are a higher-rate or additional-rate taxpayer.

You may be able to minimize your overall tax and National Insurance bill by paying yourself just a small salary and the rest of your income in the form of dividends. But HMRC have been attacking this arrangement in an increasing number of ways:

- *personal service companies and partnerships*: you may be charged tax and National Insurance on a 'notional salary' even though it was actually paid to you in dividends.

- *shares acquired on or after 2 December 2004*: if HMRC can show that the main purpose, or one of the main purposes, of issuing the shares is to avoid paying tax or National Insurance, dividends from the shares can be taxed as if they are earnings.

- *managed service companies*: under tax avoidance measures introduced in the 2007 Budget, if you are a shareholder in a company that is managed for you by someone else, any income you get from the company will be taxed as salary even if it is paid to you in the form of dividends. The managed service company should deduct the correct tax before handing the money over to you.

- *income shifting*: HMRC has pursued a long campaign against companies where a husband and wife both hold shares and receive dividends but only one of the spouses generates the main income of the company. It pursued a test case (*Jones* v. *Garnett*, also known as Arctic Systems) which went all the way to the House of Lords and was won by the taxpayers. HMRC subsequently issued draft legislation proposing to change the law, but withdrew the proposals possibly due to criticism from the tax profession that the rules would be unworkable. The government has stated that it will 'keep this issue under review'.

See Chapter 30, 'Tax', for more information about tax.

Summary

By choosing the right combination of salary and dividends, many businesses can cut their overall NICs and tax bill by opting for a company structure rather than self-employment or partnership. However, this will not apply in all cases and is being increasingly attacked by HMRC.

7. Claiming state benefits

Class 2 NICs paid by sole traders and partners entitle you to claim certain state benefits. These are the state basic retirement pension, maternity allowance and employment and support allowance (which replaced incapacity benefit from 1 October 2008). They also entitle your widow or widower to bereavement benefits. Class 4 NICs do not give you any benefit entitlement.

Employees (including directors) who have earnings at least equal to a lower earnings limit (£5,304 a year in 2011–12) are entitled to all state benefits listed above. In addition, they can also claim contributory job-seeker's allowance and are building up the state second pension. Note that employees entitled to these benefits may be earning less than the limit (£7,225 in 2011–12) at which Class 1 NICs become payable.

Summary

Provided you pay yourself a salary of at least £5,304 a year, you are entitled to more state benefits as a director of a company than you would be as a sole trader or partner. This is the case even if your salary is below the limit at which Class 1 NICs become payable.

8. When you pay tax

If you are in business as a sole trader or a partner (including an LLP), you will pay tax on your profits for the accounting year ending in the tax year in up to three instalments: interim payments on 31 January and 31 July and final payment (or repayment) on 31 January the following year.

With a limited company, on your salary you pay tax each month under the PAYE system. On the profits of the company, you pay tax nine months after the end of the accounting year.

Summary

There is little to choose between business forms.

9. What you can do with losses

If you are a sole trader or in a partnership (including an LLP), you can normally deduct losses from:

- future profits of the same trade.

- other income or capital gains either in the year of the loss or the year before. This includes any personal income you may have.

- other income in the previous three years if the losses occur in the first four years of the business.

If you form a limited company, the relief is not so generous. You can deduct losses from company profits of the previous year, future profits of the company and any capital gains the company makes.

Summary

If you are likely to make losses in the first year or so, you would be better organizing your business as a sole trader or partnership, if you have another source of income.

10. Providing yourself with a pension

If you save for retirement through a pension scheme, you can usually get tax relief on contributions equal to the higher of £3,600 a year or the whole of your UK earnings paid into any type of, or combination of, pension schemes. There is also an overall annual limit on your contributions of £50,000 a year in 2011–12. Therefore, provided you have reasonably high UK earnings (which includes profits from self-employment or salary as a director, but not dividend income), you have the scope to make sizeable pension savings whatever form your business takes. See Chapter 32, 'Pensions and retirement', for more information.

If you organize your business as a company, the company (your employer) can make broadly unlimited contributions to a scheme on your behalf. These contributions qualify for relief from corporation tax provided the contributions are 'wholly and exclusively' for the purpose of the business. In practice this means that your whole remuneration package, including salary and pension, must be in proportion to the value of the work you do for the company. If you would prefer to take a large proportion of your remuneration in the form of pension contributions rather than pay, you could arrange a 'salary sacrifice' where you formally give up part of your pay in return for pension benefits.

Self-invested personal pensions (SIPPs), which can be taken out by anyone, and small self-administered schemes (SSASs), which can be set up by a company for its employee(s), can be used to invest in a wide range of assets including, for example, the premises from which your business operates. This can have tax advantages but it is a complex area so get advice from an independent financial adviser (IFA)*.

Summary

There is little to choose between business forms.

11. Raising money

As a sole trader, your options for raising money for your business are fairly limited and are basically getting an overdraft from your existing bank or a loan from your own or another bank. As an outside possibility, you may find an individual to lend you the money. In a partnership, you may be able to find a new partner to bring in some extra capital.

But if you form a company (and it must be a PLC if you wish to raise money from the public), the choice is wider. You may find a business angel willing to invest money for part of the business. On a larger scale, you may be able to raise venture capital from a fund or a venture capital trust. Or you may be able to raise funds under the enterprise investment scheme. You may also be able to raise money from your bank secured with what is known as a floating charge on your assets. For more about these methods of raising money, see pp. 322–31.

Summary

Your choices for raising money are wider if you form a limited company.

12. Selling part of your business

This can be slightly tricky if you are a sole trader or in a partnership. One way of solving this could be to take on a partner (or a further partner), but this obviously means you must have trust in the person. If part of your business is easily separated, you might be able to sell it as a going concern on its own.

It should be somewhat easier to sell part of your business if it is in the form of a limited company. You could sell some of your shares, although it can be difficult selling shares in a private company.

See Chapter 30, 'Tax', for information about tax on the proceeds of selling your business.

Summary

Selling part of your business may be easier if it is a limited company.

How to set up as a sole trader

It is really very easy and straightforward. You need to:

- register for National Insurance with HMRC* by filling in form CWF1 (which you can download from the HMRC web site using its 'Find a form' service), by phoning the Newly Self-Employed Helpline*, or by registering online through the Business Link* web site. You must do this promptly after starting up, otherwise you are likely to be charged a penalty – the amount is based on the amount of tax you owe as a result of registering late and the degree of negligence or dishonesty involved. On the plus side, once registered, you'll be sent a guide on starting up in a business and have access to an HMRC local Business Support Team.
- check with the Planning Officer* that your workplace is suitable (p. 202).
- if you decide to trade under a name different from your own, you must put your own name on your headed paper (p. 136).
- consider whether you have to, or whether you should ask to, register for VAT (p. 420).

How to set up as a partnership

The fundamental drawback of a conventional partnership is that each partner is jointly liable with the other partners for all the debts and obligations that each partner incurs. This financial responsibility can include all your own personal assets, which could be seized to pay partnership debts (which might have happened as a result not of your actions but of your partners').

You must be able to trust your partners. Do not drift into an informal partnership. Make sure you and your partners have discussed difficult problems right at the start and come to some clear agreement.

There are several different sorts of partner, but only two are suitable for consideration in a business partnership:

1 A full partner, who will share in the profits and losses in an agreed proportion and will be part of the management.
2 A sleeping partner, who will have no part in the management of the business but will still be held responsible for the debts. (But see p. 410 for how loss relief is restricted for this type of partner.)

The partnership agreement

This is a job for a solicitor* (and find out about the Lawyers for Your Business* scheme, on p. 217). The agreement and its details, whether for a conventional partnership or a limited liability one, can be kept private. Briefly, an agreement should include among other points:

■ the names of the partners, the name of the business and its activity.

■ the date the partnership starts and how long it will last.

■ the capital and the interest on it.

■ the profits split.

■ management and control of the business.

■ holidays.

■ what happens on retirement, on death and if one of the partners leaves.

Forming a limited liability partnership

You need to submit an application document (form LLIN01) to Companies House*. This requires:

■ the limited liability partnership's name. There are restrictions on the names you can choose (in the same way as for companies – see Chapter 12, 'The right name', on p. 132) and the name must end in the words 'Limited Liability Partnership' or the letters 'LLP' (or, if incorporating in Wales, 'Partneriaeth Atebolrwydd Cyfyngedig' or 'PAC').

■ the location of the registered office (England, Wales or Scotland).

- the address of the registered office.
- the name, full address and date of birth of each member.
- which of these members are the designated members (minimum two) or that all members are designated members.

A designated member has certain duties, such as appointing an auditor, signing the accounts, delivering the accounts and annual return to Companies House, and notifying Companies House of changes to the members, registered office addresses or name of the LLP.

There are certain rules about displaying information. The name of the LLP must be displayed outside every place of business and on all its notices. On all its letters, order forms and web sites must be shown the LLP's place of registration and registration number, the fact that it is a limited liability partnership and the address of its registered office.

How to set up as a company

You can set up a company yourself, in which case get the guidance booklet, GP1, from Companies House*. But it's simpler to pass the job to a solicitor*, accountant* or specialist company formation agent. Forming a company from scratch can take several weeks, although there is now a fast-track one-day registration service. You could form a public company – this would mean you must put PLC after its name. It must have an authorized share capital of at least £50,000 or €65,600 (you must choose which currency to denominate the shares in), and at least one-quarter must be paid on each share, plus any premium. This means you need at least £12,500 to form it. Or you can form a private company (which is any company that is not a public company). A company, whether public or private, must have at least one director. Normally a company must also have a secretary (who may be a director) but, since 6 April 2008, private companies have been able to opt not to have a company secretary (see p. 41).

A company cannot start to trade until registered with the Registrar of Companies at Companies House. If you use a solicitor, accountant or other agent, they will handle this for you. Otherwise, you need to send in:

- form IN01, *Application to form a company*. This asks for details, such as the company name, its registered address, the name and address of the company secretary (if any) and directors. Directors' residential addresses do not need to appear on the register of companies that is open to the public – instead, a 'service address' can be given, i.e. an address where documents can be delivered and a receipt given if required. You might want to use a service address if, say, you fear adverse public reaction to the type of business your company carries out. Form IN01 also includes a statement of capital, setting out the number, type and value of shares in the company and details of the initial subscribers to the shares.

▩ memorandum of association. A short document recording the intention of you and any other people concerned to form a company.

▩ articles of association. These set out in detail the internal rules for running the company. You can opt to adopt model articles that have been produced by Companies House. Alternatively, you can choose to adapt the model articles or draw up your own bespoke articles. If you do not send in any articles of association, by default your company will be treated as adopting the model version.

▩ registration fee of £40, or £100 if you are using the same-day service (or £14 or £30, respectively, if you go through a firm using software filing, or £18 if you register online through Business Link*), payable to 'Companies House'.

It is no longer necessary for either the memorandum or the articles to set out the objects of the company, so (unless it chooses otherwise) there are no restrictions on the company's activities.

Instead of forming a company from scratch, you can buy a ready-made one. This is a quicker process, but it may take three or more weeks to change its name to whatever you want to call your business: however, if there is no problem with the name it normally takes about five working days. If you are willing to pay extra, you can even be up and running within 24 hours. In general, to change a company's name you need to convene an annual general meeting or extraordinary general meeting and pass a special resolution. However, private companies can choose to pass most types of resolution, including a name change, without calling a meeting. The resolution must be in writing, circulated either as hard copy or electronically, and agreed by the majority of members. Whichever route is used, a signed copy of the resolution should be sent to Companies House with a registration fee of £10. Companies House offers a same-day name change service, although the fee for this is higher at £50. But the fee is reduced to £8 (standard) or £30 (same-day) if you can go through a firm using software filing.

There are certain rules about displaying information. For example, the Certificate of Incorporation and the registration date need to be displayed publicly. On your stationery, web site, e-mails and order forms for example, you need to show the full registered name of your company, either all or none of the names of the directors, the place of registration (for example, registered in England and Wales), the registration number, and the registered office address (marked as such) as well as the trading address of the company. You must normally put the company name outside your office premises.

There are rules on what name you can give your company – see Chapter 12, 'The right name', on p. 132.

What directors must do

In practice, a director's general obligations are not much worse than those for a sole trader or partner, and indeed they can be better. This is because by forming a company you can separate your own assets from the business assets (in theory at any rate). But this separation is conditional on what could be called, in layperson's terms, responsible business behaviour. However, a director also has to cope with some technical, more detailed requirements, for example sending in your accounts, which aren't there to trip up a sole trader.

The Companies Act 2006 spells out the general duties of directors (previously, they had built up through case law). As a director, your general duties are to:

- act within the powers given to you by the company's constitution and only to exercise your powers for the intended purposes.
- promote the success of the company for the benefit of the shareholders as a whole. This means considering the long-term consequences of any decision, the interests of employees, the need to foster good relations with suppliers and customers, maintaining a high reputation for the company and so on.
- exercise independent judgement.
- exercise reasonable care, skill and diligence. This will be judged in terms of the knowledge, skills and experience both that you personally have and that would be expected of a director.
- avoid conflicts of interest. You are expected to avoid situations that could put you into conflict with the interests of the company, in particular regarding any property, information or opportunity, unless the matter has been specifically authorized by the directors of the company.
- not accept benefits from third parties that are given because of your

role as director or anything you have done in that capacity, unless the acceptance cannot reasonably be regarded as creating a conflict of interest.

■ declare any interest in a proposed transaction or arrangement to the directors.

If a company is insolvent, and the directors have failed in their duties and obligations, they could be declared 'unfit' and disqualified from being a director of any other company for up to 15 years.

Most of the big firms of accountants* and the Institute of Directors* have booklets explaining what a director's responsibilities are. You can also get insurance to protect yourself; this is known as directors' and officers' liability. Ask your insurance broker*, see p. 287.

Forming a cooperative

A cooperative is a group of people operating through a jointly owned and democratically run organization. The type of cooperative varies. For example, this could be a group of workers who own the organization they work for, or consumers who join together to buy more efficiently, or an agricultural cooperative where farmers join forces to strengthen their bargaining power. Cooperatives are underpinned by strong values, such as self-help, democracy and equity. To foster these, most cooperatives adhere to seven principles:

1 Voluntary and open membership.
2 Democratic member control. Many adhere to one member, one vote.
3 Member economic participation. Members all contribute to the organization's capital and democratically control its use in the business. Often the capital itself cannot be distributed to individual members and, even on winding up, would be given to charity or put to some community use. Profits may be distributed to members, kept within the business or used in some other way agreed on by the members.
4 Autonomy and independence. Cooperatives can enter into agreements with other organizations and raise money from external sources, provided the democratic control of the members is maintained.
5 Education, training and information. These are provided by the cooperative to its members so they can contribute effectively to its development. The cooperative also has a duty to inform the public about the nature and benefits of cooperation.

6 Cooperation among cooperatives (through local, regional, national and international bodies).

7 Concern for the community.

Cooperatives are being given a big boost by the government's new 'right to provide' initiative. This is encouraging public sector workers to leave their current jobs and instead form employee-owned mutual organizations – in other words, cooperatives. The idea is that these new not-for-profit businesses will be contracted back by government departments and local authorities to provide the same services that the cooperative's members used to provide as employees. In Spain and Sweden, such cooperatives are commonly used to provide social care and childcare services. The government has suggested that eventually one in six of the UK's public sector employees might switch to working in this way. The idea may seem attractive, enabling work to be organized and managed in a less bureaucratic way, giving you more control and greater job satisfaction. But, although you will understand the nature of the work intimately, don't underestimate the new challenges of working as a business rather than as an employee. For information, contact the Mutuals Information Service* or Employee Ownership Association*. For professional advice in setting up this type of mutual, consider the fee-based service from Public Service Mutuals*, which is a joint venture between a law firm, a consultancy group and the Co-operative Group (the UK's largest mutual organization).

You will need to get legal registration or incorporation for any cooperative you set up. There are four possible legal forms.

First, you could form a partnership. The disadvantage with this is that there is no limited liability. And the business could be sold for the benefit of its members; this is not in keeping with a fundamental principle of a cooperative. On the other hand, you can form a partnership with only two people, whereas to form a cooperative society you need seven.

Second, you could form a limited company; but the aims of a company run counter to some of the basic principles of a cooperative, so it would be difficult to organize.

Third, you could seek registration with the Financial Services Authority* as a cooperative society under the Industrial and Provident Societies Act 1965. You will need seven founder members. You will find registration will be quicker if you apply through a 'promoting body', such as Co-operatives UK*, which is the trade body for cooperative enterprises.

Finally, you could organize the cooperative as a company limited by guarantee. This needs only two people to form it.

You can get information on, and support with, setting up a cooperative, including a public-sector mutual, from Co-operatives UK and the Employee Ownership Association.

Summary

1 A limited company has several advantages: limited liability, greater credibility, lower tax, better pension rules, more avenues for raising finance and easier disposal of part of your business.
2 Sole trader and partnership have much simpler admin arrangements, less onerous rules about accounts and better tax treatment of losses.
3 If you are forming a partnership, get a solicitor's help to draw up a written partnership agreement.
4 The simplest way of all to start a business is to begin as a sole trader.
5 If you work in the public sector, you may want to explore setting up a mutual organization under the 'right to provide' initiative.

Other chapters to read

12 The right name (p. 132); **25** Raising the money (p. 316); **29** Keeping the record straight (p. 370); **30** Tax (p. 381).

5

Are you sure?

Every would-be entrepreneur should take stock before undertaking the final commitment; reassessments are a vital part of the decision process. Are you the right person? Have you got the necessary skills? Will you be able to earn enough to live on? Is your idea the best one?

What is in this chapter?

This chapter draws together all the key points made in the previous four chapters, presenting them in a series of four checklists. This should allow you to reconsider previous decisions to confirm that you are on the right road. The checklists are you (p. 56), your family (p. 58), your skills (p. 60) and your idea (p. 63).

Checklist: you

Underline the word in each answer that best describes how you fit each question. You can also ask friends, colleagues or relatives to fill in the checklist about you, so that you can obtain an external view of your character and fitness for self-employment.

1 Can you work long hours?
(1) Always   (2) Sometimes   (3) Occasionally   (4) Never

2 Do you have persistence and stamina?
(1) Always   (2) Most of the time   (3) Occasionally   (4) Rarely

3 Is this business more important than, for example, leisure or family?
(1) Completely   (2) Much more   (3) As important   (4) Less important

4 If the business struggled for five years, would you keep going?
(1) Yes, easily   (2) Yes, fairly easily   (3) Yes, with difficulty   (4) No

5 Is financial success your main guide to what you have achieved?
(1) Completely   (2) Mainly   (3) Partially   (4) Not at all

6 Are you thought of as a survivor?
(1) Always   (2) Usually   (3) Occasionally   (4) Never

7 If you were in a tight corner, would you be able to come up with an original way out?
(1) Frequently   (2) Sometimes   (3) Rarely   (4) Never

8 Do you keep going until a task is completed?
(1) Always   (2) Usually   (3) Sometimes   (4) Occasionally

9 Are problems a challenge?
(1) Always   (2) Usually   (3) Sometimes   (4) Never

10 Can you live with insecurity about job and income?
(1) Yes, easily   (2) Yes, fairly easily   (3) Yes, with difficulty   (4) No

11 Are you self-confident?
(1) Yes, always   (2) Yes, usually   (3) Sometimes lack confidence   (4) No

12 How do you view failure?
(1) Opportunity to learn   (2) A disappointment   (3) A setback   (4) A disaster

13 Can you take criticism?
(1) Always listen; may reject   (2) Always accept   (3) Don't like it
(4) Always reject

14 Do you ask for comments on your performance so that you can do something better next time?
(1) Always   (2) Usually   (3) Sometimes   (4) Rarely

15 Do you believe your success will be dependent on outside factors?
(1) Strongly disagree   (2) Disagree   (3) Agree sometimes   (4) Agree always

16 Do you like being the leader in situations where you can be assessed?
(1) Very much   (2) Quite a lot   (3) Not really   (4) Not at all

17 Are you good at finding the right person or source to help you to achieve what you want?
(1) Very good   (2) Quite good   (3) Not very good   (4) Poor

18 Do you recognize when you need help?
(1) Always   (2) Usually   (3) Sometimes   (4) Never

19 Do you set your own high standards to compete against?
(1) Always   (2) Usually   (3) Sometimes   (4) Never

20 In the past, which sort of risks have you preferred taking?
(1) Calculated   (2) High risks   (3) Low risks   (4) Seldom take risks

21 Can you identify which decisions are important and which not?
(1) Yes, always   (2) Yes, usually   (3) Yes, sometimes   (4) No

22 Can you delegate to others?
(1) Yes, when appropriate   (2) Yes, sometimes   (3) With difficulty   (4) No

23 How is your health?
(1) Very good   (2) Good   (3) Quite good   (4) Poor

When you have completed the checklist, look at the pattern of underlined words. The more underlined answers 1 and 2, the greater your probable success as a business owner.

Checklist: your family

If you are single, you may not need to consider this section. But if you have a husband, wife, partner and/or children, involving them in the decision to go it alone is important. Starting a business is an all-embracing existence, and your family life is unlikely to remain the same after taking the plunge. They will need to understand that the home atmosphere should be very supportive, particularly during the early business problems.

Your family may also turn out to be an important business resource. They can provide extra input in all you do: clerical, manual, problem solving, for example. With a family, deciding to found an enterprise is likely to be more successful as a family decision. Having said that, many succeed without the support of their families; but, in this case, the strain can be severe. In the extreme, the choice may be your business or your relationship.

In the following checklist, cross out whichever is inapplicable:

1 Have you discussed your thoughts about starting a business
with your family?   *yes   no*
2 Are they willing to help out if necessary?   *yes   no*
3 Will they live easily with job or financial insecurity?   *yes   no*
4 Have they accepted that there may be a permanent drop in
living standards?   *yes   no*

5 If you need to raise money using your home as security, do they understand the full implications?   *yes   no*

6 Is your family self-sufficient; that is, can they manage without you to do the shopping, gardening, decorating?   *yes   no*

7 Does one of the members of the family earn a living in another way, which can be used to tide the whole family over?   *yes   no*

8 Have you worked out a family budget to see how you will cope? If you have not, the *pro forma* cash flow below may help you. Remember to use conservative estimates of your likely income and allow for all the costs.   *yes   no*

9 Have you talked to your bank manager about your intended business and shown him your cash flow to demonstrate how you hope to cope in domestic finance?   *yes   no*

When you have completed your family checklist, the more times you have answered 'yes' the better prepared you are for starting your business.

Pro forma cash flow

Month	1	2	–	11	12
Balance in bank at start of month	. . .	. . .	–	. . .	. . .
Income					
Estimated from business	. . .	. . .	–	. . .	. . .
Other family	. . .	. . .	–	. . .	. . .
Total income	. . .	. . .	–	. . .	. . .
Expenses					
Mortgage/rent	. . .	. . .	–	. . .	. . .
Loan interest	. . .	. . .	–	. . .	. . .
Council tax	. . .	. . .	–	. . .	. . .
Pension	. . .	. . .	–	. . .	. . .
Life insurance	. . .	. . .	–	. . .	. . .
Tax on business income	. . .	. . .	–	. . .	. . .
Electricity/gas/telephone/fuel	. . .	. . .	–	. . .	. . .
Travel/car	. . .	. . .	–	. . .	. . .
House: insurance/repairs	. . .	. . .	–	. . .	. . .
Food	. . .	. . .	–	. . .	. . .

▶

Month	1	2	–	11	12
Clothes	. . .	. . .	–	. . .	. . .
Subscriptions/newspapers/magazines	. . .	. . .	–	. . .	. . .
Other:					
. . . .	. . .	. . .	–	. . .	. . .
. . . .	. . .	. . .	–	. . .	. . .
. . . .	. . .	. . .	–	. . .	. . .
Total expenses	. . .	. . .	–	. . .	. . .
Balance in bank at end of month	. . .	. . .	–	. . .	. . .

Checklist: your skills

This checklist should help you to look honestly at what you can do well and what you do badly. If there are skills you lack, this does not mean that you cannot go ahead. But you need to compensate:

■ be trained or seek advice from an enterprise agency or other advice body.

■ fund the business so you can employ those skills that are lacking.

■ use professional advisers, if appropriate.

Financial

As you answer each question, underline the appropriate word or words:

1 Have you kept accounting books, for example sales and purchases daybooks, cash books (see p. 372) or used a simple software program?
many times   *on a few occasions*   *not at all*

2 Have you had to chase bad debts owed by your customers (p. 345)?
yes, frequently   *yes, sometimes*   *no, not at all*

3 Have you ever installed a system of credit control (p. 342)?
yes   *no*

4 Have you ever negotiated credit terms with a supplier (p. 344)?
yes   *no*

5 What is your experience of drawing up cash flows (p. 296)?
extensive   *a little*   *none at all*

6 Do you understand the importance of controlling cash (p. 339)?
yes   *no*

7 What is your experience of drawing up budgets (p. 338)?
extensive   *a little*   *none at all*

8 Is break-even analysis a technique you have used before (p. 334)?
yes, frequently   *yes, sometimes*   *no, not at all*

9 Do you know when and how you would use:
(a) An overdraft (p. 319)?   *yes*   *no*
(b) Leasing (p. 210)?   *yes*   *no*
(c) Factoring (p. 346)?   *yes*   *no*

10 What is your experience of estimating and raising long-term financial needs (p. 316)?
extensive   *a little*   *none at all*

11 Do you know what are the sources of long-term funds, for example venture capital (p. 329)?
yes   *no*

12 What is your experience of drawing up business plans (p. 66)?
extensive   *a little*   *none at all*

13 What is your experience of presenting your plan to financiers (p. 331)?
extensive   *a little*   *none at all*

Marketing

14 Do you understand the different ways you can establish prices (p. 184)?
yes   *no*

15 Do you know how to analyse market sectors (p. 14)?
yes   *no*

16 What is your experience of identifying product benefits (p. 17)?
extensive   *a little*   *none at all*

17 What is your experience of:
(a) Direct-response advertising (p. 144)?
extensive   *a little*   *none at all*
(b) Public relations (p. 149)?
extensive   *a little*   *none at all*
(c) Face-to-face selling (p. 162)?
extensive   *a little*   *none at all*

(d) Direct mail (p. 158)?

extensive   *a little*   *none at all*

(e) Telephone selling (p. 161)?

extensive   *a little*   *none at all*

(f) Marketing through the Internet (p. 151)?

extensive   *a little*   *none at all*

18 Do you understand how to build relationships with customers (p. 172)?

yes   *no*

Operational

19 Do you know how to introduce a stock control system?

yes   *no*

20 Do you understand all the ins and outs of your product; that is, how it works, what it does?

yes, very well   *yes, somewhat*   *no, not very well*

21 Do you understand the effect that control of costs can have on profits (p. 352)?

yes, very well   *yes, somewhat*   *no, not very well*

22 Do you understand the manufacturing process of your product (if applicable)?

yes, very well   *yes, somewhat*   *no, not very well*

23 Do you know how to use a database to gather information?

yes, very well   *yes, somewhat*   *no, not very well*

24 Do you understand how to integrate the use of information technology in your business?

yes, very well   *yes, somewhat*   *no, not very well*

General management

25 What is your experience of staff recruitment (p. 222)?

extensive   *a little*   *none at all*

26 What is your understanding of employment law (p. 244)?

extensive   *a little*   *none at all*

27 Do you know how to set goals and objectives for employees?

yes   *no*

28 What is your experience of project management?

extensive   *a little*   *none at all*

Once you have finished assessing your skills and abilities, you will have some indication of what improvements you should make. A first step is reading the relevant chapters of this book.

Checklist: your idea

This is an opportunity to have a final check on your idea before you start becoming involved in the actual formalities and expense of forming your business. Note that where the word 'product' is used, this could also be 'service' or 'skill'.

		Yes	*No*	*Does not apply*
1	Have you defined your product ideas?	. . .	. . .	. . .
2	Have you carried out market research into your idea?	. . .	. . .	. . .
3	Have you discerned a market sector or niche that you will sell to?	. . .	. . .	. . .
4	Is that segment big enough for you to build a business on it?	. . .	. . .	. . .
5	Have you researched the characteristics of your likely customers?	. . .	. . .	. . .
6	Have you identified what are the benefits and advantages not yet available to that segment?	. . .	. . .	. . .
7	Will you be able to supply a product that meets those needs?	. . .	. . .	. . .
8	Do you know how your product will be different from the competitors'?	. . .	. . .	. . .
9	Have you estimated how much your likely customers will buy and when that will be?	. . .	. . .	. . .
10	Have you found out how the product will be sold, for example e-commerce, direct mail, direct selling, retail, distributors?	. . .	. . .	. . .
11	Have you made a realistic forecast of the market share you can attain?	. . .	. . .	. . .
12	Is the market likely to grow in the next few years?	. . .	. . .	. . .

	Yes	No	Does not apply
13 Have you talked to potential customers, and do they like your product?	. . .	. . .	. . .
14 Have you carried out any test-selling and has it confirmed your estimates of sales?	. . .	. . .	. . .
15 Will the product live up to the reputation you intend to project?	. . .	. . .	. . .
16 Have you estimated a price you can sell for?	. . .	. . .	. . .
17 Do you know how the product will be made?	. . .	. . .	. . .
18 Can you work out an approximate cost?	. . .	. . .	. . .
19 Do you have an initial idea of overheads for the business, for example rent, telephone, heating and lighting?	. . .	. . .	. . .
20 Have you made an approximate guess at the profits and when they will be earned?	. . .	. . .	. . .
21 Will this give you an income you can live on?	. . .	. . .	. . .
22 Will you need to raise money, and is this a realistic amount?	. . .	. . .	. . .
23 Have you thought carefully about what the principal risks are to your business?	. . .	. . .	. . .
24 Can you put an estimate on the likelihood of these risks occurring?	. . .	. . .	. . .

Now you have completed this checklist; the more times you answered 'yes', the better prepared you are and the greater the chance of success.

What next?

If you have worked carefully through these four checklists, you are now faced with one of three options:

1 Give up because you are not the right person to be self-employed or start a business or the idea is not suitable.
2 Carry out further research or training or seek a better idea.
3 Proceed.

To proceed, you need to make several decisions and carry out actions. These include choosing advisers, formulating a detailed business plan, deciding the form of your business, working on what your business or product will be called. Chapter 7, 'Timing the jump' (p. 72), should guide you through the maze.

Other chapters to read

1 You and your ideas (p. 1); **2** Who will buy? (p. 13); **6** The business plan (p. 66).

6

The business plan

Life can be very chaotic when you are starting or running a small business. The telephone calls to make, the letters to write, the decisions to take – all the day-to-day emergencies can push aside the long-term strategic planning that is essential to keep your enterprise on the right track. Do not let short-term problems divert you from your longer-term objectives.

Writing a business plan is merely encapsulating your longer-term objectives, estimates and forecasts on paper. Once you have put down your plan, do not necessarily accept that it is set in concrete. Forecasts and objectives change as new bits of information and your better experience emerge. The important point is to incorporate your best estimate, given your current state of information. There is nothing like writing something down to help to clarify your mind and reveal your uncertainties and weaknesses.

What is in this chapter?

- the objectives of the plan (p. 66).
- how many plans? (p. 67).
- who should do the plan? (p. 68).
- what should be in the plan? (p. 68).

The objectives of the plan

The two most important reasons for producing a written plan are:

1 To show to outsiders to help to raise money.

2 To use within the business to keep yourself on your planned course or to alert you to things that are not going according to your strategy. This use is discussed in more detail in Chapter 26, 'Staying afloat' (p. 333).

To persuade someone to lend or invest enough money in your business to enable you to achieve your strategy, you will need to:

- show that the lender or investor stands a good chance of being paid back or getting a good return on their investment.

- instil confidence about your abilities to manage the business and, if applicable, show that you already have the beginnings of an experienced management team.

- demonstrate that there is a good market for your product or service.

To achieve these objectives you must bring out what is exciting about the prospects of your business, combined with a thoroughly prepared presentation of the back-up figures and research.

Beware of filling your plan with nothing but turgid facts and figures; you must allow the reader of your plan to see instantly what is so interesting about your business. You need to do this to persuade your reader that it is worthwhile studying the detailed forecasts, which can be very time-consuming. Lenders and investors can be presented with so many plans for consideration that unless yours grabs the reader's attention it could be consigned to the bin before your carefully prepared figures are looked at.

How many plans?

As there are two reasons for having a written plan, will one plan suffice? The answer to this depends on who is advising you. A bank manager, or other financial backer, may say there should be only one plan, as they would like to know the absolute truth about what is happening in your business. But some small businesses adopt a different strategy and have two plans. One is for outsiders; this plan must be one that will not fail, so it will be fairly conservative about projected sales and costs. The reason for adopting a conservative approach with outsiders is that you must not be seen to fail as this can erode confidence in you and your judgement. This could make it difficult to keep the support of your bank manager when you need it later. If your plan is being used to raise money, your figures must achieve a balance between optimism and realism if you are to persuade banks and others that your business will be successful and so worthy of a loan or an investment. You must always remain confident that the figures are achievable; if you are misleading the lenders and investors, you are also misleading yourself.

The second plan is for your own use and will set higher targets, although you must believe you can do that level of business. If you pitch the figures too low, you might not achieve as much as is possible. The well-known fleas-in-the-box analogy applies to your plan; if you put a lid on the box, the fleas learn to jump to that height only, but, if there is no lid, they jump as high as they are capable of doing. Your plan should set that lid higher.

Who should do the plan?

It is your job. You will know the product and the market better than anyone else. You have to be prepared to present the plan to banks or other sources of finance, so you need to be fully confident about all the statements and forecasts. You will have that confidence if you have provided the data.

However, as it is so important for your plan to look professional, consider seeking advice and help on its production. These are available from:

- Business Link* and training courses. Many counsellors can help you put your plan together (see Chapter 3, 'A spot of coaching'). This help is often free.
- accountants* or financial advisers* can help you to prepare the figures (see Chapter 19, 'Professional back-up').

Use a computer program to help you to produce forecasts and to examine the effect changes will have on the results. Computerized spreadsheets can make short work of a lengthy task and let you investigate different scenarios.

What should be in the plan?

1 Summary of your plan (one to two pages).
   Highlighting the attractions of your business.
   (a) What is the business?
   (b) What is the market?
   (c) Potential for business.
   (d) Forecast profit figures.
   (e) How much money is needed?
   (f) Prospects for the investor/lender.

2 The past (one page plus an appendix).
   (a) When the business started.
   (b) Summary of past performance (last three years' accounts in appendix).
   (c) Indication of how relevant or not past performance is to future progress.

3 Management (as many pages as are needed).
   This is the crucial section.
   (a) Your past employment and business record. Identify achievements, not just a chronological statement.
   (b) The record of other people working with you.
   (c) If there are obvious weaknesses in management, how you'll deal with them.

4 The product or service (two pages plus an appendix).
   (a) A simple description of what it does. Avoid technical words – if essential, technical descriptions can go in the appendix.
   (b) Why the product is unique or distinct.
   (c) Brief survey of the competition.
   (d) How the products will be developed, what new products are being considered, when replacement will be needed for the existing product range, what competitive products may emerge.
   (e) Any patents applied for.

5 Marketing (three or four pages with detailed statistics in an appendix).
   The market:
   (a) Its size, its past and future growth.
   (b) Analysis of market into sectors; identify sector your business is aimed at.
   (c) Likely customers: who, type (industrial or consumer), size, how they buy.
   (d) Your competitors: who, their size, position in market, likely response to your challenge.

   Selling:
   (a) How you will sell (Internet, direct mail, telephone, intermediaries and so on).
   (b) Who will sell.
   (c) Some idea of your sales pitch (for example, benefits of your product).
   (d) How you will price.

6 Operational details (length depends on nature of business).

  (a) Where you will be based – location, premises.

  (b) Suppliers.

  (c) Manufacturing facilities.

  (d) Equipment needed.

  (e) Information technology strategy.

7 Financial analysis (two to three pages; data in optional appendix).

  (a) Summary of forecasts.

  (b) Monthly profit and loss forecast for two years.

  (c) Profit forecast for further three years.

  (d) Monthly cash flow forecast for two years.

  (e) Cash flow forecast for further three years (optional).

  (f) Forecast balance sheet for two years.

  (g) Audited accounts for last three years (if available).

  (h) The assumptions behind your forecasts.

  (i) What are the principal risks that could affect figures?

  (j) SWOT analysis – strengths, weaknesses, opportunities and threats.

8 The prospects (one or two pages).

  (a) Your objectives – short-term, long-term.

  (b) The finance needed and what it is needed for.

  (c) Shareholdings suggested (if appropriate).

  (d) Prospects for the investor or lender (if appropriate, including possible value of business if floated on the stock market or sold, so investors may cash in).

The length of the plan

In the outline above, suggested maximum lengths for each section are given. If your need for finance is small (£25,000, say) and your business simple, these would be too long. Probably all you will need for your bank manager is two or three pages plus the financial forecasts – a bit more if it is not your own bank manager. However, if you need a large sum of money, you may have to put rather more in than the above suggestions. But keep at the forefront of your mind that you need to get across to your reader what is interesting about your business.

One possible way around the conundrum of giving all the necessary information without boring a potential investor would be to include a note of what other figures and data are available, if requested.

Presenting your plan

Financiers will assume that if your presentation to them is unsatisfactory, your presentation to customers is equally unsatisfactory. So while it may seem obvious, your plan will look better if it is given a clear layout and presented in a smart folder. The information will also be easier to understand if you do not try to cram too much on one page. How you should present your plan and who you should approach for money are covered in Chapter 25, 'Raising the money'.

Summary

1 If you want to raise money for your business you will need to have a well-presented, carefully researched business plan to support your request.

2 Producing a business plan also helps you to keep control of your business by allowing you to look at how your actual performance differs from your forecast performance – and forcing you to explain the differences.

3 Preparing the plan can help you to clarify your thoughts about the success or failure of your business venture. It can also help to highlight in your mind the important steps that need to be taken.

4 Consider whether one plan will suffice for outsiders and inside use, or if two plans will be more helpful to you.

5 Your plan must get across to readers what is interesting about your business. Stress your management ability and demonstrate carefully the market for your product.

6 An ideal format for your plan for outside use is to have between three and ten pages of text that draw out the important points, plus a series of financial figures. Excessive detail should be confined to appendices.

7 You can get help to produce the plan from an advice agency or an accountant. It is crucial to try out your plan on someone independent before you try it out on the financiers.

8 Use the checklist starting on p. 68 to help you to decide what should be in your business plan.

9 Your plan should be typed and neatly presented in a folder.

10 Include cash flow forecasts, profit forecasts, and possibly a balance sheet forecast. The more money you wish to raise the more detail your forecasts need to have and the greater period they should cover.

Other chapters to read

24 Forecasting (p. 295); 25 Raising the money (p. 316).

7

Timing the jump

Starting a business can be a confusing operation: so many decisions to take, so many actions to carry out. It can be important to keep to the right path. If you fail to take one step when it is necessary, this can delay your start.

What is in this chapter?

This chapter should help you to keep to the critical path. It sets out 60 steps. Not all will apply to every business – decide which are critical for yours and which you can ignore. You might find it convenient to combine two steps even though one does not need to be done until later. But, in general, carry out the steps in the approximate order given. The steps are divided into four sections:

1 Initial preparation (p. 72).
2 Getting into greater detail (p. 73).
3 Setting up (p. 75).
4 Ready to trade (p. 76).

Initial preparation

1 Carry on in your job, if you are in paid employment; carry on drawing Jobseeker's Allowance, if unemployed. You can undertake the initial preparation and research while still doing this. If you have been unemployed for some time, you may be eligible for some help in starting your business through the New Enterprise Allowance – talk to Jobcentre Plus*.

2 Analyse your character and abilities. Are you the right person to start on your own (p. 56)?

3 Discuss with your family the possibility of starting a business. Are they aware of what it will mean to family life? Will they be committed (p. 58)?

4 Come up with a shortlist of ideas for a business. Do you have the necessary skills? Does the market look promising (p. 63)?

5 Briefly define product ideas (p. 11).

6 Brush up inadequate skills. Apart from reading the relevant sections of this book, consider training courses and counselling (pp. 29, 32).

7 Consider whether you should start the business with someone who has complementary skills, that is, who is strong in those skills in which you are weak. Negotiate who gets what share.

8 Decide how big a business you want. Will it be large- or small-scale? How much growth potential do your business ideas have? Do you have the essential management skills to opt for a fast-growth route?

9 Did your self-analysis suggest that you needed ongoing help? Or have you been unable to come up with a sound business idea? What about a franchise? You need at least one-third of the purchase price (p. 105).

10 Investigate the possibilities of buying a business if you have the necessary funds or can raise them (p. 83).

11 Carry out detailed market research into a shortlist of ideas (p. 14). Do this whether you are starting from scratch, buying a franchise or buying a business.

12 Identify a market sector (p. 13). Establish what will be different about your product (p. 17). Estimate all of these: market size, market share, market structure, market trends (p. 19). Investigate the competition and their products (p. 20).

13 In steps 11 and 12, narrow down possible ideas to a leading prospect.

14 Work out your principal selling method – e-commerce, direct mail, intermediaries, for example.

15 Forecast amount and timing of sales.

16 Review yourself, your skills, your family, your idea (p. 56). Take the decision to proceed, do further work or abandon. It is better to drop the idea now than carry on with doubts.

Getting into greater detail

17 Draw up an initial business plan. Forecast sales, costs, cash flows. At this stage, figures will be very approximate (p. 295).

18 Make a preliminary decision about your need to raise money. Roughly, how much will you need? Who is the likeliest lender (p. 322)?

19 Discuss with your family what you will be able to invest. Consider what security you can offer (pp. 58, 322).

20 Seek out and employ the advisers you need. These could include solicitor*, accountant*, bank, design consultant, IT specialist, database experts and web designers (p. 212).

21 Decide how much you will spend setting up, but keep a margin of safety. Tailor the amount to how much you are willing to risk yourself, as the funds you can raise will be a multiple of what you can invest.

22 If you are currently employed, are you able to give the necessary effort to get the business going? Or do you need the extra income? Consider giving up work.

23 Test your product to confirm its performance. Test-market your product or service, if possible (p. 26).

24 Apply for a patent to protect the product or register the design or trade mark, if applicable (p. 123).

25 What form will your business take: for example, sole trader, partnership or limited company (p. 38)?

26 Decide your IT strategy – consider your needs for hardware and software: accounts package, spreadsheet, e-mail, database and so on.

27 Name your product and business (p. 132). Keep in mind your sector of the market and the product's benefits. The name is part of your selling effort.

28 Register the company name, or change the name if buying a ready-made company (p. 96). Check there is no other company with that name. Sole traders and partnerships need take no action.

29 Draw up a partnership agreement, if applicable (p. 48).

30 Come up with some initial ideas about letterheads or consider those put forward by a designer (p. 218).

31 Develop ideas about how to sell your product or service. Identify the product benefits and advantages. What means will you use to get your message across: leaflets, brochures, etc. (p. 141)?

32 Identify possible suppliers. Begin your negotiations.

33 Develop a pricing strategy (p. 180).

34 Refine a business plan (p. 66). Be pessimistic about sales and costs.

35 Ask an adviser or colleague to go through the plan with you, challenging all the assumptions and figures. Have you identified the principal risks?

36 Review the plan yet again. Does the business look viable? Will you go ahead, research further or abandon? All the momentum is to push forward because of all the work and commitment put in so far. But if the idea does not hold water, the right decision is not to proceed but to research something else.

Setting up

37 Consider what equipment your business will need. Investigate how to pay for it: cash, hire purchase or leasing (p. 209).

38 Establish guidelines on what credit to offer, what credit to take from suppliers, how you will control cash (pp. 339–50).

39 Find out what insurance you will need for your business (p. 287).

40 Estimate the amount of initial stock and production run.

41 Make first approaches about raising money.

42 Decide if you will start trading before you raise the money or if you will wait until you have finalized. Remember with complicated finance, it can take several months.

43 Register for VAT if you are forced to and, if not, consider whether it would be beneficial (p. 419).

44 Set up a simple accounting record system (p. 370).

45 Work out what your accounting period should be. There is some advantage in a year end early in the tax year if profits are rising (p. 385).

46 Consider the virtues of trading from home, even if several of you are joining together to start the business. E-mail can help you to communicate from several locations. Otherwise, start the search for premises.

47 Finalize decisions about letterheads and order stationery, once you have found premises and know your business address.

48 If you will need staff when you start trading, start the search now.

49 Carry on developing your ideas about image (p. 143), how to sell (p. 157) and how to get your message across (p. 141).

50 Draw up terms and conditions of sale, if applicable. Set up your database for actual and potential customers.

51 If you will be selling direct yourself, develop a sales dialogue. Train by carrying out role-play with your spouse or a colleague (p. 166).

52 Set up a financial control system, that is, how you will compare actual performance with budgeted performance as drawn from your business plan.

53 Finalize your decisions about brochures, literature mailers, telephone scripts.

54 Draw up contracts of employment for any staff.

Ready to trade

55 Finalize premises, fitting out, employing staff, sales methods.

56 If you are still employed, hand in your notice. If you are unemployed, contact your local Business Link* or Jobcentre Plus* to find out whether you can get any financial assistance from the start of trading.

57 Tell HM Revenue & Customs (HMRC)* if you are to be a sole trader or partner (p. 48).

58 If you are forming a company or taking on staff, ask HMRC for information on how to operate the PAYE tax system (p. 257).

59 Set up a reporting system for your staff.

60 Plan the opening.

Summary

1 Use this step-by-step guide to help to start your business in the right way.

2 The guide is in approximate order; in particular, actions may vary depending on whether you decide to postpone trading until you have raised the money you need.

8

Less than 100 per cent

Businesses don't have to be all-consuming. Many self-employed and small businesses are run on a part-time or less than full-time basis. The increase in the number of these types of enterprise reflects the restructuring in society and the economy that has occurred over the past two or three decades. There are a number of typical scenarios.

First, you might have some sort of business idea but be uncertain whether you want to give up your relatively secure paid employment to commit yourself to surviving on the idea. It may strike you as sensible to test the water a little bit in your spare time or to find out more about the idea before you commit yourself further.

Second, you could be a permanent toe-dipper. Perhaps you have to stay at home, for example to look after dependants, children or elderly parents and you are looking to make some money on the side. The amount of time you can devote to your enterprise might be fairly limited, and you need to select your business idea with care.

Third, you may come into the category of 'greys' who have taken early retirement or redundancy and you are looking to establish a business that will supplement your other income without taking away all your spare time.

Fourth, at the other end of the age scale, you might be a young person starting a business while still in full-time education.

Fifth, a number of businesses are being set up that are 'virtual' businesses. People are opting for a different lifestyle from the driven corporate existence and choosing to establish businesses based around the home, possibly with others in a similar position, for example forming a network of consultants.

Finally, it is very common nowadays for individuals to establish themselves as self-employed with a portfolio of work based around their contacts from their experience in corporate life.

What is in this chapter?

- testing the water (p. 78).
- toe-dipping (p. 79).
- a 'grey' business (p. 80).
- young business (p. 80).
- a 'virtual' business (p. 81).
- portfolio work (p. 81).

Testing the water

There are drawbacks to trying out your business idea without devoting all your time to it. If you are in full-time employment, you will be trying to carry out your business in the evenings or weekends, when you are tired. The result may be that you give up simply because you are too weary.

The second drawback is closely linked. Because you do not have the time your business idea needs, you will not carry it out successfully; you will assess it as a failure because it has not achieved what you hoped. The real reason may be that you have not stoked the fire enough.

The third drawback is that there are not very many businesses that you can start only in the evenings and weekends, because they are not natural business hours for anyone else. Telephone answering machines, call diversion, mobile phones and e-mail do not always provide the solution.

The big advantage of toe-dipping is that you carry on earning money from your job while you are starting up. This may be essential if you have no other income, as your business is unlikely to make profits for some time.

The model way of testing the water is not necessarily to start full trading while still employed elsewhere, but to use your spare time to carry out all your market research and prepare your business plan during this period. When the initial preparation is completed, you should be able to assess whether your business idea will work and have some idea of when you should be generating an income to live on. Now would be the time to cease full-time employment. One possibility at that point is to try to raise some money to fund the business, but obviously this is not a step to be taken lightly.

Toe-dipping

Your motivation may be quite different; you may not be attempting to start a full-time business at all. You may simply want to earn more money on the side. You may be in full-time employment or you may have domestic responsibilities. In either case, the number of hours available for business is limited. And that is the way it is going to stay, at least in the foreseeable future.

You will need a very special sort of business idea. The ideal trade should allow you to fit the work into odd or irregular hours and should not need a permanent presence. Suitable ideas include:

■ *fashion, health and beauty*: hairdressing, beauty therapy, dressmaking, fashion design, knitting, invisible mending and alterations, massage, aromatherapy, physiotherapy, chiropody, acupuncture, reflexology, personal fitness training.

■ *office services*: book-keeping, word processing and desktop publishing, duplicating, addressing and stuffing envelopes, data preparation, printing.

■ *writing*: books and articles, translating, copy-editing, proof-reading, indexing, copywriting.

■ *arts and crafts*: drawing, illustrating, photography, picture framing, candlemaking, glass engraving, jewellery, pottery, soft toys and dolls, design work.

■ *home-based activities*: catering and cooking, upholstery, childminding, curtain making, garden produce, taking lodgers, rearing animals (goats, poultry, bees, rabbits), boarding animals.

■ *assembly work*: toys, lampshades, clothes, Christmas crackers, fire extinguishers, watch straps, jewellery.

■ *design work*: graphic design, interior design, web design.

■ *property*: dealing, buy-to-rent.

■ *miscellaneous*: consultancy, teaching (music, exam coaching), repairing (bicycles, china, clocks), agents (mail order, party plan organizer, telephone selling), dealing, building, decorating, electrical repairs, car maintenance, light removals, odd jobs.

A 'grey' business

There are legions of people in their 50s or 60s or even older, who are too young to cease an active economic life but who are pushed out from their established role by 'downsizing', 'restructuring', 'retreating to core activities' or simply being replaced by the march of technology. In addition, around one person in ten over state pension age currently chooses to carry on working.

Such people may not be looking to set up in a full-time business, because the package offered by their previous employer has given them a pension or other financial help. But they may be looking to supplement their income and, more importantly, remain economically and socially involved.

'Greys' can set up sound businesses. They have a number of advantages:

- they are not looking to derive a huge financial return.
- they have years of business or work experience behind them.
- they are very motivated.
- they may have some initial capital to start the business off and may not need to draw money from it until it is well established.

The disadvantage is that what might start out as a well-controlled economic activity could end up dominating their lives at a time when 'brain' work should be more important than 'brawn' work. It may also be hard to find good working space (but see p. 196 about working from home).

Young business

'Schoolboy entrepreneur nets millions' is sufficiently unusual to make headlines. But some school and university students do start their own businesses and their number could increase as a result of government policies to teach enterprise in schools. Many student businesses are Internet-based which can fit well around school hours, the demands of university and limited capital availability. There are also educational initiatives – particularly those run by Young Enterprise UK* – which enable school pupils to set up and run their own business.

There is no limit on the age at which you can start up as a self-employed person. To be a company director there is a minimum age of 16. However, at age 16, you might find it hard to gain acceptance as a credible business because of your youth (although with an Internet-based business your age will not necessarily be apparent). You will normally be unable to get trade credit or external funding if you are below the age of 18.

A 'virtual' business

Information technology has transformed the way business can be carried out. Businesses can seriously be run and grown without infrastructure and without employee overheads. Such a business fits neatly into a lifestyle for someone looking to spend less than 100 per cent of their time developing it. You could develop, say, a network of consultants, which operates without an office and without employees. Communications can be by e-mail; meetings can be held via the Internet or conference telephone; demonstrations or presentations can be given using the phone and the Internet. Meetings with clients can be held at their offices, in coffee shops or in a hired room.

The advantages of a 'virtual' business are that the overheads are low, the lifestyle is flexible, the work is home-based, and the content is mostly intellectual, with a minimum of time devoted to administration and low-quality work. The disadvantages are those typical of a home-based business: face-to-face contact can be missed, self-discipline is required to work, and meetings with clients are not in ideal situations.

Portfolio work

Typically the person who retires early from middle or senior management might look to build a portfolio of work. A good start for such a life of enterprise might be to obtain a contract from your previous employer. This gives you a good base income but now gives you the freedom to organize your time in the way you want to. This also gives you the opportunity to start using your network of contacts to produce further work. A portfolio approach to business might include the following elements:

■ consultancy.
■ non-executive directorships or chairmanships.
■ project work.
■ buying and renovating property to sell or to let.

The advantages of portfolio work are that the income can be relatively secure (especially if the first contract is with your former employer), the diversity of contracts also adds a quality to your earnings, the work is varied and the lifestyle is flexible. However, be careful of your employment status when you first set out on this course. HM Revenue & Customs (HMRC*) has clamped down on people who leave an employer one day and return the next claiming to be 'consultants' either working through their own company or on a self-employed basis. Expect HMRC to look carefully at your status – see p. 405. If it decides you are, in reality, still an employee, you will be charged tax and National Insurance on that basis.

Summary

1 Trying to start a business while still in a job can lead to failure. Instead, use the time while you are employed to do the basic research about the market and your likely sales and costs. After this, decide whether to take the plunge or not.
2 If you know that you only want spare-time earnings, not a full-time business, choose your business idea carefully to allow you to fit it in with other commitments.
3 Older people starting businesses have a number of factors in their favour.
4 Think about how you can set up a business keeping the overheads and infrastructure as low as possible. Use modern technology to enable you to do this.
5 Starting out with a contract from a former employer gives you a head start in building a portfolio of work.

Other chapters to read

17 Choosing your workplace (p. 192); 18 Information technology – and other equipment (p. 204); 30 Tax (p. 381).

9

Off the peg

At some stage in thinking about your business ideas, it probably flickers across your mind that it would be simpler if you could buy a ready-made business. Your reasoning might be that this would get you off to a flying start and cut down the period needed to establish a business from scratch.

But would it? The truth is that there is no easy way to having your own business. Either you must accept that there is a hard slog ahead of you, building up your own business, or, if you decide to buy an established business, you must expect to pay for someone else's work in having built it up successfully. What is more, if you decide to buy, you might end up paying too much for a business that still needs you to work very long hours. If you want to buy a ready-made business because you think it will be easier, you should seriously examine your motives in wanting to take on a business.

The real temptation to buy a business from someone else is that you might buy a bargain, perhaps because the owner is desperate to sell, or because the business has been run badly and you can see a few easily applied steps that could transform its profitability.

There are three main ways you can get yourself off to a flying start: you can buy a franchise (p. 105), buy into a partnership (p. 89) or buy an established business (p. 84).

What is in this chapter?

This chapter looks closely at buying the whole or part of an established business or buying into a partnership. Franchises are dealt with separately in the next chapter.

There are several ways to buy into an existing business (a 'going concern'). The first part of the chapter looks at buying outright and managing the business yourself. It considers:

■ search for a business, a guide (p. 84).

■ the business profile you want (p. 84).

■ finding a business for sale (p. 85).

■ investigation (p. 87).

■ changing the business (p. 96).

■ setting a price (p. 97).

■ tips on negotiation (p. 100).

Alternatively, you could invest as a 'business angel' in someone else's business. This is looked at on p. 101. Finally, you could buy into a business with funds raised from a venture capital organization through a management buy-in (MBI) or, as an employee, a management buy-out (MBO). These are considered on p. 102.

Search for a business, a guide

1 If you are already in business, pinpoint your overall objectives, the missing factors in your present business and what is holding back growth.
2 Develop a profile of the type of business you are interested in acquiring – either all of it or a stake (p. 84).
3 Carry out the same market research as you would do if starting a business from scratch (p. 13).
4 Research the businesses available for sale (see p. 85) and produce a shortlist of the likely contenders.
5 Investigate the shortlist of businesses carefully (p. 87).
6 Consider what effect your purchase would have on the business (p. 96).
7 Establish a price for the business; or, better still, a price to open the negotiation and a maximum price you would consider paying (p. 97).
8 Plan the negotiation carefully (p. 100).

The business profile you want

You should try to avoid the random search for a business to buy or a good deal to make. If you were starting your own business, you would set out your thoughts and ideas. This is exactly what you should do when considering which type of business you could run successfully if you were to buy one already set up.

To help to clarify your thoughts, it is a good idea to write down in specific terms a profile of the ideal business. This should include the following, among other points:

- the ideal market (or even more specifically, the segment). This choice should follow from a review of your own skills (p. 56), coupled with some market research, which should enable you to pinpoint a market providing you with the opportunities any successful business needs (see Chapter 2, 'Who will buy?').
- the products or services that fulfil this marketing strategy.
- the main factors in a business that could enable you to be successful.
- the price of the business, the maximum you could pay and how that would be financed.
- the ideal size of the business you are looking for.
- where it would best be located (for business and personal reasons).
- whether the business needs to be successful already or whether you are looking to make it profitable through your extra management skills.
- the minimum level of profitability you could accept and the minimum level of income you require from the business.

Once you have drawn up this profile, you should use it to judge the suitability and likelihood of success of all the prospective businesses you see.

On the whole, do not be tempted to abandon the principles enshrined in your profile because you see what you think will be a bargain. It is safer to adhere to the outline you elucidated in a calm, rational manner when you were not under any pressure to do a deal.

Finding a business for sale

There are two basic (but not mutually exclusive) approaches you can adopt:

1 Look at businesses that the owner is advertising for sale.
2 Search out suitable businesses that the owner may not have decided to sell, but that fit your profile.

The advantage of the second method is that you may be more likely to find the business you want; the disadvantage is that you may not be able to persuade the owner to sell, certainly at a realistic price. If you carry out this research, be prepared for several false starts.

Where are businesses advertised for sale?

Increasingly, the Internet is a good place to start your search. Web sites, such as *www.businessesforsale.com*, *www.daltonsbusiness.com* and *www.nation widebusinesses.co.uk* help you search by business sector and location. Many sites let you search for free, but others charge a subscription or fee. Some newspapers and magazines can also be a good source. If you are looking locally, your local newspaper may have a section for this. Another possible source is trade magazines, for example *Dalton's Weekly*. If you know the business area you want to trade in, also take a look at trade journals for that sector.

The details given in the advertisement will be very brief; it may only include the market, the general location and some indication of the income from a business. Note that a number of the advertisers may be the receivers of the business, trying to sell it as a going concern. If the advertisement is by a liquidator, the aim will be to sell off the assets or bits of the business, as it will not be possible to sell it as a going concern because there is no goodwill.

Another source to try is business transfer agents and estate agents. They carry details of small businesses for sale; estate agents will be mainly concerned with retail businesses. You can find the names and addresses of agents in the area you are interested in by looking in *Yellow Pages* or using the 'Brokers & Agents' section on the *www.rightbiz.co.uk* web site. These agents are not independent advisers but are acting on behalf of the business being sold.

Finally, try asking around in the area you want. Try accountants*, solicitors* and banks. These sometimes maintain a register of businesses for sale. You can also try someone already in the industry for ideas of what might be for sale. Advertise in the local newspaper or trade magazine for a business you want.

Conducting a search for a business

You may be able to identify other possible businesses not yet put up for sale by studying the market segment you want to enter. Carry out market research into that sector, identify the competitors and investigate the backgrounds. You may well find that the businesses already for sale are the worst buys. On the whole, go for what you want and not for what is available. There are also a number of organizations specializing in helping you to find acquisitions. These include some of the big firms of accountants. Other useful sources include:

■ the membership lists of relevant trade associations.

■ *Yellow Pages* and *Business Pages*.

■ databases such as Extel cards* and MINT UK (from BvDEP*) – try business or academic libraries.

■ trade exhibitions and trade journals.

Investigation

Once you have a shortlist of two or three businesses you could be interested in, the next step is to investigate thoroughly and then to investigate all over again. It is crucial to be absolutely confident that you know all the pitfalls as well as the good points of the business you are buying. Do not be hurried into an acquisition for fear of losing that so-called bargain.

Investigation is largely a question of using your common sense and being very distrustful about what you are buying. Guidance in this section is very much of the 'Don't forget to do this or that' or 'Look out for' type, but it cannot be an exhaustive list of what you must do. There are also specific investigations that need to be made for each business you look at; some of these will be exclusive to that business.

What help can you get with an investigation?

It would be wise to employ an independent adviser to help you analyse a potential purchase. The most likely candidate for the role of adviser will be an accountant*, as a considerable part of the investigation will be analysing existing accounts and assessing asset values. However, accountants may be expert at the quantitative aspects of a business but miss the qualitative aspects, such as how crucial present employees are to the business. Help and advice from someone in the industry can be invaluable.

Why is the business being sold?

This can be difficult to establish satisfactorily. For example, if it is being sold because the present owner doubts that it will prove to be profitable in the future, you are not likely to be told this. Your investigation of the business prospects must try to identify this type of reason.

A frequent cause of a sale is that the owner wishes to retire. If this is the case, you need to keep your eyes open for signs that the business is running out of steam as the owner's retirement nears. It is also possible that the business and its equipment are now out of date.

Sometimes you may come across small businesses that are being sold by larger companies. The reason given may be that it does not fit with the strategy or pattern of the larger business. The real reason may be because the large company cannot make it profitable, so you need to look for the warning signs. Look carefully at the past history and the accounting policies used.

In the current slow economy, with banks continuing to focus on strengthening their own balance sheets, many small businesses are running into difficulty because of problems renewing or raising bank loans, putting pressure on working capital. Although such businesses may be sound in the long term, you need to consider what makes you better placed than the current owners to ride out or solve the current problems.

If the business is in the hands of a receiver, it will be advertised for sale as a going concern. You cannot take for granted that this is so. Investigation needs to pinpoint whether the assets are actually owned by the owner, whether any genuine goodwill exists and, obviously, the reasons for the financial difficulties.

A sale for any of these reasons may present opportunities for the right business person. The ability to turn around a run-down or unprofitable business is a management and business skill, which you may possess. The important point in acquisition is to know the real reason for the sale before you negotiate to buy. Then you can price the business correctly and assess the impact you could make, post-purchase.

What is being sold?

What you are buying depends on the legal form of the business. If you want to buy a business operated by a sole trader or partnership, you are strictly buying its assets, excluding what the previous owner owed and was owed. You could buy all or only some of the assets. If the business has traded under a different name, not the owner's personal name, you might consider buying the right to carry on using this. This is a wise decision only if there is some goodwill attached to the business name. Your agreement should be very specific about the assets you buy and the price you pay.

On the other hand, if the business is a limited company it has a life of its own, separate from the shareholders. In this case, you could be buying only assets or you could be buying the company itself. If it is the latter, as the new owner you will acquire a business that has obligations and liabilities, such as contracts and debts, as well as assets.

Partnerships

An added ingredient if you are buying a share in a partnership is the necessity to investigate the prospective partner (or partners). All the other business aspects – for example, track record, business prospects, assets – need careful study, but it is also essential to find out what you can about the partners. This is for two reasons.

First, as a partner you are jointly and severally liable for the debts of the partnership. In practice, what this means is that if there are bills to be paid and your partners do not pay up their share, either because they do not have the assets to cover the debts or because they refuse, you can be made to pay for the whole debt, not just your share of it. You must satisfy yourself that the new partners hold some assets that would cover the likely value of their share of any debts and find out their track record of paying bills. A history of unpaid bills or lack of assets of any value (for example, a house) might raise question marks in your mind about their suitability as partners.

Second, the ability to coexist amicably in a partnership is crucial. Personality conflicts can be crippling and may mean, whatever the economic sense of the partnership, the future of the business would be in jeopardy.

If you are buying a share in a partnership in which there are already two or more partners, be prepared for the negotiation to take a long time. Two or more people have to agree; it is not just one person deciding, as would be the case if you were buying from a sole trader.

Use a solicitor* to help you to draw up a written partnership agreement or to vet the one offered to you by the partnership (see p. 49 for an idea of what needs to be covered). It might be wise to attach a note to the partnership agreement that would cover areas such as how the business is to be run, who has responsibility for what, what is the extent of the decision-making for each partner and so on. These are not strictly part of a written formal agreement, but it is crucial that each of you has a clear understanding of how the business will be run.

The accounts

The past accounts of the business are written evidence of what has happened in the last few years. But how good is the evidence? The minimum you should insist on seeing is the accounts for the last three years; these should be handed over to your accountant for stringent analysis. However, there are some points you should bear in mind. If the business is a sole trader, partnership or small company (see p. 38), accounts do not have to be audited. Indeed, the only reason that accounts need to be prepared is for tax purposes, and the accounts need only be a statement of sales and expenses; a balance sheet is not necessarily required. The evidence about the track record could be decidedly patchy and even inaccurate.

The fact that the accounts are prepared for tax purposes may suggest that the sales are understated; indeed, vendors may claim just that. But you should be wary of accepting that profits are really higher than stated in the accounts.

As well as published accounts, ask to see all the management accounts and accounting books, debtors' and creditors' lists and bank statements.

Once your accountant has examined the accounts thoroughly, you should begin questioning whether there are any specific reasons why, for example, the profits were high during the period reviewed. Was there no competition? If so, is there now? If the business is retail, has the pattern of shopping facilities altered to make the location less attractive now than formerly? Will there be a rent review, with a likely increase in rent, which will make a dent in future profits? And so on. Query anything that you think might have affected the results of the present owner, favourably or unfavourably.

Land and buildings

With land and buildings you need to consider the following points:

■ *position*: this is particularly important for shops. You need to study a shop's location very carefully. What are the other shops in the immediate area selling? Direct competition need not be a disadvantage, as customers sometimes like to have a choice and will go to a location with two or more shops selling similar products. The population of the shop's immediate catchment area could be crucial to the success of the business; you should not assume that you can persuade people to travel far to your particular store. What type of population lives nearby? Is there high unemployment? Are inhabitants likely to have high purchasing power?

The future plans for the area, if any, need to be discovered. Are any redevelopments planned? Any road changes mooted? Has planning permission been given for facilities that might undermine your trade – for example, a superstore nearby – or enhance it – say, a new leisure centre that might draw extra trade to the area, or a large new housing estate. The effect of these needs to be considered.

An important consideration for many types of retail business is how many potential customers will pass the shop each day, for example on the way to work or to do other shopping. Test this out for yourself by standing outside the shop on days that are likely to be busy for the business and on days likely to be quiet.

■ *tenure*: if the property is not freehold, what are the terms of the lease? For how much longer does the present lease run? When is the next rent review due, and is there any indication of the likely increase? Who has the responsibility for maintaining the exterior of the building? Check that the seller has the right to transfer the lease. Would you be able to sell or sublet at some future date? With a freehold property, bear in mind that the current owner might own it outright. If you'll have to borrow, you would need a higher level of profits than the current owner to make the business viable, because you'll have interest payments to cover.

■ *business rates*: these are based on the property's estimated rentable value not the profits you generate. Make sure they seem reasonable given the level of trade you are likely to attract. For example, rateable values for shops in a run-down high street are often still assessed on the basis that this is a prime retail area even if the bulk of trade has moved elsewhere. If the property's rateable value is less than £18,000 (or £25,500 in London), you may be able to claim Small Business Rate Relief. Other reliefs are also available, for example, if you locate in one of the new enterprise zones announced in the 2011 Budget. For information, see Chapter 30, 'Tax'.

■ *condition*: pay for a survey to be carried out to establish the extent of your likely bills for the property. Run your eye over the decoration and shop or office fittings. Are there any improvements you could make that would improve the potential of the property, and what would these cost?

■ *space*: what is the useful selling space? Is this sufficient to stock the quantity and range of goods you intend to carry? Will there be any surplus space? Could this be used profitably – by you or some other business?

- *insurance*: what insurance currently covers the property? Is this relatively expensive or cheap?

- *valuation*: take expert advice on the value of the property. You should also ask your solicitor to check the title, any covenants that apply and the likelihood of planning changes.

Plant and equipment

With plant and equipment you need to cover the following points at least:

- *condition*: is the plant and equipment old or badly maintained? Is the technology outdated? What volume of business or production levels could the equipment deal with? Can it cope with periods of maximum demand?

- *value*: this can be a problem to establish to both vendor's and buyer's satisfaction. The vendor may well seek to be paid a value based on the cost of the equipment. As a potential buyer, you need to look closely at the market value, as this may well be less than cost. Indeed, if the equipment can be used in that business only, the market value may be very low, although the value to this business may well be higher than that. You will have to negotiate a price.

- *future commitments*: if you are buying a company, you should investigate what capital expenditure has been contracted for which you would be responsible. This may also apply to any advertising expenditure to which the company is committed.

Stock

Stock is likely to be the major area of disappointment after a purchase. Opt for ruthless reductions in the value in the accounts or make an agreement to buy, subject to certain conditions being met, if you can. At least, check:

- *how much*: first of all, establish that the amount of stock in the business agrees with the figure in the accounts (particularly if you are buying the business, not just selected assets). Once you have established how much stock there is, you need to analyse whether this is the right amount and the right sort for that business. Get guidance on the mix of stock from an expert in the industry. Be wary of buying too much stock, even at apparent bargain prices. Keep an eye out for any outdated or damaged stock as well. You should also check if the business has had a proper stock control system. If it has not, this should raise questions about quoted amounts. It can also be worthwhile to find out whether it is possible to return any stock items to suppliers.

■ *value*: as with plant and equipment, it is likely that the seller will hope to be paid the higher of cost or market value for the business stock. You, on the other hand, may only be willing to settle for the lower of cost or market value (and that may be a very low figure indeed). You should not deviate far from your value of the stock.

Debtors: the customers who owe you money

Your investigation should cover:

■ *how old?* your main query about debtors must be: 'Will they pay and when?' Ask the seller for what is known as an age analysis of debts. This should show how much is owed and how long it has been owing. Very old bills may suggest they will not be paid or simply that the owner is very dilatory about collecting money. You need to know which.

■ *credit rating*: the analysis of debtors should pinpoint which customers owe the larger sums. Assuming that you were to keep these customers if you purchased the business, it is worth checking the credit backgrounds of those businesses (p. 342). You do not want to buy a business that relies heavily on a few customers who are bad payers.

■ *credit collection*: investigate how the existing owner collected debts. An improvement in this could enhance the profitability of the business.

■ *value*: once you have made a careful analysis of unlikely payers and allowed for the cost of collecting the debts, you should be able to arrive at an estimate of the value of the debtors.

Other assets

There are a range of other assets that the business may hold:

■ *cash*: confirm the level with the bank or wherever the cash is held.

■ *patents, trade marks, etc.*: investigate their status; for example, is the trade mark registered? You should find out what would happen to these 'intangible assets' if the business should fail. They may prove to be unrealizable assets if the rights revert to their original owner, for example. (Patents and trade marks are dealt with in Chapter 11, 'Beating the pirates'.)

■ *investments*: if the business holds investments, perhaps in other companies, your accountant should ensure that an appropriate value is placed on them.

■ *goodwill*: the price you will eventually fix is unlikely to be the sum of the values you set on the individual assets. Negotiation may result in a price above the asset value. The surplus is known as goodwill. Goodwill can also be described as the reputation of the business and what you are paying to acquire that reputation. Valuing goodwill is a very uncertain process. Will the goodwill disappear once the present owner is no longer part of the business? Will customers and suppliers stay with the business on the same terms, assuming those to be satisfactory?

Liabilities: what the business owes

The main liabilities to be investigated are:

■ *loans, debentures and overdrafts*: establish the amount, the conditions, the period of the loans and the interest rate.

■ *creditors*: an examination of an age analysis of creditors should give you some idea of the sort of credit periods suppliers have been extending to the business in the past. If the business has paid very slowly, it may suggest that its reputation with suppliers is fairly low.

Sales

To estimate the potential of the business, you will need to look carefully at the sales figures. Carry out a product or service analysis. Does one product account for the vast bulk of the sales? What is the profit margin on this product? Does your analysis suggest scope for streamlining the product list?

Your study of the debtors will also have thrown up information about the customer structure. Does the business rely on one or a few customers? Do those customers account for the major portion of the profits as well as the sales? An over-reliance on a few can mean the business may be fairly risky and prone to sudden downturns should a customer cease using the product.

Crucial information about sales potential can be ascertained by talks with the major customers. These may throw light on the quality and reputation of the business and product. Further evidence can be obtained by a study of the level and nature of credit notes and a study of the percentage of substandard goods produced.

Look for any special relationships that exist with major customers, such as an extended credit or returns arrangement.

Other aspects of the sales figures you should study include:

■ the element of windfall sales that are unlikely to be repeated.

■ the sales by territory or area.

■ the pricing and discount structure, including the existence of fixed-price or fixed-volume contracts, particularly if buying a company.

■ the distribution of the product.

■ competition.

■ the seasonality.

The products

If the business is the manufacture or distribution of a product, you will need to find out more about it. The areas you should concentrate on are:

■ *cost*: ask yourself if there are any reasons why the costs should rise or fall in the near future. Have there been any changes in the prices of raw materials, and are there seasonal variations? Is there a shortage of skilled labour to make the product? Are any changes likely among the suppliers? Are there any key supplies that need careful management?

■ *profit margin*: an examination should also be made of the cost of each individual product compared with its price. Do all the products cover direct costs and make a contribution to overheads? Which gives the highest contribution and which the lowest? What is the pricing policy? Have discounts been offered? Turn to Chapter 27, 'Moving ahead', for information about profit margins, contribution and overheads and Chapter 16, 'How to set a price', for pricing.

■ *orders*: if it is a company, what is the quantity of advance orders? Will these all be retained if ownership of the company changes hands?

Employees

If the present owner has staff, you will have to find out what your obligations will be to them. If the owner is a sole trader and you are buying some of the assets, there will probably be no legal obligation to offer continued employment; but there may be if you are carrying on the business. If the business is a company, you will most likely have legal obligations to the employees. This is particularly important if it is your intention to replace

the staff or make them redundant. You will need to ask your solicitor*
for advice.

Even more crucial than the legal responsibilities for employees can be the
extent to which the business relies on key personnel. You need to understand
their calibre, attitudes and responsibilities – before the deal. It is vital to sustain
their enthusiasm and commitment through the period of ownership change.

Changing the business

Finding out what has happened in the business in the last few years and
what changes are likely to occur as a result of external factors does not give
you a complete picture. It ignores the fact that you intend buying the business and have some ideas of how it could be improved. You need to consider
what changes you would like to impose on the business, what they might
cost and what improvement in profits you estimate they would make.

Realistically, you should also recognize that a change in ownership may
mean lower profits rather than higher. This might occur if the business
is heavily dependent on personal contacts. The previous owner may have
established an extensive network of relationships, which means that,
in a shop, for example, a substantial proportion of the customers come
because of the owner's personality rather than because of its location, its
prices or its range of goods. No matter how confident you are that you
will handle customers courteously and cheerfully, you may not have that
magic ingredient your predecessor possessed and some customers may
drift away.

On the other hand, you may estimate that, in a business where personality
is important, the previous owner has not been ideally suited to the nature
of the work and that you will be able to bring a change for the better
because of your own character.

Other changes you may introduce are more tangible, and you will be able
to estimate the effect and cost of their introduction. The three main ways
you can increase profits are by cutting costs, increasing prices or selling
more. See Chapter 27, 'Moving ahead', for some ideas.

Bear in mind that you may need planning permission if you intend to
change the use of the premises. If the change of use might be controversial
– for example, opening a workshop in a primarily residential area – it could
be a good idea to apply for permission before deciding to buy.

Some changes may involve you spending money: for example, redecorating or refitting a shop, reorganizing the production facilities, buying new equipment, restocking. Include these in the cost of acquiring the business. This allows you to set a realistic price that you can pay for the business.

Setting a price

The right price for any business does not exist as a theoretical calculation. The only price that is 'right' is the price that both the buyer will pay and the seller will accept. It is all down to negotiation. This may bear no relation to the prices calculated as a result of the value of the assets or the earnings potential that the business gives you. The first step is to jettison all notions about real value. The second step is to throw out of the window all notions that the price given in the agent's details, for example, is the price you will have to pay. Negotiation is everything.

However, you should enter any negotiation with two prices in mind. If you are the buyer, the lower price will be the price you use to open the negotiation; the higher price is the maximum you will be willing to pay. You should not start negotiating unless you have a clear idea of this maximum price. If you are the seller, the lower price is the minimum you will accept for the business and the higher price the one you adopt initially.

Nevertheless, it is vital to have used a number of methods of arriving at a price. These can give you a benchmark for establishing lower and upper prices. You must have a base point to work from. The accountant who is advising you should carry out these calculations for you, but you should know the basis for the figures. You can set a value by asset value, earnings multiple, or return on capital employed.

Asset value

Your investigation will have helped you to set values for individual assets. If you are buying the whole business or it is a company, the figure you are interested in is the net asset value, that is, the value of the assets less the value of the liabilities. There is no rule on whether you should use the cost of the asset or its market value as a basis for your price estimate, although you will be wise to choose the lower of the two.

The final value agreed upon is unlikely to be a simple sum of the individual assets; any additional value is called goodwill.

If property forms a major part of the business, you may automatically think that the price you pay is asset value. However, it is very important to look at what sort of profits those assets will be able to earn for you. See Example 1 in the box below.

Earnings multiple

A second way of valuing a business is to apply some multiple to the earnings from the business, perhaps two or three times. Clearly, you will not take the present owner's figures for earnings at face value; apart from investigating whether they are a fair reflection of what has happened, you also need to take into account in your calculations what interest charges you would be paying after the purchase of the business. This should include loans for any improvements you intend making. See the following Example 2.

Example 1

George Gabriel is interested in buying a health food store.

The details he has been given are:

Price for the freehold of the shop and flat	£160,000
Price for the stock	£9,500
Goodwill	£6,000
In total, he is being asked to pay	£175,500

George needs to carry out his own investigation. First, he looks at the shop. The size is reasonable – 500 sq. ft (46.5 sq. m) – for a specialized business and the location is excellent. However, the shop has been fitted in an idiosyncratic way, not especially suitable for the type of business. Although the condition of the fittings is good, George would want to replace them; in particular, he would like to include facilities for serving takeaway food, including hot food, which the shop does not have at present. He estimates that the cost of these alterations will be about £36,000, £18,000 of which is for the additional food facilities.

When it comes to the living accommodation, this seems in reasonable condition. He asks a valuer to give some idea of what an alternative two-bedroom flat would cost in the area and is given an estimate of £90,000 to £110,000.

A close examination of the stock reveals that some of it is damaged but, most importantly, there are very big stocks of a few slow-moving items. George would place a value of only £4,000 on the stock acceptable to him. Nor is he convinced that there is that much goodwill associated with the business; the present owner's odd personality has militated against this.

George's value for the business based on asset values would be £160,000 less £18,000 fittings that need replacing plus £4,000 for the stock. This makes £146,000 for the business, rather than the £175,500 asked.

Example 2

George Gabriel (see Example 1) now works out a value for the business based on an earnings multiple. He has been told that the present owner derived an income of £30,000 a year from the business. George estimates that, with the improvements he intends, he can increase this figure to £35,000 in the first year; he hopes to push it up to £40,000 subsequently.

George has £100,000 of his own; he intends to spend £5,000 on extra stock plus £36,000 on improvements. This leaves £59,000 towards the purchase of the business. He'll have to borrow the rest of the purchase price – an additional £87,000 if he buys the business for the £146,000 valuation above. At an interest rate of 8 per cent a year, this means interest charges of, say, £6,960 a year (exact amount depends on amount borrowed, which will vary with the purchase price).

So George's approximate earnings figure for the last year would be:

$$£30,000 − £6,960 = £23,040$$

And for the current year:

$$£35,000 − £6,960 = £28,040$$

And once the shop has reached its full potential:

$$£40,000 − £6,960 = £33,040$$

These figures give the following values of the business:

2 times multiple: £46,000, £56,000, £66,000

3 times multiple: £69,000, £84,000, £99,000

For negotiation, George should refer to the past year's earnings figure only and go for the two times multiple. This gives a much lower figure for valuation than the asset value basis does. In fact, the range of values he obtains suggests that, on the whole, the asset value basis will result in a figure that is too high for him to get the return he needs on his investment. From these figures, his negotiation should start at £46,000 and go up to £69,000, say.

There are a couple of other factors that might influence his decision; one increases the value he would be willing to pay, the other lowers it. These are:

■ the savings he will obtain from living above the shop, for example rent or mortgage payments.
■ the loss of interest his £100,000 was earning.

Return on capital employed

To assess value on this basis you need to decide in advance on a rate of return that you require on the money you invest. This should certainly be more than the rate of interest you could get from leaving your money in a building society account. Once you have decided, you work out what the income before interest and tax is as a percentage of the capital invested.

If the figure you get as a result of this calculation is less than your required rate, you would decide not to buy or to lower the figure you were prepared to pay.

Tips on negotiation

The negotiation is the key to future prosperity. This may well be the only time you are involved in negotiating to buy a business, so there is no opportunity to practise negotiating skills. But negotiation must be done if you are to buy the business at the right price for you. Follow these tips:

1 An obvious point, but do not agree to the price first quoted.
2 Open the negotiation at the lowest price you can. This price must be one that you can back up with credible reasons, so a good deal of planning is needed before negotiation begins. A shock opening bid can lower the seller's expectations and undermine resolve.
3 Look carefully at apparent bargains. If the seller accepts your first low bid, perhaps given the seller's better knowledge, your opening price was too high. Think again.
4 During the negotiation, you can undermine the opposition's confidence by asking a lot of 'what if' questions. For example, 'What if the government changes?' 'What if your major customer goes bankrupt?'
5 Do not fall into the trap of making a concession for the sake of the goodwill of the negotiation. The opposition will most likely strengthen his or her resolve to hold out for the highest price possible.
6 Do not answer questions of how much you can afford to pay, at least until you wish to use it as a negotiating tactic at an appropriate time. Answering the question at the timing of the seller's choice may lead you into discussion of helping you to foot the bill by loans or easy instalments. Later you can use what you can afford as a limit on price.
7 Sometimes, you will find that if you start out as a tough negotiator, the reaction from the other side is a soft response. A tough reply to a tough opener is more unusual.
8 Never be offensive and over-critical; it draws a defensive response.
9 Keep your reactions very low-key; never indicate whether the news is good or bad. Keep calm.
10 If the other side makes a concession, do not feel you must respond in kind. Stay tough. There is no law that if you make an agreement with the seller, the agreement should be midway between the two initial positions. On the contrary, the purpose of negotiation is to try to make sure the pendulum swings your way.

11 If you are probing for solutions that will allow you and the seller to agree, always begin your possible concessions with 'If'.

12 Planning your arguments and rehearsing them before the negotiation will give you confidence in the strength of your bargaining power.

13 Try role-playing before the negotiation occurs with a colleague or spouse acting as an objectionable seller.

14 Whatever the treatment meted out by the seller, do not let it get to you and your confidence in your own bargaining position. Do not be affected by the other's apparent wealth, status, success or attitude.

15 The best way to counter any threat is to indicate that you are indifferent to its being carried out. Making threats yourself can be unproductive.

16 If it is possible to produce some outside authority who limits your bargaining position, do so. This could be your spouse, your partner or the person lending you money.

17 Keep in mind whether the goodwill of the previous owner is needed after the change of ownership.

18 It is often useful to link part of the price to future performance. This reduces the risk of failure against forecast.

Business angels and agreements

If you don't want to purchase the whole of a business and be responsible for running it yourself, an alternative is to be a business angel. A business angel is looking to invest money in a private company, but an angel is not the main driving force of a business. The angel is looking to invest risk capital (not usually a loan) in exchange for owning part of the business (becoming a shareholder). An angel is also usually looking to work in the business, bringing additional skill, contacts and experience.

Before you invest as a business angel, you will need to carry out all the investigation spelt out earlier in this chapter. In addition, you need to negotiate your role in the company and a shareholder agreement to give you some protection in the event of disagreement. You need the protection because it is likely that you will be a minority shareholder (own less than half the shares) and thus could have little power over how your investment is spent or your role in the business. The agreement should cover:

■ what the business activity is and what it can be in the future.

■ no competing business to be carried on by the management.

- the issue of further shares to other shareholders and the right to buy the shares of any other shareholder who wants to sell.
- what happens if the existing shareholder gets into financial or legal difficulties.
- board meetings and who is on the board of directors.
- ensuring that the management cannot move assets out of the business.
- level of management salaries and how much time management gives to the business.
- your right to look at financial information.
- who can sign cheques and up to what amount.

As you can see, a solicitor* should carry out drawing up a shareholder agreement. But don't get bogged down in legal niceties and remember that you want to work with the management after you have reached an agreement. A shareholder agreement is just to protect yourself from an unscrupulous management and should not divert you from your prime aim, which is to make the business more successful with an investment by you.

Brief guide to management buy-ins and buy-outs

In recent years, there has been a growing number of management teams 'buying in' to another business or 'buying out' and running the business in which they were previously employed. Buying into another business is known as a management buy-in (MBI), and the purchase of the business will be funded by a venture capital organization, in addition to your own money.

You can make an MBI on your own or with one or more members of a team. You need to get the backing of one or more venture capital organizations before you can go ahead. Backing is only likely to be there if you have solid management experience, usually in a large company.

A management team buying out a company that they already work for is known as a management buy-out (MBO). There are three main occasions when this occurs.

First, a large organization decides to sell or close down a subsidiary. This could be because:

- the business does not fit the strategy of the organization.

■ the business does not give the rate of return required by the organization, or it could even be unprofitable.

■ the parent company does not have the resources to provide the funds needed by the business or it simply needs to raise cash.

Although we are concerned here mainly with buying a private company, these are also the sort of reasons that apply in the case of the government's 'right to provide' initiative under which, if you work in the public sector, you may be able to swap your employment for running the same service as a mutual organization – see p. 17. As a mutual, you will be expected to deliver services more cheaply and/or to improve quality compared with the existing publicly run service.

Second, a private company may want to sell out *in toto*. This may be for personal reasons, such as the family not wanting to run the business any longer or the need for cash.

Third, the company may have gone into receivership. There may be a part of the business that could be profitable if separated.

Raising money is likely to be the major problem for a management buy-out, as the management team may not be able to finance more than 10–20 per cent of the business. There is also a need to raise the money quickly before the opportunity slips. Lenders and investors will want to go through the same process as with any investment or lending decision (see Chapter 25, 'Raising the money'). A large proportion of the money put up to buy the business will be interest-bearing loans, which can be an onerous burden for a company.

Some MBOs opt to organize as cooperatives with all the workers contributing part of the capital needed and all participating democratically in the way the business is run (see p. 53).

Summary

1 Do not be tempted into paying too much to buy a ready-made business because you want your business life to get off to a flying start.
2 Clarify your thoughts about the market you want to enter, the size of business you want to run, the type of product or service you want to offer and how much you want to pay before you start searching for a business to buy. Summarize it in a business profile.
3 Consider seeking out a business that fits your profile as well as investigating all those currently advertised for sale.

4 Use advisers to help you to investigate a partnership or business.

5 Adopt a sceptical approach to investigation; query and question everything about the business.

6 Be realistic about the effect of a change in ownership; there could be changes for the worse as well as the better.

7 Set two prices before you go into negotiation: the lower one with which you start the bidding, a higher price beyond which you will not go.

8 Negotiation is everything. There are no rules; there is no right price for any business. It is up to you to summon your facts and marshal your arguments to keep the price as low as possible.

9 Use the negotiation tips listed on p. 100.

Other chapters to read

1 You and your ideas (p. 1); **2** Who will buy? (p. 13); **10** Franchises (p. 105); **25** Raising the money (p. 316).

10

Franchises

It would be lovely if there was a way you could start your own business with a much greater chance of survival than most people. And this is just what is claimed by the franchising industry. The statistics seem to back this up, although they are rather patchy. What information is available suggests that a franchised business has a much greater chance of surviving the first three years (the danger years) than other new businesses.

Clearly, you don't get something for nothing. The price of choosing the franchised route can be high. It is up to you to weigh up the costs of buying a franchise and the risks of starting from scratch.

Some of the costs are obvious: you may have to pay a lump sum at the outset as well as paying an amount each year to the person selling the franchise. Less obvious is the cost if you buy a franchise in which you have to buy products from the seller's company at a price determined by it; in this way, you cannot benefit from shopping around to buy your supplies at the lowest possible price.

One of the economic theories behind the success of franchising is that the franchised business can earn for the product as a whole higher-than-normal profits. The intention of the seller of the franchise is to cream off the above-normal bit of the profits, for example by charging a percentage of sales each year, leaving only the normal bit of the profit for the person who buys the franchise. These higher-than-normal profits can build up a brand image for the product or business by carefully positioning the product in the market and using advertising and PR to promote it. In this way, the end-user of the product, the consumer, will pay higher prices than for an equivalent product.

What is in this chapter?

This chapter looks mainly at what happens if you buy a franchise (become a franchisee) and only briefly touches on how to form a franchise to sell to others (become a franchisor). It concentrates on what is called *business format franchising*. This sort of franchising is where you buy a complete business system or way of trading. All the franchisees trade under a common name, appearing to be branches of one large firm, rather than a whole series of independent businesses. The chapter includes:

- a brief guide to franchises (p. 106).
- the pluses and minuses (p. 107).
- a guide to choosing a franchise (p. 109).
- how a franchise works in detail (p. 110).
- the contract (p. 118).
- setting up as a franchisor (p. 121).

A brief guide to franchises

This brief guide to a typical franchise describes what happens in the different stages of a well-organized and properly developed franchise; occasionally, there may be a franchise that is not developed in a model fashion, and you should beware of buying one of these. Use the guide on p. 109 to sort out the wheat from the chaff.

In the first step, a business is developed or set up. It could be based on a novel or revolutionary product, a comprehensive and well-organized business method, particular marketing style and so on. The business (or pilot) will have run for a couple of years, so that all initial problems have been sorted out. Preferably there should be more than one pilot, which demonstrates that the business idea can be repeated.

Next, the owner of the business (the franchisor) decides to expand, not necessarily by creating more branches but by selling franchises to the business format already developed in the pilot operation. Note that the two forms of expansion, selling franchises and opening branches, can be carried on at the same time. The franchisor develops the franchise operation, which should be a mirror of the successful pilot. The franchisor should produce an operating manual to show how each franchise should be set up and run.

Once the format has been developed, the franchisor will try to find a suitable person to buy the franchise (a franchisee) for a particular territory. There will be careful investigation by the franchisor to make sure that the franchise is sold to a suitable person who will develop the particular territory successfully. A prospective buyer should investigate the franchise, the pilot operation, the contract, operations manual and so on to ensure that the franchise will be worth buying. Mutual suspicion should rule.

When the franchise is bought, the contract (p. 118) will be signed and the buyer will usually pay an initial fee to the franchisor. After opening, the franchisor should continue to provide advice and should advertise and market the product name. The franchisee will normally pay a fee each month. The product will usually be purchased from the franchisor, which may be another way that the franchisor makes his or her profit instead of the percentage on sales. The franchisor has the right to make visits to the franchisee's business to examine the accounting records. At the end of the contract, which lasts five or ten years or more, the franchisee can usually renew, subject to the franchisor being satisfied with performance.

The pluses and minuses

Your main consideration before buying any particular franchise is whether it will work as a business for you and provide you with the sort of living you require. Assuming that you have found such a franchise, there are advantages and disadvantages of which you should be aware.

The pluses

1 It is your own business.
2 If the business format has been well worked out and tested in the pilot operation, many of the problems experienced in setting up a business can be sidestepped. This reduces your risk.
3 You receive ongoing advice and support.
4 You hope you are buying a product with a recognized brand name. To create a brand image all by yourself can involve considerable resources. But in the case of a franchise, the franchisor should carry on promoting it, using the management service fee (or royalties) or possibly an advertising levy (p. 112), which all the franchisees will pay. So the brand name of your business will be getting a bigger selling push than could be achieved by each franchisee's individual contribution.

5 In the case of many franchises, you need no knowledge of the industry before you start your business. The training given by the franchisor should be sufficient to overcome any ignorance.

6 Franchisors, because of size, have greater negotiating power with suppliers than you do on your own, although not all of them pass this benefit on to the franchisees.

The minuses

1 While it is your own business, you are expected to act in the best interests of other franchisees and the franchisor. You could find this irritating and restrictive.

2 As well as the initial fee, part of your profits will have to go each year in a payment to the franchisor. You might find this galling.

3 Often the continuing fee to the franchisor is based on your sales rather than profits. This could lead to problems if you are struggling to make profits, perhaps because the costs are too high. This will not be reflected in the level of the fee.

4 The franchisor has the right to demand that you send in sales statistics and other documents promptly, plus the right to come to your business premises and inspect your records. This might seem intrusive.

5 You have to adhere to the methods laid down in the franchisor's operating manual. This could be restrictive and allow little room for you to exercise your own initiative and enterprise.

6 You may have to purchase all your stocks from the franchisor. This allows little room for you to seek competitive alternatives. Again, you could find this stifling if you want to run your own business.

7 Should the franchisor fail to maintain the brand name by promotion or fail to meet commitments about training and the search for better products, frankly there is little you can do about it. If this is all buttoned down in the contract, however, you may be able to get somewhere.

8 If you want to sell the franchise before the end of your contract, the franchisor has to agree.

9 The franchise runs for a certain number of years. Normally, if your performance is satisfactory (whatever that means, see p. 119), you will be able to renew for another period; but you may have to commit to spending more money on refurbishment and more modern equipment. What happens about further renewals is not always clear. You should assess the return on the money you invest over the first period of the franchise only. If, for some reason, you are not able to renew, you may have little to sell, because you cannot sell the name or the goodwill.

A guide to choosing a franchise

1 Be sceptical about franchises, franchisors and franchise specialists.

2 Make your own choice of advisers; do not use those suggested by the franchisor. The most unbiased advisers are likely to be a high-street bank – some of which have specialized franchise units giving independent advice – and the solicitor* and accountant* you employ to advise you.

3 Get your accountant to examine the forecasts given to you by the franchisor and to advise you on how realistic they are.

4 Ask your solicitor to go through any contract carefully to bring out clearly the restrictions and also the ways in which the franchisor will be making money. A legal affiliate to the British Franchise Association (BFA)* will have specialist experience.

5 Find out how many franchises have already been sold and how long they have been going.

6 Find, visit and talk to existing franchisees. Do not allow yourself to be restricted only to the franchisor's choice of references.

7 Be particularly careful if the franchise you are interested in is one of the first to be sold. You will need to study the pilot operation with a fine-tooth comb. Does it mirror your likely business? Does the manager of the pilot have the same sort of knowledge and skill as you? Are the premises and their location much the same? Is the stock identical?

8 Watch out if the initial fee is relatively large and the continuing fee relatively small. It is essential for the franchisor that the business continues to be promoted and properly managed. The success of your business depends on how effective the franchisor is in marketing and purchasing.

9 Look carefully at the arrangements for purchasing equipment and stock. You do not want to be forced to buy new equipment if unnecessary; nor do you want an arrangement in which the franchisor can increase the mark-up on products sold to you. Can you buy from alternative sources?

10 Investigate the franchisor. The continued existence of the franchisor's business is important to you, because it carries out the marketing, purchasing and other centrally organized functions. Get references and credit ratings. Ask the franchisor to give you a copy of the latest accounts and ask your accountant to study them.

11 Be careful about buying a franchise from a franchisor who is not a member of the BFA. Membership does not guarantee the success of

your business or the franchisor's business. And a number of quite reputable franchisors do not belong to the association. However, members agree to abide by a code of ethics. Ask a franchisor why it is not a member, if it is not.

12 Check that your territory is properly marked out (and you receive a clearly defined map of it). What market research has been done to ensure the territory is promising enough to provide the estimated sales? Do your own analysis – don't rely on the franchisor.

13 Examine what will happen if you die, want to sell your franchise, disagree with your franchisor or want to renew the franchise (see p. 119).

14 What sort of product is it? It must have a useful life of at least the length of the franchise that you are purchasing.

15 Carry out market research in exactly the same way as if you were setting up the business on your own. Chapter 2, 'Who will buy?', should help you to do this. Do not rely on market statistics or views passed on by the franchisor.

16 Check that the product has been patented or the name registered as a trade mark, otherwise the franchise you buy could be worthless.

17 How will the advertising levels be maintained? Does the franchisor contract to spend certain amounts on promoting the brand name?

18 What is the quality of the field force run by the franchisor? How often will they visit? Are they competent to give sound business advice? What will happen if your business runs into difficulties?

19 The relationship between franchisee and franchisor may, in a few cases, prove difficult to maintain at a harmonious level. What are the lines of communication? Do you think that you will be able to build a good relationship with this particular franchisor?

20 If it is a good franchise, you will face competition from other would-be franchisees. So you should expect a grilling. If you are not closely investigated, this may indicate that the franchisor is short of buyers.

21 Many points on which you need information before you tie up an agreement with a franchisor are listed in this chapter. Make sure you cover them in your discussions, and check the franchisor's response.

How a franchise works in detail

Cost

The cost to you could be made up of one or more of the following. There will be the initial cost of a franchise, including the initial fee, and most likely there will be a continuing fee (also called royalty or service fee). There may also be an advertising levy, a mark-up paid on goods or equipment supplied by the franchisor and a mark-up if you lease premises from the franchisor.

You also need to look out for any hidden costs of financing, which may occur if the franchisor obtains a commission on introducing you to a business providing finance or to a leasing company, if you lease equipment. It is only a cost to you if you could have arranged cheaper finance elsewhere.

■ *initial cost*: the range of prices for all franchises is wide; it could be as little as £25,000, for example, or as much as £5 million. Usually, the initial fee is between 5 and 10 per cent of the total investment but can be as much as 40 or 50 per cent. The latest annual survey by NatWest and the BFA (2010) found that the average initial outlay for setting up a franchise was £63,900, though this varies greatly according to the business sector concerned. Six out of ten franchisees borrowed money to set up, with the average loan being £51,000 in the 2010 survey (slightly up on the £49,000 reported in 2009 but well down on the £70,000 average in the 2008 survey), but over a third of franchisees borrow more. The fall in the average may reflect tight bank lending conditions, with franchisees having to find more of the initial outlay from their own resources.

There is no typical start-up package, but below is an example of the sort of items that could be included in the initial cost:

Shopfitting	£20,000
Equipment	£22,000
Initial stock	£11,000
Initial franchise fee	£15,000
TOTAL	£68,000

The initial fee is what you are paying to be given the right to use the brand name within a certain territory and to be trained and provided with advice.

■ *service fee*: the service fee payable can also vary quite a lot, from nil up to 20 per cent of sales, but was on average around 11.2 per cent according to the 2010 NatWest/BFA survey. This is a big jump from the 8.2 per cent average in the 2009 survey. The service fee could be paid weekly or monthly. The fact that the service fee is nil does not necessarily mean that all you are paying will be the initial start-up cost. Franchisors can also be paid by using mark-ups on products and equipment and there is usually an advertising levy (see below).

A low service fee is not necessarily an advantage for you. It is crucial that the franchisor retains an ongoing interest in promotion and improvement of the business format, and that will only be achieved by the reliance on some sort of continuing payment from the franchisee.

The franchisor prefers to base the service fee on sales rather than profits. This is because monitoring the franchisee accounts to ensure that the franchisor is receiving the proper amount can be time-consuming and expensive. If the fee is based on profits rather than sales, the monitoring has to apply to costs as well as sales, doubling the difficulty of the task.

However, a fee based on sales can be disadvantageous to the franchisee. If the costs of the enterprise prove to be higher than forecast, paying the service fee could be an onerous burden for the franchisee.

You should not underestimate the size of the service fee, because it is based on sales not profits. If, for example, your costs are 60 per cent of your sales value, a service fee of 10 per cent of sales translates into a service fee of a quarter of the profits you make. Work out the figures before you sign.

One point to watch out for is what happens at the end of the original franchise contract if you want to renew. Does the contract allow the franchisor to increase the size of the service fee? Try to negotiate on this, as you do not want a bigger percentage of your hard work to be passed over to the franchisor.

■ *advertising levy*: a number of franchise packages charge an advertising levy as well as the service fee. This is usually calculated as a percentage of sales and paid at the same time as the service fee. The 2010 NatWest/BFA franchise survey found the average advertising levy was 2.6 per cent of turnover. (This partially reverses the steep rise to 3.9 per cent in the 2009 survey compared with 1.9 per cent the year before.) The existence of an advertising levy could be regarded as an advantage for a franchise if promotion of the brand name is a very important part of the franchise success. If an advertising levy is made, look to see if this will be audited separately in the franchisor's accounts so that you can see that it has indeed been used for that purpose and that alone, not just disappeared into the franchisor's pocket. If there is no separate advertising levy, the franchisor may undertake to spend a certain proportion of the service fee each year. The other common alternative for advertising is that the franchisor will undertake to advertise as and when needed. With some franchises, the franchisee is expected to advertise as well as, or even instead of, the franchisor. This could lead to promotions that are at odds with each other – and may mean that the prestige of the franchise name deteriorates.

■ *mark-ups*: one apparent advantage of grouping together can be that buying in greater bulk can mean bigger discounts and cheaper supplies. This should also apply to franchises, where supplies are often an important part of the cost of the enterprise. However, some franchisors put on mark-ups that deprive the franchisees of any benefit from bulk purchase.

■ *hidden costs of financing*: it is not unusual for companies to pay commission to someone who introduces a new customer to them. This does not necessarily mean that you will get a bad deal if your franchisor helps you to arrange finance. But it does mean that you should shop around to satisfy yourself that you cannot organize a more attractive deal elsewhere. In practice, you may find it difficult to arrange finance except through the franchisor, but you should examine the possibility.

Finance

Raising money to finance the purchase of a franchise is treated in the same way as raising money to start any new business. All the clearing banks have specialist franchise units and, on the whole, they appear to look more favourably upon the average franchise application than on the average start up. This is because a franchise is believed to offer a lower risk to a lender.

However, any bank will require that a prospective franchisee contributes a proportion of the start-up capital, usually around 40 per cent. The remaining 60 per cent could be financed by the bank. Don't forget that the lower the level of your borrowing the greater the chance of your business surviving.

A loan will need to be repaid by the end of the franchise term; however, there may be some leeway on the initial repayments of capital. For example, a repayment holiday could be arranged until the business is in profit.

If the bank requires security, this could be provided by a charge on the business assets, such as premises or equipment, but only if you run the franchise as a limited company. If you remain a sole trader, a mortgage on your house may be acceptable.

Territory

The interests of the franchisor and franchisee may clash when it comes to the allocation of territory. The franchisor would like the option to introduce another franchisee to the area to maximize sales and profits. The franchisee, on the other hand, does not want to be competing with another business on the same patch, selling identical goods.

Whatever is granted in terms of rights, it is important to have clear identification of the territory. Check that it is clearly specified in the contract. The delineation of the territory should also be relevant to the particular trade. If it is a shop, perhaps a certain number of miles from the site would be relevant. If it is a service franchise, perhaps a *Yellow Pages* division of territories would be more suitable.

It is also important to ensure that the territory is large enough to support a business of the type proposed. If you have any doubts, do not buy.

Premises

There is no set practice on whether the premises are owned or leased by the franchisor and sublet to the franchisee or the premises are owned and leased by the franchisee. It varies from franchise to franchise. Controlling the premises has advantages either way. If the franchisor owns the site, and if the franchise is not renewed, a valuable, well-placed site is not lost, as far as the franchisor is concerned. Conversely, if you are the franchisee and the premises are in your name, when it comes to renewal, you can use the site for another business if you would prefer.

Whatever the position about tenure, the location of a site, especially if it is for a shop, needs to be examined carefully, in exactly the same way as for any other business (p. 192). Do not take the franchisor's word for it.

Operations manual

This is where the franchisor puts all the know-how of the business; it should incorporate the essence of the business format you are buying. One of the terms in the contract will be that you must adhere to the manual.

It should include details on everything: accounting systems, recruitment, how to carry out the actual process of the business (for example, grill a hamburger, print a leaflet or unblock a drain), reporting systems and so on. You should see a copy of the manual before you buy. Make sure you understand what is in there; it is how you will have to behave in your business while you own the franchise.

An indicator of the ongoing interest of the franchisor can be how frequently the manual is updated. Ask how often this has been done.

Training

Training is an important part of what a franchisor is offering. Before you sign the contract, you need a clear idea of how much training there will be and how long it will take – two months is the average, according to the NatWest/BFA 2010 survey. You should expect training in all the basic business skills you will need to run a business. This includes financial methods, stock levels, operating the equipment, carrying out the process of the business, working out accounts and PAYE, employment law, VAT and so on *ad infinitum*.

Opening

The franchisor should help you to start your business. If it is a retail business, once the premises have been found, the franchisor will help organize the shopfitting. Indeed, it may be part of the agreement, as it may be that the shopfitting has to conform to the brand image: the colours, style of counter, type of shelves and so on.

Additionally, advice will be available (it may even be a requirement to follow it) on the equipment and amount and mix of opening stock you should have. Find out before you sign what the franchisor's policy is on this and satisfy yourself that you are not being cornered into a policy of over-equipping and over-stocking.

To have a successful opening, you need publicity and perhaps an opening ceremony; you should get help and advice on how to advertise and arrange media coverage. Find out the franchisor's level of commitment on this.

Ongoing support and supervision

This could consist of six elements:

1 Refresher training (see p. 115).
2 Product research and development (see p. 115).
3 Troubleshooters and supervisors who pay regular visits (see p. 116).
4 Updated operations manual (see p. 114).
5 Advertising the brand as a whole (see p. 112).
6 Advice on an individual level about promotion (see p. 116).

Products do not last for ever. So for any business there needs to be continuous assessment of the product to see how well it meets its customers' needs, not just in the past, but now and in the future. Any market trends need to be taken into account, and the product may need altering over the years to meet the new criteria. Or a completely new product may need to be evolved. For a franchise to be successful, the franchisor should devote some energy to this. Check what your franchisor's policy will be on this before buying.

The downside to this is that any innovations or alterations could end up being costly for the franchisee. Try to establish what the future plans of the franchisor will be and check what the agreement says about implementation of any new developments.

Another element of support and supervision by the franchisor is the help available if you or the business are in difficulties; for example, are there troubleshooters to provide guidance? The sort of questions you want the franchisor to answer include:

- how often will support visits be made, and what is the calibre of the support staff?
- if the business is struggling to break even, does the franchisor have special troubleshooters? If not, what sort of help will be available?
- what happens if the equipment does not work properly? Are there maintenance facilities, and what is the response time?
- if you are ill, is an emergency staff team available to take over?

As well as the positive side of providing support, you must recognize that the supervisory team also fulfils the role of monitor for the franchisor. You will have to accept that they will want to examine your records and books on a regular basis, check that you are not understating sales (or whatever it is that the service fee is based on) and ensure that the service fee is paid on time.

A final element of support that you need to investigate before you buy is the advice available on promotion of your business. While it is a better arrangement for the franchisor to carry out the advertising and promotion of the product name on a national basis, you may feel that there are opportunities that allow you to boost your business by advertising and promoting locally. The franchisor may be able to advise on this. In fact, the franchisor may insist, as part of the agreement, that you promote locally. For example, is the amount of expenditure specified, and will it prove onerous?

Franchising and pyramid selling

You need to check that the franchise does not get caught by the Trading Schemes Act 1996, which is intended to curb pyramid selling. The two main caveats that would exclude a franchise from the terms of the Act are:

1 If all the franchisees are registered for VAT; or

2 The franchise operates through a single tier only. For example, if there is a single franchisor for the UK and all franchisees are recruited by that single master franchisor, the scheme could be exempt. But if there is a layer of several different franchisors for different regions of the UK who each recruit franchisees, the scheme would be caught by the Act. Similarly, if the franchisees themselves recruit further franchisees or even if they contract self-employed people to carry out their work, the scheme would be caught by the Act.

Finding and buying a franchise

At the time of the 2010 NatWest/BFA franchise survey, there were 845 active franchises in Britain in 2009. There are 137 full members of the British Franchise Association (BFA)*, 79 registered associates and 63 companies with a provisional listing. Associate members have begun franchising but do not yet have a track record; full members are longer-established franchisors. Companies that are new to franchising can get a provisional listing as long as they can show that they are taking all reasonable steps to develop their business properly and test its viability for franchising.

To start your search for a franchise you could contact the BFA. It provides guidance on its web site to buying a franchise, as well as through a range of published guides and DVDs (costing between £10 and £20 each) available from the BFA bookshop. The BFA* also organizes one-day seminars on becoming a franchisee at various locations across England and Scotland (£75 plus VAT).

There are a number of organizations operating as franchise consultants that say they will give advice on finding a franchise. Before you use one, be absolutely certain that it is not an organization concerned solely, or even mainly, with finding franchisees for one or two franchise companies. If this is the case, the impartiality of the advice can be discounted. There are a couple of franchise directories* that may give you a head start. Web sites advertising businesses for sale – for example, *www.businessforsale.com* or *www.daltonsbusiness.com* – usually include franchises.

Work out some rough guidelines for the type of business you would be happy to be in and the sorts of areas of the country you would be prepared to move to. Estimate the sort of price you could pay, bearing in mind that you should be able to invest at least one-third, while borrowing the remaining two-thirds is a possibility.

Write to a shortlist of five or six franchise companies, asking them to send you the details you need. This should include projections of the likely level of business and a draft contract, as well as the areas where the company currently has a franchisee vacancy.

Once you have received the information, the hard work begins. Consult your solicitor* and accountant*. Carry out your own very thorough research, investigating, among other aspects, marketing, advertising, product lines, financial aspects and supervision. Use the guide on p. 106 to assess each franchise. It is important to remember that if the franchise is a good one, the franchisor will be able to pick and choose from applicants. Treat the negotiation with the franchisor from two points of view:

1 The need to investigate and assess the worth of the franchise.
2 The need to sell yourself as an ideal applicant to the franchisor.

For a good franchise, you will need to provide references along with much more information about your suitability as a franchisee.

While you are negotiating, you may be able to reserve a particular territory by placing a deposit. The amount of the deposit and whether it is partially refundable or not varies from franchise to franchise. Sometimes the deposit is set against the initial fee on signing. Check the terms and the franchisor's references before you pay it.

The contract

This is the kernel of all franchises. Once you have signed it, it will rule your life. Do not skimp on independent legal advice, although it is unlikely to be negotiable as the franchisor will want to ensure that the same conditions apply to all franchisees.

The contract will attempt to ensure that you run the business along the lines specified by the franchisor. The contract should cover these areas:

■ the type of business, its name and the use to which it can be put.

■ the territory where the franchisee has the right to use the name.

■ how long the franchise will run.

■ what the franchisee will have to pay (the initial fee and service fee).

■ if the franchisee wants to sell.

■ if either the franchisee or franchisor wants to end the agreement.

■ what both the franchisor and franchisee have agreed to do.

The type of business, its name

This part of the contract will describe the franchise. It will indicate that the franchisor has registered any relevant trade mark or patented any invention. The franchisee will probably have to agree not to handle any trade mark, product or service belonging to a competitor of the franchisor.

The territory

The contract may specify a right to carry out your business in a particular area, defined by a map or postal code, for example. Unfortunately, it is very difficult to stop another franchisor, or indeed any competitor, encroaching upon your particular area.

How long the franchise will run

The average length of time a franchise has been running stood at nine to ten years, at the time of the NatWest/BFA 2010 survey. The contract may specify a minimum initial period – say, three, five or even 20 years. Normally, you can renew the franchise at the end of the original agreed period, but this may be subject to satisfactory performance. You should certainly want an option to renew and you should try to ensure that the legal wording about what constitutes a 'satisfactory performance' is clear to you, fair to you and can be enforced by you. This is essential, because unless you have the lease on the premises, you would have very little to show for your work at the end of the initial franchise period. You would not be able to sell the business as a going concern, because you would no longer have the rights to the name or to use the business format, and without these there is little goodwill to be attached to the business.

Some contracts specify that if you do not wish to renew, the franchisor will buy the business from you, including a value for goodwill. The value put on the business will be set by an independent accountant.

If you have an option to renew, the contract may specify that certain sums of money are spent to update the premises and smarten the business. The details of this commitment need to be buttoned down in the contract. In any case, the option to renew may well be to renew on the terms currently on offer to franchisees; these may be less favourable to a franchisee than the terms on which you originally signed.

If you have decided not to look for another agreement with the franchisor, the contract may restrict your activities. It may specify that you cannot carry on a similar or competing business for a certain length of time.

What the franchisee will have to pay

The contract will specify the amount and the nature of the fees that will be paid: that is, the initial fee, the service fee (or royalty) and, if applicable, the advertising levy.

If the franchisee wants to sell

Most agreements include some arrangement whereby the franchisee can sell the business during the course of the term. The contract may specify that the franchisor will be entitled to first refusal. Additionally, one of the conditions will be that the franchisor has to agree that your buyer is properly qualified to run it. Your buyer will have to receive training and probably have to be prepared to sign a new agreement. However, it will be difficult to give the same sort of rigorous vetting that the franchisor can do for the initial holder.

Watch out for the sort of agreement that allows the franchisor to charge high transfer (or other) fees on a sale. This type of condition could effectively block any sale you might make, except to the franchisor on poor terms.

A contract should also include the terms and conditions that apply if you die during the agreed period of the franchise.

If franchisee or franchisor wants to end the agreement

It is possible that you want to end the agreement, if you find that the business is hard going, for example. In those circumstances, it may be difficult to find a buyer. On the other hand, it is not especially in the franchisor's interests to insist on keeping you to the agreement if you are not making a success of it. The contract should deal with what can be done in these circumstances. You need to satisfy yourself that the contract would treat you fairly.

The contract will also specify the conditions under which the franchisor can end the agreement. This could occur if you break the agreement that you sign and fail to meet your obligations under it. Conditions might include:

■ minimum performance target.

■ agreement to purchase minimum amounts of goods and merchandise.

■ the requirement to bring your unit up to standard, if necessary.

Experience is now indicating that, with a good franchisor, renewals are made and some are now on their third or fourth term.

What franchisee and franchisor have agreed to do

The contract will stipulate what both of you must do to keep your side of the bargain. For example, for the franchisor the rules about training, supervision, advertising, support and maintenance and management services should be specified.

The franchisee will have to operate according to the manual and allow the franchisor's staff to monitor the business activities. There will be a requirement not to handle the trade marks, products and services belonging to any competing business of the franchisor's or possibly to trade in any other area allocated to another franchisee.

Setting up as a franchisor

This aspect of franchising is beyond the scope of the guide, although your interests can be interpreted from what is said about the franchisee's interests. Here are a few brief guidelines:

■ you need to have proved in practice that the business format works. This is done by establishing a pilot operation, which should be run exactly along the same lines as the proposed franchise. All the systems and products should be tried out here and all the wrinkles ironed out before selling any franchises. Ideally, the pilot should have run for two years. It goes almost without saying that the pilot has to be successful, otherwise you will not be able to sell any franchises.

■ the business format needs to be distinctive in its image and/or its way of operating.

■ it must be possible to pass on the format successfully to others.

■ the format needs to be capable of earning high enough profits to give both the franchisee and franchisor an adequate living.

The British Franchise Association* has *The Franchisor's Handbook*, which costs £18.50 (including postage and packing) and runs seminars on franchising an existing business.

Summary

1 The main advantage of starting a business by buying a franchise is that a lot of the initial start-up problems have already been sorted out; this means there should be a greater chance of survival than starting a business from scratch yourself.

2 The main disadvantages are that there is a loss of independence because of your commitments to a franchisor; you also lose the possibility of earning exceptionally high profits, because the profits are divided between the two of you.

3 Use the guide to choosing a franchise on p. 109 to help you to sort out the good from the bad.

4 The franchisor should provide support and development throughout the franchise.

5 Because of uncertainty about what will happen at the end of the initial agreed period of the franchise, your decision to buy or not should be based on the initial period only.

6 Use your own advisers, for example bank, solicitor and accountant, and carry out your own research into finance, the market, the product, the franchisor, the location and the detailed terms of the franchise. Do not rely on the word of the franchisor.

Other chapters to read

2 Who will buy? (p. 13); 5 Are you sure? (p. 56); 25 Raising the money (p. 316).

11

Beating the pirates

Successful small businesses do not need to be founded on an invention or an original design. A much more important factor is that there is a market that wants to buy your product. The ultimate in good indicators for success would be a strong market and an original product. But often there is not a ready-built marketplace waiting for inventions. You may need to educate customers. This can be expensive as well as time-consuming.

However, if you have thought of an invention, a trade mark or an original design that could form the kernel of a successful small business, it is worth trying to protect it with the law. For example, if the idea can be turned into profits, someone else may try to copy it and you should obtain the best protection you can, so that you make the profits, not the imitator.

The law cannot protect alone. First, you have to be vigilant in watching out for infringements. Second, and more importantly, the best protection of all is guaranteed by carrying out effective marketing: this can turn a product based on an invention, for example, into the market leader (p. 141).

What is in this chapter?

- what to do with an invention (p. 124).
- what to do with a design (p. 126).
- what to do with a trade mark (p. 128).
- what to do with copyright (p. 130).

What to do with an invention

What is an invention that can be patented?

There are four requirements for something to be regarded as an invention for patent purposes. These are that it must:

1 *Be new*: it must not have been published or made known anywhere in the world previously.
2 *Involve an inventive step*: by and large this means that it must not be obvious to another person with knowledge of that particular subject.
3 *Be capable of industrial application*: an idea that cannot be made or used will not be counted as an invention.
4 *Not be excluded*: there are various categories that are excluded by law. These include something that is a discovery (that is, you found out about it, but did not invent it), scientific theory or mathematical method, mental process, literary, artistic or aesthetic creation, playing a game, presentation of information or a computer program. Also anything that would be regarded as encouraging offensive, immoral or antisocial behaviour, a new animal or plant variety, or a method of diagnosis or surgery for animals or humans.

What is a patent?

A patent of invention is granted by a government body. It gives the owner of an invention the right to take legal action against others who may be trying to take commercial advantage of the invention without getting the owner's permission. This right is granted in return for complete disclosure by the owner of his/her invention.

The body that grants the UK patent is the UK Intellectual Property Office* (IPO), formerly the Patent Office. A UK patent can last up to 20 years from the date on which you first hand over documents to the IPO. After the first four years, you have to pay a yearly fee to keep it in force. Note that the four years start from the date you first applied for the patent. A national patent gives protection only for the country in which it is granted.

If your invention is of a type that you believe you may want to exploit throughout Europe, not just in the UK, it could be cheaper to take advantage of the European Patent Convention. This allows you to obtain patent rights in a number of European countries. You need to make only one application (still to the UK Intellectual Property Office), whereas if you applied for a UK patent first, you would then need to apply for patents in each of the individual countries you thought important.

Can you get a patent?

The main criterion for granting a patent is whether or not the invention meets the four guidelines about what an invention is (see p. 124).

One area you have to be particularly careful about is not telling anyone – apart from, in confidence, a patent agent* (also called a patent attorney) which would be a good idea – or publishing information about your invention before you file your application at the UK Intellectual Property Office. If your invention is not kept secret, it may mean that, even if no one else has thought of it, you will not get a patent.

Occasionally, even if you have been granted a patent, you may find that someone challenges it. This could be on the grounds that someone else had already thought of the invention and had made details of it public before you filed your application for your patent. The other person may have decided not to bother to apply for a patent. Making details of it public would include describing it in a trade journal, or exhibiting or selling it.

What does it cost?

When you first file your application, there is no fee. Within a year, you will have to pay a fee of £180 (postal) or £150 (online) for a preliminary search and examination. If you go ahead with your application there is another fee of £100 (postal) or £80 (online). To keep the patent in force for up to 20 years, there is a yearly fee, which increases. For the fifth year it starts at £70 and rises to £600 for the final year.

You'll pay more if you want to patent your product in other countries as well. Because the UK has international agreements with European and many other countries, the cheapest route is often to obtain a UK patent first and within 12 months file applications to extend your rights abroad.

However, many inventors use a patent agent to help with the application. You would have to check the fees before employing one.

A guide to obtaining a UK patent

1 Keep mum about your invention, unless to a patent agent.
2 Complete and file patents form 1 in the UK Intellectual Property Office (there is no fee unless you are also applying for a search). With the form should be sent a description of the invention drafted in accordance with UK Intellectual Property Office rules, which specify the exact format. It must describe the invention fully and clearly enough so that a competent person could follow the description and

build it or carry out the process. Enclose two copies, preferably typed and on A4-size paper. (If you regularly apply for patents, you could use the IPO's online filing service.)

3 You will receive a receipt with the date of filing and a number. This gives you your priority date, which gives you precedence over the same invention being filed later. But this is no guarantee that the same invention has not already been publicized elsewhere by another person (see p. 125).

4 During the next year, examine the commercial possibilities and decide whether to press on with your application or let it lapse.

5 If you make an improvement to your invention, you cannot add it to your first application but would have to file a new one. However, as long as you do this within a year of the priority date, that date will apply to whatever is in the new application that was also in the first application. The first application can now be allowed to lapse.

6 Within a year of the priority date you need to file a request for a preliminary search and examination on patents form 9, together with the required fee. If you do not do this, your application lapses. You will also need to file the patent 'claims', which define in words the monopoly sought and an 'abstract', a short summary of the invention.

7 Once the search has been carried out by a UK Intellectual Property Office examiner, a search report will be issued. This is a list of relevant documents so you can compare your invention with others and decide whether your application is likely to be successful.

8 If you do not withdraw your application at this stage, your application will be published by the UK Intellectual Property Office without any changes.

9 Within six months of publication of the application, you have to file the next form (form 10), plus the required fee. There is now a much more detailed examination of your invention.

10 As a result of this substantive examination, amendments may be required by the examiner. If these are carried out satisfactorily and within the required time, the patent will be granted. Typically, it takes two to three years from application to grant of patent.

What to do with a design

Sometimes the success or failure of a product depends not only on how it works but also on what it looks like. The outward shape or decorative appearance of a product can also be protected, either by:

■ relying on the automatic protection of design right; or by

■ registering the design, by applying to the UK Intellectual Property Office*. This gives stronger protection, but not all designs can be registered – and it takes time and money to register.

What protection does design right give you?

Design right means someone else cannot copy the shape or configuration of an article if it is an original, non-commonplace design. Design right does not apply, for example, to items such as wallpapers or textiles (but these may still be protected by copyright and you may be able to register them).

Design right protection lasts for the shorter of ten years from the end of the year in which you first start selling articles made to the design, or 15 years from the end of the year in which you created the design.

You have an exclusive right for the first five years after you start selling the articles, and in the remaining five years others can obtain a licence to the design – but you don't have to hand over drawings or know-how.

The limits to design right are that something you design to fit or match an article designed by someone else won't get protection, and design right protection applies in the UK only. However, some countries accept UK registration as equivalent to a registration in their country too or as establishing a priority date for a local application.

What is a registered design?

Registering a design gives you a monopoly right for the 'look' of an article or set of articles manufactured from the design. The protection lasts for 25 years, but you must renew it every five years.

You can't register a design either if the outward appearance of the article is not important or if the shape of the article is determined by the shape of another item. And the design must be 'new', otherwise registration won't be granted. For this reason, it is important to keep the details of the design secret before you register; if you have not done so, it will not count as new.

What does it cost?

To register a design as soon as possible, you pay £60 for the first design and £40 for each subsequent design applied for on the same form. If you are happy to defer the publication of your design(s) by up to 12 months, the costs are reduced to £40 for the first design and £20 for each subsequent one. You can register a design for protection throughout the European Union via the UK Intellectual Property Office (in which case, there is a handling charge of £15 on top of the fee) or direct with the Office for Harmonization in the Internal Market*. Initial registration is for five years and costs €350. Registration can be renewed in five-yearly blocks up to a maximum of 25 years.

A guide to registration of a design

1 Keep mum about your design, except in confidence to a patent agent.
2 Tell the UK Intellectual Property Office what the design is and what is going to be made from it. You must do this with a copy of the design, for example a drawing or a photograph, in accordance with their rules. Remember to send the required fee.
3 The UK Intellectual Property Office carries out searches and assesses whether the design is original and new. If it is, registration is granted.

What to do with a trade mark

What is a trade mark?

A trade mark is something that identifies a product in the eyes of the consumer. The consumer will know who has manufactured the goods or who is selling them. Trade marks are closely linked with the idea of building loyalty among customers, so that they will choose your product or service over another similar one.

A trade mark can be a word or a symbol, such as a logo. Since 1994, distinctive smells and three-dimensional shapes can also be registered as trade marks. Obviously, what you use as your trade mark should be carefully considered, as it needs to fit in with the image of your product and business that you are trying to put across.

In the past, you have not usually been able to register your own name as a trade mark if it is a fairly common name. But, in a recent case, the European Court of Justice found no reason to treat names any differently from other trade mark applications. As a result, an application to register a name as a trade mark will be judged on criteria specific to the sector in which it is to be used.

How can you protect it?

You can register a trade mark with the UK Intellectual Property Office* (IPO). To be eligible for registration, the mark must be distinctive. A made-up word or a new symbol would be considered distinctive. Ordinary words would not; although after a number of years, with the advertising you put behind such a trade mark and the reputation for the product and business that you build up, the mark can acquire distinctiveness. Consumers will now recognize what was formerly an everyday word or name as identifying your product.

Registration entitles you, and only you, to use the mark. It gives you the right to take action against someone else to prevent their using it.

You can also obtain an EU-wide trade mark effective in all the member states of the EU by applying to the Office for Harmonization in the Internal Market*.

There are also some simple steps you can take to help to protect the mark yourself. For example, put TM beside the mark when you use it in advertisements or sales literature. It can also help to include a sentence such as 'Microtops is the trade mark of Matthews Computer Stores'.

What does registration cost?

The cost will be £200 (£170 online) but could be more if anyone challenges the mark. You can opt to use the Intellectual Property Office's RightStart scheme (£200) which lets you pay half the fee when you first apply, with the other half payable only if you decide to go ahead. However, this would only be for one class of goods, and there are 45 altogether. If you intend to use your mark on more than one product, you may need to apply for registration in more than one class at £50 per extra class.

A guide to registering a trade mark

1 Consider whether the mark will distinguish your product from another. Is it similar to another mark? Could it confuse consumers about the nature of the product or service? Even if the mark is an ordinary word or name, do you believe that your reputation has built it up into a distinguishing feature for your product or service?
2 Apply to have the mark registered with the IPO. Include the required fee and a description of the goods on which your mark will be used.
3 The IPO considers the application; if there are any objections you will be told, so that you can decide what to do. If you have opted for the fast-track service, the IPO reports back to you within ten days.
4 After about 15 months from the application, the IPO will advertise the mark in the *Trade Marks Journal*. If there is no opposition, the trade mark is registered.

What to do with copyright

What is copyright?

Generally, you have copyright in any creative literary, musical or artistic work you create. This can include not just books, films, photographs, recording, and so on but also, for example, content you create for your web site, computer programs and databases you create if they have an original element. Copyright is automatic – there is no need to register – and usually lasts from the time the work is created until 70 years after the year in which the author dies. (Databases can also be protected by database right which is similar to copyright but lasts only 15 years.)

Copyright gives you the economic right to benefit commercially from the work you have created. The benefit might come from your own use of the work. Alternatively, you might sell (assign) your copyright or, for a fee, license others to use your work. Copyright usually also gives you moral rights to be identified as the author of the work and to be protected from misuse of the work that would damage your reputation.

How can you protect it?

There is no official register for copyright and no need to register it at all. Some private firms run their own registers and offer to register your work for a fee, but there is little advantage for you in using these services unless the firm offers extras, such as legal help defending your right.

Wherever you use the work, it is sensible to mark it with the copyright symbol (©) followed by your name and the date the work was created.

Copyright is a private right and, if someone else uses your work without permission, it is up to you to decide what remedies to take. You could go to court but this is generally costly and time-consuming. The best first step might be to write a strongly worded letter to the offender, requiring them to stop using your material, with the threat of legal action if they do not. If the offender has used your work on a web site, print off the relevant screens so you have a record of the offence even if the web site is subsequently changed.

If someone disputes your claim to be author of the work, you may need to provide evidence that you are. You can establish the date at which the copyright material was created by posting yourself a copy using special delivery and leaving the package unopened. However, this does not prove you were the creator, so you should also keep drafts and any other evidence that supports your claim to be the author.

The Digital Economy Act 2010 includes measures to help copyright owners take action against people who infringe copyright by illegally downloading material from the Internet. For example, Internet service providers can be required to monitor and provide a list of incidents where your copyright has been infringed in order to help you bring court action against the perpetrators. Measures under the Act are due to come into force by 2012.

What does it cost?

Nothing. Copyright is automatic without any need to register or pay fees.

Summary

1 The strongest way of protecting an invention, design or trade mark is to use effective marketing (Chapter 2, 'Who will buy?', Chapter 11, 'Beating the pirates' and Chapter 13, 'Getting the message across').

2 Patents and registration provide protection; but the law cannot achieve this alone. You need to follow up infringements of your rights.

3 With inventions and designs it is crucial to keep quiet about them before you apply for a patent or design registration.

4 Mark original work you create with the © symbol and be prepared to challenge anyone who uses it without your permission.

Other chapters to read

2 Who will buy? (p. 13); **12** The right name (p. 132); **13** Getting the message across (p. 141).

12

The right name

At an early stage in your planning, the question will come up: 'What am I going to call my business?' or 'What am I going to call my product?' You may be tempted to plump for your own name or your initials and quickly move on to other tasks. But this would be a mistake.

Choosing a name is a long-term decision, which is all wrapped up with working out what you are trying to sell and identifying why customers will buy from you rather than your competitors. Your company or product name should encapsulate a message to potential or existing customers. This will not happen overnight; it takes many years to build up a name to carry the message you want. But one thing is for sure, you cannot change horses midstream. The name you plump for now should be the name you still have in five or ten years' time.

Choosing a name

Before you start the search for a name, there is quite a lot of background thinking to do about your marketplace, competitors and product.

Why do people buy from you?

If you analyse why people buy a particular product or service, the list might include things such as it is cheaper, the product has a special feature that others do not have, the service is nearby and very convenient, its running costs or maintenance is less, and there is 24-hour guaranteed service. These are all rational reasons, capable of proof. If your product or service has one feature, or more, that is like this you have a primary benefit. You may be able to achieve your sales on this alone.

The list of reasons why people buy a product might also include it is better, it looks good, the quality of the service is high, it is believed to be very reliable, it is better value for money, and the design is excellent. These are all emotional reasons, which may be real or imagined. But they reflect how customers feel about a product.

A combination of the emotional and the rational reasons gives a product its reputation (or brand image).

How does your product rate?

Your product may have some unique element; if so, you are probably unusual. The chances are that there is nothing that much different or better about what you are going to do than your competitors' offerings. But that does not mean you will not be more profitable, make more sales and get a bigger share of the market than someone with a product that does have unique features.

Creating a 'good feeling' among buyers about your product can give you a better general reputation and can make you better thought of and more widely known. Giving your business an identity can make you successful.

However, creating an image of quality and reliability for a utilitarian product can lead to a downfall if your product or service does not live up to it. The product must be good even if it is not the best; the service must be reliable even if not the most reliable.

Where does name come in?

You want the name of your business or product to summarize all the emotional and rational feelings about the product. So if a potential customer hears the name, it instantly gives a good connotation. On day one of your business, this will not happen. You must plan to achieve it over a number of years.

Your first step is to select a name that does not, by itself, cause any feeling of antipathy. Ideally, the name on its own should give a clue to your image. You should at least aim for the name to generate neutral feelings in the early stages, until you have built the image from scratch.

One name or two?

Should your business and product share the same name? There is no clear-cut answer to this one, and for a small business it may not be very important. You will not have the resources to create two brand images, one for the product and one for your business. In any case, it could be confusing. So even with separate names, you will be promoting only one.

If I'm selling to industry, do I bother with image?

Yes. You may be selling to a buyer from an industrial firm but, with the other hat on, the buyer is also a normal human being. This means that he or she will probably have the same number of prejudices as a member of the general public buying soap. It is as important to create a good feeling about your product with an industrial customer as with a domestic one.

If my product has a unique feature, do I have to bother with image?

Yes. You may have some original feature, but once you have launched it on the market, your competitors will be beavering away to make sure that it does not stay unique for very long. And, on the whole, you cannot patent an idea, only a mechanism, so you may not be able to rely on protection (p. 123). If you do not concentrate on the image of your product, and your competitive advantage is subsequently eroded because other products are improved, the future of your business may not look so rosy. Building an image for your product is a low-risk safety route.

What image do you want to create?

This is all linked up with the market research you will have done (p. 14), a crucial stage of your planning. You will have found that there are sectors within the market. For example, if you were considering opening a picture-framing business, you might find the following sectors: do-it-yourself, speedy service, mail-order, high-quality frames, and a service with advice from a designer or artist.

Your research will identify the size and growth of each sector, where the competition lies, and what are the prime demands by customers in each sector. In turn, your decisions will be to go for one or more sectors, to look at your service compared with the competitors' and to focus on what your customer wants. This will give you guidance on what sort of image to build for your business.

Logo – a no-go?

A logo or logotype may be nothing more than a word, the name of your company or product, always shown in the same typeface or in the same colour, or, perhaps, within a simple shape. It could also include an unusual or memorable shape; one that people will recognize quickly and eventually come to associate with all their perceptions of your product.

Using a logo can emphasize your name and get greater customer awareness. If you can afford to do it, do it. But do not rely on your printer. Paying a designer may be worthwhile (p. 218). In your dealings with your designer, specify that the logo must be cheap to reproduce, as once you have got it, you will use it on everything you can. So you do not want to end up with a beautiful logo that costs you an arm and a leg every time you want new quantities of stationery.

Do not make snap decisions on logos; if you can, try a little bit of market research on potential buyers to assess their reaction or possibly ask colleagues, family or friends.

Tips on choosing a name

1 Made-up words can make good product or business names. They may not arouse any positive feelings about your business, but they are also unlikely to create negative ones. If you are going to register that name as a trade mark, there is more chance of coming up with something distinctive and less chance of objections from firms already named something similar if it is a made-up word (p. 128).
2 If you are going to use an existing word, if possible try it out on potential buyers to check that you will not create a bad impression simply because of the name.
3 Use brainstorming sessions with family and friends as well as colleagues to produce a list of names for consideration.
4 Check that the name you prefer is not used by another product or business in the same or a similar market. (There is no automatic search for similar names when you seek to register a trade mark, but anyone already using a similar name can apply to block your registration.)
5 Avoid initials: it is difficult in the short term to create a comfortable feeling about a business or product with initials.
6 If you think that some of your business will come through *Yellow Pages* or other alphabetic listings, choose names beginning with A.

7 Check that the name you choose does not mean anything nasty in a foreign language (for example, look it up in dictionaries in the library). If you are interested in selling throughout Europe, consider whether your proposed name is suitable.

8 Very complicated words need careful consideration. If a customer has to ask you to spell the word when it is first mentioned, this can be a positive reinforcement for recognition in future. But if it is just too difficult, it may be a disadvantage.

9 A name that uses all capital letters, for example FLAG, can stand out in a chunk of written text, giving the name prominence.

10 Finally, ask yourself if the name seems right for the image you want to project.

What the law says about names

With a limited company or a limited liability partnership (LLP) (see p. 40), you will not be allowed to register names:

- that are considered the same as that of an existing company or LLP. You can check this by looking at the index at Companies House*.
- that contain 'limited' or its equivalent anywhere else in your company name but at the end.
- that could be considered offensive or illegal.

And you're unlikely to be able to register a name that could give the impression of a connection with the government, the devolved administrations, a local authority or other public authority. There is also a range of words that require the agreement of the Secretary of State or various other bodies before you can use them. Examples are Abortion, British, Charity, Royal, Windsor, National and English. There are around 145 of these words altogether. There are other rules about company and LLP names, so advice from your solicitor* would be helpful. Guidance on names for companies and limited liability partnerships is given in the booklets GP1 *Incorporation and names* and GPLLP1 *Limited liability partnerships, incorporation and names*, available from Companies House.

If you are a sole trader and want to use a business name other than your own surname, there are certain rules you have to observe, and the same names which are prohibited or sensitive for company or LLP use (see above) also apply in this context. You are not required to register your business name anywhere, but you must disclose your own name in various ways. You must put your own name and address legibly on all business letters, on written orders for goods and services, on invoices and on written demands for payments of debts. You must display your name and address prominently at your business premises or at any place to which your customers and suppliers have access. And if anyone with whom you are discussing business asks you to disclose your own name and address, you must do so immediately in writing.

If you are going to trade under a name that is not your own, consider registering it as a trade mark (see p. 128). You won't be able to register a name that is descriptive of your product or service (because this would be too restrictive for other businesses), but if you choose a name that is made up or unusual you may be able to do so. And registering it as a trade mark would give you some sort of protection for the investment you are making to build a brand image.

If you will be trading under your own name, you could apply to trade-mark it. This might be especially worth doing if you have built up a reputation that would enhance the image of your business – say, you are a sports personality selling sports equipment. Following a European Court ruling, an application to register a name as a trade mark is now more likely to be successful than in the past, even if it is a relatively common name.

Building your reputation

Once you have selected your business or product name, your next strategy is to devise means of getting your name noticed by as many of your target customers as you can. Obviously, you do not want your name to be associated with any bad news, so you may find that you do not want to take up every opportunity to publicize your business name. What you should aim for is that your business or product name comes instantly to mind in your potential buyers, but with a favourable impression.

Letterheads

This is the single most important way for most of the self-employed and small businesses to create some type of image about themselves. Poor-quality paper suggests cheap, poor-quality service. Spend more on the paper to create that good impression.

It is tempting, especially if you know little about marketing or design, to play safe and choose white paper with black type for your letterheads. But consider experimenting with some draft versions before making your choice; it may cost a little extra, but if it helps to create the image you are seeking you should do it. Your local instant print or photocopying shop can be very helpful, either printing small-run samples of different types or positions or at least letting you rearrange elements (name, logo, address) and photocopying the permutations. Consider:

- different colour paper.
- different colour type.
- different positions for your business name (for example, the centre or to the right).
- different typefaces for name and address.
- big- or small-sized typefaces.
- adding a ruled line to give a more finished appearance.

Once you have settled on your letterhead, look carefully at your other stationery needs. If your work is the type where you send out few invoices for large sums of money, you may not need separate invoices but can use ordinary stationery. Will you need compliments slips, or will business cards suffice if you will only need them for a few occasions? Whatever stationery you do require, the colour and typeface should be uniform throughout the range. If you have a logo, it should be included on all your stationery.

If you are in retailing, you may decide that letterheads are not an important tool for you in creating an image. While this may be so with customers, letterheads are still needed to create that right image with suppliers, on whom you rely for credit.

Labels and stickers

If you can see any opportunity for using labels and stickers on your products, seize it. These can also carry the message you want. There must be continuity with your chosen letterheads: colour, style, typeface and logo – if you have one – all identical to your stationery. In a shop, you might consider having price stickers. On garments or other material items such as rugs, tableware and so on, labels should be sewn in.

Packaging

The package says lots about the goods, so take the opportunity to reinforce the message you are sending to customers. The style of the packaging should be consistent with all the other items for promoting your image, and with your chosen image itself. Packaging is an extension or even an integral part of your products.

Your own web site

You may decide to have your own web site or to rent space on someone else's. Branding on your web site should be an extension of the branding on your product, letterheads and so on. And the address for your web site (the site name or URL) ideally should be the name of your product or company to strengthen your branding further. Web site names are registered with Nominet UK*. See p. 151 for ideas on how to maximize the number of people who find your web site.

Other ideas

These can all help to build your reputation:

- advertising.
- public relations.
- appearance of salespeople.
- how you answer the telephone.
- vehicles: their cleanliness and livery – i.e. the colour or markings on them.

Summary

1 People buy particular products for rational and emotional reasons.
2 You should aim to create a 'good feeling', a brand image, a reputation, about your product among customers. Make sure that your product can live up to this.
3 Industrial or unique products still need brand images.
4 Analyse your market and customer requirements to decide on an image.
5 A business or product name will be built up over the years to summarize what your image is all about.
6 If you can afford it, have a logo designed for you.
7 Try to encapsulate as many pleasant (or positive) associations in your name as you can.
8 Letterheads are a most important way of projecting messages about your business. Keep the style consistent with web site, labels, stickers and packaging.

Other chapters to read

2 Who will buy? (p. 13); **4** Your business identity (p. 38); **13** Getting the message across (p. 141); **14** Getting new customers (p. 157); **15** Building customer relationships (p. 172); **19** Professional back-up (p. 212).

13

Getting the message across

Do you know what message you want to say about yourself, your product and your business? If you do not, how can your customers know? But knowing the message is not the end of the story. You have to decide who to send it to and how you are going to do it. If your message is not received loud and clear, your customers will not understand why they should buy from you or what it is they are getting. If they do not know the reason for buying, there will be no sales; if they have the wrong reason for buying, there will be dissatisfaction.

If you do not manage to communicate effectively the benefits of your product or service, your business will fail. The message, and getting it across, is crucial. Broadly, marketing is all about getting your message across. But marketing can be a very expensive habit if it is undirected, too ethereal and without a clear purpose. Small businesses need to market, but more and more the marketing should be focused on generating direct responses, on building communications with your target group of customers rather than broad-brush image generation.

What is in this chapter?

This chapter focuses on how you can get potential customers to be responsive to your business message: to soften them up until you can close the sale. It covers:

- the message: who, what, how? (p. 142).
- building up your brand (p. 143).
- direct-response advertising (p. 144).

■ public relations (p. 149).

■ marketing through the Internet (p. 151).

The message: who, what, how?

Who is the message to?

If you do not know what your target market is, you really do not deserve to succeed. You need this information at your fingertips from a very early stage of planning your business (see Chapter 2, 'Who will buy?'). Defining the target market necessitates sorting out its characteristics: the number, the location, the spending power and the class structure (if consumer).

Knowledge of the target market is needed to help to refine the message and select the most useful way of communicating it to that particular group.

What is your message?

You need to work out what message you want to send to customers. The two main constituents of your message are:

1 *The long-term reputation* you want to build for your product or business. This can be things such as good quality, reliability, quick service and good value. There is more about reputation in Chapter 12, 'The right name'.
2 *The specific message* you want to get across now. This may simply be part of building your reputation, as above. Or it could be that you want to describe your product, giving customers information to make a buying decision. Or it could be some specific offer you have available. Or it could be an item of good news about your business. The list is endless.

How to send the message

There are numerous ways of trying to get across your message to your target market. The trick is to select the most cost-effective way of reaching your group. The cost of communication should be measured by what you have to spend to reach each potential customer or, if possible, by the number of sales leads each pound spent generates. Obviously, any cost-conscious small business has to look at the total figure too. But it would not make good sense to plump for a way of sending the message on the grounds that the overall cost is least, if few customers are reached. What matters is how many possible buyers receive the message compared with the total expense. Very broadly, you can communicate with your customers by:

■ *writing the message*: this includes direct mail, advertising, web sites, press releases, blogs and materials such as brochures.

■ *speaking the message*: this includes telephone selling, carrying out demonstrations, attending exhibitions and face-to-face selling.

■ *implying the message*: this does not give any specific details but gives an impression about your business or product. For example, the quality and design of your letterhead, a business gift or a van sign send an implied message to anyone who sees them. You should recognize that all ways of communicating the message, such as selling and advertising, also include an element of this. An advertisement does not simply have a picture and some words describing a benefit; the whole adds up to more than this, or it should. It should build up the general impression you want to give.

Building up your brand

All the means you use to get your message across contribute to building up your brand. The methods described above for writing, speaking and implying your message build up the strength of your brand. The aim should be to receive instant recognition of your product (or company) name and an understanding of and favourable reaction to your business among your potential customers. This is explained in more detail in Chapter 12, 'The right name'.

Brochures, leaflets, flyers and data sheets

These can be used to send out in response to sales enquiries or possibly mailings to generate interest. But beware the unfocused, general, corporate brochure that has no specific product to sell. If it is not informative and specific, such a brochure may simply be consigned to the bin.

Brochures can be relatively cheap, and there is no need to make them glossy or over-complicated. You can use a brochure to describe your product as well as drawing attention to the benefits. But while you need to be careful not to make it too general, you also need to avoid filling a brochure with a mass of technical details. If the only recipients are going to be highly technical people, consider cheaper forms of product information, such as leaflets or data sheets. Or keep the brochure jargon-free and tuck a one-page technical sheet in the back.

Leaflets are cheaper still, as they may be only one or two pages or a foldover. But again, the style should be consistent, and the leaflet should not look low-quality. A leaflet can be used more widely than brochures, given out at exhibitions, sent out in mailshots or dropped through letterboxes. A leaflet should try to attract attention and increase awareness for your name and product. What is likely to catch a target reader's eye will be a benefit from your product that is something your target customer is interested in.

Flyers are a good, sensible option for small businesses. You could have an A5 one-page flyer, or an A4 flyer folded into three to fit into a standard DL-size envelope. The flyer could be four-colour on one side to incorporate your logo or illustrations of your product, and mono on the reverse to give the details.

Data sheets are simpler still, can be printed at your office, and supply product details without a big selling message. They are for information.

You need to work out your costings very carefully before going for a full-blown brochure. Instead, look closely at the options of flyers, leaflets and data sheets. A cheaper alternative to a brochure may still generate as much interest and so be much more cost-effective.

If you have a web site, you should include a downloadable copy of your brochure and any factsheets on your site, for example, as PDFs (Portable Document Formats). Clearly show in the navigation on your home page where these documents can be found.

Direct-response advertising

What can you expect advertising to do for you? Sell more. Unfortunately, it does not seem to work quite like this. The direct link between spending money on advertising and generating more sales is sometimes difficult to establish; the linkage is there, but measurement can be fraught with problems. General advertising is an investment decision, as are all the other ways of trying to get your message across. Spend money now in the hope of more sales later; but the outcome and the return are not certain.

Your advertising strategy should aim to move the potential customers from ignorance about your product to purchasing it. It should:

- get attention for your product.
- help them to understand the product or service.
- get them to believe in the benefits.
- establish a desire for the product.
- generate action.
- improve the reputation and general impression of the product.

You should not expect one particular form of advertising carried out at one particular time to achieve all this. To expect it might be counterproductive if it leads you to cram too many objectives into one small piece of advertising. Your strategy should be to use a mix of different forms to achieve these aims over a long period of time.

If you can sell as much as you want by personal contact, do not waste money on advertisements, PR or literature. With large-value items sold to a few buyers, spending more on direct selling might be a better use of money.

Apart from the obvious form of advertising – advertisements in newspapers and magazines – there are other forms that small businesses will probably find more useful.

Generating a direct response

The type of general corporate advertising that large blue-chip companies indulge in is not an option for small businesses. You need to focus on how you can generate a response from the reader because you want details of that reader in your database of potential customers. You may also be able to sell products off the page by generating enough interest so that they phone up and purchase direct (you will need to have organized credit card facilities to achieve a proper off-the-page sales plan). Here are some ideas for generating response:

■ use eye-catching headlines.

■ offer some incentive for people to contact you, such as a sample copy or version of the product.

■ offer a discount.

Using a media buyer

If your product has a national market and if you would advertise in national papers, or even in specialist publications with a national readership, consider using a media buyer. This is a business that specializes in buying advertising space. A media buyer can get much cheaper space from publications than you can buying direct and is paid by the publication rather than by you. Discounts of up to two-thirds of the rate card advertised by the publication can be obtained by media buyers.

If you are going to advertise, you may need to have copies of your advertisement ready for the publication and produced in either hard-copy or digital format. Your agency can advise you.

Publications may have very cheap slots available at the last minute. A media buyer could advise you to have advertisements made up and ready so that if a slot comes up you could send over your copy at once to catch the empty (and very cheap) space.

Where can you advertise?

You can advertise in:

- local newspapers and directories.
- technical or special interest magazines.
- local radio, cinema or TV.
- local shops, pubs and so on.
- national newspapers and magazines.
- reference handbooks and trade directories.

TV advertising will be too expensive for most small businesses and would be appropriate only if you are looking for volume sales nationwide. You can often target a national audience more effectively and more cheaply if you pick a specialist publication aimed at your target audience. If you run a locally based business, local advertising is clearly most appropriate and there may be numerous opportunities – for example, sponsoring the printing of raffle tickets for a local school or charity in return for your ad on the back of all tickets, ads on boxes used by a local video library, special features in your local newspapers. Clearly, which form of advertising suits you will depend crucially on the nature and scale of your business.

Before embarking on an advertisement, every small business has to decide:

1 Which newspaper, magazine or directory?
2 What size and position of advertisement?
3 What goes in the advertisement?
4 When do you advertise?
5 How often do you run this, or any other, advertisement?
6 How do you get the advertisement drawn up?

1. Which newspaper, magazine, directory?

Choosing the right place to put your advertisement is crucial. To be cost-effective, the ad must be placed where it reaches the biggest possible section of your potential customers. The journal or paper must be read by the people or businesses you want to talk to and by people at the right level in the organizations or in the right class grouping in the population.

Two important statistics you need to find are the number of copies sold and the readership. Larger magazines have their circulation figures independently audited by the Audit Bureau of Circulations (ABC)*, although it may be necessary to rely on publishers' claims for smaller magazines. Rates charged for space usually bear some sort of relationship to circulation. Do not assume that the cheapest or the most expensive will be the best bet. Try to estimate the cost per reader for any ad you want to put in.

A listing of magazines and journals accepting advertising, together with the prices charged for space, can be found in *British Rate and Data* (BRAD)* or its online version *www.bradinsight.com*. Look in your local reference library for the hard-copy version.

It may be important in your type of business to pay for entries in various directories, the commonest of which is *Yellow Pages*. Before you commit yourself to paying for an entry, investigate how many copies of the directory are sold and to whom. The longer-established directories may be the ones with the biggest usage by potential customers. If you expect to find most of your customers locally, there might be a town directory (check with the library or chamber of commerce*) that would be suitable – often a simple listing is free, and charges for display ads may be modest. Directories tend to be published once a year, and entries need advance planning. Some towns have community magazines published, say, monthly or bi-monthly that carry display ads and go to every household.

2. What size and position of advertisement?

Clearly, the cost of your ad is affected by its size and its position; the bigger the ad and the better the position, the more expensive it will be. For example, an ad on the front page will be seen by more readers and an ad that does not have to compete with others on the same page will be more easily seen too. There is no clear-cut advice that can be given about whether to go for bigger and better. In a trade magazine, a good rule of thumb is:

- in the first third of the magazine.
- on a news or editorial page.
- on a right-hand page.
- one-third the size of the page.

3. What goes in the advertisement?

Here are some general guidelines, none of which is sacrosanct:

- have a clear, straightforward message.
- do not be afraid of white space in an ad.
- use as few words as you can to get your message across, unless you are trying to sell off the page.
- steer clear of humour; readers may not share your sense of what is, or is not, funny.
- do not copy other people's ideas.
- remember that you are speaking to your customers, and to no one else.
- the reader is more interested in the message than in your name, so do not put your name at the top of the ad.
- an ad is easier to read if the words go left to right and top to bottom.
- make sure your ad complies with relevant voluntary codes of practice and any legal requirements – see below.

4. When do you advertise?

There may be seasonal fluctuations in your business, and an advertising strategy may need to take this into account, using ads at the start of the summer for summer goods and at the start of the winter for winter ones.

5. How often do you run this, or any other, advertisement?

One isolated ad on its own may, frankly, achieve little. If that is all you can afford, you may be better concentrating on the other ways of getting your message across. To achieve objectives such as increasing awareness, generating further action or reminding existing buyers, an ad may need to be repeated several times. A different ad may be required to follow the first one to consolidate the improvement in awareness and, ultimately, in sales.

6. How do you get the advertisement drawn up?

If you want help producing the ad (the copy, design and layout), you may want to use an advertising agency. There are lots of small agencies or free-lancers willing to work for small businesses.

Keeping it legal

The Consumer Protection from Unfair Trading Regulations 2008 impose a blanket legal ban on unfair commercial practices and also outlaw 31 specific practices. The regulations are very wide-ranging and apply to your advertising as well as other marketing and selling practices. For example, your ads should not give false or deceptive messages, or fake credentials or endorsements, omit important information, use scare tactics or guilt, confuse advertising with editorial and so on. Contravening the regulations can result in disruptive investigations, prosecution and fines. It is important to familiarize yourself with these regulations – see the guidance on the Office of Fair Trading* web site.

There are also a number of important voluntary codes that apply to advertising. The most important of these are the British Codes of Advertising and Sales Promotion published and enforced by the Advertising Standards Authority*. As well as a general requirement for all advertisements and promotions to be 'legal, decent, honest and truthful', the codes contain sections dealing with specific areas, such as health products, financial products, children and tobacco. Since 1 March 2011, the Advertising Standards Authority also regulates online marketing messages (whether paid for or not).

If you are involved in particular types of business, such as providing credit, your advertisements may also be subject to legal requirements, for example under the Consumer Credit Act 2006. The sale of and advice about many financial products, including investments, mortgages and insurance, are subject to advertising and promotion rules set by the Financial Services Authority*.

If you plan to target your customers with direct mailshots, consider joining the Direct Marketing Association*. Its members are required to comply with a code of practice. You must also comply with the Consumer Protection (Distance Selling) Regulations 2000. Among other things, these require you to give customers all the relevant information they need and to fulfil orders within 30 days. Your customers have a statutory right to cancel an order and receive a refund within seven days of receipt. Further details are available from the Office of Fair Trading.

Public relations

This can be a low-cost method of getting across a message to the marketplace, although it can be time-consuming. The basic aim is to get information or news about your business into magazines or newspapers in the form of an article or news item, or to get a mention in the online blogs of respected bloggers, such as national journalists. Increasingly, too, you might consider how social media, such as Facebook and 'tweeting', could spread news of your product or service 'virally'. See 'Marketing through the Internet' below. If you can achieve this, such items are seen as very credible and 'true', in a way that advertising is not, because readers place greater trust in the objectivity of journalists and other consumers. Sometimes a newspaper or magazine will accept editorial material only if it is accompanied by an advertisement, which obviously you have to pay for. If it is obvious that you have paid for an ad to get a placing for some editorial, it dilutes the effect of the editorial.

The main ways of achieving this use of the press are to:

- *issue press releases* when there is a news item. You will have to write this yourself, or pay someone else to do it. If you do the latter, you are losing one of the benefits of public relations, which is its low cost.

- *get to know the editor or journalist*: in this way, if you have a story, you could ring your contact before issuing a press release, to see if they would be interested because it is 'exclusive'. This may well be a more successful way of publicizing your story than issuing press releases.

- *try writing suitable small articles*: for example for trade or technical papers, and sending them in.

To write a press release yourself, keep to the facts, brief and salient. The length of the press release should be as short as possible and summarize all that you want to say in the first paragraph, as this may be all there is room for in the journal. Somewhere in the press release, put your name and telephone number, where editors and journalists can speak to you.

If there is a good quote that you can include from yourself or the person in your business responsible for this item, this can be an excellent way of lightening the copy and making it more readable. If there is any other personal or human angle that might appeal to the public, do not forget to introduce that. Do not be too optimistic about the chances of getting your press release in – hundreds will be sent each week.

Press releases stand a better chance of publication if there is a photograph attached. It can be a good investment to have some interesting photos of you and the business, which can be appended to the release.

Marketing through the Internet

It can be very tempting when everyone else is rushing around putting up web sites to think that you should have your own web site too. It's worth going carefully over the pros and cons before you decide that you need to be up on the Internet.

First of all, ask yourself why anyone would want to come to your web site. Customers would come only if:

■ they know your web site exists.

■ your web site is interesting.

■ your web site is a convenient way of purchasing your product.

The major problem for most small businesses is making potential customers aware of the existence of your business and your product. If you throw in your web site as well, you now have a third element that you have to promote and market. So setting up your own web site could simply increase your costs and increase the amount of effort that you need to put into marketing rather than be the source of a lot of extra revenue.

The argument goes that by browsing, potential customers will find your web site and visit it. But there is a growing body of tactics to showing up on browsers plus alternative approaches such as using social media to create awareness of your products and traffic to your web site. Moreover, once people do reach your web site, the visit won't last more than one second if your site is not interesting. Your site could interest customers if there is some free and useful information on it. Although you may be able to deal with all these aspects yourself and many of the tools available online are free, there can be a big cost in establishing and maintaining your web presence in terms of the time you need to devote to these activities in order to make them pay off. If you accept orders through your web site, you also need to ensure they can be processed smoothly and are promptly picked up and fed through to your fulfilment system. All these could be a major extra cost of a web site, not immediately apparent to you.

Promoting your web site

If you are convinced that a web site would be a crucial element in your business, you need to work out how to bring it to people's attention. First of all, you have to get it onto what are known as search engines. These are sifting software programs that will give you a list of sites of interest if a customer types in a topic. Typically, someone browsing will not go further than the first page of a search engine output; the brief information they read about your site must be relevant and punchy enough to persuade them to click through and your site needs immediately to deliver something relevant if they are not to click away.

Companies such as Google maintain large databases that match sites to the keywords that people type into search engines. They rank the sites in order of importance using complicated algorithms that include the popularity of a site – in other words, the more people already use your site, the more likely you are to get further hits. That makes life tough if you are starting out, since it is not enough to design your web site with well-placed and relevant keywords; you must also think about a strategy to get your site known. There are two main approaches: making sure that real-world marketing – your direct-mail brochures, flyers, press ads and press releases – all contain your web address, and using online marketing techniques. These might include 'pay-per-click' where you buy a prominent position on a search engine listing page every time someone searches using a keyword you specify and the amount you pay depends on the number of people who click on your link as a result. However, pay-per-click can be expensive. Cheaper options include persuading other trusted sites to link to yours and social media marketing.

Social media are websites, such as Facebook, Twitter and LinkedIn, where people build relationships, exchange information and chat, and in the process create content. This is a very different environment from traditional marketing. When you send out a leaflet or place an ad in a newspaper, you control the content; with social media, content is created by the dialogue between everyone taking part and no single person or firm controls it. On the plus side, if people like your firm or product, they will pass that information on, so that reaching some people directly means your message may then be cascaded to many others. Key steps in making good use of social media include, for example:

- Decide who you are trying to reach and identify the social media sites most relevant to you. For example, if you are selling to retail customers, Facebook and Twitter may be good places to start, whereas if you are selling to businesses LinkedIn might be more suitable. Create accounts with the sites that you think will work for you – this is typically free.

- Identify and join groups on those sites that are relevant to your product or service. Expect to be ignored or rebuffed if you now simply plug your product. This is a social medium. Just as you would not launch into a sales pitch at a dinner party, it is not etiquette to do so here. But what you can do is to engage in dialogue with the other users in the group by, for example, asking and answering questions, passing on handy tips and highlighting interesting news and information. In the process, you can introduce your company and products and include a link to your web site. You may also be able to manage the content to some extent, for example, by responding openly and helpfully if users post adverse comments about your company or product.

■ Create content that can be used on your web site and easily reversioned to appear on social media sites. For example, you might consider having a blog on your web site with short posts that can be reproduced on Facebook or snippets of news (140 characters at most) that can be reused on Twitter.

■ Consider content and offers that you could place on social media sites to encourage traffic to your web site: for example, referring to free guides or podcasts available on your web site, or a prize draw for people who click through.

Once your product is established, you might consider setting up a fan page on Facebook, where customers can exchange comment relevant to your product or company and where you can provide information and answers direct to customers. But do not expect much traffic to a fan page if you are only just starting out.

You can get some free information on optimizing your use of social media web sites, for example, from *www.seop.com/social-media-marketing* but you may want to engage a specialist firm to help you create and implement your online marketing strategy (see p. 220).

Apart from building popularity, the other strand to getting a high place in search engine listings is to make sure your web site is visible to search engines and includes relevant keywords. Some things to think about include:

■ To a search engine, the links to your site and between the pages on your site are like pathways. The search engine crawls along these pathways looking at each page as it goes.

■ Search engines only look at web page content that is written in html, the special mark-up code for Internet content. They do not see at all any information contained in, for example, images, Flash or Java plug-ins, podcasts or PDFs. So make sure important information is given or repeated in text – for example, include a transcript for a podcast or a brief explanation of what a Flash calculator can do, and do not embed links only in PDFs.

■ Be aware that your entry on a search engine will include the title of your site (called the title tag, which appears for example on the web browser tab above your web page) and a brief description (usually the meta-description which is some special text you write that does not actually appear on your web site but gives a pithy description of it). These two items essentially become the ad for your business that appears in the search engine listing, so like all advertising, they need to be immediately relevant and engaging. They should also contain keywords. For example, suppose your business involves selling products handmade with locally grown lavender. Your title tag might be 'Perfumes and foods from lavender' while your meta-description could be 'Lavender products for all your senses from relaxing and sensual perfumes to subtle and delicately flavoured foods'. Keywords that feature prominently here are 'lavender', 'perfume' and 'food'.

The whole area of increasing your chance of a high position in search engine listings is called search engine optimization (SEO). You can find a useful beginners' guide to SEO at *www.seomoz.org/learn-seo*. It includes details of some of the tools available online that can help you check how your web site appears to a search engine and how popular different keywords are. Be aware that search engines and SEO techniques are evolving and changing all the time. Rather than try to get to grips with this area and keep abreast of the changes yourself, you might prefer to hire an SEO firm to do the job for you (see p. 220).

Bear in mind that, however good your SEO, potential customers will be quickly antagonized if your web site does not quickly and efficiently deliver the information or services they were expecting.

Other ways of marketing through the Internet

You could consider advertising on someone else's web site. But take care, as browsers and users of the Internet find advertisements irritating and turn them off, so you may pay on the basis of a number of visitors but find that your ad is not seen by the number you expect.

You could take space in someone else's web site. For example, there are sites devoted to people wanting to buy second-hand cars or organize travel arrangements. The owners of the site are faced with the problem of promoting and marketing the site and ensuring that there are enough visitors, and you may pay for a page or an entry or whatever. If the site really does generate the audience claimed, this could be your most satisfactory way of marketing on the Internet.

Take the claimed number of page impressions with a pinch of salt. Look carefully to see how the claim is made up. Dissect the claims before estimating how many people are likely to see your particular page. You can work out how cost-effective the entry is.

If you are marketing locally, you might be able to get a link to your site from your local authority's web site or any online local directories.

Designing your site

If you have decided that your own site is important, consider these points:

■ *visitors to the site don't want to waste time*: usually they have come for information. Illustrations and graphics simply slow the site down, and many net users turn them off. Focus on your site being quick rather than over-elaborate.

■ *enable visitors to enter your site easily*: don't block them by requiring them to register first.

■ *encourage visitors to register at a later point in the site*: for example by offering them an e-mail newsletter or advance notice of special offers. In this way, you can gather information about your site visitors, including their e-mail addresses, and you may be able to use this for direct mail.

■ *offer something genuine*: to be of any value to potential and existing customers, your site needs to offer real service and real value (and this is a cost you should quantify and allow for in your business plan).

■ *how to pay*: if you want customers to be able to buy your goods or services through your web site, you'll need to think about how to receive payments. Specialist companies can either help you to design secure links for accepting payments direct or link you up with third parties who can handle the payment side of things for you.

Summary

1 To communicate your message about your product's benefits, you need to know who you want to talk to, what your message is and the best way of getting your message across.

2 Look at flyers, leaflets and data sheets as a way you can convey information about the benefits of your product to your target customers.

3 Advertising can create attention, inform, remind, prompt sales and improve the image of your product. But the return from advertising is uncertain. It costs more and takes longer than you think.

4 Focus on direct-response advertising, which encourages readers to contact you about your product. You can enter details in your marketing database and send offers to them until you convert them into customers.

5 Do not rely on one form of advertising to achieve your objectives. If you can afford it, use a mixture and try to organize a spread of advertising over a period of time (unless you need specific timing for your product).

6 Advertising must be consistent with the impressions of your product and business that you are endeavouring to foster among potential buyers.

7 Think carefully before you set up a web site. You may spend as much time and effort marketing the web site as you do marketing your product.

Other chapters to read

14

Getting new customers

The simple truth is that if you do not make any sales, you do not have a business. This chapter looks at how you get new customers by selling direct.

Every part of your business will be involved in selling, in the search for more customers. This extends from answering the telephone to your notepaper and literature, to any person or activity in your business that may one day come into contact with an existing or potential customer. Train everyone who answers the telephone the correct way to do it: they must be prompt, polite, friendly and helpful. If necessary, provide them with a script to follow. But also read Chapter 12, 'The right name', which gives lots of useful tips on building your reputation: from choosing the right name to the right note-paper. Chapter 13, 'Getting the message across', gives some simple and cheap ways of getting your company or product message across to potential buyers.

The first step in gaining sales is to plan and organize. The key to gaining new customers is to gather data and information about people who fit the profile that would be interested in your product. Databases are funda-mental to the development of sales, so you need to select database software and work out how to design it to meet your needs.

What is in this chapter?

- direct mail (p. 158).
- telephone selling (p. 161).
- face-to-face selling (p. 162).
- indirect selling (p. 170).

Direct mail

An increasing amount of sales activity takes place by direct mail, either via post, fax or e-mail – see pp. 149 and 176 to check out the law. Even if you will close the sale by a face-to-face meeting, direct mail will be the first stage in the sales process to filter and screen the prospects.

However, many products can be sold simply by direct mail without any follow-up stage. The key to a successful direct mail campaign to attract new customers is to have a very clear idea of your likely customer and to select a mailing list to match that profile. The second most important factor is to be careful about the letter or mailshot that you send, the offer that you make, the envelope, even the postage that you use. All these details can be incredibly important in raising or lowering response rate.

The trick with any list, any offer and any mailshot is to test first, before you roll it out on a larger scale. A minimum test to be economic is probably 5,000 names. But you can start lower if you print and fulfil in-house.

The list

You can compile lists yourself from different sources, carefully chosen to include what you believe to be potential customers. Or you can buy a licence to use lists from list owners or through list brokers. In this case, you are buying the right to use the list usually either just once in a 12-month period or multiple times during a specified period. Increasingly you can buy lists online for immediate download from web sites such as *http://marketingfile.com* (consumer and business lists) and *www.businessmailing.co.uk* (business lists).

Try to make sure that any list you buy is responsive: i.e., the people on it are proved to have bought previously as a result of direct mail. The list should also be recent; lists over six–12 months old decline in responsiveness.

The price for a consumer list that is recent and responsive might typically be around 16p to 22p per entry for single use (so £160 to £220 for every 1,000 names) and, say, 28p to 44p per entry for multiple use. But watch out, because list owners tuck in all sorts of other expenses and selections that increase the price.

Response rates of 1 or 2 per cent for mailing a list that you have bought or compiled would be good.

Lists should be regularly cleaned and the names of people who have died, moved away or have asked for their names to be taken off should be deleted. When you buy a list, if you find that the number of returns is less than 2 per cent, say, you should be able to get a refund. Unfortunately, the amount of the refund is likely only to be for the names, not the wasted postage or mailshot.

The offer

Typically, you devise an offer that makes what you want to sell look attractive. For example, you might be able to offer a discount. Or you might be able to offer some sort of extra. The idea is to give recipients the feeling that this offer is particularly good and not likely to be bettered.

You might also offer a free product or sample of something if the recipient responds within a number of days, say seven, 14 or 21. The difficulty with direct mail is to generate action by the person receiving it. So the notion that something extra is on offer for a prompt reply is attractive.

The mailer (mailshot)

Gradually, you will find out what style of mailer best fits your target market. But it could be something simple like a letter with a flyer. Or it could be much more elaborate.

There needs to be some sort of strapline to attract the reader's attention and prompt your mailer to be read. Otherwise, it might be consigned to the bin, like the other 99 per cent. And the copy can be highlighted to emphasize particular words.

The envelope

Some mailers include messages on envelopes to encourage people to open them rather than stick them in the bin. You could mail using stamps or franking to give your mailer more of a personal touch, but this is expensive. There are now 55 licensed postal operators in the UK (including Royal Mail*) and they offer a variety of cheaper mailing options. For example, you may get discounts if you pre-sort your mailshot into postcode areas.

Mailing services are cheaper if envelopes are not personalized or individually addressed. But this might lower the response rate. You have to weigh up what is more important for you.

The web site of Postcomm* (*www.psc.gov.uk*), the mail regulator, has a useful list of mail industry suppliers, outlining the direct mail and other services they offer, with links to their web sites.

The law

Anyone collecting or using data lists needs to establish whether they need to register with the Information Commissioner*. You will not have to register if you collect data or buy data lists solely for the purpose of marketing your own goods and services. But, regardless of whether you need to register, you must comply with the principles of data protection – see p. 175 for more information.

Steps to help you to organize a mailshot

1 Build up your mailing list from all past, present and potential customers. You can get names from personal contacts, through existing customers, following up requests for information, from exhibitions and so on.

2 Add to your mailing list by checking trade directories, members of trade associations, in fact any likely place for finding potential members of your target market.

3 Consider renting or exchanging mailing lists with other organizations. If you can buy a list it means you can use it as often as you like, but few organizations sell them. If you are going to rent or exchange, the other organization may insist on using a specialist mailing service, so you cannot copy the list. The organization may also want to see what you are going to send out, so that they can approve what is going to their customers. If necessary, ask a list broker to help to find suitable lists for a fee. Always test a list first. If the test works, on the second occasion you use the list, don't use more than three times the size of the initial test.

4 Weed out all 'gone aways', 'cannot be founds' and 'died' from your mailing list. To achieve this, you need to keep working on your mailing list on a regular basis and feeding in any information that comes in. But keep a separate note of old sales leads in case they resurface.

5 Find out the name of the most suitable individual to receive your message. If you are sending to businesses, do not simply send to a company or to a position, for example the chief accountant. Finding out names may mean telephoning the company first.

6 Always include a letter addressed to the individual and, if possible, signed personally by yourself or someone in your business, not pp'd (that is, signed by someone else on your behalf).

7 Remember what image you are trying to build. Choose good-quality literature, paper and envelopes.

8 Look carefully at what you are sending. If it is a letter, do not make it too long; probably one or two pages is the maximum. Nor should it be too cluttered with jargon. Try to grab your reader's attention in the opening sentence or headline. Make sure that the letter ties up with any other material, such as leaflets or catalogues.

9 Consider how you can increase the response. Would reply cards or coupons be a good idea?

10 Test your mailer first, if you think it necessary. Learn from your mistakes and improve your full mailshot.

11 Work out the cost. Try to assess your likely response rate. Only 1 or 2 per cent is considered to be a good response. A poor mailing list could mean even fewer enquiries. Calculate the cost for each response by dividing total expenses by number of likely enquiries or follow-ups. Is this a cost-effective way of reaching potential customers?

12 Do not forget to find out about any cheap rates on offer to new businesses and for large postings from Royal Mail and other business delivery services.

Telephone selling

The past few years have seen a huge growth in the amount of telephone selling (and call handling generally). More and more tasks are being handed over to telephone operators – fixing up insurance policies, giving details about bank accounts and so on.

Face-to-face selling is partially being superseded by the use of the telephone. Face-to-face selling is being made more effective by the qualifying of prospects by telephone before appointments are made. People's time is one of the most valuable resources for a business. Anything that reduces the wastage of that time is beneficial.

If you have not sold by telephone, and even if you don't intend to be selling yourself by telephone, it makes good sense for you to be trained in how to do it. The trick is to try to establish a relationship with the person at the other end of the line.

Telephone selling requires you to have carried out the research into your prospect, preferably to have already sent a letter or an e-mail setting out your proposal, and ensuring that the specific offer you are making is likely to be of some interest to the person you are calling, perhaps because it helps to meet some sort of business objective.

The stages of a sale are the same as for face-to-face selling: opening stage, building the sale and closing the sale; see p. 167.

Consider what communications equipment and services you need if telephone sales will be important to your business. For example, you could buy software or a hosted dialling service that schedules and manages outbound calls. In some industries, for example financial services, you are required by law to record telephone calls; even where this is not a legal requirement, recording can provide a useful legal safeguard and potentially valuable information. You can either record, store and retrieve calls using your own equipment or you could buy into a service that hosts and manages your recordings on a remote server. Contact business telecommunications companies to find out what services they can offer.

If you intend to record telephone calls, familiarize yourself with the law in this area. In general, recording of calls is banned but there are exceptions for lawful business practices as set out in the Telecommunications (Lawful Business Practice) (Interception of Communications) Regulations 2000. This allows you to record calls, for example, to comply with regulatory requirements or ensure that quality standards or targets are met. If your calls are for other purposes, such as marketing, you will need to get the recipient's consent.

Face-to-face selling

The first stage in acquiring new customers is to work out a possible list by market research and other methods. You may, for example, start with the raw list that you use for doing mailings. But you could not possibly follow up and sell direct to everyone on this list; your efforts would not be effective, because you would not be pinpointing those most likely to buy. So the list needs narrowing. This is done in many ways:

- *following leads*: leads are those people who have approached you, either as a result of your advertising or mailers or having seen your business at an exhibition. They may have asked for your literature or for a demonstration or simply expressed interest.

- *using referrals*: ask your existing customers if they know of other businesses that might be interested in your product or service. On the whole, referrals are more likely to lead to a successful sale than a lead, because you have several advantages. You already have an introduction, you know something about the person, and your existing customer may have already expressed satisfaction with your business.

■ *by qualifying potential customers*: when you are starting up your business, you may not have any referrals or leads to follow. All you may have is a list you have built up from market research. To reduce the list to the best prospect for you, you need to qualify. Find out the name and position of the decision-taker. Look for information about the potential customer's business. Work out what are likely to be the main factors that mean a business is likely to buy your product or service. You also need to know if the potential customer is considering buying a product like yours or has recently bought one.

Two important aspects of sales organization are:

1 Recording the information you have about each potential customer.
2 Devising a strategy for following up at regular intervals those potential customers who are not interested now but may be in the future.

There are two possibilities to carry out direct face-to-face selling: you, directly as a salesperson, or using a sales representative.

You

When you are starting your business, or if it is a very small one, it is more than likely that you yourself will be selling. If you have not previously worked in this role, the prospect may be fairly daunting. But you are likely to start with one major advantage – complete product knowledge – which is very important for selling. It is possible to acquire and develop many of the personal selling skills that you need, and many courses are available. If you are doing the selling, it would be a mistake to think that you do not need to organize and plan because you have stored it all in your head. You need the same information, sales systems and records as any sales rep.

If yours is a very small business, you might include your mobile phone number in your advertisements. This is fine if you do not expect a high volume of enquiries, but you'll find it hard to get on with your job if you're constantly being interrupted by phone calls. Bear in mind that you will need to hand some means of noting down the callers' details.

Sales representative

At some stage, you may decide to employ someone else to carry out or help with the selling. To enable a sales rep to work effectively, you need to make several decisions:

■ how will the rep be paid?

■ how much training is needed?

■ what sort of back-up organization and systems will be needed?

■ how to control the rep's activities.

Pay

Most salespeople will have an element of business-related remuneration. The purpose is twofold. First, commission or bonuses can be a motivator for salespeople to achieve greater sales. Second, it allows you to keep your over-heads lower by not having to pay a greater fixed salary. However, be aware of a possible conflict of interest if you use commission-based remuneration in an industry where your customers will be relying heavily on advice from your sales reps in coming to a decision about whether or not to buy. In this situation, commission may tempt reps to give inadequate or misleading advice if it generates more sales. In the long term this could damage your business reputation as well as leading to claims for redress. You may need to foster and possibly monitor high ethical standards – see 'Control' and 'Personal selling skills' on p. 165 and 'Keeping it legal' on p. 170.

Three of the possible combinations of salary and commission are:

1 Basic salary, plus commission on all the sales the rep makes. The rate of commission could vary depending on the volume of business already achieved, that is, the more sold the greater the rate. Commission could be based on value of sales, or if there is some discretion on pricing, possibly the amount of gross profit achieved by each sale.
2 Basic salary, plus commission on sales once a certain level (or quota) has been achieved.
3 Commission only, that is, no basic salary and every sale made triggering commission payments.

Training

Unless you yourself as the business owner are a sales specialist, it would be unusual for a small business to take on someone who needs basic training in selling skills. If you do employ a trainee, you need to be prepared to wait for a long period before the person is achieving a good level of sales.

However, even if you employ only experienced salespeople, you may find it difficult to employ someone who knows your particular market and product in great detail. You must be prepared to provide good product training, plus detailed analysis of the strengths and weaknesses of competitive products. If you fail to do this, your sales are likely to be disappointing.

Back-up organization

There need to be a number of systems and records in place to enable the sales effort to work effectively.

1 Sales staff spend a lot of time out of the office. This is incompatible with the need for existing and potential customers, as well as new leads, to be in contact. You should have a well-organized way of recording telephone calls: for example, name, position and company of caller; date and time call received; brief message about purpose of call and what response was promised at your end. Any good sales rep will keep in touch with your office to ask what calls have been received and follow those up.
2 Every sales rep needs a comprehensive and up-to-date price list, plus copies of any literature, press releases and publicity material.
3 If yours is the sort of business that has to issue quotes to customers, try to standardize these as much as possible. This cuts down the amount of time the rep has to spend on paperwork. This also applies to any other sales job that can be standardized. Sales letters, follow-ups to those not currently buying, and terms and conditions of the sale can be standardized. Terms and conditions can be printed on the back of the order form.

Control

You need to exercise effective control over your sales staff. This can be difficult if they spend most of the time out of the office. You must insist on a weekly sales meeting with prepared information, such as number of telephone calls or sales visits made, demonstrations carried out, quotes issued and orders received. The sales rep should be able to give you an estimate of the probability of receiving an order from each potential customer and when it is likely to be received.

The information provided by salespeople is crucial in helping you to plan your business. You may be able to produce 'conversion ratios' to help you to predict your likely level of sales. This would be something like a percentage of initial telephone calls that become a sales visit, a percentage of sales visits that move to the quote stage, or a percentage of quotes that turn into orders.

Personal selling skills

Many people regard salespeople as liars, cheats and commercial vultures. Some salespeople may be like this, while others can be more successful by being honest and responsible, and by paying attention to every small detail and developing their own selling style to match the product, as well as their own character.

What you need to do to improve your selling skills is develop a sales strategy, which can be simple but which should be applied to every sale. One approach is to produce a series of lists. These should include:

- main features of your product.
- major benefits it offers.
- most likely objections and your planned response.
- advantages and weaknesses of competitive products.
- the key characteristics of your potential customer.
- in what ways your product meets the customer's needs or wants.

There are also simple rules you can follow that will vastly improve your selling ability:

- know your product.
- listen to your buyer.
- relate what you are selling to your customer's needs and wants.
- plan your sales strategy for each prospective customer so that you know what you want to achieve at each stage of the negotiation.
- have clear and well-worked-out sales presentations, demonstrations or telephone calls.
- make sure at all times that you know who the decision-maker is in your prospective client's business.

Developing your own sales approach

The first time you try out your selling approach should not be in a potential customer's office. It is important to feel confident in your dialogue and handling of the client. This means practice. Ask a relative or a colleague to take part in a role-playing session. The best practice for you will be obtained if the customer is played by your relative or colleague as hostile, vindictive and uncooperative. Try to carry out role-playing sessions many times before you come face-to-face with a genuine customer so that you can develop confidence in your style.

The stages of a sale

There are three stages to making the sale:

1 Opening stage (often a telephone call making an appointment to visit).
2 Building the sale (including sales presentations, demonstrations and dealing with objections).
3 Closing the sale (recognizing buying signals and asking for the order).

Opening stage

Your objective at this stage will usually be to make an appointment to visit a prospective buyer of your product and commence the negotiation. Obviously, you do not want to spend the time doing this unless you have already qualified this potential customer and satisfied yourself that there is a chance of selling your product.

The most efficient way of arranging appointments is to do so by telephone. The first hurdle may be to get past the buyer's secretary. Do not allow your name and telephone number to be taken with a promise of ringing back. Instead, ask when your prospect will be free to take a telephone call.

The purpose of the telephone call is to make the appointment, not sell your product at this stage. Try to keep it fairly brief and plan ahead what you are going to say. It may run along these lines:

■ an opening statement.

■ any qualifying questions you would like to put (such as 'Are you likely to buy this product in the next three months if it meets your requirements?' or 'What is your budget?').

■ why your prospective customer should arrange a meeting to see you and your product.

■ be prepared with a list of answers to the possible objections your prospect might throw out.

■ offer alternative times for the appointment.

■ finish the telephone call.

Jot down the important parts of the conversation while you are speaking on the telephone or straight afterwards.

Building the sale

You must plan in advance any sales call, presentation or demonstration. Carefully analyse your potential customer's needs and requirements and decide the relevance of your product or service to these.

The opening phase is important. First impressions are important, so make sure that your appearance fits in with your customer's, as well as being neat and clean. Do not waste too long on social trivialities but establish why you are there and awaken your listener's interest in your product. Before making your detailed sales pitch, ask about the customer's needs, so you can sell to these.

Important points you want to communicate to your listener are:

- the good reputation of your business and product and yourself.
- the benefit your potential buyer will gain if your product or service is purchased.

This suggests that you are talking while your possible buyer is listening. But this is unlikely to achieve your sale. Salespeople have a tendency to talk too much. Instead, you should spend over half the sales call listening to your prospective customer. If you do not do this, you cannot judge the chance of making the sale and you cannot relate your product to the customer's needs. You must be able to see yourself, your product and your company through your prospective customer's eyes. This involves listening.

It also implies that your prospective customer will talk. Some try not to, which can be disconcerting. Prepare a number of open questions that you can put during the sales call. An open question is one that cannot be answered by 'yes' or 'no'.

References to other customers who are already dealing with you can be very powerful, as long as your buyer sees the reference as relevant. So the reference must be to a comparable business and use.

At some stage, the subject of your competitors may be raised by your buyer. The traditional stand-by advice is 'Don't knock the competition!' On the whole, the advice is sound; criticizing the competition may have an adverse effect on your listener, because it tends to make you sound rather weak. However, do emphasize any benefits that you know your competitors do not have, as long as they are important to your buyer.

Demonstrations can be an effective selling device but need careful preparation. Make sure everything works before you leave your office for the appointment. Handle the equipment carefully during the demo and if possible involve the buyer in using and handling it during the demo.

With some products or services, quite a lot of investigation needs to be done by you before you can suggest a solution and give a quote. If yours is this sort of complicated sale, before you make a proposal you should carry out the following steps:

- make sure you are investigating the right problem.
- ensure you have all the facts you need by speaking to everyone involved.
- keep an open mind about the solution you will propose.
- keep in touch with the decision-maker and talk through your proposed solution before committing yourself to paper.

The sales proposal should be a restatement of what has already been said. Little has been said so far of your potential client's reactions. If there is to be any chance of making a sale, at some stage objections will be raised. Do not view these negatively as a nuisance. An objection displays that your listener is interested in the negotiation process. An objection should be treated as a request for more information. It would be a mistake to respond to sales resistance by becoming too persistent or pressuring too much.

There are some general guidelines to follow:

- do not contradict or argue and remain calm at all times.
- do not allow the objection to become too important by spending too long replying to it or making several attempts to reply.
- if possible, anticipate the objections and prepare a response.
- the best way of dealing with an objection is to turn it into a sales benefit or to agree with the prospect, but counter with a benefit.

Closing the sale

It is important to ask for the order at the right psychological moment. This could be after overcoming an objection or if your potential buyer is showing buying signals. These might include asking about delivery terms or financial terms, arguing about price or asking about extras available.

If your prospective customer is hesitating, extra pressure is unlikely to be effective. Instead, try to create a relaxed atmosphere to have a discussion and assume the decision will go your way. Talk about what will happen in the future and assume that there will be a continuing relationship between the two businesses.

Once you have got the order verbally, do not relax – you can still lose it. Do not count it as an order until you have received written confirmation; in particular, do not order materials until you have the order in writing. If it is a new customer, it is financially prudent to take up references or find out credit ratings before you accept the order. The last thing you want is to do all the work and find that you will not be paid.

Indirect selling

Your particular industry may still use various intermediaries to make sales. The advantage from your point of view is that it is a management problem passed to someone else. The disadvantage is that you are far more concerned about revenue of your products than some outside firm.

Agent

Agents are not employees. They are in business on their own. They are likely to be agents for several products, but you should insist that they are not agents for any competing products. They work for commission on each sale, often between 7½ and 15 per cent. The agent does not buy the product from you; instead, you invoice the customer direct.

The advantage of an agent is that you do not have to fund the overheads: no salary, car, office space and so on. The disadvantage is that you may find it difficult to control the agent's activities. If you have a continuing responsibility for your product, be careful the agent does not sell to unsuitable customers.

To mitigate the disadvantages, you need a written agreement, which you should enforce carefully. The agreement should include the details on territory, products, type of customer, commission and the duration of the agreement.

Distributors

Wholesalers and distributors are not the same as agents. They are your customers. They buy direct from you. When they sell on to their customers, they expect to be able to put on a mark-up of at least 30 per cent, if not more. If you choose this route for your business, it cuts out most of the costs of direct selling, as you will probably deal with only a few distributors. However, you have no control over their selling effort.

Keeping it legal

The Consumer Protection from Unfair Trading Regulations 2008 impose a general ban on unfair commercial practices and also outlaw 31 specific practices. Unfair commercial practices are broadly any that fail to meet the honest practices and good faith that can be expected of traders in your field. The specific practices that the regulations ban include:

■ making personal visits to the consumer's home and ignoring the customer's request to leave or not to return.

■ making persistent and unwanted, unsolicited telephone, fax or e-mail contact.

■ falsely stating that a product or particular terms will only be available for a very limited time.

■ falsely claiming that you are about to close down or move premises.

■ promoting a product in such a way as deliberately to confuse it with some other manufacturer's product.

■ falsely claiming or creating the impression that you are not acting for purposes relating to your business.

■ demanding immediate payment for or the return or safekeeping of unsolicited products.

Contravening the regulations can result in fines and up to two years in prison, so make sure you familiarize yourself with these regulations – see the guidance on the Office of Fair Trading* web site.

Summary

1 Direct mail can be an effective way to sell some products. Test your lists, offers and mailshots before mailing in volume.

2 Telephone selling is an increasingly important sales means. Consider being trained yourself for your own calls.

3 Qualify all potential customers to avoid wasting time and effort. Narrow down your list to those most likely to buy from you.

4 If you employ salespeople, you will need some back-up organization and system. You need to be able to record information about customers to help with negotiations and to help you to plan, control and forecast.

5 If you are doing the selling, try to develop personal selling skills. There are some hints about starting sales negotiations, developing them and closing the sales on pp. 165–9.

Other chapters to read

2 Who will buy? (p. 13); 12 The right name (p. 132); 13 Getting the message across (p. 141); 15 Building customer relationships (p. 172).

15

Building customer relationships

Who is more likely to buy from you? An existing customer? Or a passer-by on the street who has never heard of you, your business or your product? The answer to this is pretty obvious. An existing customer is many more times likely to buy.

For a business to be secure and to produce high-quality long-term earnings (and provide you with a good, steady income), it needs to focus on retaining its customers. It also suggests that this should be part of your initial strategic thinking. A business that relies on one-off purchases is building a steeper cliff to climb than a business that targets a group of customers and develops products that can be sold more than once and has much spin-off potential.

Clearly, when a business is starting, every customer is a new one. Potential customers need to be sold to in a number of different ways to generate confidence in your product. But once your business is up and running and has been going for some time, sufficient for your product to be known, tested and liked, your organization needs to be ready to cope with the next part of your strategy, customer retention. Any well-run small business should have as its motto, 'Once a customer, always a customer'.

What is in this chapter?

- customer care (see p. 173).
- data gathering (p. 174).
- new offers, new products and repeat purchases (p. 178).

Customer care

It's all too easy when you're struggling with the finances, the production or the employees to regard customers as 'just another problem', 'a nuisance' or 'getting in the way'. But you need to drag yourself back to reality. Without customers, you have no business, no matter how slick your financial control or how good your man-management.

Put yourself in your customer's shoes. What would you expect if you were buying this product? How would you want to be treated over the telephone if you are phoning with a query? You won't be able to satisfy all customers, but you should struggle to satisfy all reasonable customers, because you want them to carry on buying from you.

When a new customer signs an order, this is not the end of the selling story. You should aim to build up a long-term relationship, because, in most businesses, you will be hoping for repeat orders or for additions to the original order. These will not come to fruition if you do not follow up orders, see they are delivered on time, or, if they are going to be late, warn your customer in advance. You need to give prompt attention to any problems or criticisms.

If your business depends on a few sizeable customers, establish a network of contacts in the customer's business, not just the buyer.

Response times

As a starting point, set up response times for the care of your customers. How quickly is the telephone picked up? Within one ring? Two? Four? Or longer? A telephone line dedicated to customers that avoids the switchboard or general business line would provide a better service. It would mean that customers get directly through to the correct person to deal with queries or complaints. You could even look at providing an 0800, 0808 or 0500 freephone number for customers.

Also set up required response times for replying to letters, e-mails or faxes.

Complaints handling

In some industries, money-back guarantees are commonplace – and in any case if you sell your products by credit card, you will find that if a consumer complains to the credit card company, the money will almost always be refunded to the customer to your cost. Distance selling means that a customer is legally entitled to a seven-day cooling-off period in which payment has to be refunded.

Perhaps you could adopt a money-back guarantee or some sort of guarantee of customer satisfaction. Businesses are happy to offer these guarantees, because the number of complaints or people who ask for refunds is usually tiny, but it encourages more people to buy from you in the first place.

If your sort of business cannot offer this sort of customer guarantee, you will need a clear policy and procedure on complaints and how they will be handled. Depending on the number of customers, there are also software programs developed specifically to deal with customer complaints. In some industries – for example, if you are an insurance or mortgage intermediary – you must comply with regulations that require you, among other things, to have a formal complaints procedure and to belong to an independent complaints handling body.

As a basic premise, you should follow the policy that complaints are valuable feedback and a customer who has complained but has been dealt with satisfactorily can turn into one of your most loyal and supportive customers. A survey for the (now superseded) National Consumer Council in 2007 found that 44 per cent of consumers have wanted to complain but don't and 52 per cent of consumers who feel let down or annoyed by a company simply take their custom elsewhere. Research among Australian consumers suggests that an unhappy customer will tell up to eight other people about their bad experience, potentially damaging the company's reputation further. By contrast, 70 per cent of customers who complain and whose complaint is resolved satisfactorily will carry on buying from the company or 95 per cent if the complaint is resolved immediately. Bear in mind that the impact of poor service or complaints handing can be even more disastrous if it is discussed on social media sites (see p. 152). This is another reason why you might want to get actively involved with such sites. That way, even if you do have a bad patch with handling customers, you may then have an opportunity to respond online directly to disgruntled customers to show that you care and explain what you are doing to put matters right.

Developing the concept of a club

If you can convince customers that their input and opinion matter, they will feel as if they belong to a select group or a club. This feeling of belonging can help to increase the responsiveness from your customers to anything else they might be offered by you. So work on ideas that can reassure them of their value to you – special letters, special offers, or inducements offered only to them as one of your valued customers. A simple way to establish a club could be to set up a fan page on Facebook. Make sure you actively engage with the followers who sign up, preferably letting customers get to know you as a person rather than just being an anonymous company representative. Customers may feel flattered and special if they feel they have direct access to the people in charge.

Customer referrals

Another important reason for building up a good working relationship with your present customers is that they can often be the source of your new business too. They may be able to suggest others in the same line of business who may be considering buying a product or service similar to yours. They may even be willing for you to use their name as an introduction. If the customer is very satisfied with your service or product, they may be willing to act as a reference for you, although obviously you must ask first. A reference means that you can give their name to potential customers and they will be prepared to discuss your business with them.

Data gathering

A very important part of building relationships with customers is data gathering. Databases are the key foundation for any business trying to put the emphasis on customer retention. All communications with customers (or potential customers) should be recorded.

If you get an enquiry from someone not yet a customer, it should be logged, along with name, mailing address, e-mail address, telephone number and any other details that come up. A note of the communication should be made. Thus, whenever this person subsequently contacts you, you need only to ask for their surname and postcode and you can find that record and build on it.

Similarly, if you have a web site, once potential customers have had a chance to look around, invite them to register so that you can create a data record for them. Be aware that you will always lose some visitors at the registration stage. Think about what added value you can offer to encourage registration – for example, access to a useful guide or a free gift.

When someone becomes a customer, you may be able to build a little more information, such as age or occupation, although you can't constantly bombard people with demands for information that appear to them to be irrelevant and intrusive.

The basic premise, though, is to gather and capture whatever data and information you can about potential and existing customers. As you gain more experience, building up a picture of your current customers allows you to select lists to mail to attract new customers with greater certainty for a higher response.

Data warehousing and data mining are two jargon phrases used by the data and direct mail industry. Warehousing is putting together lots of names with appropriate information, for example from the electoral rolls or from shareholder registers, which are lists that have to be available legally to the public. Data mining is searching through those names to target those that match your customer profile.

Individual records

The record will need to be tailored to your individual business or product, but more than likely it should include:

- name, address, e-mail address, telephone number.
- customer's type of business (if any).
- what the customer has bought from you, how frequently and in what quantities.
- the name of the decision-taker and the names of other contacts and their positions.
- the customer's credit rating or information about paying.
- any complaints and how they were resolved.

Checking out the law

The gathering and holding of personal data is tightly regulated. You are required by law to comply with the following eight principles. Data must be:

1 Fairly and lawfully processed. This means you must have a person's consent – usually this is done by including a tick box on any forms that gather data. Unless the information is sensitive, it is usually enough to give a person the right to opt out of your data lists. But where the information you collect is sensitive (for example, ethnic origin, political or religious beliefs) you must have the person's express consent to be included. Fair processing includes observing people's rights to confidentiality.

2 Processed for limited purposes. This means using data only in ways that are compatible with the purpose for which you collected the data.

3 Adequate, relevant and not excessive. In other words, you should stick strictly to the data you need for your purpose.

4 Accurate. You must ensure the data you keep are accurate and up to date.

5 Not kept longer than necessary. If you don't need a person's details or a particular category of information any more, delete it from your list.

6 Processed in accordance with the data subject's rights. This includes preventing processing if a person has indicated this could be damaging or distressing, and preventing processing for direct mailing purposes if the person has requested this.

7 Secure. You must have adequate measures to prevent unauthorized use of the data and to guard against loss or destruction.

8 Not transferable to countries without adequate protection. If you intend to transfer data to countries outside the European Economic Area, you must first check that the country has adequate data protection measures.

These principles apply to all databases, whether held on computer or manually. If you hold a computer database, you may in addition be required to notify the Information Commissioner* so that your name can be added to a public register of data controllers. There are exemptions from notification, including the processing of data only for the marketing purposes of your own business. Failure to register if you do need to is a criminal offence. If you hold manual data lists, you do not need to register, but you can do so voluntarily. For businesses with fewer than 250 staff, registration costs £35 a year (no VAT).

Be on your guard if you are contacted by an 'agency' that says you must be registered and that they will organize this for a fee (typically £95 or more). They have no official standing. You can find all the details you need on the Information Commissioner's web site and, if needed, sort out your own registration for the standard fee.

There are bodies with which people can register if they do not want to receive unsolicited mail, telephone calls, e-mails or faxes. Becoming a member of the Preference Service (Mailing*, Telephone*, E-mail* or Fax*) allows you to check their lists and so eliminate from your database those people who will not welcome your unsolicited advance. Under the data protection legislation, you do not have to belong to any of these bodies, but the Information Commissioner strongly encourages membership. If you belong to a direct marketing trade body, you may well find that its rules require you to be a member of the Mailing Preference Service or its equivalent bodies.

Using questionnaires

You could try sending around a simple questionnaire for your customers to complete. Don't make it too elaborate or too long (not more than two sides), and offer an incentive to encourage people to complete it, for example a prize draw for a free product. Questionnaires can give you a huge amount of information about your customer base, what they are really looking for from your product and other general information. Responses of 10 per cent of your customer base would be very good and would be considered a sound basis for making decisions.

New offers, new products and repeat purchases

This is where the real benefit to your business will emerge from adopting a proper customer care policy and being ruthlessly efficient at data gathering.

New offers

If you mail a list of existing customers with a new offer, you should expect a much higher response rate than from a list of people who have never heard from you before. A response of 1 per cent would be good to bring in new customers; but to sell something to existing customers you might look for a response of 3 or 4 per cent. A very targeted and specific offer might bring in a higher response than that, up to 10 per cent say. What this means is that your business suddenly becomes much more profitable.

New products

Successful customer care and data gathering should mean that the launch of new products can be infinitely less risky and more successful if you have a good existing customer base. For a start, you would choose your new products to appeal to your existing customers, as well as targeting other potential purchasers. Indeed, you might offer different products to different sections of your customer base.

The benefits of this should be obvious. Launching new products may even become cash-flow-positive. At any rate, the period between launch and the product becoming profitable should be considerably shortened.

Repeat purchases

A much higher proportion from a list of existing customers will make second or further orders of the same product (assuming it is a product that has a life of more than one purchase) compared with first orders from a list of potential customers. For example, a magazine or publication that has succeeded in getting a response rate of 1 per cent on the initial direct mail campaign could get a second-year subscription rate of between 25 and 75 per cent, say, without any marketing or selling costs.

Summary

1 Develop a long-term strategy of building sales with recurring purchases to existing customers.
2 Develop policies on response times and complaint handling to improve customer care.
3 Make data gathering and data capture a priority.
4 Making very specific offers to existing customers should be very profitable.
5 New products should become profitable after a much shorter period if you target an existing customer base.

Other chapters to read

2 Who will buy? (p. 13); 13 Getting the message across (p. 141); 14 Getting new customers (p. 157); 27 Moving ahead (p. 351).

16

How to set a price

There are four ways you can increase your profits. You can cut your costs, you can sell more, you can change your product mix or you can increase your prices. Clearly, your aim should be to set your prices initially at the level that gives you your highest profits possible. Needless to say, as with everything else to do with your business, it is easier said than done. There is no clear-cut or agreed method of establishing a price for your product.

Some people use the level of costs as a way of fixing price. This may seem a straightforward calculation but it has drawbacks. For example, if your costs are very low, does it automatically mean that your prices should be low too? And even working out the cost can be fraught with possible errors.

Other people argue that the price should be set by what the market can bear. But there are no quick and simple calculations that can tell you what this should be. Instead, you have to establish the price by looking at the market you are in and the particular part of it your product appeals to. How does your product rate against others competing in the same marketplace? There are also different strategies you can adopt depending on whether your product is a new or old one. Often overriding all your plans can be the effect that your competitors' pricing policy has on yours.

It is probably more realistic to think in terms of a range of prices. The lowest price you should consider setting will be fixed by the cost. You should not go below this price; if you have to, it would be better not to be in business at all. There are a couple of exceptions, where temporarily it may make sense (p. 182). The highest price will be the highest the market can bear without sales disappearing altogether. Between the two will be the price that will give the highest possible profits.

What is in this chapter?

- ■ the price range (p. 181).
- ■ setting a price (p. 184).
- ■ pricing with more than one product (p. 190).

The price range

There is a range of prices open to you to charge for your product or service. Your aim should be to get as near as possible to the price that is going to give you the biggest profit. But this is a long-term strategy; there may be short-term considerations that imply another price is appropriate.

The highest price

This strategy means you have decided to go for the cream at the top of the market. In marketing jargon, it is called price skimming or prestige pricing. You are pricing your product to appeal to those of your potential customers with the highest incomes or those seeking the snob value of a high-priced item. You can also carry out price skimming if you have a product with a genuine technical advantage or if it has novelty value.

Adopting a price-skimming policy usually implies that you are accepting that you could make bigger profits if you lowered the price, because you would sell correspondingly more. Nevertheless, this strategy can be very appealing to small businesses. To sell more you may need to invest in bigger production facilities or employ more staff. This could involve raising funds to be able to do so. And you may find that this bigger business is harder for you to control. Creating a specialist niche could be ideal for the self-employed and small business owner. While it may not give the highest possible profits, it could make you a very acceptable living.

A pitfall to watch out for is that high prices attract competitors. Your profitable niche may soon be invaded by those offering lower prices or a better service or product. You need to allow for this competition in a price-skimming strategy. This applies particularly if you are adopting a price-skimming policy because your product is new with a technical innovation. It is unlikely to remain unique for long. Your strategy needs to involve either reducing prices in the longer term or concentrating on other advantages or benefits so that your product establishes its own image. This allows it to carry on commanding a higher price even when the technical advantage no longer exists.

The lowest price

The lowest price you should consider accepting for your product is the one that covers your direct costs and contributes something to the cost of your overheads. But this must be regarded as a last resort and not to be accepted if you can obtain business at a higher price.

How is it worked out?

You need to find the direct costs of your product or service. Direct costs are the costs that you would not have if you were not producing that particular item. Your business will also have other costs, indirect costs or overheads. You will still have to pay these whether you produce the item or not.

Example

Sidney Smith knows that the cost of producing his stationery pads is as follows:

Direct materials (paper, glue)	10 pence
Direct labour	5 pence
Total direct costs	15 pence

The lowest price Sidney should consider accepting for his stationery pads is 15 pence plus something towards the costs of overheads, for example, 16 pence a pad.

Note that the terms direct costs, indirect costs and contribution to overheads are explained in much more detail in the section 'Break-even point' on p. 334.

When should you use this price?

As little as possible must be the answer. You would need to sell very large volumes of your product to have enough contribution to cover the cost of your overheads, never mind make a profit.

The main circumstance in which you can justify selling as cheaply as this is if you have spare capacity, with very little prospect of using it for product or services selling at a higher price. If this is the case, anything you sell that helps to contribute to the cost of your overheads should be considered.

However, making this decision can have longer-term effects that must be considered. If you are operating in a market that is very competitive or in one in which your customers tend to be in contact, you may find that you are being forced to sell all your products or services at this very low price. Raising or maintaining your prices can be very difficult in these circumstances.

Selling your product at the lowest price, even on a one-off basis, can have an even worse effect on your business if it triggers off price-cutting by your competitors. This could well occur if customers use your low price to force the competition to lower their prices.

The moral is only sell something at this contribution price if it is a one-off product, perhaps not part of your normal range of goods, and if you are very confident that it will not lead to secondary effects on your other products or the competition. You must only consider this price if you have spare capacity. If you do not have any spare capacity, choose the price that gives you the biggest contribution.

Can you go lower than this price?

Only in exceptional cases, such as if you need to clear excess stocks or low-selling lines. If this is the case, try to clear these outside your main selling channels so that it can have no counter-effect on your normal selling activity.

Why you should not use cost as a basis for establishing your normal price

Many businesses work out their prices by calculating what it costs to make the product or service and adding on what they consider a suitable profit margin. But this approach is not satisfactory for two reasons:

1 It is surprisingly difficult to work out what it costs to produce an item.
2 The cost of an item tells you nothing about whether customers will
   buy it at that price at all or whether they would have paid much more.

There are various different ways of working out the cost of something, but very often businesses use some variation of a standard costing system. Typically, it looks something like this:

Direct materials	£100.00
Direct labour	£75.00
Indirect materials (50 per cent of direct materials, say)	£50.00
Indirect labour (30 per cent of direct labour, say)	£22.50
General overhead (40 per cent of direct labour, say)	£30.00

▶

Total cost	£277.50
Profit margin (add 50 per cent)	£138.75
Price	£416.25

Of course, various discounts may be offered on this price.

The problem with this system is the difficulty of working out how much of the indirect costs and overheads should be added to each product to work out the cost. To attribute a certain percentage to the product, you need:

■ some idea or forecast of the total amount of overheads and indirect costs for the year; and

■ some idea of the total amount of product you will sell during the year.

In other words, a pricing system based on cost is based on your best fore-casts. Obviously, forecasts can be wrong. You may find that you have not sold at a price high enough to cover the costs of overheads, because either your sales are lower or your overhead costs higher than your forecast.

The problem is multiplied if you have more than one product or service. How do you decide how much of the indirect costs and overheads should be apportioned to each product? There is no clear-cut answer.

Setting a price

There are several influences that will determine how near the top or how near the bottom end of the price range your product should be placed:

■ how your product compares with competing products.

■ the life-cycle of the product; that is, how new or mature.

■ how price-sensitive your customers are.

■ what price conveys to your customers.

■ what position your product has in the market.

How your product compares with competing products

Assuming that you face competition in your chosen market, it is realistic to assume that the price you can place on your product will, to a certain extent, depend on the competition. This does not mean that if your com-petitors price very low, you have to follow suit. But it does mean that you should analyse your product carefully in relation to the others. The sort of characteristics you should look at include:

■ what your product looks like and how it compares with the others.

■ how it is packaged and presented.

■ what the availability is.

■ whether your delivery and after-sales service is better or worse than that offered by your competitors.

■ how customers pay.

■ whether your product has a better image or reputation.

If your product compares favourably with the others, you may be able to justify a higher price than the competition, even if you are relatively new into the market. Do not be afraid of putting a higher price than the competition. If your product really does have benefits, such as better delivery and service, or a better image, the marketplace may well accept that your price should be higher.

Stage in the product life-cycle?

If it is a new product, one not before produced, there are two possible strategies to adopt. One possibility is a price-skimming policy (p. 181), which goes for a high initial price. The other possibility is to try to secure a very large share of the market for your product before the competition appears on the scene. This would be achieved by setting a low price, known as the penetration price (p. 188).

How price-sensitive your customers are

If you put up your prices, do you have any idea how many of your existing customers would switch to another supplier? Or if you dropped your prices how many new customers you would acquire? How great an effect change in prices has on the amount you sell is called price sensitivity (or elasticity of demand). If customer response to price changes in your product is not that great, you can push nearer the upper end of the price range.

Broadly speaking, if your product is not bought that frequently, that is, one purchase will last quite a long time, the sales of it will not be so sensitive to price changes. On the other hand, if it is bought at regular intervals, sales may react much more strongly.

If it is difficult to differentiate one product from another in your market, this also implies that it will react much more strongly to price changes. If, on the other hand, your product can be differentiated from others by perceived benefits such as image and delivery, sales will be more resistant to price changes.

What price conveys to your customers

Price alone can conjure up ideas about your product in your potential customers' minds. The consumer often associates higher quality with a higher price; paradoxically, a high price can help the image or reputation of your product. If this applies to your market, a lower price will not generate more sales.

In general terms, a product that has the greatest market share is unlikely to be the cheapest. These products may generate high sales, because despite their high price they are thought by consumers to offer the best package of benefits (or best value for money).

What position in the market?

Often, your ability to set prices may be limited by the market in which you operate. There may be a going rate established in the market and, unless your product becomes the market leader (see below) or is definitely a better product, it may be difficult to establish any other price.

The price of your product needs to fit the market position planned for it. This is the place that the product occupies, compared with competitive products, in the eyes of your existing or potential customers.

A guide to setting prices

1 Analyse the position your product holds in the market. Are your target customers those who are looking for reliability? Has your product already achieved an established image in the eyes of the market? Do buyers view it as good quality, prompt service, stylish, say?
2 Analyse your product. Are you planning modifications or alterations that could alter its reputation or relative position in the marketplace?
3 Analyse the competition. How do their products rate against yours? What is the relative price structure in the market?
4 Decide your pricing strategy. Where in the price range are you going to pitch your price? Is it going to be average for the market, 5 per cent less than the average, 5 per cent above the average or a premium price, 25 per cent above the average?

5 Choose some specific prices. Estimate volume of sales, profit margin and costs to forecast the level of profits for each price.

6 Choose your price.

7 Would you be able to test-market the price in a small area of your market? This would allow you to gauge customer reactions.

Price near the top of the range

There are two possible reasons why you may be able to justify a price near the top end of the range:

1 The product is the market leader.

2 The product is set apart from the competition by non-price benefits.

Market leader

The market leader will be the biggest-selling product in the market. There are several advantages to being the market leader, so it is a position worth aspiring to. The advantages include being able to charge a higher price than the average, making greater sales, having more power over your suppliers and competitors, and being less risky in poor economic conditions.

There is no easy way to become the market leader. Some of the guidelines to achieve the premier position are:

■ try to be one of the earliest entrants into the market (not necessarily the first).

■ develop, by careful marketing, selling and advertising, what is different about your product or business.

■ be ruthless about efficiency and costs.

■ be sensitive to changes in the market.

■ compete intensively on all sales.

■ look for profits over a long period, not the short-term fast buck – so lengthen your horizon.

Non-price benefits

The price you put on the product tells prospective customers something about it. On the whole, a higher price implies high quality, a lower price low quality. You are unlikely to build a business offering a low-quality product at a high price; on the other hand, you are throwing away profits if you offer high quality at a low price. You have to decide where your product is placed in the market compared with competitors and price accordingly.

You will be able to justify a higher price, near the top end of the range, if you decide to offer a high-quality product. You must not be frightened into thinking that the only thing that matters to buyers is price; they are interested in other aspects of your product too.

In your marketing and selling, build an image or reputation for quality, efficient service, reliability, prompt delivery, and effective sales and technical literature. This will allow you to raise prices and generate higher profits.

Price near the bottom of the range

There are three main reasons why your pricing policy might be near the bottom end of the range:

1 Fear (because you mistakenly believe that the main factor in buying is price – but see above).
2 A strategy of grabbing market share.
3 Severe price competition.

Market share

A legitimate strategy for a business is to sacrifice the level of profits in return for an increased market share. To achieve this, you would pitch the price near the low end of the possible price range (in marketing jargon, a penetration price) in return for selling more of the product. The intention in the strategy is to increase your market share, consolidate your position and increase your prices gradually while retaining the share you have established. Essentially, the aim is eventually to become the market leader with higher unit sales at a higher price. A number of dangers are inherent in this strategy:

- you may find it exceptionally difficult to raise your prices without demonstrating an improvement in the product in compensation.
- you may find that new customers do not remain faithful to you when you increase the price but return to their original supplier.
- you may trigger off a price war with your competitors.

The likeliest use of the strategy occurs when you are introducing a new product to the market, and the competition is weak. In this case, you can establish a large market share without attracting strong competition because of the large profits to be made.

Few small firms will have the financial and managerial resources available to achieve this strategy of establishing a large market share successfully; it is really too risky to be considered. Instead, they should look more closely at devoting the available resources to promotion or advertising.

Facing severe price competition

Low prices or a price-cutting war is an advantage to very few people: you do not want it, other small competing firms do not want it; in the long run, customers do not want it, if it means a reduced number of suppliers and less choice. It may only be in the long-term interest of a large company, if that is your main competitor. So, whatever you do, try to avoid triggering it off.

If one of your competitors cuts prices, what should you do? Try to avoid the instant reaction of following prices downwards. Instead, try to concentrate your customers' minds on the non-price benefits (see p. 187) of doing business with you. If you have carried out some market research, you will know which are the non-price factors that buyers rate most highly, and these can be emphasized.

However, if you operate in a market that is very price-sensitive and does not differentiate between products, there is little choice but to match the price cuts. In this case, your survival will depend on savage reduction in your costs.

Selling at more than one price

If you have a range of different customers, you may be able to sell your product at a higher price to some of them and a lower price to others (called 'price discrimination'). For example, a solicitor or accountant might have one rate for individuals and another for corporate customers; an entertainment provider might have a reduced rate for, say, children, students and elderly people; a farmer might have different prices for sales direct to the public, sales to distributors, and sales to firms that are going to further process the product; a supermarket in a large town where there are many competitors might charge less than one in a rural area with far less competition; you might have to charge less for overseas sales than for sales in the UK.

Price discrimination is possible where you can divide your likely customers into distinct groups that are willing to pay different amounts. Yours must also be the sort of product or service that cannot be readily resold. This is more often the case with services. For example, if you are a landscape gardener, there is no real way for one customer to purchase the work you have done for another. In general, unless you have a monopoly over the supply of your product (which is unusual for a small business), you can discriminate on price only if other suppliers are doing the same – otherwise, by charging a higher price, you will simply lose customers to your competitors.

Successful price discrimination should boost your revenue above the level you would have had charging a single price to all customers. This is because setting a single price would lose customers unwilling to pay that much and give an unnecessary discount to others who were willing to pay more.

Pricing with more than one product

If you have more than one product, the sales could be interlinked if they are:

- competing with each other; or
- complementary to each other.

You need to ensure that your pricing policy is consistent across the range of your products. With competing products, the prices need to make sense. There needs to be a recognizable gap in the prices if one is a high-quality product while the other is of lower quality.

The pricing considerations are different if your products are complementary, that is, if you sell one, you are likely to sell the other. Once your customer is hooked, there will be lots of scope for charging high prices on a complementary item, as long as it is not so blatant that it puts off buyers from the starting product.

Summary

1 There is a range of prices that you can charge.
2 The lowest price is set by the contribution to overheads that it makes. Never go below this price. Only accept this price if you have spare capacity and there is no prospect of selling your product or time at a higher rate. If you have little or no spare capacity, choose the sale that gives you the biggest contribution.
3 Do not use costs as the basis for setting your prices, at least not without first trying to price the product according to what customers will pay.
4 If you go for the highest price possible in the market, you will restrict the amount you can sell. It will not give you the maximum

possible level of profits. However, a specialist niche of this type can be attractive to a small business.

5 When it comes to setting a price, you have to compare your product with others, establish how responsive sales are to a change in prices, work out your strategy if it is a new product or coming to the end of its life, analyse what price conveys to your customers and decide what position your product is aiming for in the market. Use the guide on p. 186.

6 The market leader has several advantages; the main ones are that it means you can achieve more sales at a higher price than the competition.

7 Justify a higher price by stressing non-price benefits, such as quality, reliability and delivery.

8 Avoid pitching your price too low through fear or misunderstanding of what buyers are interested in.

9 A strategy of increasing market share through low prices is dangerous for a small business.

10 If you are facing severe price competition, try to distract attention from price by emphasizing the product benefits.

11 If your customers can be divided into distinct groups, you may be able to increase revenue by charging several different prices.

Other chapters to read

17

Choosing your workplace

One of the jokes that can be made about people starting small businesses is that the first thing they want to do is to search for premises. It is an understandable desire, as premises are tangible proof of the creation of an enterprise. However, today it is possible to run a business, even with several people, without ever having separate business premises.

The concept of 'the virtual business' is no longer a joke. Given the communications now available – e-mail, broadband, fax, telephone and mobile phone – it would now be possible for several people to group together, operating from their respective homes, and to create a business, communicating regularly and at length. You could also use freelancers and subcontractors, again operating from their homes, rather than employees.

At a stroke, a 'virtual business' removes the burden of two major overheads, rent and employees, and many enterprises are discovering the benefits that this brings. You could adopt this strategy as an initial phase until the business is more established, or as a permanent way of operation.

If you decide that your business cannot operate without premises, it is a very important step to take. Finding the right premises at just the right location for just the right price can prove to be extraordinarily difficult.

Unless you have decided to retail only through the Internet, a large part of the setting-up process for a retail business will be devoted to the search for a good location. And you cannot afford to compromise and take premises that with a bit of luck will be OK. You have to be satisfied that the premises meet all your criteria; if they do not, carry on the search until you find the right site.

What is in this chapter?

Where is your business to be located?

An important first exercise would be to start with a blank piece of paper and think about location from first principles. What is the ideal location for the type of business you have in mind? At a later stage, you can introduce the constraints placed on location, such as home and family. You should know the ideal location so you can estimate the effect of concessions you are making to these outside non-business constraints. There may be further constraints, such as the lack of finance, which may cause you to compromise.

Communications

How dependent is the success of your business on communications: road, rail, air, bus? This could be important if:

■ you deliver your product.

■ your business is service-based to particular areas of the population.

■ you sell your product direct, using salespeople.

■ your business is dependent on import and export.

In these and other categories of business, an ideal location would allow easy access to the relevant parts of the country. For example, if import/ export is your trade, a location within reach of a major airport could be an advantage. Or, if you sell direct to the whole country, you need access to motorways.

Labour

If your business is dependent on the use of certain skills, you may find that one part of the country is more abundantly endowed with potential employees who have already acquired those skills than other parts. On the other hand, skills may be irrelevant; what you may need is a ready pool of unskilled labour, in which case some areas have higher unemployment than others.

Centres of population

Your business may need to be located near particular centres of population. If you are trying to sell your product in large volume, being in a large centre of population may be an advantage. Or you may want to choose an area with a specific structure of population if your product or service is sold only to particular sectors. For example, if you plan to open a bookshop, you typically need a town or catchment area of a certain size. You also need a population, or substantial visitor base, well endowed with the particular characteristics of those who buy books. Your market research will help you to identify what those characteristics are.

Business clusters

Sometimes there is an advantage in setting up in an area where there are already competitors. This may be the case if customers have to travel some way and are more likely to come if there is a choice of different outlets, especially where there is a great deal of variation in the individual items being sold. This is why shopping centres are attractive destinations, but it can equally apply to, say, clusters of antique shops or restaurants.

Another reason for a cluster can be access to specialist labour – for example, a science park that draws on expertise from a nearby university – or to foster joint ventures.

Suppliers

Your business may depend on supplies of a particular raw material or some other product. Costs would be lessened if your business was located near the source of supply. This could be either the main distributor of the item or where the item is grown or produced.

Government and local authority assistance

Your business may be location-independent. Thus, you can look at some of the deals that the government and local authorities produce to stimulate the founding of new businesses in specific regions.

The government has designated some poorer regions of the UK as assisted areas until at least December 2013. These are parts of Cornwall, West Wales and the Valleys, the Highlands and Islands of Scotland, the whole of Northern Ireland, and various parts of England, for example, Yorkshire, Tyneside and the Wirral. If you locate your business in one of these, you may be eligible for grants. You can get a list of assisted areas from Business Link* or the equivalent organization. A Business Premises Renovation Allowance was introduced from 11 April 2007. Under this scheme, you can get tax relief in the year you incur the expenditure for the full cost of renovating or converting business premises in an assisted area to bring them back into commercial use where they have been vacant for a year or more.

In the 2011 Budget, the government announced the establishment of 21 new enterprise zones. Businesses setting up in these zones will qualify for tax breaks, including business rate reductions up to £275,000 over five years, simplified planning rules and access to super-fast broadband. At the time of writing, eight specific locations had been announced: Nottingham (the Boots campus), Liverpool (Liverpool and Wirral Waters), Manchester (Airport City), London (Royal Docks), Birmingham (City Centre), Leeds (Lower Aire Valley), Bristol (Temple Quarter Zone) and Sheffield (key sites along the M1). A further three will be established somewhere in: the Black Country, Tees Valley, and North Eastern. Ten more zones are due to be announced in summer 2011.

There is a range of support and funding schemes for new businesses not dependent on where you locate (see Chapter 25, 'Raising the money'). Some are targeted at specific sectors, including the Rural Development Programme for England* which provides help for farmers, foresters, landowners and other businesses located in rural areas. You can get details from either Business Link or *www.rdpenetwork.org.uk*.

At the time of writing, England is divided into nine regions, each with its own Regional Development Agency* (RDA). The RDAs for each of the other countries of the UK are Invest NI*, Scottish Enterprise*, Highlands and Islands Enterprise* and the Welsh Assembly Department for the Economy and Transport*. The RDAs coordinate economic development and regeneration in their region. Many of them have adopted a 'cluster concept' which means they focus on a specific industry – often one which has historical links to the area. The aim is to bring together businesses relating to the chosen industry to foster growth and cooperation. For example, the relevant RDAs are currently promoting Manchester, Newcastle, York, Bristol, Nottingham and Birmingham as 'science cities'. Locating in an RDA area that supports your particular industry could give you access to funding, a skilled workforce and suitable premises.

The RDAs in England will all be dismantled by March 2012 with many of their powers and duties shifting to new Local Enterprise Partnerships* (LEPs). LEPs will be responsible for setting and delivering local growth and regeneration strategies. They take the form of partnerships between local authorities and local business and cover natural economic areas rather than following administrative boundaries. For example, where it makes sense for two adjacent local authorities to combine forces, they will both be in the same LEP. Some funding for growth will not be available directly to businesses. Instead, LEPs will bid for funding, possibly for major projects but also for packages that bring together a variety of local initiatives. It will then be for local businesses to apply to their local authority for individual support out of such funds.

To find out what help is available regionally, contact Business Link* (England), Business Gateway* (Scotland), Business Wales* (Wales) or Invest NI* (Northern Ireland). There are interactive search tools on their web sites. If you have a specific area in mind already, you could contact the local authority for that area and the RDA office or LEP to check out what help might be on offer. Be wary of firms specializing in telling you about grants – some of them are cowboys, and you could end up paying a few hundred pounds or more for information you can get free from Business Link or an equivalent organization.

The final choice of location

It would be unrealistic to assume that domestic constraints are not important in locating a business. The extra benefits gained from moving to another area may simply not outweigh the domestic upheaval and cost of moving house when you want to start your business.

If you decide not to move your home, it makes sense for your offices to be close to your home, as long as other business considerations do not apply. If it would not adversely affect your business to be near your home, it can be an advantage as it cuts down on your wasted travelling time from home to office when you probably need all your time for business problems.

Working from home

Many small businesses will start off in the back bedroom. Some, especially if they are part-time businesses, may stay there permanently. Working from home has several advantages: it is free, it involves no travelling, the work can be combined with any domestic tasks to be done, there are no fares or expensive lunches to be bought, you can wear what you like, and it protects your home and business from burglars.

However, working from home involves an extraordinary amount of self-discipline. It is all too easy to find some domestic job that needs doing. It can also be frustrating to have your work interrupted by callers or other members of the family. And your work never goes away; you cannot leave it behind when you walk out of the office door. This can lead to extra worry.

Ultimately, you may also find it lonely, and you may find the lack of stimulation from fellow workers and colleagues very dispiriting. And another disadvantage of using your home as working premises is the poor impression it could create on customers if they need to visit you.

Good organization is the key to being able to work successfully at home. Your work space needs to be separate from the rest of the house; a room is ideal, but a corner set aside for work is better than nothing.

You should also try to be strict about the time set aside for work. Try to start at a definite time each day. Persuade friends that you are serious about your work and you will be hard at it between certain times. To solve the problems of loneliness and loss of stimulation, try to build a network of others working from home or in your business field.

The obstacles to turning your home into a successful workplace could include the possible need to get planning permission. This may occur if your business alters the residential character of your home. This might be the case if you convert part (a garage, say) into a workshop, your business is noisy or involves hazardous materials, customers will visit your home or you will have employees working there. But provided your business is unobtrusive, you probably will not need permission. If in doubt, contact the planning officer* at your local authority.

Other possible obstacles include:

■ the existence of restrictive covenants on the land (ask your solicitor*).

■ the existence of a mortgage (check with building society or bank).

■ restrictions on insurance (check with insurance broker* or company).

■ problems with the environmental health department if your business is food production, for example.

Working from a home that you own may mean that some capital gains tax will be due when you sell it (p. 400). Check with your accountant*. But you should be able to organize things so that this does not happen. You might be liable for business rates on the part of your home used for business (and the band your home is in for council tax might then be reduced) but not if your business does not alter the essentially residential character of your home (p. 402). Contact the Valuation Office Agency* for guidance. You will also need to consider insurance for an office you run from home. An increasing number of insurers will let you cover business equipment as an extension to your normal house contents insurance. But, more usually, you need to take out separate insurance to get additional cover, for example for business interruption (see Chapter 23, 'Insurance').

What other sort of premises?

After settling on a location, your search can home in on the premises you need. There are two aspects. First, you need a tighter specification of location, for example town, district, neighbourhood or even street. This very tight specification mainly applies to retail business. Most of the considerations you need to take into account are explained on p. 90. The second aspect is the type of premises. The factors that influence your choice include:

- *appearance*: if customers and suppliers are likely to come to your offices, appearance can affect your credibility and your image.
- *parking or public transport*: if you have staff or visiting customers and suppliers, you'll want either good transport or parking. The planning officer* (see p. 202) may need to be satisfied that you have adequate parking, unless there are good public transport links.
- *cost*: you obviously want to keep your costs as low as you can, consistent, that is, with achieving your business objectives. Keep an eye on business rates.
- *size and layout*: your business activity may impose constraints on the amount and exact physical layout needed.
- *physical environment needed for maximum work efficiency*: cold, noise, dirt and dark can all mean people do not operate at their best.

The type of business may well dictate your choice of premises between office, factory, workshop or warehouse, for example. But a number of specialized options are open to small businesses.

Managed workshops and small business centres

In many places, there are centres designed especially for small businesses. These provide small offices, workshops or factory space. There may well be an element of joint services thrown in, for example a telephone answering service or secretarial facilities. There could even be an advisory team to help you with initial management problems.

Sharing accommodation in this way with other small businesses has its attractions; there can be mutual support and business introductions, for example. You may also be able to run a more efficient business because of the shared facilities than from an office on your own.

Some workshop groups are organized as 'business incubators' designed to foster rapid growth through an entrepreneurial and learning environment, high profile and access to mentors. Contact UK Business Incubation*.

Science parks

Finding premises in a science park has its attractions for high-tech businesses. Most science parks are attached to universities. The theory is that by grouping innovative businesses together and in close proximity to the research facilities of the university, this will provide a breeding ground for new ideas. Whether this happens or not, your business may be able to project a high-tech image as a result of being located in a park. For information, contact the UK Science Park Association*.

Searching for premises

There are two aspects to searching for premises. First, you have to find out about premises that are vacant. Second, you have to decide whether any of the premises you see meet your needs.

There are several places to look to find vacant premises:

- local newspapers or web sites, such as *www.startinbusiness.co.uk*.
- estate agents. You will find that not all estate agents handle commercial property. The estate agent dealing with a particular property may not be local at all but could be based many miles away.
- the local authority*. Many of them keep lists or registers of vacant industrial or commercial property within their boundaries. Some have

disused public buildings for sale. Indeed, it can be worthwhile having a discussion with the local authority, for example the industrial development officer, as there may be special schemes to help you within certain areas of the authority.

■ Local Enterprise Agency* or equivalent (see Chapter 3, 'A spot of coaching').

Once you have gathered together information about premises for renting or buying in the area, the next step (before you go to see any of them) is to draw up a checklist of the priority points your premises need:

1 *Space* How many sq. ft do you need? For offices, allow roughly 100 sq. ft per employee.
Office ....
Storage ....
Factory ....
Retail ....

2 *Working environment* What is the importance of these factors?
Appearance for customers and suppliers ....
Light ....
Noise ....
Cleanliness ....
Smells ....
Fire hazards ....
Neighbours (type of work) ....

3 *Ease of access* What do the premises need?
Good access for pedestrians ....
To be near a bus stop or railway station ....
Good parking facilities ....
Delivery facilities ....

4 *Services and facilities* Would you like these already installed?
Partitions/fittings ....
Telephone/broadband ....
Burglar alarms ....
Central heating ....
Lighting/electricity points ....
Air conditioning/ventilation ....
Cooking/refrigeration ....
Computer network ....

5 *What about cost?*

Rent per sq. ft ....

Rates per sq. ft ....

Maintenance ....

Running costs ....

Rent reviews ....

Premium for getting in ....

Rent-free period ....

Decoration ....

Fittings needed ....

Telephones, electricity, security, etc. ....

Length of lease ....

When you have worked out a shortlist of properties that you want to see, it can be useful to draw a quick sketch-plan of the premises. At your leisure, you can mark where the various parts of the business will be put and get some idea of how comfortably your particular business fits into those premises.

Investigating and negotiating

Before you sign anything, there are several steps to take to investigate the premises further. These steps are to estimate costs, to check the structure of property (if it is freehold or a repairing lease), to investigate the legal side of things, and to look at local authority requirements.

To estimate costs

There are a few things to investigate before estimating costs. First, do not rely on the measurements given by the estate agent or landlord. Measure the premises yourself. There is a chance that the area is less than they said, which could mean lower rent for you if you have been quoted a rent per sq. ft.

Second, it would be a good idea to look at the premises a number of times on different days and at different times of the day. This should allow you to get a better idea of decoration, heating, lighting or noise insulation needed.

Third, make sure you estimate or allow for all the running costs as well as alterations and improvements you would need to make.

It is always worthwhile trying to negotiate a lower rent and, in particular, asking for a rent-free period of three, six or 12 months if there is a lot of vacant property around, as for example in a recession.

To check the structure of property

Many leases make the tenant responsible for the repairs and maintenance of the premises. Get a survey from a member of the Royal Institution of Chartered Surveyors*. You can also use a survey to negotiate that the landlord pays for certain improvements before you take the premises.

To investigate the legal side of things

Your solicitor* should be asked to undertake a perusal of the lease. The sort of points to look out for are:

- can the premises be used for the type of business you have in mind?
- how long is the lease? Commonly, it is between three and 20 years.
- will you have the right to get a new lease when this one runs out?
- are the premises listed? This can restrict the way you adapt and extend them to suit your business needs.
- are there rent reviews, and when are they?
- can you sublet part or all of the premises?
- who is responsible for the repairs and the insurance?
- is the lease actually owned by the person trying to sell it?
- are the premises likely to be affected by any road or town improvements or alterations?
- who is paying for the landlord's legal costs? It is general practice for you to pay them, but it is always subject to negotiation. At any rate, agree beforehand that you will only pay a reasonable amount.
- is it possible to rent the premises on a weekly agreement, rather than sign a long lease? This gives you flexibility, but you lose security. An informal arrangement like this may be possible at times when there is a glut of vacant property.
- does the landlord want you to give a personal guarantee? Your solicitor should spell out to you the implications of doing so and help you to negotiate to try to avoid this.

To look at local authority requirements

A simple step you can make for yourself is to call the planning and building control officer to find out what is the current approved use for the premises. If your intended use is the same, you may need to do nothing more. If a change of use is required, your solicitor* should be able to help. The planning officer can also advise you if your premises have listed building status.

Depending on the nature of your business, you may need to consult:

■ planning and building control officers.

■ environmental health officers.

■ fire officers.

■ the Health and Safety Executive*.

Summary

1 Could your business be a 'virtual business'? Improved communications means that a business could be started by several of you, each working from home.

2 Look at location with an open mind. Would your business get off to a better start moving to a different part of the country? Locations with assisted area status can offer considerable benefits and some RDAs/LEPs specialize in supporting businesses in particular sectors.

3 As well as conventional premises, small businesses can also look at shared workshops and offices, and setting up in a science park.

4 Before you inspect any premises, draw up a list of what you think are your business needs.

Other chapters to read

8 Less than 100 per cent (p. 77); **18** Information technology – and other equipment (p. 204).

18

Information technology – and other equipment

Fifteen years ago, small businesses could get by without investing heavily in information technology (IT). Since then, two changes have occurred. First, the price of all IT equipment has plummeted, so for a small outlay a small business can become efficiently and comprehensively equipped with fast computers, clever software and communications with the outside world. Second, the way of doing business has changed dramatically. Face-to-face selling and contact and networking at meetings or at the golf club were the main means of arranging business deals. These are still important today, but a whole new way of doing business has emerged. Communications are now by e-mail, by telephone or on the Internet. Such a sea-change in culture is a major boost for small businesses. Using information technology wisely allows small businesses a much greater reach to customers and suppliers, and allows a business to put across the appearance of efficiency and control – attributes normally associated with larger companies.

Small businesses now need an IT strategy. Investment in IT should be a priority, but there are two particular types of business where this should be given even greater emphasis.

You can now run a 'virtual' business from wherever you are based, whether it be in a remote part of the country, a farm in Sussex or a loft in an inner city area. Using IT allows you and other members of your team to remain in locations where you want to live, each of you using your own home as your particular base, and yet build a business together.

The second category where IT is especially important is for growth businesses. Growth businesses invest heavily in IT because they are constantly searching for ways to carry out their work more efficiently, to give faster and better service to customers, to rid their businesses of the endless paper trail, and to keep the overhead burden caused by taking on employees to a minimum.

What is in this chapter?

■ choosing information technology (p. 205).

■ choosing other equipment (communications, furniture, cars) (p. 207).

■ how to pay for equipment (p. 209).

Choosing information technology

The first question you need to ask is what you want a computer to do in your business. Quite apart from specialist functions such as computer-aided design, a range of general business tasks can be carried out, such as:

■ *word processing*: a computer can be invaluable if in your business you send out a lot of routine letters, such as sales letters, quotes or mailshots. A computer with a word-processing program can be time-saving and produce a high-quality service.

■ *accounts*: there are a number of computerized accounting packages, including some simple software designed especially for small businesses.

■ *financial control and planning*: the programs range from cash management to sophisticated systems for working out forecasts and updating them at regular intervals. A software program can considerably simplify the task of forming and updating cash flow and profit-and-loss forecasts and helping you to manage your cash. Some of the banks now give business planning software and accounting software away free as part of an introductory package.

■ *database-type work*: if you have a large list of potential customers and send out mailshots or want to record information about them, using database software can improve your efficiency dramatically.

With the move in sales methods towards direct selling, often by mail or telephone, the use of databases becomes more and more important. And if you are adopting a strategy of building a group of customers with like needs and interests and developing products to meet their requirements, database software is the only answer.

Choose your database package with care and if necessary use an IT expert to set it up correctly for you before you start building your business. Altering your database structure after you have been in business a while is expensive and problematic.

You must comply with the requirements of the Data Protection Act – see p. 175. If you are going to hold personal data, you may need to register as a data controller with the Information Commissioner*.

- *stock control*: this can be important for retail outfits. Some computer systems link up to the cash till, so that levels of stock and need for re-ordering are worked out automatically.
- *information gathering*: if yours is a research-based business, you can now access a huge amount of information via the Internet. And all businesses may find it useful to check or gather information from, for example, government web sites, trade bodies and Business Link* or its equivalent organization.
- *selling*: the Internet may be a suitable medium for selling your product, in which case you will need a web site.

A computer system is made up of hardware and software. The hardware is the computer and peripherals such as printer, modem, router and scanner. These are now mass-market products, and you can easily shop around to get the cheapest deal. If you have more than one computer, you will probably want to network them to improve efficiency and allow you to share data between computers and to share printers. The software is what makes the computer carry out various tasks. There are two types of software: operating software, which makes the computer go; and application software, which does the specific job, for example cash management, word processing or e-mail. This software can come as a 'package' with your hardware. Don't even consider having software written specially for you, although you can get simple adaptations to the packaged software by using what are called 'scripts', 'macros' or 'templates'.

Both aspects of a computer system are important, although with the development of cheaper and better hardware, choosing the software becomes the prime task. You can buy computer systems from high-street stores, computer superstores, the Internet or computer dealers who specialize in business computers and software.

In conclusion, it's crucial to have a fast computer. Buy one off the shelf that comes with ready-made packages, such as word processing, spreadsheet, accounts package, database software, e-mail and access to the Internet. But if you know particular aspects are more important to you, choose the specific software package and install it yourself.

You will also need to select a printer, and you can choose either a laser printer (the best quality) or a good ink-jet. If you design your letterhead with care, for example in black only, you can print it yourself. Even if your letterhead is in colour, unless you want a large quantity, you can get cheapish colour printers to print in-house. But don't just look at the initial capital cost; also consider the cost of 'consumables' (such as ink or toner cartridges and drums), which can vary a lot from one printer to another so that the running costs can easily outweigh any saving in initial outlay.

If there is more than one of you in the business, you need to set up a network with a server. A network allows you to switch documents from one machine to another without making paper copies, and it allows more than one of you to work in the same application software at the same time.

Get advice from an IT consultant on the best way to set this up so it works properly. Don't use gifted amateurs or friends. Ask your Business Link* or equivalent organization adviser to recommend an IT consultant.

Choosing other equipment

The right communications

Computers these days come with an internal modem as standard. This enables you to link to the Internet and send and receive e-mails and faxes through your ordinary telephone line. But this is a slow way to connect. These days, most firms opt for broadband – an 'always-on' connection for which you pay a flat, monthly fee.

Broadband is now widely available even if you live in a rural area. Make sure you choose a broadband package that suits your intended usage. Cheaper deals usually limit the quantity of information you can download each month. If you are a heavy user, go for a deal with a high download limit (say, over 5 gigabytes per month) or unlimited download. But be aware that most unlimited download services have a 'fair usage' policy which means you can be asked to cut back your usage if you persistently download very large amounts each month.

If you will be out and about a great deal, you may want to consider mobile technology. There is now a continuous spectrum from laptops and netbooks through to tablets (such as the iPad and its Android rivals) and smartphones.

You can link a laptop or netbook to the Internet using a 'dongle' – a gadget you plug into your computer that connects you via a mobile phone account. Alternatively, you can 'tether' your computer to your mobile phone which then acts as a Wi-Fi hotspot.

A further option is to abandon your computer altogether and opt for a tablet or smartphone. These are both hybrids that act as mobile phones but also have many of the features of computers. You can use them as self-contained units or you can link remotely to your network back at the office. Alternatively, you could choose to locate all your files in the 'cloud' (i.e. on remote servers owned by third-party firms) rather than on the hard drive of your office computer, in which case you will be able to access them from anywhere through your tablet or mobile phone.

This is a fast-moving area and, before you buy, you should catch up on the latest developments, through computing magazines, such as *Which? Computing**, or on sites such as *www.pcmag.com*.

Landline telephone systems are also important. Even if you are working at home, and there is only one of you, consider a separate business line. Bear in mind that with a broadband Internet link, you can use your telephone and the Internet simultaneously.

On your telephone system if you are working from home, you may want all the services such as call diversion, call waiting and voicemail. These allow you to present a more professional image to the outside world. Once your business is beyond the one-person stage, spend some time researching to find a telephone system that meets your requirements, as an inadequate system leads to inefficient working.

For receiving faxes, consider a plain-paper fax that can double as a photocopier if your only need is for the odd one or two pages to be copied (if you'll need to copy a lot, get a dedicated photocopier). Alternatively, many printers now double up as a copier (and also scanner). If you regularly need large amounts of copying, consider buying your own photocopier. You can set up your computer to send and receive faxes. This will not suit everyone. For example, sending handwritten comments on a document can be more cumbersome because you'll need to scan in the document first.

The right furniture

Choosing the right furniture for your business depends essentially on the type of business. Cheap, second-hand desks and chairs may not be good business sense. If you think it possible that customers or suppliers will visit your premises at regular intervals, it is crucial to select furniture that projects the image you have planned for your business. If you need to spend a lot of time at a computer, your chair and desk arrangements should be ergonomically sound to reduce the risk of developing health problems.

The right car

A car can arouse great emotions. It is one of those peculiar purchases where it can be difficult to disentangle desires from needs. The car you drive somehow projects something about your own personality; it is often regarded as an extension of it. Nevertheless, caution is needed before personal desires get confused with business needs.

It is often argued by business owners that a prestige car is needed to project an image of credibility, for exactly the same reasons outlined above for furniture. But a cool, hard look is needed at that claim. Will customers and suppliers really see you driving into their car parks? To project the image that is needed, is the souped-up version essential? Will not the same effect be created by the slightly cheaper version? The argument that one car will cost only £50 more a month to lease than another is weak. You need to look at the cost over a longer period of time, say two years, or however long you intend to keep the vehicle. It would be a mistake to swing too far in the opposite direction and choose a second-hand car that is rusting or requires excessive maintenance.

If you run your business as a company, you will either have a company car or be using your private car on business. Either way, the tax system encourages you to choose a fuel-efficient vehicle (see p. 397).

How to pay for equipment

There are four main ways you can pay for equipment – buying outright, hire purchase, leasing and contract hire.

Buying outright

This does not necessarily mean buying it with your own money; you could use a bank loan or overdraft to finance the purchase of the equipment.

The advantage of buying outright is that you own the asset, which will be entered in your balance sheet. This will make your balance sheet stronger. Also, the tax system is very favourable for most types of equipment, often allowing you to write off the whole cost in the year of purchase (see p. 395). The disadvantage of outright purchase is that it uses up large lumps of cash, maybe when you are short of funds.

Hire purchase (or credit sale)

Ultimately, you will own the asset outright at the end of the hire period. This means that hire purchase confers some of the same advantages of buying outright. As with outright purchase, you can claim a capital allowance from the time you start using the equipment, and you will be able to take the equipment into your balance sheet as an asset, with what you owe as a liability on the other side.

Using hire purchase also means that you are not laying out such a large sum initially, compared with buying outright, which can be helpful for cash flow. However, the payments you make will consist of capital, as well as interest. You get tax relief only on the interest part of the payments. If you are a sole trader or small partnership, hire purchase deals up to £25,000 are within the scope of the Consumer Credit Act 1974 (as amended by the Consumer Credit Act 2006) but larger hire purchase deals, and deals of any size if you operate as a company, are not covered. The Act provides protection against unfair terms and access to the Financial Ombudsman service in case of dispute.

Leasing

If you lease equipment, you are not the owner of it, although you may be able to buy it at the end of the lease. The company that organizes the lease is the initial owner. The main advantage of leasing is that there is no capital outlay, so it can be a big help to cash flow.

In general, you do not claim the capital allowance for the equipment; the company organizing it claims the allowance. However, all the payments you make are treated as expenses, so you get full tax relief on them.

There are different types of lease. If the lease is a closed-ended one, it means there will be a fixed period of one to five years. At the end of the agreed period, there may be an option to buy or to take on a further lease for a nominal rent. An open-ended one means you can end it when you like after the expiry of an agreed minimum period.

Contract hire

This is a form of leasing, mostly used for financing a fleet of vehicles. In this case, what is in the contract is not a specific vehicle or vehicles but the use of an agreed number of the specified type. The length of the agreement is usually shorter than the estimated life of the equipment. Use of the vehicles can be provided with or without the maintenance. You may be able to arrange to buy the vehicle at the end of the agreement.

Summary

1 A good computer, tablet or smartphone, giving you access to e-mail and the World Wide Web, is crucial.
2 An IT strategy needs to be developed if your business is to grow.
3 Choosing the right communications equipment can be important for the efficiency of your business.
4 The furniture and fitting out of your premises can have an impact on your credibility with customers and suppliers.
5 Your car may affect the image of your business less than you believe.
6 You can pay for equipment by buying, hire purchase, leasing or contract hire.

Other chapters to read

8 Less than 100 per cent (p. 77); 17 Choosing your workplace (p. 192); 30 Tax (p. 381).

19

Professional back-up

Luck can make a lot of difference to the success or failure of an enterprise, but you cannot sit around waiting for luck to land on your doorstep. You must take all the steps you can to ensure success. Weaknesses in specific skills must be covered; you may be able to obtain advice and guidance from Business Link*, equivalent organization or an enterprise agency. But there may still be some skills for which you must seek outside professional help.

The time to seek out and engage professional advisers will be fairly early in the planning stage. Thus, their expert advice can be taken before your plans are firmly formulated. If the adviser is good, this should help you to avoid making the sort of expensive errors and misjudgements that could mean your business begins with a permanent disadvantage.

The sort of adviser that could be helpful to you includes:

- accountant and book-keeper (p. 213).
- bank (p. 214).
- solicitor (p. 217).
- surveyor, estate agent (p. 218).
- designer and web designer (p. 218).
- financial adviser (p. 219).
- IT and web specialists (p. 220).

Accountant and book-keeper

The advice that accountants* may be able to give ranges from the basic services, such as book-keeping, to the more sophisticated, such as tax planning or raising funds. Not every accountant will offer every sort of advice. For example, a big firm of accountants is unlikely to undertake weekly book-keeping functions; an accountant working alone may not have the expertise to help with raising funds.

Some of the areas of advice are:

■ *accounts*: doing the book-keeping, setting up accounting systems, advising on computerized accounting packages, preparing your annual accounts, auditing for a limited company.

■ *finance*: managing cash, helping to raise finance and to negotiate with the bank manager, raising venture capital.

■ *business purchase*: investigating possible acquisitions, analysing franchise opportunities, negotiating purchase prices.

■ *tax*: preparing income tax, corporation tax and VAT returns, carrying out PAYE and National Insurance requirements for employers, personal and business tax planning, advice on raising funds under the enterprise investment scheme.

■ *general business advice*: preparing business plans, budgets and forecasts and advising on the form of your business; that is, whether you should be a sole trader, in partnership or form a limited company.

■ *preparation of prospectus*: to raise money from the public.

Quite a lot of accountants, particularly the large firms, also have management consultancy divisions, which can advise on the setting up of internal systems, computerization and so on.

How to choose

The term 'accountant' does not necessarily mean that the person so described has any formal accountancy qualification. If you want to employ someone who is a member of a recognized body, you should look out to see if there are letters after the name. The main organizations that will be of interest to you as a small business are:

■ the Institute of Chartered Accountants in England and Wales* and the Institute of Chartered Accountants in Ireland*, whose members put ACA or FCA after their name, and the Institute of Chartered Accountants of Scotland*, whose members put CA after their name.

■ the Association of Chartered Certified Accountants*, whose members put ACCA or FCCA after their name.

What you gain by using a member of one of these bodies is the knowledge that a required course of training has been followed and certain exams passed. In addition, if you want to appoint an auditor, you must appoint someone who is a member of one of these bodies, which have all been recognized as auditing bodies.

If you need to find someone who will help with your book-keeping and preparation of your tax returns, and your business is fairly small-scale, employing fully qualified accountants may be the equivalent of cracking a nut with a sledgehammer. You may be able to find someone else quite competent to carry out the limited range of jobs you have in mind, but obviously at a much cheaper rate.

The only satisfactory way of choosing an accountant is by recommendation and taking up references. Ask your bank manager. Colleagues and friends who use the services of accountants are also possible sources of recommendation. References should always be taken up.

There is a case to be made for opting for one of the bigger firms of accountants if you want to raise money from outside organizations or the public. Investors may look at the proposal with more confidence if your financial advisers are well known, rather than from a small firm of accountants (however good at their job).

As with any business negotiation, there should be a discussion about the scope of the work to be done and clear agreement on what this is and what it will cost. Really you must satisfy yourself, before any work is begun, that the accountant knows what you want and is capable of doing it.

If it is management consultancy that you are interested in, find out if the consultancy is a member of the Institute of Consulting*. An important point to check is that the consultant has experience of the problems of small businesses.

Bank

Banks obviously can offer a wide range of financial facilities, such as current accounts, provision of overdrafts, longer-term loans, leasing and factoring, and import and export assistance. There is more detail about the provision of finance in Chapter 25, 'Raising the money'. However, it has been noticeable since the global financial crisis that banks are being much more cautious about lending to small businesses. If you are choosing a business bank account, you may want to discuss with each bank its attitude towards lending to businesses like yours before you decide. Most of the banks also have specialist services for small businesses and networks of small business centres or advisers. Some of the banks offer free banking for the first year or longer if you open a business account with them.

The role of adviser sits rather uneasily with the provision of finance. Some small businesses may hesitate to discuss business problems completely frankly in case it should affect the bank's judgement about extending an overdraft, for example. However, this worry may be illusory, as most bank managers or advisers should be competent enough to spot problems from the figures presented.

Following a review of business banking in 2002, banks were required to make a number of improvements to their services in favour of business customers. These include:

- either the payment of interest on current account balances (of at least base rate less 2½ per cent) or exemption from transaction charges on items paid into and drawn from the account. These price controls were lifted from December 2007 onwards. If your bank does not offer competitive price deals you should consider switching your account.

- unbundling services so that, in particular, you can take out a bank loan without having to open a current account at the same bank.

- faster and easier transfer from one bank to another, including portable credit histories available on CD-ROM.

- making charges and interest more comprehensible with a view to enabling league tables of accounts to be published.

- investigating the feasibility of branch sharing so that from a single outlet you have a choice of banks.

Most banks have to abide by conduct of business rules set by the Financial Services Authority (FSA)*. These rules apply to small businesses (called 'micro-enterprises' in the rules) as well as retail customers. In this context, the FSA defines a 'micro-enterprise' as a business 'which employs fewer than ten persons and has a turnover or annual balance sheet that does not exceed €2 million, including self-employed persons, family businesses, partnerships and associations regularly engaged in economic activity'.

How to choose

The bank that holds your personal account may not be the automatic answer. There can be a strong case made for separating your business and personal affairs so that one cannot influence the other.

If your business is planned to be on a large scale, for example you are raising substantial funds and are looking for very fast growth such as profits of £200,000 to £300,000 within five years, it may make sense to put your account with one of the larger branches. This is particularly so if you can build up a relationship with the bank manager. The manager of a large branch will have more discretionary power; this means that fewer decisions will need to be referred upwards to regional decision-makers within the bank, thus losing the personal touch.

There is probably no advantage in opting for a larger branch if you are likely to be working on your own or on a small scale. Convenience will be more important.

You may not want to bank with a branch at all. With many business accounts, you can bank by telephone or online. If you bank online, take care to have good IT protection (firewall and anti-virus software) to protect your account from online crimes.

Many small businesses find it convenient to pay suppliers by cheque or accept payments from customers this way. You may have been worried by reports that cheques were due to be phased out by 2018. However, this plan has now been abandoned and cheques will remain in use at least for now. However, you may want to consider whether alternative methods of payment would be suitable for you. For example, payment by telephone using a debit or credit card, payment by direct debit or automated bill payment, or instructing payments online are all options.

The British Bankers' Association* in conjunction with Moneyfacts publishes comparative tables of business current accounts on its web site to help you to choose an account on the basis of transaction charges and interest paid.

Solicitor

Solicitors* can be particularly useful during the formation of your business. The specialist advice they can give includes:

- *business advice*: on the legal form of your business (that is, sole trader, partnership, limited company), on personal guarantees, steering you through the maze of employment law, helping with debt collection by advising on writs and winding-up orders.
- *contracts*: conditions and terms of sale of your product, leases, franchise contracts, for example.
- *legal entity*: forming companies and drawing up partnership agreements.
- *preparation of prospectus*: to raise money from the public.
- *product protection*: helping to obtain a patent or register a trade mark or an industrial design.
- *protection of intellectual property*: increasingly important in this era of 'knowledge-based' businesses, copyright and design right protection.

Many solicitors belong to the Lawyers for Your Business* scheme. This offers a free initial consultation for those running young or growing businesses, plus a clear indication of the cost of further advice.

How to choose

Very similar considerations apply to the choice of solicitor as to that of your accountant. Solicitors specialize in different branches of the law, so you should ensure that the firm can give you the advice you need on specialized topics. If the specific partner you deal with cannot do this, another partner in the same firm may be able to do so, but it is your responsibility to question abilities closely to satisfy yourself that the advice will be soundly based. A wise precaution can be to take up references.

As with accountants, some businesses would be advised to choose a large firm because of the credibility the name would add to your quest for raising large sums of money.

For whatever you want doing, ask for an estimate of costs; if the answer is that it is not possible because the solicitor does not know how long the work will take, ask for the daily rate. But a solicitor who cannot give you an estimate is not impressive. Many solicitors offer a package price for jobs such as forming a company.

The law requires solicitors' fees to be 'fair and reasonable'. When you receive the bill, if you do not understand how it is made up, your solicitor will have to get a certificate from the Law Society declaring the bill to be fair and reasonable if you demand it.

To find a solicitor in your area, you could contact the Law Society of England and Wales*, Law Society of Scotland* or Law Society of Northern Ireland*.

Surveyor, estate agent

You may at some stage want the help and advice of a surveyor or estate agent in your search for suitable premises. This may include:

- structural surveys. This could be important if you are considering buying a freehold or signing a lease that includes the condition that you carry out repairs and maintenance.
- finding and assessing suitable premises and negotiating with the landlords or vendors.
- advice on whether planning permission or the landlord's consent for change of use is required and helping to make the application for you.

How to choose

For advice on structure, repairs and maintenance use a qualified surveyor, that is, a member of the Royal Institution of Chartered Surveyors*.

Designer and web designer

Design can be a crucial element in the success of a business. It may not appear as obvious as the need for accounting or legal expertise, yet it is. Designers can give help and advice on the visual elements of your business and product. There are specialists in:

- setting the image of your business or corporate identity (p. 132).
- fitting out premises, where this is important for customers or suppliers (p. 209).
- designing what your product looks like or product positioning (p. 16).
- designing your web site (p. 155) – also see 'IT and web specialists' on p. 220 for help in getting prospective customers to your site.

- selecting what your employees wear and what your vans look like (livery specialists).
- using letterheads, logos, brochures and leaflets (pp. 137, 143).
- packaging.

Using a design shop can be a more cost-effective alternative than an advertising agency for a small business, especially as you are likely to adopt other means of getting your message across than straight advertisements.

You may find that some printers have designers working with them, and this could be the most cost-effective of all. However, cheapness is not the best option if you fail to achieve your objectives because of the poor quality of advice. You must still assess how good the advice is.

Before you approach a designer, you should have a clear idea of what you want, although you should be prepared to listen to suggestions. You should ask the designer to show you a wide range of ideas in what is called 'scamp' form, which is a very cheap way of letting you see what sort of impression the idea will give. Settle on two or three ideas that you think are consistent with your product or business and ask the designer to work in more detail on these.

How to choose

The best way of finding a designer whose advice you value is to ask friends and colleagues for recommendations. Another approach is to keep an eye open for work you admire that other businesses have, for example a logo you think good or an effective premises fitting. Most businesses will be flattered if you ask who helped design it. Whichever way you choose of finding some names of designers, ask for references and see examples of the work done.

Financial adviser

As well as advising on the financing of businesses, financial advisers* can act as an intermediary between those wanting funds and those with money to invest, such as venture capital funds or business angels (private individuals with the funds and the willingness to invest in private companies).

They may also be able to give advice on raising money and floating on the Alternative Investment Market or AIM (the junior market for young and small companies of the London Stock Exchange*). There is also a trading facility called PLUS Markets*, which your adviser might be able to introduce you to.

Financial advisers will look into a business plan and proposal, and their sponsorship of it should carry some weight with investors, but this applies only if their reputation is sound. Many large firms of accountants, stockbrokers and merchant banks have specialist corporate finance sections.

Financial advisers may be able to:

- advise on the organizational structure, in particular whether there are gaps in the top management and how the structure can be strengthened to attract investors.
- check your projections, advise on the strength of your business plan.
- advise on the amount of money and how to raise it.
- help to produce a prospectus that can be issued to the public or other investors.

How to choose

There are those who are very good and those who are awful, but, unfortunately, there is no clear-cut way of finding the name of a good financial adviser. Probably the best way is to ask other people how they raised funds and if they would recommend the person who helped. Magazines that are aimed at those running small businesses may have articles about who has raised money and how much. Contact the managing director of the firm that raised the funds and ask for a recommendation. However you get the name, always ask for references.

A financial adviser may charge a flat fee or a fee dependent upon the sum raised, say, between 2½ and 20 per cent of the money raised. But there may also be demands for shares or options on shares and directorships.

IT and web specialists

It's crucial with a small business to incorporate what you need from IT to allow you to operate your business as efficiently as possible, thus allowing you to keep your headcount on the low side. An IT specialist can offer the following advice:

- advice on hardware, software, setting up networks.
- accounting and spreadsheet packages.

- databases and how to set them up to gather as much data as possible from your business.
- web sites and how to incorporate them into your business model, including creating a strategy to promote traffic to your web site and to enhance your prospects of appearing prominently in search engines.

How to choose

You can ask Business Link* or the equivalent organization to recommend a specialist. Or you could ask among your local business networks, such as your local chamber of commerce*, or look in trade magazines (always take up references). If you search online, you will also find many specialist firms in social-media marketing (generating traffic to your web site through networking sites such as Facebook and LinkedIn) and search engine optimization (SEO), but the quality may be variable. Do some homework on the topic first (see pp. 151–4) so you understand what they are offering.

Summary

1 You can improve your chances of success by using professional advisers with their expert knowledge. Select your advisers at an early stage in your business planning.
2 Agree with your advisers at the outset what work they will do for you. Make sure you both understand and agree the scope of the work.
3 Take up references and ask for estimates of costs before the work begins.

Other chapters to read

3 A spot of coaching (p. 28); **23** Insurance (p. 287); **25** Raising the money (p. 316).

20

Getting the right staff

Deciding when to take on an employee is a delicate balancing act. On the one hand, if you increase your staffing levels, you might not be able to cover increased costs straight away. On the other hand, extra manpower could free you to spend more time on other activities, such as marketing or planning, which should, in the end, mean increased profits.

A useful rule of thumb for choosing the best time to increase your staff is to ask yourself if you can generate enough extra sales to cover the cost of taking on that extra employee. If you will not be able to increase your sales straight away, you could still employ someone; but, in this case, you will need to be able to keep your business going until you have been able to build your sales up to the new level you need. It all sounds straightforward, but in practice it is very tricky. It is like being on a seesaw. One step in the wrong direction can tip the balance against you.

If you are clever enough, or lucky enough, to get your timing right, you will not want to throw away your advantage by employing the wrong person. The whole process can take several months, so finding you have made a mistake and having to recruit again can throw your business off its planned course. Nor should you underestimate the emotional problems of getting rid of an unsuitable employee, which can unnerve the toughest of businessmen or businesswomen and unsettle other employees.

What is in this chapter?

This chapter looks at how to recruit. It should help you to answer these three questions:

1 Do I know what I'm looking for?
2 Will I recognize it when I see it?
3 Can I make sure that, if I offer the job, it will be accepted?

There are sections on the job that needs doing (p. 223), the employee you want (p. 225), getting the right person to apply (p. 230) and interviewing (p. 235). The cost of employing staff is covered on p. 239.

The job that needs doing

Before you plunge into adding that extra employee, look carefully at the work to be done. It is very important to sort out in your own mind what the job entails. Once you have done this you can define the person you need. If you fail to do this preparatory work, you might find yourself employing someone who is not capable of doing the work. This list of topics might help you to organize your thoughts about the job:

■ *level of skill*: when you decided you needed an extra pair of hands, was it because you needed work done that you did not feel competent to carry out yourself? Does the work require a special skill?

■ *training*: if you have the skill to do the job, but not the time, would it take a lot of training to employ someone without that particular skill and teach them on the job? Would you have the time to carry out that training?

■ *length of time*: do you estimate that this extra work will need doing for a long period of time? Or is it a temporary bulge? Watch out for mistaking a backlog of work that can be cleared up quickly for a permanent increase in activity.

■ *how much extra work*: can you quantify how much time will need to be spent by someone to carry out the work? Is it a full working week? Do not assume that if you find the work difficult and time-consuming, because it is outside your range of skills, a skilled employee will take as long.

■ *experience*: do you think the job requires a lot of experience? Would the employee need to be able to make independent judgements? Or is it intended that the work will be closely directed by yourself or another?

■ *responsibility*: how much responsibility will the employee have? Will the employee be required to man the office alone? If the job is selling, will the person be required to go out selling unsupervised? Will the employee handle money? Or be responsible for other staff? To whom will the employee be responsible?

- *tasks*: list the things that need to be done by your new employee. Work out for whom the tasks will be done and the importance of the tasks.

- *authority*: work out what your new employee can do without asking you or someone else for permission – for example, making appointments, spending money up to a certain limit.

- *contacts*: will your new employee need to deal directly with the general public or your customers? Will the contact be face-to-face, on the telephone or by letter? If the contact is by e-mail/Internet, you need to make clear the authority of your employee and how far he or she may be able to commit your business.

- *special circumstances*: does the job involve working during unsocial hours? Will your new member of staff need to do much travelling away from home? Will the working conditions be unpleasant or dangerous?

- *future developments*: consider how the job might develop and expand in the future. You need to assess a job hunter for this potential too.

Setting out your thoughts in this way may seem like overkill if the job is relatively simple. But hiring and firing a succession of unsatisfactory people will be more time-consuming and disruptive to your business than spending an hour or so defining the job; and marshalling your thoughts in this way will also help you to decide whether there really is a job that needs doing.

Another way of examining your needs would be to fill in a job description form. Try using the simple one below:

Example: job description

Job title: ....

Purpose of job: ....

Whom the employee works for: ....

Who works for the employee: ....

Main tasks: ....

1. ....

2. ....

3. (and so on) ....

What authority the employee has: ....

1. ....

2. ....

3. (and so on) ....

Duties: ....

1. ....

2. ....

3. (and so on) ....

Contacts: ....

Internal: ....

External: ....

Possible development of the job: ....

The employee you want

Your next task is to match the employee to the job. Decide if you need someone full-time or part-time. Think about what experience, qualifications and personal abilities are needed to do the job.

Full-time employees?

Conventionally, most employees are permanent, full-time and salaried, but this may not suit your business. Do not ignore other ways of getting the job done. Look closely at help from your family, contract or temporary staff, part-time staff, commission-only salespeople or agents, and/or fixed-term contracts.

If you have time to offer training and support, instead of looking for an experienced full-time employee, you might consider taking on an apprentice. Under the government's Work Place Training scheme, you have to pay the full salary costs (the national minimum wage for apprentices is £2.60 per hour from 1 October 2011) but the government will fund part or all of associated training costs. How much depends on the business sector you operate in and the age of your apprentice. Full funding is given for apprentices aged 16 to 18 and half-funding for 19–24-year-olds. You may get a contribution towards the training costs for an older apprentice. The funding normally goes direct to the training provider rather than you. See *www.apprenticeships.org.uk* for further information and a 'return on investment' calculator that estimates the costs and benefits to your business of taking on an apprentice including an indication of the level of funding you may get.

Your family

Do not overlook the possibility of your spouse, civil partner or a relative helping out. Employing your family may not be the permanent solution you seek, but it may help to tide you over until you are confident that taking on an extra employee is justified.

Freelance staff

For quite a number of jobs it is possible to get people who are happy to work on a freelance basis. This means you will pay an agreed fee but have no responsibility for National Insurance contributions, sickness payments or holiday pay. And if the extra work comes to an end, you need feel no responsibility towards finding more work for a contractor, as long as you made it clear that the work was temporary or was a contract for a particular piece of work or period of time, but less than a year.

A further advantage of using freelance staff is that it can be a good opportunity for you and the person to size each other up and see if you could work together before you offer a permanent job.

There are two main disadvantages of solving your extra workload in this way. First, it can cost you more than taking on permanent staff to get the particular piece of work done. If the job involves a skill that is widely demanded and in short supply, a self-employed contractor's rate is likely to be correspondingly high. And if you are using a temp, you will have to pay a fee if an employment agency introduces the temp. Second, while some contractors or temps may be keen and enthusiastic, others may be less so.

Your legal obligations to temporary freelance workers or to people who contract out their services is rather hazy. You may also find that someone you regard as a freelance is considered an employee by the HMRC*. Seek advice so you do not get this wrong.

Agency workers

Another alternative to employing permanent staff is to hire temporary workers through an agency. This has the advantage of flexibility: for example, you can take people on just to cover a short-term or seasonal increase in workload.

You pay the agency a fee for providing the worker. Hiring arrangements vary, but for tax purposes the worker is treated as if they are employed by the agency rather than you. This means the agency deals with tax and National Insurance, saving you these administrative tasks. It is also the agency that has to ensure the worker is paid the national minimum wage (see p. 253), and the agency, not you, is also responsible for providing statutory sick pay, statutory maternity pay and similar payments to workers who qualify. However, all these elements will be reflected in the amount you must pay the agency. Moreover, these arrangements do not mean that you have no responsibilities towards the worker. Some of your key responsibilities are:

■ Health and safety. You must ensure that the worker understands and is protected from hazards in your workplace. Bear in mind that temporary workers may be particularly at risk because they are unfamiliar with your business.

■ Working time. You must ensure that the hours the person works are not longer than the law allows and that they get proper breaks as required by law (see p. 260).

■ From 1 October 2011, from the first day they join you, agency workers have the right to access all the same facilities as comparable permanent staff, including for example car parking, childcare facilities, canteen and so on. Access should be on the same terms – for example, if permanent staff have to join a waiting list to get a parking space, the agency workers have the right to join the list too. They also have the right to receive information about relevant job vacancies you have.

■ From 1 October 2011, agency workers also have a range of new rights once they have completed 12 weeks in their job with you. The 12-week period starts either from 1 October 2011 or from the date you hire them, whichever is later. The new rights are:

  – the same pay as your permanent employees doing comparable jobs. This includes basic pay, overtime rates, holiday pay, bonuses and so on. There are various items that do not count as pay. Important exclusions mean that temporary workers do not have the right to redundancy pay or notice pay, or to join any occupational pension you offer (though agency workers will be covered by new rules from 2012 – see p. 259).

- the same basic conditions, for example, annual leave and overtime. So they know what pay and conditions they are entitled to, you will need to give temporary workers a copy of your standard employment terms and conditions.

- if pregnant, paid time off for ante-natal appointments.

If a temporary worker leaves you before they have been in the job 12 weeks, the clock resets. There is nothing in the legislation to prevent you taking on temporary staff for less than 12 weeks at a time. See Chapter 21, 'Your rights and duties as an employer' for information about your legal duties towards employees generally.

Part-time staff

If the work you want to be done does not add up to a full working week, consider getting someone in on a part-time basis. Your duty as an employer is pretty much the same whether your staff are full- or part-time – see Chapter 21, 'Your rights and duties as an employer'.

Commission-only salespeople or agents

Do not automatically think in terms of a salaried employee if you are looking to boost your selling effort. You may be able to find someone competent who would prefer to be paid by getting a commission on each item sold. Again this will cut your risks – no sales means no pay. However, the commission you will pay will be greater per item than to a salaried employee who also gets commission on sales.

Fixed-term contracts

You may need people to carry out specific projects that cannot be undertaken by your full-time employees.

Whatever category you decide to utilize, you need to ensure that, where appropriate, the national minimum wage is being paid (see p. 253). It is illegal to treat fixed-term employees less favourably than permanent employees. For example, they must be employed on the same terms, in most cases offered the same training opportunities and so on. You may need to seek further advice concerning this.

Who is right for the job?

Try to develop an idea of the sort of person who will perform well in the job and in your business. Use the groups of characteristics listed below to help you sort out what is important for the job and what is not. You can use this to help you to specify the person you need for the job and to help you collect your thoughts while interviewing.

Here are some useful ways of grouping characteristics:

- *physical make-up*: this covers the employee's health, physique, appearance, manner and speech (take care that you do not inadvertently discriminate on grounds of sex, race, disability, religious beliefs, sexual orientation or age).
- *achievements*: what education, qualifications and experience do you expect?
- *general intelligence*: this is rather difficult to judge if you are not a psychologist, but what sort of reasoning ability should the person have? How quickly do they understand what you are saying?
- *special aptitudes*: what particular skills do you need, for example mechanical, verbal, numerical or manual skills?
- *interests*: what are the person's hobbies and leisure activities? Are there any particular hobbies that would be more or less suitable for the person who is needed to do this job? Check how much time is spent on interests. Is this likely to conflict with the job?
- *circumstances*: include only those factors that are essential to the job.
- *personal characteristics*: this covers the slightly tricky area of whether the person has the right personality to cope with that particular type of job. Avoid focusing on characteristics that can be met only by certain sections of the population.

It would be a good idea to pick out of the list those characteristics that you think are very important and those that would be an advantage but are not crucial for this particular job. It is always tempting to demand very high qualifications, experience and so on, but it is wiser to be fairly flexible in your requirements and not overstate what is needed to carry out the job satisfactorily. In any case, you should always remember that employing someone who is over-qualified for a job may lead to a rapid staff turnover, as the employee may soon get bored.

As well as picking out those characteristics that you need or hope to find, it is equally important to sort out those that would be a definite disadvantage to someone carrying out the job.

Getting the right person to apply

Once you have completed the essential preparation and so got a clear idea of what job you need doing and what sort of person you would like to fill the job, your problem now becomes: how can I find the person I want?

The main ways you can tell job hunters about the job on offer are:

- by advertising direct, on the Internet or in newspapers or magazines.
- through recruitment agencies and consultants.
- through friends, existing employees and business contacts.
- by recruiting direct from colleges.

Use more than one method to fill a job as it will widen the field.

Advertising direct

You can get in touch with the local Jobcentre Plus*, if the vacancy is suitable. Failing this, you can advertise direct in the appropriate newspapers, magazines or web sites. This could be tricky if writing is not your strong suit. However, there are certain guidelines you can follow to help you.

Remember that the purpose of the ad is to attract someone who will be able to do the job very well and who will settle down happily in your business. You have to tell job hunters enough about the job to stimulate their interest and make them feel it is worth having a closer look; equally, you want to use the ad as a starting point of the selection process. So you want to make it clear to those applicants who would be suitable that they should apply and to those applicants who would not be suitable that they should not. Finally, the ad should be interesting enough to attract attention compared with what else is on offer in that newspaper or magazine the same day.

From research that has been done on what attracts people to join a company, some of the more important points are listed below in order of priority:

- the prospects for interesting and creative work.

■ the prospects for promotion and pay.

■ the quality and reputation of the company's products or services.

■ the opportunity to use 'brains'.

■ the security of the job.

■ the company's past financial record.

■ a congenial working environment.

How do your business and the job you are offering rate against these points? In your ad, draw attention to your strong points. Most small and new businesses would score highly on giving lots of scope for interesting and creative work and the opportunity to use 'brains'. In particular, an employee would be given the opportunity to be part of the whole business and not just in one department. However, if it is a new business, there may be little reputation built up for its products, and its financial record may be short.

When it comes to writing the ad, the style could be important in attracting job hunters' interest. Be informal and friendly – but not too friendly. Use 'you' and 'your' when you are speaking about the person needed and 'we' and 'our' when talking about your business, but avoid over-chatty comments and stick to the facts.

Checklist: what should be in the advertisement

■ *company name*: put in the name and logo, if you have one.

■ *job title*: use a title or description that will mean something to a stranger.

■ *pay*: state what salary can be expected. Job hunters interpret phrases such as 'salary negotiable' as meaning a low salary.

■ *place*: state where the job is. If you are not offering moving expenses, this is very important. In any case, people like to know what the environment of the job is.

■ *the work*: describe the work to be done and say what authority the job has.

■ *the company*: state what your company does and what size it is. Avoid clichés about dynamism, fast-growing and so on; all companies use them.

■ *the person*: state your requirements, such as experience needed, qualifications and other qualities.

■ *how to apply*: name the person to write to, not just the job title. Tell the job hunter how you want them to give details of experience and qualifications – for example, send in brief CV, write for application form.

■ *when to apply*: give a closing date for applications, if possible allowing two to three weeks from the appearance of the ad.

■ *the law*: check that your ad is not breaking the sex, race, disability, age, religious belief or sexual orientation discrimination laws (see Chapter 21, 'Your rights and duties as an employer'). And make sure the information is accurate, as the ad may form part of the contract between you and your new employee.

How to apply

Asking for too much information from job hunters can deter people from applying, and you should remember that your business is competing with all others for the best talents. Keep your demands to a minimum. Asking applicants to write in has the advantage of letting you see what their written work is like, but you do need to allow people to contact you by telephone if they are unable to write (due to disability).

If you do give a telephone number that job applicants can ring, make sure it is always manned – and by someone who knows what they are talking about. You can use the telephone to sift out people, as well as to give them information. This can be done by preparing a shortlist of key questions that you can ask over the telephone. Keep a written record of why you have filtered people out so that you can explain the reasons if ever challenged.

An application form has the advantage of allowing you to compare information presented in an identical format. But specify an alternative method if individuals are unable to complete the application form. In any case, drawing one up would take you some time and may not be worthwhile, unless you are considering employing many people.

Where to put the advertisement

It depends on the job. Different newspapers, magazines and web sites will give you the response you need for different jobs. There are trade magazines that may have cornered the market for job ads in a particular specialization, for example computing. For jobs that are not so specialized, local newspapers may provide a good response, for example for clerical staff. A publication called *British Rate and Data* (BRAD)* lists newspapers and magazines and gives details of the cost of advertising and a profile of the readership. Your local library should be able to tell you where to see a copy.

Increasingly, jobs are advertised on the Web. Some newspapers also offer you a web position as well as an ad in the newspaper. But there are an increasing number of web sites devoted solely to advertising jobs.

Apart from formal advertisements, increasingly the Internet is also being used for recruitment via social networking sites, such as LinkedIn. Searching groups relevant to your business will give you access to profiles of people who might be suitable. You can then either make contact through that web site's facilities or use the information gleaned (for example, current workplace) to establish contact directly. This might be particularly appropriate if you are looking for a freelancer, but could also be a route to finding permanent staff.

The best market research about where job hunters look for jobs may be to ask people who work in that field where they would look for a new job.

The cost of advertising

The bigger the circulation of the newspaper or magazine or the number of hits on a web site, the more they charge for advertising. You have to weigh up the cost against the benefit of getting the size of response you need. Sometimes if the response is too high, it can overwhelm you.

Recruitment agencies and consultants

If you do not have the time to handle the advertising and to sift through all the applications, you can use an agency. Obviously, you have to pay for this, so you must be sure it is worth the extra cost; and do not forget that you will have to spend time in selecting the right agency, so the time saving may not be as great as you think. Nor can you afford to skip any of the preparatory stages; you will still have to decide what the job is and what type of person you want so that the agency can do its job.

There are several different types of agency:

■ Jobcentre Plus*.

■ private employment bureaux (Adecco, Brook Street, Office Angels or Reed, for example).

■ selection consultants.

■ search consultants (or headhunters).

■ web sites.

Using Jobcentre Plus is free and can be a useful source of applicants for manual and clerical jobs, but do not expect too much from the screening process. The private employment agencies charge varying amounts ranging from 6 to 20 per cent of first year's earnings, depending on the agency and type of job to be filled.

You can get a list of members of the Recruitment and Employment Confederation (REC)* to help you to pick out an agency. You should also look in trade magazines to see which agencies advertise which types of job.

Friends, existing employees and business contacts

If you do get a strong recommendation from someone, do not rely on the friend's advice. Ask your prospective employee for a *curriculum vitae* (CV) and give them a copy of the job description (p. 224) and the advertisement you would have used. Observe all the necessary precautions by conducting a full and careful interview (see more about all this below).

This method of finding your new employee is not to be ignored, as it has several advantages. First, it is cheap. Second, if it is through a friend, you will start off knowing something about the abilities of the new person. Third, a new employee recruited in this way may find it easier to settle down in your organization.

The main disadvantage arises if the appointment proves unsuccessful; this can be embarrassing if the contact was made through a friend and disruptive to a previously harmonious working relationship if the recommendation came from an existing employee. You also need to be careful that you do not miss out on possible good applicants because they are not known to you.

Recruiting direct

If you are looking for someone who does not need experience in your particular field or skill, you could try going direct to further education colleges. The types of skills you might be able to recruit direct in this way include secretarial, hotel and catering, and retail management.

If the type of job you have in mind could be done by a young school leaver to whom you could give on-the-job training, consider whether you could use the apprenticeship scheme. Visit the Apprenticeships* web site for information.

Interviewing

An interview has two purposes:

1 It helps you to choose your new employee.
2 It helps your new employee to choose you.

It is important to remember that you should structure the interview process to enable you to find out what the applicant is really like and to allow the job hunter to find out about you and your company and decide that this is the job he or she wants.

Before you get to the interview stage you will have to sift the applications and decide who to select for a closer look.

Who should you see?

If your ad was successful, the sifting process will not be a case of eliminating totally unsuitable candidates; rather it will be to rank the applications according to how closely they match your ideal. If you are tempted to see someone who does not fit the bill but looks interesting, think twice. It means either that the requirements you set for the job were not the right ones or that you will be wasting your time on an unnecessary interview.

Once you have ranked them, choose to see the top five, say. If you do not find anyone in that group, you could try the next five. After that second-ranking group, if you still have not found the ideal person you may have to accept that your ad has been unsuccessful. You will need to reconsider how to find the person you want. Keep a written record of interviews so that you can return to consider a candidate later if necessary and justify why he or she has not been selected.

Setting tests

Setting a test can be a very useful way of checking how a prospective employee will tackle a task in a pressure environment and what level of skills has been attained. The task set must be relevant to the job proposed to provide you with any useful information. The results of the test can be discussed and analysed in the interview.

Getting ready for the interview

There are two stages. First, you must gather together the essential information you will need to give the job applicant. This can be conveyed in written form or orally, in which case you need the facts at your fingertips if you are to sound organized and efficient to the job hunter.

The questions you might be asked could be about:

- *holidays*: you need to be able to say how many days, when they can be taken and any restrictions you intend to impose.
- *illness*: explain what will happen if your employee is away from work because of illness.
- *starting date of the job*: if this has been decided.
- *hours of work*.
- *salary matters*: such as when they are paid, any rules on overtime, bonuses or commission, if applicable.

The second stage of preparation is to work out what key questions you want to ask. One type of question would give you comparable information about the people you see. This could be a test question, such as describing a typical event in your business and asking what each person would do in those circumstances.

The second type of question is to help you to pinpoint each candidate's strengths and weaknesses. The only way this can be done is by good preparation, reading the candidate's CV or whatever. There is no short cut. What you should look for is anything that seems odd or is not a smooth progression. Watch out for any unexplained gaps in the person's story; this may give you hints about poor health, or unsatisfactory jobs or character. Notice very frequent job changes, as this could raise questions in your mind about job success, as could a failure to match in employment the level of achievement suggested by educational qualifications.

Useful interview questions

1 What is the best part and worst part of your present job, and why?
2 What bit of your work do you find difficult and what bit the easiest?
3 How do you rate your present boss?
4 Describe your ideal boss.
5 What do you consider to be your greatest success and why?
6 What do you consider to be your greatest failure and why?
7 When were you last angry at work? What caused the anger? What form did your anger take?
8 What is most important to you about the job you are looking for?

 9 What will your family and friends think of your new job?
10 What are your greatest strengths?
11 What are your weaknesses?
12 What worries you most about the job?
13 What excites you most about the job?

These are all examples of the kind of open question that should prompt the candidates to reveal a bit more about themselves; use whichever seems most appropriate. As well as these questions, there are more straightforward ones about the present job, career, education and so on that need to be asked.

Holding the interview

Some thought needs to be given beforehand to where the interview should be held and who should be present. The person you are interviewing will feel more relaxed if the interview is private and uninterrupted, so try to find somewhere where you will not be overlooked or overheard. If you are not going to be the new employee's boss, perhaps the person who is should sit in on the interview. If this is not possible, arrange for the new person's superior to see the candidate separately, if necessary on another day, before deciding to offer the job.

What should happen in the interview?

Roughly, a useful interview could run along the following lines:

1 Spend a few minutes putting the applicant at ease, for example by talking about his or her interests.
2 Ask open questions, which the person you are interviewing will have to answer with more than a yes or no. The questions you ask should allow you to get some idea of whether the person could do the job well.
3 Also ask closed questions designed to test a candidate's knowledge and skill, specific questions such as 'On what date . . .?' and hypothetical questions, 'If you were . . .'.
4 Try using silence sometimes as a way of getting the person to expand. For example, once the person has finished explaining something, do not always leap in with another question but remain silent. Sometimes, the person being interviewed will be prompted to be more revealing.
5 Keep in control of the interview while doing little talking, perhaps less than a third of the total time.

6 Concentrate on listening and observing your applicant. This helps you to judge the replies and to pinpoint areas where you need to probe more. You should also reflect on what the person has said and feed it back to them.

7 Be flexible; do not stick rigidly to a planned script. Try to develop what your interviewee has said.

8 Take notes. They do not need to be very comprehensive but sufficient to jog your memory when assessing the interview afterwards (bear in mind that the applicant has the right to see your notes – see below).

9 Give a little detail about the job and how it fits in your business. You can miss out this and the next stage if you have already concluded that the person is not suitable and thus save wasting time. It is important not to do this stage before asking the questions. If you do, you may have fed the person with sufficient information so that he or she knows how to answer your questions.

10 Ask the job applicant if there are any questions, or if he or she wishes to tell you anything else about suitability for the job that has not been brought out by the questions.

11 If the person seems promising, spend some time making sure that the job would be accepted if it was offered. After all, the person is selecting a new job in the hope that it will last for a while and will want to be confident that your job really is the best choice.

After the interview

Summarize the interview in writing straight afterwards while your memory is fresh. The aim of the summary will be to allow you to look back when you are choosing between the candidates, and to judge how closely each person matched up to the job you want done. In particular, you will want to remember later the person's strengths and weaknesses. And you may be challenged as to why you recruited a candidate and would need a written record to defend any discrimination allegations. Under the Data Protection Act 1998, a candidate has on request a right to see any interview notes you hold.

There are some other important actions to be taken before someone joins your staff. First, always take up references. It can be much better to speak to a referee direct on the telephone than to interpret what the written word may be hiding; people can be much more unguarded 'off the record'. Always ask the direct question, 'Would you re-employ this person?' Second, if the job is an important one, consider having a medical done. It might throw up a problem that you would want to know about before hiring.

Third, if the job involves driving, always ask to see their driving licence; do not be fobbed off by excuses.

Making the offer

Always make sure your written offer letter is conditional upon satisfactory references and medical, if applicable. Remember that this letter (and the ad) forms part of an employee's contract of employment (p. 250).

When the new employee joins

A new employee will feel more positive when starting a new job if presented with a planned induction and training period. It is well worth the extra effort on your part to prepare this in advance.

If it all goes wrong

Sometimes you can make mistakes. If it is a really bad one, you will need to know how to deal with it. In Chapter 21, 'Your rights and duties as an employer', there are details about the law on dismissing staff.

It could be worthwhile to interview a job leaver to see why it did not work out from the employee's viewpoint. You can learn from your mistakes and make a better choice next time.

The cost of employing staff

The costs can be divided into two groups:

1 One-off costs of employment, such as advertising. There is also the time you spend interviewing or sifting through applications and the time and possible expenditure spent on training a new employee.
2 Continuing costs of employment, such as salary, employer's National Insurance (NI) contributions, fringe benefits you offer and extra office equipment. There will also be the extra costs created by the person carrying out the job, such as more stationery, petrol or telephone use.

What is your break-even point?

Your break-even point is the point at which your business is making the right amount of sales to give you enough profit to cover your overheads, which include rent and rates, heating and lighting. Sometimes employee costs are overheads and sometimes they are not. It all depends on what they do. If what the employee does is related to the level of sales, their costs will be called direct and are not part of overheads. Examples would include staff whose time is paid for by customers, or employees who are directly involved in making a product. But if the employee's job is something like accounting, marketing or general clerical duties, their costs will be included in overheads. In your business there may be a grey area in which it is difficult to decide whether the employee's costs are direct or not.

The purpose of finding your new break-even point is to work out how many extra sales you need to make to cover the cost of your new employee. You can see how to work out the break-even point in more detail in Chapter 26, 'Staying afloat'.

Finding your break-even point

First, you have to find what your gross profit margin is. This is your gross profit as a percentage of sales. You work out gross profit by deducting the amount of your direct costs from the value of your sales. Direct costs will be the purchases you need to make to supply your service or product and the costs of any labour directly associated with your sales.

Once you have worked out your gross profit margin, your second step is to work out the amount of your overheads (for example, rent, rates, heating, lighting, telephone costs, professional fees or labour costs, such as secretarial or book-keeping).

To find your break-even point, your third step is to divide the amount of your overheads by the gross profit margin. This will give the level of sales you need to make to cover your overheads.

Example

Jeremy Jones needs someone to act as a secretary and book-keeper. He used the checklist below to work out the extra cost involved. The calculation is quite simple and looks like this for the full year:

Salary	£14,000
Employer's NICs	£956
Extra use of telephone, etc.	£595
Total	£15,551

Jeremy now works out how it will change his break-even point:

He has estimated sales of £45,000 for this year with direct costs of £20,000. This gives a gross profit of:

£45,000 − 20,000 = £25,000

And his gross profit margin is:

$$\frac{£25,000}{£45,000} \times 100 = 55.56\%$$

His overheads, without taking on an assistant, come to an estimated £5,000, and after would come to £20,551 (£5,000 + £15,551).

Jeremy finds his break-even point before he employs someone. This he gets from the following equation:

$$\frac{\text{overheads}}{\text{gross profit margin}} \times 100 = \frac{£5,000}{55.56} \times 100 = £9,000$$

of sales to cover his overheads. If he employed an assistant, the break-even point would become:

$$\frac{£20,551}{55.56} \times 100 = £36,992$$

Jeremy needs sales of £36,992 − £9,000 = £27,992 to cover the extra overhead created by employing his new assistant. As he has estimated his sales at £45,000 (compared with the £36,992 he needs), he decides he can afford to employ an assistant at this time.

Checklist: work out the extra cost of employment

	This year £	Full year £
Salary or wages (including holiday pay)	. . .	. . .
Estimated commission, bonuses, overtime payments	. . .	. . .
Employer's NI contributions (see p. 257)	. . .	. . .
Other possible costs or benefits:		
■ employer's pension contributions	. . .	. . .
■ use of car	. . .	. . .
■ payment of subscriptions to professional societies	. . .	. . .
■ cost of sick pay insurance	. . .	. . .
■ others	. . .	. . .
	. . .	. . .
	. . .	. . .
	. . .	. . .

▶

	This year £	Full year £
Additional office space required	. . .	. . .
Additional equipment needed	. . .	. . .
Extra use of telephone, stationery, heating, lighting and so on	. . .	. . .
Total	. . .	. . .

Notes

1 Most small businesses will not be providing many fringe benefits, but you may need to consider doing so if you want to employ an experienced and skilled member of staff, for example an accountant or salesperson. At present, you do not have to pay anything towards an occupational or personal pension for an employee. However, the government is proposing a new national system of auto-enrolment into pension schemes (and new pension accounts called NEST – the National Employment Savings Trust) from 2012. After a transitional period, even small employers will be required to make pension contributions to this on behalf of most employees (see Chapter 32, 'Pensions and retirement').

2 You will need to break down these costs into monthly expenditure (p. 295).

3 This breakdown of costs assumes that you rent, lease or hire any additional equipment, rather than buying it outright. For help in deciding which is the right way for you, see p. 209.

Summary

1 Work out the costs of employing an extra person and watch the effect on your break-even point.
2 Make sure there is a job to be done.
3 Look to see if the work can be carried out in a non-permanent way, for example by temporary staff, contract or freelance worker.
4 Draw up a job description, no matter how simple or low-level the job seems.
5 Get a mental picture of the person for the job. Do not overstate your requirements. Pick out the characteristics that would be a disadvantage in doing the job well.
6 You can save money by drafting your own ad. Use our checklist to make sure you include the necessary information.
7 Prepare thoroughly for interviews.
8 Ask open questions to get the job applicant to talk. Keep notes.
9 Don't forget to insist on a medical, if necessary; check all references and see the driving licence, if driving is part of the work.
10 Work out an induction and training programme. Do not put all

the effort into finding the right person for the job and then, by not training them properly, end up with employees unable to function effectively and productively in your business.

Other chapters to read

21 Your rights and duties as an employer (p. 244); **26** Staying afloat (p. 333).

21

Your rights and duties as an employer

The idea of employment law can conjure up images of the Gorgon. You, as an employer, turned to stone when faced with the legal pitfalls of employment. The myth remains that you cannot sack anyone. Well, it is not true.

By and large, you can employ whoever you want. You can set up your own criteria about who you want to employ, but there should be good reasons for it – not solely because of sex, race, disability, marital status and so on. You can normally dismiss unsatisfactory employees. But the law sets out that it should be done fairly. If you do not do so fairly, then you may have to be prepared to pay compensation. Moreover, there are rules about how you treat employees while they work for you. If disgruntled employees leave, they may claim your actions amounted to constructive dismissal, which could again result in you facing a bill for compensation. So it makes sense to have a good working knowledge of employment law.

This chapter should give you some guidelines about how to:

- take on an employee (p. 248).
- pay staff (p. 252).
- provide a safe and healthy working environment (p. 261).
- avoid discrimination (p. 263).
- treat an employee if pregnant or a parent (p. 269).
- dismiss them if unsatisfactory (saying goodbye) (p. 275).

If you need more advice and guidance, contact the Advisory, Conciliation and Arbitration Service (ACAS)*, or for Northern Ireland the Labour Relations

Agency*, or see the Employment & skills section of the Business Link* web site (*www.businesslink.gov.uk*). If your worry concerns discrimination, contact the Equality and Human Rights Commission (EHRC)*, which, since 1 October 2007, has replaced the three former equality bodies: the Equal Opportunities Commission, the Commission for Racial Equality and the Disability Rights Commission. The EHRC is responsible for all types of anti-discrimination, including newer areas such as age discrimination. The EHRC produces a range of free guides to the various areas of employment law. Some are listed in this chapter. They can be obtained from the EHRC or Jobcentre Plus*.

Employment law is very complex. It is also changed frequently. However, in order to help businesses to keep track, the government introduces most changes to laws affecting businesses (including employment law) from either of two common commencement dates each year: 6 April (coinciding with the start of the tax year) or 1 October. Through the Business Link* or Business Gateway* web site, you can arrange to have regulatory updates e-mailed to you. This chapter can do no more than give general guidelines, and the coverage cannot be considered comprehensive.

Bird's eye view of your rights and duties

In general terms, apart from what is in the employment contract, what can you expect from your employees, and what can they expect from you?

Your rights

1 Employees should be honest and obedient and not act against your interests.
2 They should not disclose confidential information about your business.
3 They should take care of your property.
4 Any patents, discoveries or inventions made during working hours generally belong to you.
5 Your employees should be competent, and work carefully and industriously.

Your duties

1 You should behave reasonably in employment matters.
2 You should practise good industrial relations and provide, for example, a written statement of terms of employment, including disciplinary procedures and grievance procedures.
3 You should pay your employees when you agreed to do so.

4 You should take reasonable care to ensure the safety and health of your employees.

As well as these general rights and duties, your employees acquire certain rights by law – see 'Legal life-cycle of an employee' (below), which applies to full- and part-time permanent workers. If you employ temporary staff through an agency, the rules are changing from 1 October 2011 – see p. 227 to check which of the rights and duties apply.

What is in the rest of this chapter?

The rest of this chapter fills out the details. But it cannot cover every single employment possibility.

Legal life-cycle of an employee

How long employed	What you must do
New starter	1 Do not dismiss for automatic unfair reasons such as maternity, health and safety, or asserting a statutory right such as the right to written terms and conditions. There are many statutory rights, and these are increasing with new legislation – seek advice.
	2 Do not discriminate on racial grounds or, since 1 October 2006, on the grounds of age (pp. 265, 266).
	3 Do not discriminate on grounds of sex (p. 264) or against married people.
	4 Do not discriminate on basis of sexual orientation or religious or similar belief (pp. 264, 265).
	5 Pay equal salary to men and women (p. 256).
	6 Do not discriminate because of trade union membership (p. 267).
	7 Do not treat part-time employees less favourably.
	8 Pay statutory sick pay (SSP) when required (p. 255).
	9 Give maternity leave when required (p. 269).
	10 Make sure you pay the national minimum wage (p. 253).
	11 Provide access to a stakeholder pension scheme (unless exempt) (pp. 259, 436). From 1 October 2012, a new system starts under which employers have to contribute to a pension scheme for each employee unless

the employee opts out (pp. 259, 436). The system is being phased in, starting with the largest employers. Existing small employers (50 or fewer employees) will be brought into the system between August 2014 and February 2016. If you take on your first employee on or after 1 April 2012, the earliest you will be brought into the system is March 2016.

12 Do not discriminate against disabled people (p. 265).

13 Give an itemized statement with pay (p. 253).

14 Give paid time off for ante-natal care (p. 269).

15 Consult a recognized trade union about redundancy (p. 279).

16 Do not dismiss unfairly because of pregnancy (p. 269).

17 Give written reason if dismissing because of pregnancy.

18 Do not insist an employee works more than 48 hours a week and give 20 minutes' rest break after six hours of work (p. 260).

19 Give 5.6 weeks' paid holiday (p. 254).

One month or more

20 Give the minimum notice periods required by law (p. 280).

21 Pay guaranteed pay if you have no work (p. 256).

Within two months

22 Give a written statement of the main terms and conditions (p. 251).

Six months or more

23 Give paternity leave and adoption leave if requested by new parents (p. 269).

24 Pay statutory maternity pay (SMP), statutory paternity pay (SPP) and statutory adoption pay (SAP) to employees who qualify (pp. 269–73).

25 Seriously consider requests by parents for flexible working (p. 274).

One year or more

26 Give written reasons for dismissal (other than pregnancy), if requested.

27 Do not dismiss unfairly (p. 276).

28 Give paid time off work to look for work in redundancy.

29 Give job to employee back from maternity leave, unless original/alternative unavailable (p. 272).

Two years or more

30 Pay redundancy money (p. 279).

Taking on an employee

The most important part of employing someone is to select the right person for the right job in the first place. The techniques of job description, advertising the job, selecting for interview and interviewing are covered in Chapter 20, 'Getting the right staff'. However, there are certain legal points to look out for to ensure that you and your employee get off to a happy start.

What you must do

1 Do not discriminate because of sex, marital status, disability or race in ads, interview and job descriptions. You must also avoid discrimination on the grounds of sexual orientation, religious or similar beliefs and age.
2 Check that the person is legally entitled to work in the UK.
3 Tell your tax office when you take on an employee.
4 Give your employee a written statement within two months of starting work.

Avoid discrimination

You should be careful that sex, racial or other sorts of discrimination do not creep into ads or interviews. Avoid using job titles that imply one sex or the other – 'foreman', for example. If you use this sort of job title, include in the ad a note that you welcome applications from both sexes. Avoid using 'he' or 'she' to describe a job applicant in an ad as it suggests you want applications from men only, if you use 'he', or women only, if you use 'she'. And be careful that illustrations don't give the impression that the job is a man's or woman's. In an interview avoid asking women about their husband, their marriage or family responsibilities or whether or not they intend to have a family.

You must also take care not to discriminate, either directly or indirectly, in ads and interviews on the grounds of age unless there is a justifiable reason for recruiting someone within a particular age range. This means, for example, making sure you place ads in publications that are likely to be read by a spread of people of different ages. Note that advertising for a younger person simply because you think they would be cheaper then an older worker will not count as a justifiable reason. If you advertise for graduates, you need to make clear that graduates of any age are welcome, not just people in their twenties. Advertising for people with a minimum number of years' experience would exclude younger applicants, so you need to be certain you have objective grounds to justify the experience requirement. In interviews, avoid age-related questions, such as how the person would feel managing older or younger workers.

Check eligibility to work

From 29 February 2008 the law changed to make employers play a key role in preventing illegal working in the UK. You can be fined up to £10,000 if you employ someone aged 16 or over who is subject to immigration control and does not have permission to work or do the type of work you offer. You can get the fine put aside if you have a 'statutory excuse', which you acquire by making checks of the worker's documents before you take them on.

You must not discriminate on the grounds of race and, since ethnicity and country of origin are not reliable guides to immigration status, it makes sense to build an automatic check of documents into your recruitment system and apply this to all prospective employees. You could ask to see the documents either when shortlisted candidates come for interview or before making a firm offer to the successful candidate.

You must ask the worker to provide original versions of either one or two of the specified documents that prove their right to be in the UK and work here. For a full list of the acceptable documents, see The Immigration (Restrictions on Employment) Order 2007 available from the government legislation* web site *www.legislation.gov.uk*. They include:

- British passport.
- European Economic Area (EEA) or Swiss passport or national identity card.
- Home Office residence permit or other document indicating permanent residence for an EEA or Swiss national.
- biometric immigration document issued by the UK Border Agency indicating permission to stay indefinitely in the UK.
- passport or travel document endorsed to show exemption from immigration control or right to be in the UK indefinitely.
- birth certificate issued in the Channel Islands or Isle of Man together with an official document giving the worker's permanent National Insurance number and name.
- passport or travel document endorsed to show the holder may stay in the UK and is allowed to do the type of work in question without issue of a permit.

■ a work permit issued by the Home Office or UK Border Agency which indicates that the holder may stay in the UK and is allowed to do the type of work in question.

If the worker's document(s) show they have indefinite leave to be in the UK and work here, you just need to make the check once. If the worker has only limited permission to be in the UK, you must repeat the check every 12 months.

You must check that the details on the documents (such as birth date and any photograph) match the appearance of the worker and tally with information given on the job application. You must take all reasonable steps to ensure that the document(s) are valid and that the worker is the rightful owner. Photocopy or scan the documents and store the copies securely. To comply with the data protection legislation (see p. 176) do not keep the copies longer than necessary, which is generally taken to mean three years after the employee has left.

For more information, contact Business Link* or the equivalent organization, or see the UK Border Agency* web site at *www.ukba.homeoffice.gov.uk/ employers*. The Business Link web site includes an interactive tool to help you check the status of prospective employees.

Other starter rules

The job should be described accurately in the ad and in the letter offering the job. These two can form part of the contract of employment. When you do take on an employee, you should tell your tax office. Remember to get your new employee's P45; if your employee does not have one, fill in a P46. By the time your employee has been with you for two months, you must have given them a written statement of the conditions and terms of the job (see below).

It would be wise to take note of the actual day on which your employee starts. The date can determine whether you may be able to dismiss your employee fairly or not, if things do not work out. Remember that dismissal because of sex, marital status, disability, race or age require no qualifying period and will be unfair from day one.

What is the contract of employment?

The words 'contract of employment' conjure up thoughts of a written document. But the terms of your employee's contract of employment can be made up of anything you write or indeed say. It can include what you say in the ad, in the interview, in the offer letter, when your employee starts work and any subsequent chat you have about the terms and conditions of the job.

The basic contract is offer of employment, acceptance of employment and agreed amount of payment; these can be oral or written. Anything else makes up the terms. It is far better to have the terms in writing, which are then signed by both the employee and the employer. There is a legal requirement to provide a written statement of terms within eight weeks of the start of employment.

What you have to put in the written statement

The statement should include your name and your employee's name. You have to say when your employee's present job began and when your employee's period of continuous employment began.

You also have to give information on various terms and conditions. The terms and conditions are:

■ the scale or rate of pay, including how it is worked out.

■ at what intervals payments will be made (weekly, monthly, etc.).

■ hours of work, including normal working hours.

■ holidays, including public holidays, and holiday pay, including how it is worked out.

■ place of work.

■ your employee's job title or a brief outline of the work.

As well as the statement, you must give further information on:

■ sickness or injury and sick pay.

■ pensions and pension scheme.

■ length of notice to be given by you and your employee.

■ if the contract is 'temporary', an indication of the expected duration.

■ details of any collective agreement affecting the job.

Finally, you also have to state whether a contracting-out certificate under the Social Security Pensions Act 1975 is in force that applies to your employee – see pp. 434–5 for the significance to you of being 'contracted out'. There is a tool on the Business Link web site to help you create a written statement of employment.

Who gets a written statement?

Most employees do, unless:

- you have already given your employee a written contract of employment that includes all the above items.
- the employment is for less than a month.

Booklets

- Advisory, Conciliation and Arbitration Service (ACAS), *Recruitment and selection* S06; *Contracts of employment* S02.
- Equality and Human Rights Commission (EHRC), *Straightforward answers to ... 50 difficult questions on equality and good employment practice.*
- UK Border Agency (UKBA), *Comprehensive guidance for employers on preventing illegal working*, November 2010: *Avoiding unlawful discrimination – code of practice*, February 2008; *New measures for preventing illegal migrant working in the UK – what employers need to know*, January 2010.

Pay and working hours

There are quite a lot of rules about how you can pay, how much you have to pay and what you have to give with pay.

What you must do

1 Act as collector of income tax and National Insurance contributions for the government using the PAYE system (p. 257). You may also have to deduct student loan repayments to pass to the HMRC. On the rare occasion it happens, you may also have to act to enforce a court order, by deducting sums from an employee's earnings under what is called an attachment of earnings. This may occur, for example, for paying maintenance under a Child Support Agency ruling or for paying a fine.

2 In most cases, do not deduct anything from your employees' pay unless it has been agreed in writing that you can do so, for example in the contract of employment.

3 Pay statutory sick pay, statutory maternity pay, statutory paternity pay and statutory adoption pay if due.

4 Give equal pay to employees carrying out broadly similar work or work of equal value.

How much do you have to pay?

In many cases, deciding how much and how often you pay your employee will be negotiated between you and your employee. Whatever is decided will be part of your employee's contract of employment. You can also negotiate the question of bonuses, commission, overtime, holiday pay and sick pay.

If your business was formerly covered by a Wages Council (now abolished), any employees previously covered by a wages order will retain those rights. You will have to vary their contracts to change this, and this can be a tricky procedure, so take advice.

A statutory national minimum wage was introduced from 1 April 1999. You must pay employees at least per hour:

Age of employee	Year starting 1 October		
	2009	2010	2011
21 or more	£5.80	£5.93	£6.08
18 to 20	£4.83	£4.92	£4.98
16 or 17	£3.57	£3.64	£3.68

What you can, or have to, deduct from pay

You cannot deduct anything from your employee's pay unless it has been laid down by law or unless it has the written agreement of your employee.

However, you can make some deductions if your employee has agreed in writing. For example, you can deduct a sum of money and hand it over to someone else, such as dues to a union or donations to a charity under a payroll giving scheme or contributions to a pension plan.

What you have to give your employee with the pay

You must give your employees a detailed pay statement when or before they are paid. The statement must be in writing but this does not necessarily mean it has to be paper-based. You could opt for an electronic format instead. For example, some larger employers in particular issue online pay slips that employees can download through a secure section of the company's web site. What must be written in the statement is laid down by law:

■ the amount of your employee's salary before any deductions are made.

■ if you deduct any sums of money, which can vary from pay day to pay day, you must say what the amount of each deduction is and what it is for.

■ if you deduct any sums of money that remain the same on each pay day, you can do one of two things. Either you can say how much each deduction is and what it is for on each pay slip. Or, on the pay slip, you can say what the total of these fixed deductions is and separately from the pay slip give a statement of what the sums of money are used for.

This separate written statement must be handed out at 12-monthly intervals. It must say how much, when and why any deductions are made, and you must hand it to your employee before or when they are made. If these fixed deductions are changed, you have to give your employee written notice or an amended written statement.

■ the amount of your employee's pay after all deductions.

If your employee is paid by more than one method, your pay slip should show how much is paid in each way, half in cash and half by bank transfer, for example. And remember that employees are entitled to see pay records to confirm that you are complying with the national minimum wage. So you must keep records for these purposes.

Do you have to give holiday pay?

By law, all employees are entitled to a minimum amount of paid holiday. Since 1 April 2009, the entitlement is 5.6 weeks (28 days for an employee working five days a week). Employees have this right from the first day of work. Leave accrues at a rate of one-twelfth of the annual entitlement for every month worked rounded to the nearest half-day. This statutory holiday entitlement is not in addition to bank holidays – and can include them. You therefore need to make the position clear in the written statement of terms, which can be more generous than the statutory minimum if you like. The holiday entitlement is calculated *pro rata* for part-time employees. A court case in March 2006 determined that it is illegal to roll up holiday pay and give it as extra wages instead of allowing paid time off.

You do not have to agree to an employee's request to take holiday but must give adequate notice of any refusal. The required notice is at least as long as the time to be taken off, so a week for a one-week holiday, a day for one day off and so on. You can decide when employees can and cannot take holiday but you must give notice at least twice as long as the period to be taken off or the period during which holiday is banned. You can put rules about taking holiday in the contract of employment, provided the effect is not to make it impossible for employees to take their legal entitlement.

Do you have to give sick pay?

Yes and no. If you have agreed to give your employee pay while ill, you must do so as it is part of the employment contract. How much pay and for how long should be set out by you in the written statement of employment given to your employee within two months of starting the job (p. 251).

If you have not agreed to pay your employee while ill, then your only obligation is to give statutory sick pay (SSP). Employers are required by law to pay SSP to their employees during sickness if the qualifying conditions are met. The weekly rate for 2011–12 is £81.60 for employees with average weekly earnings of £102 or more. All employers are eligible to reclaim the SSP paid out in any month where it comes to more than 13 per cent of the total National Insurance contributions (both employer and employee) paid.

Employees will qualify for SSP if they are aged 16 and over and are sick for at least four days in a row. This is known as a period of incapacity for work (PIW). All days count towards sickness, including weekends and public holidays, but you only pay SSP after the qualifying days. These are normally the days your employee does not work. No SSP is payable for the first three days of sickness in a PIW – these are known as waiting days.

For absences of four to seven days it is usual to ask your employee to sign a self-certificate form (your own or form SC1 or SC2, available free from Social Security offices). For absences of more than seven days, it is usual to ask for a medical certificate. You cannot insist on a medical certificate for absences of less than seven days. In the past, these certificates have generally been known as 'sick notes' but, from 6 April 2010, they have been replaced with 'statements of fitness for work' ('fit notes'). The doctor issuing the statement will either state that your employee is not fit for work or that he or she may be fit as long as you give appropriate support – the doctor will advise what support would be appropriate (for example, lighter duties). You do not have to give the support, in which case your employee will be deemed not fit and you will be obliged to pay SSP as usual.

Your employee is not entitled to SSP if his or her average weekly earnings before sickness are less than the lower earnings limit for National Insurance contributions (£102 from 6 April 2011).

In February 2011, the government launched a review of long-term sickness absence to explore radical new ways to cut the number of people off work sick. There have been suggestions that one option might be to replace the current statutory sick pay system with a requirement for employees to have private insurance cover instead through their employers. The review is due to report during 2011 and it is too early to say what it might suggest and what policies the government might take forward.

For more information about the SSP scheme, see HMRC* guide E14, *Employer helpbook for statutory sick pay*.

If you have no work for an employee, do you have to pay?

Generally speaking, pay is negotiated between you and your employees, without any government intervention. Whether employees are paid when there is no work or they are unable to work will be decided by negotiation. However, in most cases you will pay your employees' salary or wages regardless of how much work you have and regardless of whether something happens, such as a power cut, that means your employee cannot do the work required.

But if your employee is paid by the hour or on piece rate, you do not have to pay:

- unless you have agreed to do so in the contract of employment; or
- unless you have to make what is known as a guarantee payment.

You may have to make this payment, once your employee has worked for you continuously for a month, for any complete days when he or she is not provided with work throughout a day during which there would normally be work. Guarantee payments can apply to all workers, not just hourly and piece-rate workers. You have to pay £22.20 a day for workless days (from 1 February 2011) unless they earn less than that a day.

This payment may be made up to five times in a three-month period. The limit on the payment is reviewed, but not necessarily changed, each year.

Note that you can make a provision within the written statement of terms for lay off or short-time working.

Equal pay

You cannot pay one employee more than another because one is a man and the other a woman. For example, simply to say that a man is stronger is no defence to justify higher wages. If your employees are doing the same or broadly similar work or work of equal value, you should pay the same rate to each and give each the same terms of employment. 'Broadly similar' means that the differences between the two jobs are not of practical importance.

You can pay one employee more than another if there is a genuine non-sex-based reason for it. An example would be if one of your employees had been with you for many years and you had a scheme to pay employees a higher rate after a number of years.

Anti-age discrimination regulations came into force from 1 October 2006. In some circumstances you will still be able to pay workers of different ages different levels of pay. These include differentials that depend on length of service of five years of less, and differences that recognize loyalty and experience or whose purpose is to motivate staff.

How to operate the PAYE system

You have to act as a tax collector for the government. The government department that deals with tax is HM Revenue & Customs (HMRC)*. On each pay day you have to deduct the correct amount of tax and National Insurance contributions from your employee's pay and you have to send it to the tax collector. Here are the steps to take when you employ someone:

1 Tell your tax office. If it is your first employee, tell your own tax inspector. You will be told which is your PAYE tax office as an employer, which could be different from the office that handles your individual tax affairs. When a new employee starts they should hand you a form P45 from their last job or, if they do not have this, they should complete a P46. You must send the P45 or P46 to HMRC and you are required to do this using the online PAYE service which you can access from the HMRC web site.
2 Work out the tax and National Insurance contributions you have to deduct each pay day. Your PAYE tax office will send you the tax and NI tables or calculator you need to calculate this.
3 Fill in the deductions working sheet you have been sent by the tax office (or your equivalent software). Do this for each pay day.
4 Within 14 days of the end of each month, send the tax and NI contributions to the accounts office. You may have pay slips to send in with the money. Alternatively, you may deal with this aspect of PAYE over the Internet.

5 At the end of each tax year (5 April), you must send HMRC summarized details of the pay and benefits of each employee. You must send in these details via the Internet and by the specified date – if you don't, you'll be fined. You must give a copy of the details to your employee as form P60 no later than 31 May.

You will not have to do this if your employee earns less than a certain amount – in the 2011–12 tax year, the PAYE threshold is £139 a week or £602 a month. But, even if your employee earns less, you still have to tell your tax office.

When an employee leaves, you must complete a form P45 and give this to the employee to pass on to their next employer. You must also send the P45 to HMRC using the online PAYE system.

For guidance on your tax and National Insurance duties as an employer, contact the relevant HMRC employers' helpline or see the HMRC web site.

Fringe benefits as pay

Fringe benefits, such as a pension scheme, childcare vouchers or cheap meals, can be worth more to an employee than a salary rise. How much of your employee's pay package is made up of salary and how much of fringe benefits is generally a matter of negotiation.

Your employee may have to pay income tax but usually no NI contributions on the taxable value of the benefit. However, you have to pay employer's NI contributions (called Class 1A contributions) on most of the benefits you give your employee. There are some exceptions, such as money you pay into a pension scheme on behalf of the employee or childcare vouchers you provide.

You have to send in a form P11D each year to HMRC by the date on the notice requesting information, which gives information about fringe benefits and expenses. The form needs to be filled in for:

■ employees earning at the rate of £8,500 a year or over, including the taxable value of fringe benefits and expenses. So you might have to fill in a form for employees whose salary is much less than £8,500, if they also have a lot of perks; and

■ any directors, unless the director earns less than £8,500, including perks, works full-time for you and has 5 per cent or less of the shares, including what his or her family and friends own.

Pension benefits

If your business has five or more employees (including yourself if you are director of your own company), you must offer your employees member-ship of a workplace pension scheme. This can be:

■ an occupational scheme where you partly or wholly fund the pensions. You can require your employees to contribute part of the cost.

■ a group personal pension scheme (GPPS). This is provided by an insurance company or other specialist pension provider and your employees take out their own personal pensions through the scheme. You arrange access to the scheme through the workplace and for employees' contributions to be deducted directly from their pay and passed to the pension provider. In addition, you must make an employer contribution to the scheme of at least 3 per cent of each employee's pay.

■ a stakeholder scheme. This is similar to GPPS but each employee who joins gets a pension scheme that meets some minimum standards designed to ensure the scheme offers reasonable value. You do not have to make any employer contribution.

For small businesses, a GPPS or stakeholder scheme is currently likely to be most appropriate. For information and help setting it up, contact an inde-pendent financial adviser*.

At present, if your business has fewer than five employees, you do not have to offer any kind of pension scheme to your employees. But this is due to change with the introduction of auto-enrolment and the National Employment Savings Trust (NEST). Auto-enrolment and NEST will affect 'eligible workers', defined as aged between 22 and state pension age and earning at least a minimum amount (around £7,500 a year). The changes are due to be phased in over the period from 2012 to 2016, with employees of large employers affected first and the smallest employers last.

Under auto-enrolment, within 12 weeks of their starting work, you will be required to enrol any eligible employee in NEST or a workplace pension scheme that is at least as good. The employee can choose to opt out of the scheme if they want to. You must pay employer contributions, but only for those employees who choose to stay in the scheme.

NEST is basically a nationwide occupational pension scheme, in which employees have personal accounts.

After a transitional period, contributions to NEST or an alternative workplace scheme will be 3 per cent of pay (between a lower and upper limit, currently £5,715 to £38,135 a year) from the employer, 4 per cent from the employee and around 1 per cent from tax relief. If you are a small employer, auto-enrolment probably will not apply to you until October 2016. The transitional period will be just one year, during which your employer contribution rate will be 2 per cent, rising to the full 3 per cent from October 2017 onwards.

For more information about the 2012 changes, see the Department for Work and Pensions* (DWP) publication, *Automatic Enrolment and Workplace Pension Reform – the facts*, May 2011, available from *www.dwp.gov.uk/docs/auto-enrol-and-wpr-the-facts.pdf*.

Working time regulations

The following rules apply:

- if working more than six hours a day, employees are entitled to a minimum 20-minute break away from their work station if possible.

- for most employees, working hours must be limited to an average of no more than 48 hours a week over a reference period. The normal reference period would be a period of 17 weeks, although it can be extended in certain circumstances to 52 weeks. An employee can agree to work longer than this, but it must be in writing and the employee must be able to give notice to withdraw agreement (on a maximum of three months' notice) – this exemption from the 48-hour limit is called the 'opt-out'.

- employees are entitled to one rest day in every seven or two days in 14.

- a working day should be no longer than 13 hours, although it depends on how it is dealt with and what break there is between that shift and the next. There must be an uninterrupted break of 11 consecutive hours in each 24-hour period (although this can straddle two days).

There are also regulations concerning night workers.

Booklets

- HMRC, *Employer's further guide to PAYE and National Insurance contributions* CWG2; *Class 1A NICs on benefits in kind* CWG5; *Day-to-day payroll* E13; *Employer helpbook for statutory sick pay* E14; *Collection of student loans* E17.

- EHRC, *Code of practice on equal pay*.

■ Department for Business, Innovation and Skills (BIS), *National minimum wage guide for employers* BIS/Pub8910.

■ ACAS, *Paying employees* S10; *Holidays and holiday pay* AL03.

■ DWP, *Automatic Enrolment and Workplace Pension Reform – the facts*, May 2011.

Safe and healthy working environment

You have to provide a reasonable standard of health and safety not only for your employees but also for visiting workers, other visitors and members of the general public who may be affected by what you do. This applies to the safety of the premises as well as to any risks arising from the work itself.

Note that an inspector has the right to enter your workplace to examine it and enforce legal requirements.

What you must do

Once you have employees there are additional rules. Broadly:

1 Tell whichever organization is responsible for health and safety at work for your business what your business name and address are. If you have an office, shop, warehouse, restaurant or funeral parlour, for example, your local authority* will be responsible. For other businesses, it will be the Health and Safety Executive* (HSE) area office.
2 Get employer's liability insurance and display the certificate at each place of work.
3 Bring your written statement on your policy for health and safety at work (if you have five or more employees) to your employees' notice or create one and make any breach the subject of the disciplinary procedure.
4 Display the health and safety law poster or hand out the equivalent leaflet.
5 Make an assessment of the risks of your workplace – and keep a written record if you have five or more employees.
6 Train and appoint a first-aid officer or someone who is responsible for your policy.

Insurance

You must have employer's liability insurance to cover you for any physical injury or disease your employees suffer as a result of their work (p. 287). The latest certificate must be displayed. Electronic rather than paper display is allowed, provided your employees know how and where to find the certificate and have reasonable access to it.

Safe working environment

You must see that the place where your employees work, and the entrance and exit to it, are reasonably safe. Making a safe place of work includes things like fire exits and extinguishers, electrical fittings, storing material, machinery, hygiene, first aid; the list is very wide and covers all aspects of work.

You also have to take steps to provide a system of working for your employees that will give adequate safety. This includes making sure your employees are given adequate information and are trained well enough to carry out the work safely, for example, where the work involves use of machinery or fire risks. And you also need to check that the system of working is actually being carried out.

You must provide equipment, materials and clothing that enable your employees to work in reasonable safety. You could be held responsible if there is a defect in the things you give to your employees that causes an accident.

If there is a risk of injury from criminals or others, you must take steps to protect your employees.

Competent workers

If you know one of your employees is incompetent, and if one of your other employees is injured as a result of that incompetence, you could be held liable. And even if you do not believe your employee to be incompetent, but your employee behaves negligently while carrying out your work, and another employee or a member of the general public is injured, you can be held liable.

If one of your employees breaks a safety rule that you have publicized, you can fairly sack that employee. However, you must have made clear beforehand that breaking the rules would result in sacking, so include this in your disciplinary code. The reverse side of the coin is that if you do not take reasonable steps for the safety of your employees, an employee could resign and claim constructive dismissal (p. 279).

Paperwork

If you have five or more employees, you must have a written statement on your policy for health and safety at work and how that policy is to be carried out. This statement should be displayed so that employees can see it.

Regardless of the number of employees, you must also either display the health and safety law poster at work or hand out the appropriate leaflet. You can get these from your local HSE office.

If you have ten or more employees, you must keep an accident book to record work accidents. If you have a factory, you have to keep a book like this regardless of the number of employees. And for all businesses certain accidents must be notified to the authority that regulates your business for health and safety.

You must make an assessment of the risks relating to your work premises and identify any safety measures you need to take. If you have five or more employees, you need to keep a written record of this.

Booklets

■ Health and Safety Executive (HSE), *Essentials of health and safety at work* (Fourth edition); *The law on VDUs: An easy guide: Making sure your office complies with the Health and Safety (Display Screen Equipment) Regulations 1992 (as amended in 2002)*, HSG90; *Managing sickness absence and return to work: An employer's and manager's guide*, HSG249; *Involving your workforce in health and safety: Good practice for all workplaces*, HSG263.

Discrimination: what to watch out for

In general, you cannot discriminate on grounds of sex, disability or race, marital status, union membership, sexual orientation, religious or similar beliefs or age.

The government body responsible for all aspects of discrimination is the Equality and Human Rights Commission (EHRC)*. The EHRC publishes a wide range of guidance on the requirements of anti-discrimination legislation and what you need to do to comply.

What you must do

1 Do not discriminate on grounds of sex, race, marriage, disability, sexual orientation, religious or similar belief or age.
2 Do not refuse to allow your employees to join a trade union or dismiss them for trade union activity.

Sex and marriage

Discrimination means less favourable treatment of a man or woman on the grounds of sex or because they are married. It covers pay and conditions of the job, as well as opportunities for promotion, for example. You cannot discriminate:

- in advertising or interviews for the job.
- in the terms in which the job is offered.
- in deciding who is offered the job.
- in opportunities for promotion, transfer or training.
- in benefits to employees.
- in dismissals.

You need to be particularly careful that you do not introduce requirements for a job or promotion that are likely to be met by one sex more than the other. For example, if you insist that the person for the job needs to be six feet tall, you will be discriminating against women. The same could apply if you insist on some technical qualification more likely to be held by men than women. But you can insist on height, technical or other qualifications if you can show that these are genuinely necessary for the job.

Discrimination based on sexual orientation is also outlawed. This covers orientation towards people of the same sex, opposite sex or both but does not extend to sexual practices or preferences. The discrimination may relate to someone's actual orientation or their perceived orientation – so harassment of a worker because he or she was thought to be homosexual would still be illegal, even if the person was not in fact homosexual.

Disability

Disabled employees have the right not to be discriminated against either in the recruitment procedures you use or during the course of their employment (for example, they must be treated equally when it comes to opportunities, training, promotion and so on). As an employer, you are under a duty to take reasonable steps to remove physical barriers and to adjust your working practices so that any disabled employees can exercise these rights.

Employers with fewer than 15 employees used to be exempt from the requirements. However, since 1 October 2004 this exemption has ceased. 'Employee' includes both full- and part-time workers, apprentices, contract workers working for you and workers you contract out to others.

Race

Racial discrimination means treating one person less favourably than another on racial grounds, which includes colour, race, nationality or ethnic or national origins. As with sex discrimination, racial discrimination also applies if you make a requirement for a job that one racial group would find more difficult to meet than another group (unless this is a lawful requirement for the job). This is known as indirect discrimination and is unlawful. An example of this would be to insist on certain clothing being worn or to ask for a high standard of English when it is not necessary to do the job. And you cannot discriminate against a black employee because of how customers might react (for example, someone working in a pub).

You cannot discriminate:

■ in advertising or interviews for the job.

■ in the terms in which the job is offered.

■ in deciding who is offered the job.

■ in opportunities for promotion, transfer or training.

■ in benefits to employees.

■ in dismissals.

If one of your employees takes you to a tribunal claiming racial discrimination, it is unlawful for you to victimize the employee. It is also unlawful to instruct or put pressure on others to discriminate on racial grounds.

Religious or similar beliefs

It is illegal to discriminate on the grounds of someone's religion or similar beliefs. Until a body of case law has developed, what counts as discrimination is something of a grey area. In the first case to be decided under the new law, a bus cleaner was awarded £10,000 compensation after being sacked for taking extended leave to make a pilgrimage to Mecca. Other areas that could possibly give rise to discrimination claims might include dress code and canteen menus.

Beliefs similar to religious beliefs have not been defined in the regulations, and it will ultimately be for tribunals to decide whether particular beliefs come within the scope of these rules. A tribunal might consider, say, whether the beliefs involve collective worship, way of life or view of the world.

As with sex and race discrimination, these rules apply to recruitment, promotion, transfer, training, benefits and dismissals, and cover both direct and indirect forms of discrimination.

Age

Anti-age discrimination regulations came into effect from 1 October 2006. These ban discrimination, harassment and victimization on the grounds of age when recruiting, training and employing people. The regulations apply to all workplaces and affect the way you treat all employees, not just older workers.

A job applicant or employee who feels they have been the target of age discrimination can take their case to an employment tribunal which can award compensation of an unlimited amount. Along with the person doing the discriminating, harassment or victimization, you as employer can also be found liable for the actions of your employees. Therefore, it makes sense to have an equality policy at work which includes age, and to make sure that your workforce is aware of and trained in the practice of the policy.

See p. 248 for how these regulations can affect your approach to recruitment and interviewing. Other areas affected by the legislation include providing training, pay and benefits (see p. 252), redundancy (see p. 279) and retirement (see below).

There are some circumstances in which you are allowed lawfully to discriminate on the grounds of age. These are:

- *where you can objectively justify the discrimination*: this means having a legitimate aim for discriminating, good grounds for thinking that the discrimination will achieve the aim and no better alternative.
- *length of service*: you are allowed to offer additional rights or benefits to employees who have completed a minimum period of service of five years or fewer. For longer periods, extra rights and benefits are permissible provided that they aim to reward experience or loyalty or keep staff motivated, and you can prove that the discrimination is effective. Proof might take the form of, say, monitoring staff performance or the results of staff surveys.
- *minimum wage*: the national minimum wage (see p. 253) sets different pay rates according to age but is exempted from the regulations. Similarly, you are allowed to pay more than the national minimum wage to employees of different ages provided

you follow the same pattern – in other words with lower amounts for younger workers and using the same age bands (16 and 17, 18 to 20, 21 and over).

■ *statutory authority*: this enables you to comply with the law where, for example, it sets a minimum age for holding a licence.

■ *redundancy*: see p. 279.

■ *genuine occupational requirement*: this might apply where, for example, a theatre needs a young actor to play a particular role.

Before 6 April 2011, there was a national default retirement age of 65 after which you could legitimately retire older workers. From 1 October 2011 onwards (with transitional rules between 6 April and 1 October), the default retirement age is abolished. This means that, in most cases, you can no longer set a compulsory retirement age for your staff. You could still, as explained above, set a general retirement age or retire a particular employee, if you could objectively justify such discrimination. However, be aware that it is difficult to meet the objective justification rule and you may have to pay compensation if an employee challenged your stance and you could not provide adequate proof to back up your position. In general, you need to accept that it will in future be up to your employees to decide when they are ready to retire.

If you provide health-related insurance for your employees, this is exempt from the post-April 2011 rules. This means it is still possible to stop providing cover after employees reach age 65 (or some later age). Pension schemes are also exempt and so can still offer a full pension from a specified 'normal' pension age (which, at present, commonly is 65).

Trade unions

A tribunal will find the dismissal unfair if you sack an employee for:

■ belonging to an independent trade union (that is, a union that is not controlled by an employer) or for not being a member of a trade union.

■ taking part in trade union activities (for example, meetings) at the appropriate time, which is normally outside working hours or inside working hours with the agreement of the management. Industrial action does not count as a union activity.

Employees can also complain to an employment tribunal if you penalize them, but do not dismiss, or if you make them redundant for any of the above actions.

Since 2 March 2010, it has also become illegal to compile, supply, sell or use a 'blacklist' of people involved in union activities.

Criminal offences

In some cases, people who have been convicted of an offence do not have to tell you about it. If you ask, they can lie about it quite legally. The people who can do this are usually those who have had sentences of 30 months or less. They can keep quiet about their convictions after a specified time, which varies, but it is not more than ten years and not less than six months, and it also depends on the type of conviction.

If you employ someone who is entitled to keep quiet about their convictions and you subsequently discover their past, you cannot fairly dismiss the employee.

However, if your employee is required to drive a vehicle during work, you would need to insist on knowing about any driving conviction or disqualification. Your insurance cover would be affected by this.

There are also exceptions if your business involves working regularly with children, young people, the elderly, people with disabilities, administration of the law and certain other sensitive areas. In these situations, you are required to register with the Criminal Records Bureau (CRB)* (England and Wales), Disclosure Scotland* or Access Northern Ireland*. This enables you to ask people applying for jobs with you to apply for a CRB check (or its equivalent in Scotland or Northern Ireland), which is then sent to you and the applicant. This lists past convictions, including those that are spent, and also lesser sanctions, such as police cautions and reprimands, to help you decide whether the applicant is suitable for the job. The applicant is required to pay for the check, but it is good practice for employers to reimburse the cost. You are required to use the CRB information fairly and to keep it securely.

Health and disablement

You can refuse to employ someone if you are unhappy about their state of health. If one of your employees has been absent from work due to sickness, you may be entitled to dismiss on these grounds, providing a proper procedure is involved and subject to the length of time the employee has been absent. This involves consulting with the employee concerned, obtaining up-to-date medical evidence and considering any suitable alternatives for the employee before dismissal.

It is illegal to treat someone less favourably than other employees because they are disabled – for example, by offering them lesser benefits or fewer opportunities for promotion or training.

Booklets

■ ACAS, *Religion or belief in the workplace* EEL01; *Sexual orientation and the workplace* EEL02; *Age and the workplace* EEL03; *Working without the default retirement age: guidance for employers,* AL14.

■ BIS, *Union membership: rights of members and non-members* 06/558.

■ EHRC, *Straightforward answers to … 50 difficult questions; An employer's guide to … Creating an inclusive workforce; A practical guide to the law and best practice for employers (on disability); Top tips for small employers: a guide to employing disabled people; Age isn't an issue: an employer's guide to a 21st century workforce; Age legislation: 20 facts your business needs to know; Age diversity in the downturn; Age and the workplace; Sexual orientation and the workplace; Religion or belief and the workplace; Code of practice – sex discrimination; Code of practice on equal pay; Gender equality duty – code of practice; Statutory code of practice on racial equality in employment; Statutory code of practice on the duty to promote race equality; The duty to promote disability equality: statutory code of practice.*

■ Criminal Records Bureau, *Employing ex-offenders – a practical guide.*

Maternity and parental leave

Pregnant employees, married or unmarried, have several rights, such as the right not to be dismissed unfairly, the right to maternity leave and the right to return to work – but there are many conditions and exceptions, which can only be glossed over in this section.

In addition, working parents have a range of rights, including paid leave for new fathers and parents who are adopting a child, plus the right of parents with young or disabled children to request flexible working.

Regardless of how long the woman has worked for you, she is entitled to up to 52 weeks' maternity leave and, if she has been with you for at least 26 weeks, may claim statutory maternity pay for 39 weeks of her leave. Similarly, maternity allowance is payable for 39 weeks. Non-pay contractual rights continue to apply throughout the whole maternity leave period (not just the first 39 weeks of leave).

A major change since 6 April 2011 is that, if a mother returns to work before fully using her maternity leave and pay, the unused part can be transferred to the father.

Since April 2007, the right to request flexible working (see p. 274) has been extended to employees who are caring for an adult, as well as those caring for a young child. From 6 April 2009, this right was extended to parents of children up to and including the age of 16 (previously under six). The coalition government had announced plans to extend the right to flexible working to parents with children up to age 18 from April 2011 and to all workers from April 2012. However, possibly in response to pressure from business, the April 2011 extension did not go ahead and the government is now reviewing the remainder of these plans.

What you must do

1 Give reasonable paid time off work so that your employee can have ante-natal care. Fathers have no right to time off to accompany their partners, but some employers do voluntarily allow unpaid leave.
2 Do not dismiss your employee because she is pregnant.
3 Give your employee statutory maternity pay – SMP (see p. 271).
4 Give your employee her job back – see below.
5 Give new fathers up to two weeks' leave and statutory paternity pay.
6 Give parents who are adopting time off and statutory adoption pay.
7 Seriously consider requests from working parents for a change in their hours or work pattern.

Dismissing while pregnant

A woman will automatically be held to be unfairly dismissed if (among others) the reason for dismissal is that she is pregnant or for any reason connected with her pregnancy.

An Employment Appeal Tribunal has also found that it can be sex discrimination to dismiss a woman because of pregnancy if you would not dismiss a man who would need similar time off for an operation.

If a pregnant employee cannot do a particular job or it would be illegal for her to do so, then the employer is entitled to offer her a different job that she can perform where appropriate. An employee is entitled to receive no less favourable terms than that of her previous position. If there is no other position, then she may be entitled to be suspended on pay, but she cannot be fairly dismissed in these circumstances unless the dismissal can fit one of the legal categories and has no relation to pregnancy.

Maternity leave

Regardless of how short a time she may have worked for you, your employee is entitled to 52 weeks' maternity leave. Thirty-nine weeks of this will normally be paid leave.

The employee must normally tell you by the end of the 15th week before the expected week of childbirth (EWC) that she intends to take leave. She can then take the full 52 weeks without giving you any further notice. However, if she wants to come back to work early, she must give you eight weeks' notice of her intention.

If your employee is off work sick during the four weeks before the start of the EWC, her leave will be deemed to have started automatically. Otherwise, it starts when the employee chooses, provided this is no earlier than the beginning of the 11th week before the baby is due.

During the whole maternity leave period, your employee continues to have the same non-pay contractual rights as she did while working. What these rights are depends on the contract of employment but are likely to include, for example, the right to accrue paid holiday entitlement. The right to any contractual perks, such as a company car, also continue. The period of maternity leave counts as continuous employment for the purpose of her pension rights.

You can ask your employee to work up to ten Keeping in Touch (KIT) days during her leave. However, KIT days are optional for your employee as well as you, so she does not have to take up the days offered. She has the right to return to work at the end of her leave – normally to the same job she had before her leave started.

Maternity pay

You must normally pay statutory maternity pay (SMP) to an employee during the first 39 weeks of her maternity leave even if she is not going to return to you after the birth of her child. You pay SMP if your employee:

■ has stopped working for you.

■ is still pregnant at the 11th week before her baby is expected.

■ has average weekly earnings of at least £102 a week for 2011–12.

■ has been continuously employed by you for six months or more by the end of the 15th week before the baby is due.

The amount of SMP is 90 per cent of average earnings for the first six weeks of the period. Thereafter, it is £128.73 a week in 2011–12 (or 90 per cent of weekly average earnings if this average is less).

You can claim back some or all of the SMP that you pay out. You get the relief by deducting it from the tax, National Insurance contributions and other PAYE deductions you would otherwise hand over to HMRC. If the amount you must pay out to employees exceeds the PAYE deductions you've collected, apply to HMRC for advance funding. You can recover the SMP you pay out in full if the employer's and employees' National Insurance contributions you collect come to no more than a set amount, which is £45,000 in 2011–12. If the National Insurance comes to more, you can claim back 92 per cent of the sum you pay out (and have to fund the remaining 8 per cent yourself). If you are using payroll software, it will automatically calculate the SMP due and the amount you can reclaim. There is also a calculator on the Employer CD-ROM sent to you by HM Revenue & Customs* and on the Revenue web site at *www.hmrc.gov.uk/calcs/smp.htm*.

Right to return to work

Your employee has the right to return to work if she has worked for you continuously for one year at the beginning of the 11th week before the baby is due. (There is at present an exemption for employers with less than five employees to refuse the right to return.) Your employee may lose the right to return to work if:

■ her job no longer exists because of redundancy and there is no suitable alternative job (in which case redundancy pay may be due).

■ it is not practicable for her to return to her job and you have offered suitable alternative work, which she refuses.

It is assumed that the woman will return to work at the end of her maternity leave. No earlier than 21 days before the end of her 18-week ordinary (statutory) maternity leave, you can ask your employee to confirm that she will be returning to work, and she is obliged to respond.

You are required to consider all requests for flexible working from parents of young children (see p. 274).

Booklets

■ BIS, *Pregnancy and work: what you need to know as an employer/employee* 09/804.

■ HMRC, *Employer helpbook for statutory maternity pay* E15.

Paternity pay and leave

Fathers who have worked with you for at least 26 weeks are entitled to take up to two weeks' ordinary paternity leave following the birth of their child. Provided they have earned at least a minimum average amount (£102 a week) during the preceding 26 weeks, they are also entitled to Statutory Paternity Pay (SPP) of £128.73 a week (or 90 per cent of their average earnings if less).

From 6 April 2011, fathers may also qualify for additional paternity leave in order to take care of their newborn child. This is leave that can be transferred from the mother if she has returned to work without taking her full leave entitlement. The father can also get additional paternity pay for any part of the transferred period if the mother would have been entitled to SMP (see p. 271) and the father's pay exceeds the £102 a week qualifying limit. Additional paternity leave can last for a maximum of 26 weeks.

To apply for additional paternity leave, both the mother and father must sign a completed form SC7 and give it to you, as the employer of the father, at least eight weeks before they want the leave to start. You must respond within 28 days either to request more information (such as the child's birth certificate) or to confirm the date that leave starts. You cannot refuse the leave or pay if the father meets the entitlement conditions.

For more information, see the Business Link* web site.

Parental leave and time off for dependants

Employees who have worked for you continuously for a year or more have the right to take up to 13 weeks' unpaid parental leave to care for their child. From 6 April 2009, this right was extended to parents of children under the age of 17 (previously under six). The age limit is under 18 if the child has a disability.

Employees with at least a year's service have the right to take reasonable or unpaid leave to attend to domestic incidents/emergencies/family crises. This covers, for example, sickness, injury, a death in the family, a partner giving birth or a serious incident at school. The legislation does not include any default rules about how this right should be put into practice. So, unless you draw up your own policy and make it part of the terms of employment, there is no requirement for your employee to tell you they are taking this leave or to inform you of how long they expect to be away. You will need to make clear whether this will be paid or unpaid and how you will deal with this in practice.

Flexible working

Since 6 April 2003, parents of a child under the age of six (or under 18 in the case of a disabled child) have had the right to ask to switch to flexible working in order to care for the child. From 6 April 2007, this right has been extended to employees caring for a spouse, civil partner or relative who lives at the same address and who is in need of care. From 6 April 2009, the right has been further extended to parents of children under the age of 17. The request may relate to the hours they work, the times they are required to work and where they work (for example, from home or an office). You, the employer, must consider the request. However, you can refuse if you have good commercial reasons for doing so. These might be:

- the burden of additional costs.
- detrimental effect on meeting consumer demand.
- inability to reorganize work among existing staff.
- inability to recruit additional staff.
- detrimental impact on quality.
- detrimental impact on performance.
- insufficiency of work during the periods the employee proposes to work.
- planned structural changes.

An employee will have the right to take you to an employment tribunal if you refuse to consider a request for flexible working or you have refused the request on the basis of incorrect facts. But the tribunal will not be able to consider the merits of the commercial reasons you have given for refusal. If the tribunal finds in favour of the employee, it will be able to order you to pay compensation.

Booklets

- ACAS, *The right to apply for flexible working.*
- BIS, *Flowchart of right to request flexible working process 08/1486; Form FW(B): flexible working acceptance form 03/570Y; Form FW(C): flexible working application rejection form 03/571Y.*

Coping with the economic downturn

If you have a downturn in orders, there are several options you could consider to cut your labour costs: lay-offs, short-time working and redundancies.

Lay-offs means sending staff home for a period because there is no work, but you expect this to be a temporary situation. Short-time working means laying off your staff for a set number of hours a day or days a week.

You have the right to lay off staff or put them on short-time working only if it is written into their contract of employment, there is an agreement between you and the relevant union, there is a national agreement or you can show that it is customary in your particular industry. Normally, you must still pay your employees their normal rate even if there is no work for them to do, but you can pay them less or nothing at all if there is a specific provision in the contract or agreement to allow it. You might have to pay a minimum sum, called a guarantee payment (see p. 256).

If the only alternative is redundancy, you may be able to negotiate with your employees to accept a change in their contract to allow lay-offs or short-time working.

Where employees are laid-off on no pay or on short-time working and getting less than half a week's pay for four consecutive weeks (or for six non-consecutive weeks in a 13-week period), they have the option of claiming redundancy and any associated redundancy payment.

Generally, redundancy should be the last resort. Bear in mind that you may be losing good staff and may need their skills and experience when business picks up. If you do decide that redundancy is the only option, you must follow set procedures (see p. 279).

Booklets

■ ACAS, *Lay-offs and short-time working* (ACAS/AL01).

Saying goodbye to an employee

In most circumstances, you have got one year to assess employees (make sure you have a probationary period), and during that time you can dismiss them without any fear of being taken to an employment tribunal and accused of unfair dismissal. However, you will automatically be guilty of unfair dismissal, regardless of the length of time the employee has worked for you, if you sack him or her or if the reason for the dismissal is:

- trade union membership or activity.
- not being a member of a trade union.
- acting as a representative for negotiations about redundancy and so on.
- being pregnant or taking maternity leave.
- taking action on health and safety grounds.
- trying to enforce a statutory employment right (such as requesting a written statement or refusing to allow an employee to bring a work colleague or trade union representative to any disciplinary grievance hearing).
- refusing to do shop or betting work on a Sunday.
- acting in his or her role as a pension scheme trustee.
- reasons relating to the national minimum wage.
- reasons relating to the working time regulations.
- reasons relating to the transfer of employment rights from one employer to another.
- 'whistle blowing', where protection is given by the Public Interest Disclosure Act 1998.

And if you dismiss an employee who would qualify for paid suspension on medical grounds, you could be guilty of unfair dismissal if the employee had been with you for a month or more.

However, be careful in how you dismiss an employee who has been with you for less than one year in case he or she can claim breach of contract. The statutory minimum notice can be added to the dismissal date for the purpose of the calculation.

You are normally automatically guilty of unfair dismissal if you fail to follow a fair procedure. From 6 April 2009, there is no longer a statutory procedure that you must follow. Instead you should take fair and reasonable steps in accordance with a code of practice published by ACAS. There is also an ACAS helpline* and free early conciliation service. The ACAS code is not legally enforceable but any Employment Tribunal will take into account whether you have followed its provisions.

What you must do

1 Behave in a reasonable way when dismissing an employee.
2 Give your employee the right notice.

How you can sack an employee

There are five reasons that may mean a dismissal is fair, although you will also have to demonstrate that you have followed the three-step procedure and been reasonable in the circumstances. The reasons are:

1 *Being incapable of doing the job*: this covers skill, competence, qualifications, health and any other mental or physical quality relevant to the job. Note that you do not have to prove to an employment tribunal that an employee is incompetent, merely that you believed it to be so and that you have acted reasonably. But you must make sure that your employee is aware of the requirements of the job and why and how they are not being met.
2 *Misconduct*: for example theft, insolence, horseplay, persistent bad time-keeping, laziness.
3 *Redundancy*: see p. 279.
4 *Legal reasons*: for example, if a van driver could no longer carry out his or her duties because of losing his or her driving licence.
5 *Some other substantial reason*: for example, if it is not financially viable for the firm to continue to employ an employee.

As you can see, it is possible to dismiss an employee if you are dissatisfied. But it is very important to follow the correct procedure and to act in a reasonable way. It can save you an awful lot of time and money if you do because you can demonstrate to an employment tribunal that you have acted correctly and fairly.

Dismissal is the final step in a disciplinary procedure. You must act fairly and reasonably at all times and in the context of the circumstances of the case, and this will usually be judged by reference to the ACAS* *Disciplinary and grievance procedures* CP01 (price £2.95 for hard copy or free to download or view online).

Step-by-step guide

1 When you first become dissatisfied with the employee, investigate the matter promptly so that you establish the facts of the case.
2 If, based on the facts, there is a disciplinary issue, notify the employee in writing, giving details of the problem. You should normally provide written copies of the evidence you have gathered.

3 Meet the employee to discuss the problem and to explore constructively how things might be improved. The employee has a statutory right to be accompanied at the meeting by, for example, a trade union representative or fellow worker.

4 Consider whether the matter can be resolved informally, for example through training for the employee or extra supervision of their work. Inform the employee of how you expect them to improve, over what time period and when their progress will be reviewed.

5 If an informal solution is not possible, take formal action. You should normally follow these stages: first written warning, final written warning. Inform your employee that they have the right to appeal against your decision. Written warnings must set out the nature of the problem, the improvement or change you require and the consequences for the employee of failing to comply. At each stage, you should meet again with the employee to give them a chance to present their case. A written warning should be disregarded after a specified period without further action (say, six months, or 12 for a final warning).

6 If the employee requests an appeal, arrange a meeting to hear the appeal. Tell the employee your decision.

7 Repeat steps 3 to 6 above as necessary.

8 If the problem persists, you may decide to dismiss the employee or possibly offer them an alternative job. Make sure you give the correct notice (see p. 280). You should give your reasons for dismissal/transfer/demotion in writing, meet with the employee and give them the opportunity to appeal.

Sacking someone on the spot

It can be done, and exceptionally a tribunal may judge it to be a fair dismissal provided the circumstances were extreme (for example, gross misconduct, such as dishonesty) and you have followed a modified statutory procedure. Immediately after the dismissal, you should give the former employee in writing an explanation of your reasons for the dismissal, including the evidence for your decision, and inform the employee that they have the right to appeal. If they take up this right, you must meet with them to hear the appeal and give the employee your final decision following the meeting.

However, in most cases, you reduce the risk of problems if instead you follow the full procedure recommended in the ACAS code. Consider suspending the employee on full pay (which does not count as a discipli-nary measure) while you investigate and go through the procedure.

Can it be unfair dismissal if your employee resigns?

It may seem a paradox, but the answer is yes. It can be unfair, if it is a con-structive dismissal. So watch out. If you increase working hours without extra pay, cut your employee's fringe benefits or accuse an employee of something, such as theft, without investigating it properly, it may count as constructive dismissal.

Making an employee redundant

You can make an employee redundant if you are cutting down generally on the number of employees or if your need for a particular skill in your business ceases or diminishes. But you must make the redundancy fair; do not choose married women, trade unionists, part-timers or people over a certain age, for example, as reasons for redundancy. And you must consult the recognized trade union (if appropriate) about the proposed redundancy.

If an employee has been with you for two years, you will have to pay redun-dancy pay. The statutory amount depends upon the age of the employee and varies between ½ and 1½ weeks' pay for each year the employee has worked for you. There is a limit on the amount of a week's pay (£400, from February 2011) and the maximum number of years that can be taken into account is 20. This means the maximum statutory redundancy pay an employee can qualify for is £12,000 from February 2011. You can make a more generous payment.

Generally you will breach the anti-age-discrimination regulations if you select employees for redundancy on the grounds of age. This means, for example, that generally you cannot operate a last-in-first-out policy (which could discriminate against younger employees) or a policy of making those with the longest service redundant (which would tend to discriminate against older workers). However, age-related redundancies are allowed but only if you can objectively justify them.

The statutory redundancy pay scheme, which pays larger amounts to older workers, is exempt from the age discrimination regulations on the basis that it is harder for older workers to find similar employment elsewhere and so the larger compensation is objectively justified. If you offer more generous redundancy terms, generally your scheme will also be acceptable under the regulations if it is based on the statutory scheme (for example, based on higher pay than the statutory scheme or paying out a higher multiple for each year).

How much notice do you have to give?

You must give your employee:

- one week's notice if your employee has been with you for one month but less than two years.
- two weeks' notice if your employee has been with you for two years.
- an extra week's notice for each extra year your employee has been with you, up to a maximum of 12 weeks' notice.

If your employee's contract specifies a longer notice period, the longer period applies.

These minimum notice periods do not apply to the notice given to you by your employee, who by law has to give only one week's notice if employed by you for a month or more. So, if you want to make sure your employee has to give more notice, you must put it in the contract of employment.

What to do when an employee leaves

You must fill in form P45. Send part 1 to the tax office and hand parts 2 and 3 to your employee. If an employee dies, you should also fill in form P45 and send all three parts to the tax office.

Booklets

- BIS, *Avoiding and resolving discipline and grievance issues at work: simpler laws, better services* 09/1227; *Redundancy consultation and notification: guidance* 06/1965Y; *Statutory redundancy pay: calculation table* 09/1371.
- ACAS, *Disciplinary and grievance procedures* CP01 (price £2.95 for hard copy or free to download or view online).

Summary

1 Do not be too frightened of employment law. On the whole, you can employ who you want and sack them if they prove to be incompetent.
2 Behave reasonably towards your employees, giving them a chance to

explain their actions. If you do this, you can cut down the chances of being found guilty of unfair dismissal in an employment tribunal.

3 Use all the agencies who are set up to advise in this very complex area.
4 Seek legal advice. Getting it wrong can be expensive and time-consuming.

Other chapters to read

20 Getting the right staff (p. 222); **29** Keeping the record straight (p. 370).

22

Your business and the environment

Increasingly, even small and medium-sized businesses have to comply with a range of legal obligations aimed at reducing pressure on the environment. This chapter looks briefly at how your business may be affected by the main requirements concerning waste disposal and the efficient use of resources. While complying with these rules may seem onerous, bear in mind that taking steps to limit your waste and use resources more effectively may also save your business money.

You can get more information about your waste responsibilities from Business Link* (or equivalent organizations) and the government web site, NetRegs*.

Normal business waste

The law imposes on you a duty of care to produce, store and dispose of your business waste without harming the environment. This applies whether you work from dedicated business premises or from your own home.

Business waste is anything produced by or in the course of your business that needs to be disposed of or recycled. It may include, for example, paper if your business is office-based, empty ink and toner cartridges from printers and photocopiers, packaging from supplies you use, defective products from your processes, old items and materials that you replace if, say, you are a builder and so on.

In most cases, you will want to throw out your rubbish and have it collected. As a business, you are required to make sure that your waste is collected and handled by a carrier that is registered to do so. This applies even if you work from home – you can be fined if you are found putting your business rubbish into the normal household waste system. You can find registered waste management firms either by contacting your local authority or using the directory on the government's NetRegs* web site. The firm will issue you with a waste transfer note which, for repeat collections, can cover a period up to 12 months. You are required to keep your waste transfer notes for at least two years.

The waste management firm will provide you with rubbish sacks, bins or skips and arrange for them to be collected or emptied and the rubbish taken away. There will be a charge for this service. In general, the charge is higher according to the amount of waste you produce.

Alternatively, you can transport your waste to a waste treatment site operated by a registered firm, usually without any formalities. But, if your waste is from construction or demolition, you will need to register as a waste carrier with the Environment Agency* (England and Wales), Scottish Environment Protection Agency* or Northern Ireland Environment Agency*. When you transport waste yourself to a site, you will usually need to get a consignment note from the waste operator.

Under new rules, from 28 September 2011 onwards, whenever you get a waste transfer note or consignment note, you must sign to say you have complied with the 'waste management hierarchy'. This applies to all businesses that produce waste (and those involved in its carriage, storage, treatment or disposal) and sets out in order of priority the steps you should consider concerning your waste. The steps are:

■ First: prevention.

■ Second: preparing for reuse.

■ Third: recycling.

■ Fourth: recovery, for example, energy recovery.

■ Fifth and only as the last resort: disposal.

From 1 January 2015, some items will have to be sorted and collected or disposed of separately (in the same way that most household waste is). These items are: waste paper, metal, plastic and glass.

Trade effluent

Trade effluent is waste liquid from premises being used for business. It includes fats, oils, greases, detergents and food waste, as well as things like chemicals. In fact, the only liquids that do not count as trade effluent are normal domestic sewage and rainwater run-off. The size of your business does not affect the fact that your waste liquids are treated as trade effluent.

Before you discharge any effluent either directly or indirectly into the public sewage system, you must get a 'trade effluent consent' or make a 'trade effluent agreement' with your local water or sewerage company. You can find out which is your local company by contacting Water UK*. For some types of effluent (such as those containing potentially dangerous substances), you may also need a permit from the Environment Agency or its Scottish or Northern Irish equivalent.

Hazardous waste (special waste)

Hazardous waste (called 'special waste' in Scotland) is waste that may be harmful to the environment or to human health. Before you think this does not apply to you, check. Some very ordinary items count as hazardous, including fluorescent tubes, energy-saving light bulbs, toner and ink cartridges and old-style computer monitors (with a cathode ray tube). Some other examples of hazardous waste include car batteries, car oil, brake fluid, antifreeze, rags contaminated with these substances, aerosols, human or animal tissue, drugs and medicines, nappies, sharp instruments and so on.

You must dispose of hazardous waste at a landfill site that is authorized to accept such waste – not all are. Contact the waste management firm operating the site to check whether it can accept your waste and how much you will be charged. You must get a consignment note from the firm for each disposal and this note must be kept for at least three years.

You must register with the Environment Agency or its Scottish or Northern Irish equivalent if your business produces hazardous waste, but in England and Wales you are exempted from this requirement if you produce less than 500 kg per year.

Electrical equipment

Any waste electrical equipment from your business must be stored and disposed of separately from your other business waste. This covers, for example, computers, printers, monitors, heating, cooling and lighting equipment, automatic dispensers, household appliances and so on.

When you dispose of such equipment, you must get and keep proof that you handed it over to a registered waste management firm. You can find registered waste management firms either by contacting your local authority or using the directory on the government's NetRegs web site.

If you sell electrical equipment to end-user customers, additional rules apply, including setting up a system for taking back free-of-charge old equipment from customers for disposal. You can either run the scheme yourself or join a third-party scheme.

Portable batteries

If you supply more than 32 kg a year of portable batteries to end-user customers (directly or installed in products you sell), you must keep a record of the amount and type of batteries you supply. If you sell batteries separately from products, you must also operate a system that allows consumers to return their used batteries free-of-charge. Since batteries contain hazardous substances, you must then also make special arrangements for their disposal – you can arrange for them to be collected by the Battery Compliance Scheme*.

For more information and to calculate the weight of batteries you supply, visit the Department for the Environment, Food and Rural Affairs* web site.

Packaging waste

If you make, sell, fill or handle packaging, regulations apply to your business and you could be fined if you do not comply.

Some regulations (the Producer Responsibility Regulations) that require you to comply with recycling and recovery targets apply only if your turnover is more than £2 million a year or you handle more than 50 tonnes of packaging a year. If you think they might apply, vist the NetRegs web site for details.

The Packaging (Essential Requirements) Regulations apply more widely to any business that produces packaged products, or markets or sells packaging or packaged products. These regulations require you to minimize the amount of packaging used (but given hygiene, safety and consumer acceptance requirements) and to ensure that packaging can be recovered. 'Recovery' has a variety of meanings, for example, making packaging durable enough to be reused, ensuring it is recyclable or compostable or that energy can be recovered from it. You must minimize the use of any hazardous substances in the packaging.

You are required to keep evidence that you have complied with the Essential Requirements regulations and to keep these records for at least four years.

Packaging regulations are enforced by your local trading standards office* or, in Northern Ireland, the Department for Enterprise, Trade and Investments*.

Energy efficiency

The UK is committed to reducing its greenhouse gas emissions, and one measure aimed at this end is the climate change levy. The levy is built into the energy prices that business customers pay.

You will not be paying the climate change levy if you work from home and at least 60 per cent of your energy use is for domestic rather than business purposes. If less, you will have to pay the levy on the portion of your fuel use that is for business use.

Energy suppliers are being required to install 'smart' meters at business premises, to ensure accurate billing and so that businesses can monitor their energy use (and hopefully therefore take steps to reduce it). Larger businesses (and, in Northern Ireland, all but the smallest businesses) must have smart meters by 2014. In England, Wales and Scotland, all businesses are due to be converted to smart meters by 2020.

The tax system (see Chapter 30, 'Tax') includes a number of measures to encourage businesses to use more energy-efficient equipment and vehicles.

23

Insurance

Deciding what insurance you should have must rate as one of the least exciting decisions you have to make for your business. Paying out money to cover you against hazards, which you fervently hope will not happen, ranks fairly low in satisfaction. But it should rank quite high in priority. Failing to get the right insurance might mean the collapse and end of your business.

There are two different categories of business insurance:

1 Insurance you must have by law.
2 Insurance you could consider to cover risks and disasters.

Buying the insurance

Not only do you want the right sort of insurance, you want it at the right price and with the right company. The obvious place to start your search for your business insurance is with an insurance broker*. A broker can, in theory, deal with the full range of insurance companies and should be able to find the lowest quote for you. Note that the cost of the insurance may vary depending on the location of the business; at the extreme, you may find it difficult or expensive to buy insurance for some areas.

There are different types of insurance intermediary. Those using the name 'broker' are usually independent and can arrange insurance for you with any company in the market. Other intermediaries – for example, those calling themselves 'consultants' – could be independent but more often will be acting as agents for just one or a handful of companies. It's important to check this before you do business.

Insurance companies, brokers and other intermediaries are regulated by the Financial Services Authority (FSA)*. It is illegal for a firm to trade without being authorized by the FSA and, provided you deal with an authorized firm, you are protected by complaints procedures and a compensation scheme if anything goes wrong. Firms are also required to treat customers fairly and to comply with rules about how they conduct business, which includes finding out enough about your needs and circumstances to recommend only a suitable policy and drawing your attention to any unusual or onerous terms in the contract. Under the FSA rules, you must be given information about the main features of the policy. This may be in the form of a standardized policy summary that carries a 'key facts' logo and is designed to help you more easily compare one policy with another.

You can check whether a firm is authorized by the FSA by using the FSA Register*. You can get a list of brokers in your area from the British Insurance Brokers' Association (BIBA)*, a trade body that also sets standards of practice for its members. If you prefer to deal online, using a search engine (see p. 23) will give you a long list of online companies and brokers.

Be aware that, if you search for insurance online, comparison web sites do not necessarily cover the whole market and may be earning commission when you 'click through' to buy online. The search filters may also not reflect all the factors that are important for your particular circumstances, so you should check the terms and conditions of the insurance policy carefully before you buy to make sure it is suitable. The Association of British Insurers*, the trade body for insurance companies, has developed a code of good practice for comparison web sites, but it is voluntary, so check whether the site you are using follows it. If you do use comparison sites, it's a good idea to check with more than one before you make your final choice of policy.

Insurance you must have

1. Employer's liability

You must have insurance to pay out for your legal liability if one of your employees is injured or ill as a result of working for you and you have been negligent. The amount of cover (the amount of money the insurance company will pay out if you claim) must be at least £5 million. That sounds a lot, but might not be enough – most policies give cover of at least £10 million. The law also requires you to exhibit a certificate of employer's liability insurance at each place of work.

Premiums for employer's liability insurance have soared in the past few years. There is anecdotal evidence that some employers, no longer able to afford cover, are making do without it. Don't be tempted to follow this course. It is illegal to carry on a business in which you employ people if you do not have this cover, and you could be personally financially ruined if an employee has an accident at work and claims against you.

You do not need employer's liability insurance if you are not a limited company and the only people you employ are close family members (your spouse, civil partner, children, parents, grandparents, brothers or sisters). You do not need this insurance if you operate as a limited company, you own at least 50 per cent of the shares and you are the only employee.

2. Motor insurance

You must insure your liability to others, known as third-party liability, which occurs because of a car crash or other motor vehicle accident. This includes death or injury to anybody (but not your employees while working, as they are covered by employer's liability insurance, see above) and damage to third-party property including other vehicles.

A further addition to third-party cover that could be worth your while is fire and theft cover. Finally, if you want to get cover for accidental damage to your vehicles, regardless of who is to blame for the accident, you want a comprehensive insurance policy.

If you have a car or other vehicle for your own private and social use, and you want to use it for your business, you should tell your insurance company. You may need to pay an extra sum to get it covered for business.

Be clear about what the car is going to be used for when you fill in what is known as the proposal form (the form you fill in to apply for the insurance). You will probably have to pay extra money if the car is used for some purposes, such as by a sales rep. Failure to tell the insurance company may mean that it will not pay out if you make a claim.

3. Insurance needed by contracts

Check all the contracts you have (for example, under a lease or hire purchase agreement) to see what insurance you are committed to get.

4. Engineering equipment

By law, certain equipment, such as pressure vessels and lifting tackle, has to be inspected and passed as safe at regular intervals. You can combine the maintenance with an insurance policy to cover you against the risk of explosion, accidental damage and breakdown.

Other insurance you can get

1. Insurance against fire and other perils

This covers destruction or damage to your buildings and contents through fire. You can also be covered for other risks, such as lightning, explosion, aircraft, storm, flood, riot and malicious damage. Standard business property insurance normally specifically excludes loss or damage caused by terrorism, but you can buy back this cover for an extra premium. If you work from your own home, you will still need to get your own insurance policy and there are some special schemes available – consult an insurance broker*.

Worth getting? *Yes.*

2. Insurance for loss of profits

This covers you if your business is disrupted by fire, flood or some other insured peril. It can pay out money to pay your employees, maintain your profits and pay for the extra cost of temporary replacement premises. These 'business interruption' policies normally only cover incidents where the interruption stems from damage to your business premises. However, you can separately buy 'contingent business interruption' insurance to provide cover where the disruption to your business is from some other cause, such as an epidemic, transport disaster or a strike at your suppliers or customers. (You cannot buy cover against a strike by your own workers.)

Worth getting? *Depends* on your business. In most cases, yes to standard business interruption insurance; but if your business is small with few employees, and you could easily find somewhere to work, for example, your home, you may not consider it necessary. Note that using your home could cause problems with insurance, so check with your insurance company. Rather than insure for full loss of profits, you could consider insuring for the cost of finding somewhere else to carry on working. In the case of contingent business insurance: probably not worth getting unless your business is particularly vulnerable. You might consider other ways to manage risks, for example diversifying your supply chain or customer base to lessen the impact of third-party strike action.

3. Insurance against theft

This covers you for loss or damage to the contents of your premises. Theft for insurance purposes means that someone has forced an entry to or exit from your workplace, so if you want to be covered against theft by your employees or visitors, you'll have to pay extra and get fidelity insurance.

Worth getting? *Yes.*

4. Loss of money

Cash and near-cash, such as cheques and stamps, can be insured against theft from your premises or from the homes of directors or employees of your company or in transit.

Worth getting? *Yes*, if your takings are in cash. Otherwise, no.

5. Goods in transit

This insurance covers loss of or damage to your goods in your own vehicles, or other means of delivery, such as post or road haulier.

Worth getting? *Probably*, unless you don't sell in this way.

6. Trade credit insurance

This protects you against your customers failing to pay. You probably will not be able to get this insurance until you have been in business for some time.

Worth getting? *Probably not*, if you deal mainly in cash or payment on delivery. For selling on credit, by the time you can get this insurance, you will be able to work out for yourself how likely a problem bad debts will be. It is probably better to operate good credit control (p. 342) or use a factoring service (p. 346). However, if you have only one large or a couple of big customers, you should have credit insurance.

7. Public liability and product liability

This will cover your liability to visitors and members of the public if your business causes injury or illness to them or damages their property. Product liability insurance covers you for these risks, which occur as a result of the goods you are producing, selling or repairing up to a limit each year.

You need to make sure that the amount of cover is high enough. Damages in the courts have been as high as £1 million. You may need cover for more than this, especially if you do business in the USA.

Worth getting? *Yes*. With product liability, you may not need it if your products are very unlikely to cause damage or if yours is a service business.

8. Professional indemnity

If you are the type of business where the end-product is expert advice, this insurance can cover you against claims from your clients for damage caused by your negligence or misconduct.

Worth getting? *Yes*. These sorts of claim are on the increase.

9. Legal expenses

This insurance would enable you to pay for legal assistance if you are involved in a contractual or employment dispute, plus some other legal procedures.

Worth getting? *Probably not*. Most legal disputes are generally in the employment field. It would be far better to concentrate on getting well organized in this area to cut the risk of being taken to a tribunal and charged with unfair dismissal or breach of contract, for example.

10. Key person (keyman) insurance

If your business is heavily dependent on one or a few people for its future success, you can get keyman life insurance, for example for a sum of £250,000 to be paid to your business in the event of one of those people dying or being ill for a considerable period. To get cover, you must be able to prove the person's death would cost your firm money.

Worth getting? *Yes*.

11. Other insurance

There are some other types of insurance that you should consider, depending on your business. These include:

■ glass breakage, which is important for shops.

■ cover for frozen food.

■ computers and computer records.

■ fidelity insurance, which covers you against fraud or dishonesty by your employees.

■ business machines and equipment.

■ agricultural and fish-farming operations.

■ directors' and officers' liability.

Insurance for you and your family

If you and your family are not covered by insurance for various personal mishaps, you may find it difficult to carry on your business, so do not neglect your personal needs. Almost everyone should have life insurance, income protection insurance and a pension plan.

Make sure that you and your spouse/partner have enough life insurance to protect you in the event of your early deaths. For this purpose, do not go for the sort of life insurance that is really an investment but go for term insurance, family income benefit, mortgage protection and so on.

Income protection insurance would pay out an income if you were too ill to work and could pay for a temporary manager. You should consider this carefully. And do not forget pensions, which are covered in detail from p. 433.

Summary

1 Do not delay in taking out the insurance you need.
2 Use a registered insurance broker to act for you.
3 Shop around. Seek advice from more than one broker and ask for several quotes for each insurance you need.
4 Do not neglect personal insurance requirements. Life insurance for your family, income protection insurance and pensions should

be looked at carefully to determine the level you need. Use an independent financial adviser who is authorized to advise you on these topics.

Other chapter to read

32 Pensions and retirement (p. 433).

24

Forecasting

Forecasts are the kernel of your business. They are the basis on which you raise money, negotiate premises and order raw materials. These are only a few of the decisions that need to be made in advance with only your forecasts as guidance on how much is needed. Making a wildly inaccurate forecast can, for example, lead to raising insufficient funds. When the business fails to meet expectations and begins to run short of money, it may prove impossible to raise further funds. Lenders are very wary of handing out more when forecasting has proved to be mistaken. The result could be liquidation, or bankruptcy if you are a partner or sole trader, and the end of your dreams.

However, making no forecasts at all is even sillier. You would have no guidance on when to take certain basic business decisions.

Given the importance of attaining a reasonable estimate of future sales, costs and cash balances, it follows that making the forecasts is a process that should not be hurried or treated casually (and can usually be carried out with the help of a computer program). You must constantly strive to seek information on which forecasts can be based; you must constantly curb your over-optimism, which can lead to estimated sales figures that are too high and estimated cost figures that are too low. Question your first forecasts for the realism of their assumptions before accepting any figure as a part of the final forecasts.

Nevertheless, it is realistic to accept that some of the figures will be nothing more than a best guess given the current state of information available to you. However, your figures should have some grounding in fact, so when you present your case to your bank manager or other source of finance you can support the figure when challenged.

It is important to make the forecasts in your plan realistic so that if your business idea does not hold water, you can discover this at the planning stage. You do not want to discover two years down the track that your business will not work, after you have committed money, time and effort. Do not underestimate the mental anguish and financial problems that can be caused by a struggling business (p. 364).

What is in this chapter?

There are three forecasts you need to make:

- cash flow (p. 296).
- profit and loss (p. 302).
- balance sheet (p. 306).

Finally, on pp. 310–13, there are some example forecasts.

Cash flow forecast

The first point to note is that cash and profit are not the same thing at all, so the two forecasts may be quite different.

A cash flow forecast is a record of when you think you will receive cash in your business and have to pay it out. In your business plan, you should include monthly cash flow forecasting for at least one, preferably two years ahead. Depending on the size of your business, you may need to include yearly cash flow forecasts for a further three years.

On p. 298, there is a blank cash flow form, which shows the typical headings and layout of a forecast. Obviously, the headings will vary with the nature of the business. See p. 310 for an example forecast.

Detailed calculations for cash flow forecast

Do the cash flow forecast for your chosen accounting year. If, for example, you choose to end your accounting year at the end of April, your cash flow forecast will run from 1 May to 30 April.

It is important to make realistic assumptions about when you will receive the cash, or when you will have to pay it out. The purpose of the forecast is to throw up when your need for cash is at its greatest, so you can demonstrate what your funding requirements are.

1. Opening bank balance

This shows how much is actually in your business bank account at the start of each period. If you owe your bank money (have an overdraft), show this by putting the figure in brackets. If your forecast is made before you start trading, the opening bank balance is likely to be nil.

Your opening bank balance for one period will be the closing bank balance for the previous period.

2. Cash from sales

In here would go any cash you expect to receive when you sell your product, not in payment of an invoice you send out. If your business is a shop, most of your sales will be cash ones, so this would be the biggest element of your cash receipts. If you are registered for VAT, enter the figure you expect to receive, including VAT.

3. Cash from debtors

If you sell your product and do not receive payment at once, but instead send out invoices, you would enter here when you expect to receive the cash. Someone who owes you money (for example, has not yet paid your invoice) is a debtor. You should aim to get your invoices paid as quickly as possible, but most of your customers will expect to delay payment by at least one month (see Chapter 26, 'Staying afloat', for how to get your debtors to pay).

If you are registered for VAT, enter the figure you expect to receive, including VAT.

4. VAT (net receipts)

If you are not registered for VAT, ignore this section (see p. 420 for details of whether you should not be registered). If you are registered for VAT, you will only expect to receive cash from the VAT system if for some reason your purchases, on which you can claim back VAT, are greater than your sales on which you have charged VAT.

This might happen as a rare occurrence if you have spent a lot of money while starting up, before your sales have got going. Another possible reason could occur if your sales are seasonal but your purchases are not. It could also happen if your sales are zero-rated, in which case you do not have to charge VAT on your sales, but you can claim it back on purchases (p. 426).

Monthly cash flow forecast

(for the period 1 January 2012 to 31 December 2012)

		Jan.	Feb.	–	Nov.	Dec.	Total
1	Opening bank balance (A)	. . .	. . .	–	. . .	. . .	. . .
Receipts							
2	Cash from sales	. . .	. . .	–	. . .	. . .	. . .
3	Cash from debtors	. . .	. . .	–	. . .	. . .	. . .
4	VAT (net receipts)	. . .	. . .	–	. . .	. . .	. . .
5	Other receipts	. . .	. . .	–	. . .	. . .	. . .
6	Sale of assets	. . .	. . .	–	. . .	. . .	. . .
7	Capital	. . .	. . .	–	. . .	. . .	. . .
	TOTAL RECEIPTS (B)	. . .	. . .	–	. . .	. . .	. . .
Payments							
8	Payment to suppliers	. . .	. . .	–	. . .	. . .	. . .
9	Cash purchases	. . .	. . .	–	. . .	. . .	. . .
10	Wages/drawings	. . .	. . .	–	. . .	. . .	. . .
11	PAYE/NIC	. . .	. . .	–	. . .	. . .	. . .
12	VAT (net payments)	. . .	. . .	–	. . .	. . .	. . .
13	Tax payments	. . .	. . .	–	. . .	. . .	. . .
14	Rent	. . .	. . .	–	. . .	. . .	. . .
15	Uniform business rate	. . .	. . .	–	. . .	. . .	. . .
16	Heating/lighting	. . .	. . .	–	. . .	. . .	. . .
17	Telephone	. . .	. . .	–	. . .	. . .	. . .
18	Professional fees	. . .	. . .	–	. . .	. . .	. . .
19	General expenses	. . .	. . .	–	. . .	. . .	. . .
20	Capital expenditure	. . .	. . .	–	. . .	. . .	. . .
21	Bank interest and charges	. . .	. . .	–	. . .	. . .	. . .
22	Other payments	. . .	. . .	–	. . .	. . .	. . .
	TOTAL PAYMENTS (C)	. . .	. . .	–	. . .	. . .	. . .
23	CLOSING BANK BALANCE (A) + (B) – (C)	. . .	. . .	–	. . .	. . .	. . .

You may make your returns for VAT on a quarterly basis, so allow for this in your cash flow.

5. Other receipts

Put here any miscellaneous receipts of income that you expect to occur.

6. Sale of assets

This section is for you to record the proceeds you expect to get from selling any assets, for example a car or office equipment.

7. Capital

Put the amount of money you are going to invest and make sure you put it in the month you expect to invest it. If anyone else is expected to invest or to lend you money (not including an overdraft with the bank), slot it in here.

8. Payment to suppliers

Put in here when you expect you will have to pay suppliers for their services or materials. The longer you delay paying suppliers' invoices, the better it can be for your cash flow. This beneficial effect has to be balanced by any ill will created by late payment. A realistic assumption for your cash flow forecast will be that you will not have to pay your suppliers' invoices until one month after you receive them. Whether you are registered for VAT or not, enter the amount including any VAT you will be paying to your suppliers.

9. Cash purchases

If you have to pay cash on the spot for purchases from suppliers, estimate the amount (including any VAT) and time in this section.

10. Wages/drawings

Put here the amount after deducting tax and National Insurance contributions under the PAYE system for wages.

11. PAYE/NIC

Total the amount of tax under the PAYE system and the amount of National Insurance contributions you will deduct from your employees each month, as well as the amount of the employer's contribution. You have to send this money in to the tax collector within two weeks of the end of the month (but if your average PAYE and NIC payments are likely to be £1,500 a month or less, you can make quarterly payments, which will help your cash flow).

If your business is a limited company and you pay yourself a salary as a director, your personal tax and National Insurance contributions will be collected in this way.

If you are a sole trader or partner, your personal tax on what you pay yourself will not be collected in this way. Instead, you will pay tax, and Class 4 National Insurance contributions if you pay them, in two or three lumps, in January, July and any remaining balance the following January. Enter the amount in the section 'Tax payments'. However, your Class 2 National Insurance contributions will be collected each month, and you should reflect the amount here under 'PAYE/NIC'. For more about your personal tax and National Insurance contributions as a sole trader or partner, see Chapter 30, 'Tax'.

12. VAT (net payments)

If you are not registered for VAT, do not enter anything here. If you are registered for VAT, you should estimate the amount of tax you will be paying over to the VAT collector each quarter or other period (see Chapter 31, 'VAT').

13. Tax payments

If you run a limited company, enter the amount of tax you estimate you will pay on your company's profits and when you will pay it. Corporation tax, that is, tax on your company's profits, is payable nine months after the end of your accounting year – ask your accountant* for more information.

If you are a sole trader or partner, your tax and any Class 4 National Insurance contributions payable will be paid in three lumps – on 31 January, 31 July and the balance or a repayment on the following 31 January. For how to work out the amount of tax you will be paying, see Chapter 30, 'Tax'.

14. Rent

Enter the rent you will pay in each month or quarter.

15. Uniform business rate

Enter the amount of the business rate and when you will have to pay it – see p. 402. Do not forget you can opt to pay your rates monthly over a 10-month period. This can improve your cash flow.

16. Heating/lighting

These bills will be paid each quarter in arrears or monthly by direct debit. Remember to cater for heavy winter usage.

17. Telephone

The telephone bill will be paid quarterly or monthly in arrears.

18. Professional fees

Payment of these bills will be fairly erratic; you must make your best guess, but try to obtain an estimate.

19. General expenses

Enter an estimate for those continuing and recurring, but small, expenses. These could include postage, fares, newspapers, or whatever is required in your business. If your business is a mailing service, for example, you should have a separate heading for postage. What exactly goes in here will have to be decided by you.

20. Capital expenditure

If you are going to buy any pieces of equipment, such as a car, computer or machinery, enter the amount, including VAT, and when you estimate you will have to pay for it. If you are paying cash, put in the full amount. If you are going to buy on hire purchase or using a loan, you will enter the amount of the deposit and the monthly payments separately and in the correct months. Leasing payments will be monthly.

21. Bank interest and charges

If you have an overdraft or bank loan, estimate the amount and frequency of the interest charged. Get a quote from the bank manager.

22. Other payments

What goes in here depends on the nature of your business. It could include insurance, but if this is of reasonable size you should have a separate entry.

23. Closing bank balance

Work out the closing bank balance for the period by adding the opening bank balance to the total receipts and taking away the figure for total payments. The closing bank balance becomes the opening bank balance at the start of the next period.

Profit and loss forecast

A profit forecast should show what level of profit you expect your business to produce at the end of the period, according to the accounting records you keep. Your accounts will not be drawn up on a cash basis, so many of the figures in your profit forecast will be different from those in the cash flow forecast. Below there is an explanation of how and why the figures will differ.

Detailed calculations for profit and loss forecast

1. Sales

The figure you put in here is the sum of the invoices you expect to send out during the accounting period. It is not necessarily the sum of the cash you receive during the period (unless your business is a shop that makes only cash sales, for example). You could also describe the sales figure as the cash you receive during the period plus what you are owed at the end of the period less what you were owed at the end of the previous period.

If you are registered for VAT, you do not include the amount of VAT you charge on your sales, unlike in your cash flow forecast.

If your business is likely to be seasonal, or if you know of events coming up that might temporarily increase or decrease your sales figures, show this monthly effect. A reader of your business plan will not be impressed by a monthly figure that is level or shows a very steady rate of increase unless you can demonstrate that this is a realistic assumption.

When forecasting sales, you need to consider two factors: the number of units you can sell and the price you can get for these units.

2. Cost of sales: purchases

You are estimating for this section those costs that you would expect to vary with the level of your sales; if your sales go up, the level of direct costs goes up, and vice versa. In real life, things are not quite so cut and dried and often the distinction between direct costs and overheads is blurred. The important point is for you to have a clear idea about which you regard as overheads.

Purchases could be the raw materials you buy from your suppliers to manufacture your products. Or, if you are not a manufacturing business, they would be the items that you purchase to sell on to your customers, having added on your profit margin.

Monthly profit and loss forecast

(for the period 1 January 2012 to 31 December 2012)

		Jan.	*Feb.*	–	*Nov.*	*Dec.*	*Total*
1	SALES (A) less cost of sales	. . .	. . .	–	. . .	. . .	. . .
2	Purchases	. . .	. . .	–	. . .	. . .	. . .
3	Labour	. . .	. . .	–	. . .	. . .	. . .
4	Other direct costs	. . .	. . .	–	. . .	. . .	. . .
	TOTAL (B)	. . .	. . .	–	. . .	. . .	. . .
	GROSS PROFIT (C) Take (B) from (A) less overheads	. . .	. . .	–	. . .	. . .	. . .
5	Rent and rates	. . .	. . .	–	. . .	. . .	. . .
6	Heating/lighting	. . .	. . .	–	. . .	. . .	. . .
7	Telephone	. . .	. . .	–	. . .	. . .	. . .
8	Professional fees	. . .	. . .	–	. . .	. . .	. . .
9	Depreciation	. . .	. . .	–	. . .	. . .	. . .
10	Employee costs	. . .	. . .	–	. . .	. . .	. . .
11	Other overhead expenses	. . .	. . .	–	. . .	. . .	. . .
12	Drawings	. . .	. . .	–	. . .	. . .	. . .
13	Interest	. . .	. . .	–	. . .	. . .	. . .
	TOTAL (D)	. . .	. . .	–	. . .	. . .	. . .
14	Plus miscellaneous income (E)	. . .	. . .	–	. . .	. . .	. . .
15	NET PROFIT (F) BALANCE (C) + (E) – (D)	. . .	. . .	–	. . .	. . .	. . .

The figure you put in your profit and loss account will be different from the cash flow figures for payments to suppliers and cash purchases. For the profit calculation, you need the sum of the invoices you receive in the period for materials.

Another way of working out the purchase figure for this forecast is to say it is what you pay for supplies in the period plus what you owe at the end of the period less what you owed at the start of the period.

If you are registered for VAT, you do not include the figure for VAT that you are charged by your supplier for your profit forecast. If you are not registered for VAT, you do include the figure for VAT.

Points to look out for when you are forecasting costs include:

■ make sure that the level of costs corresponds to the amount of sales you expect to make.

■ allow for any changes in the prices of raw materials that you can reasonably expect to occur in the period.

3. Cost of sales: labour

Here include the cost of your employees who are directly involved with manufacturing your product. As with purchases, the distinction between staff who are directly involved with production and those who count as overheads can be blurred. On the whole, if you do not think that employees' wages are directly related to the amount of work you have, it may be more satisfactory to include employee costs in overheads.

Remember to include all your employee costs; this implies gross salary, your NI contributions as an employer plus any other costs.

The figures may diverge slightly from those in the cash flow forecast, as PAYE and NI contributions are due the following month. Differences will show up only when you first take on an employee or their salary rises.

4. Cost of sales: other direct costs

Estimate here any other direct costs that you foresee.

5. Overheads: rent and rates

In the profit forecast, the total for rates should be spread evenly over the whole year. With rent, you should enter the cost for each period, which may not coincide with the timing of the payments.

6. Overheads: heating/lighting

You need an estimate for the cost of heating and lighting that you will use in each period. Usually you're billed quarterly. This is the case even if you have chosen to pay monthly by direct debit, in which case the quarterly bill is set against the sum of your monthly payments.

7. Overheads: telephone

The treatment of the telephone is similar to that for heating and lighting.

8. Overheads: professional fees

The figure to include here is what it costs you in legal and accounting fees. You should include the cost in the period in which the work is done for you, even if you do not receive the bill until the next period.

9. Overheads: depreciation

Depreciation is what you deduct from the value of an asset to reflect the fact that it is wearing out. This is an item that does not appear in the cash flow forecast. You work it out by taking the value of capital equipment at the start of each period and estimating a figure for its depreciation during the period. Typically, cars and office equipment are written off over three, four or five years.

Note that you do not put in the profit forecast what you pay for capital equipment, which does appear in the cash flow forecast.

10. Overheads: employee costs

This should be your estimate of employee costs that are not directly related to the volume of your sales, see p. 239.

11. Overheads: other overhead expenses

Include overhead expenses not slotted in elsewhere.

12. Overheads: drawings

What you pay yourself.

13. Overheads: interest

Estimate the interest on loans and overdrafts during the year.

14. Miscellaneous income

Put here an estimate of the other income you might receive, not as a result of the sales of your products. For example, if you have money invested, it might include interest.

15. Working out the net profit figure

You can work out a gross profit figure (C) by deducting the figure for direct costs (B) from the sales figure (A). On p. 334 you will see how you can use the gross profit figure to work out the break-even point for your business.

Once you have arrived at an estimate for gross profit, deduct the figure for overheads (D) and add on the amount of any miscellaneous income (E) to give your forecast net profit level (F).

Balance sheet forecast

A balance sheet for your business will show what you owe and what you are owed on one particular day. A forecast one will show your estimate of that picture at the end of the period.

There is more about accounting records needed to produce the right information for a balance sheet once you are in business in Chapter 29, 'Keeping the record straight'. Your accountant should be willing to help if you find it difficult to produce a balance sheet yourself. If your business is likely to be fairly small-scale and you are only approaching your bank manager, and for a fairly modest sum, a forecast balance sheet may not be necessary.

In this section there are brief guidelines on how to work out what the balance sheet might be at the end of the period, once the forecast cash flow and profit and loss account are drawn up. And on p. 314 there is a blank balance sheet forecast for you to complete.

Detailed calculation for balance sheet forecast

One important check on your balance sheet figures is to note that the figure for total assets should equal the figure for capital and liabilities together.

1. Fixed assets

These figures are fairly straightforward to work out. You know from your cash flow forecast when you plan to buy particular bits of equipment. Include all equipment that you have received before the end of the period, even if you have not paid for it. A fixed asset is something of a permanent nature, likely to remain in use in your business for some time.

The value you put in here is not just what you paid for the equipment; you also have to allow for the fact that it will have depreciated since the period started. You can obtain the figure for depreciation from your profit forecast. Deduct these figures from the appropriate cost of each piece of equipment, or written-down value at the start of the period, and enter the figures here.

Example

Richard Petworth is working out the depreciation for the office furniture he has bought for his business. There are a number of different ways of calculating this, but for office furniture he thinks he will write off the value in equal lumps over five years; this is called straight-line depreciation.

The furniture cost Richard £2,000. This means he writes off £400 from the value of it each accounting year. The written-down value at the end of the first accounting year is £1,600.

2. Current assets

The main current assets you are likely to have in your business are:

■ cash.

■ debtors (that is, what your customers owe you).

■ stock (that is, products you have in store, either raw materials to make your product, half-finished products or unsold finished products).

Take the figure for cash straight from your cash flow forecast.

You can derive the figure for debtors from the cash flow and profit forecasts. You will have made some assumption about number of units sold in each month and how quickly you will be paid your cash. From this you can calculate how much you would be owed for sales by your customers at the end of each period. Remember to include VAT if you are registered.

The figure for stock can also be derived from the other two forecasts. Count as stock all goods received from your suppliers to be used in your product but not yet used in products sold, even if you have not yet paid your suppliers' bills. These should be shown at their 'cost' to you.

3. Capital

Put here the capital you used to start your business. The figure for profit and loss you take from your profit forecast. It is the cumulative figure at the end of the period. If you forecast a loss, put it in brackets and it will be deducted from your capital.

Example

Betty Crop and Roger Cartwright are planning to start a knitwear business on 1 January. Their aim is to design knitwear and sell in small quantities (five to ten) to boutiques. Later they hope to produce in bigger quantities selling to department stores. The knitwear will be produced by outworkers.

The final price of the knitwear in the shops will be £90–£120, but Betty and Roger will receive £50–£60. The average cost of the raw materials will be £12 and they will pay each outworker £10 for each garment, on average. They have to take into account seasonal changes in sales, although they will design a range of cotton knitwear for the summer.

They will have to buy raw materials in advance on 30 days' credit and pay each outworker on completion of each garment. They will sell to the boutiques on 30 days' credit, but realistically will allow for an average 60 days' credit in their cash flow forecast.

At first they will work from home, but later in the year would like 500-sq. ft offices – they hope to get light industrial premises at £12 a sq. ft on the outskirts of London. When they have premises they would like to employ someone for clerical work and organizing the outworkers, leaving themselves free to design and sell.

Given their forecast level of sales, Betty and Roger do not need to register for VAT. They produce cash flow (p. 310) and profit and loss forecasts (p. 312) to see how the business will shape up.

Conclusions:

Betty and Roger should take advice before going ahead with their business; their idea is not viable as it is currently presented, especially with the increase in overheads (rent for premises and assistant's wages) in the second half of the year. They would certainly need to put in more money but, even then, unless they can increase their sales figures, the long-term prospects must be fairly negative.

4. Liabilities

Loans from the bank or another lender that are not due to be repaid within one year are medium- or long-term liabilities. Current liabilities are mainly:

- overdraft.
- tax payable, including VAT.
- creditors (that is, what you owe your suppliers at the end of the period).

The figure for overdraft can be taken from your cash flow forecast.

If you have made a profit in the period, you will need to estimate what tax will be payable. You may also have to include a figure for what you owe HMRC in VAT (if you are owed VAT, you should have an entry in the current assets section for this).

In the same way as you worked out debtors, so creditors can be estimated using the two other forecasts. It is the value of the amount of goods you have that you have not yet paid for.

Cash flow forecast

(for 1 January 2012 to 31 December 2012)

	Jan.	Feb.	Mar.	Apr.	May	Jun.
Opening balance	–	9,820	7,970	8,330	9,060	8,880
Sales	–	–	1,900	1,900	1,350	1,350
Capital	12,000	–	–	–	–	–
Total: Cash receipts	12,000	–	1,900	1,900	1,350	1,350
Raw materials	380	380	270	270	110	760
Outworkers	350	350	250	250	100	700
Capital equipment	600	–	–	–	–	350
Stationery/labels	200	–	200	–	200	–
Heating/lighting	–	70	70	–	70	70
Telephone	–	300	–	–	300	–
Bank	–	–	–	–	–	–
Rent and rates	–	–	–	–	–	1,500
Assistant	–	–	–	–	–	–
Car expenses	50	150	150	50	150	50
Drawings	600	600	600	600	600	600
Total: Cash payments	2,180	1,850	1,540	1,170	1,530	4,030
Closing balance	9,820	7,970	8,330	9,060	8,880	6,200

	Jul.	Aug.	Sep.	Oct.	Nov.	Dec.	Totals
Opening balance	6,200	3,955	1,624	(2,693)	(4,974)	(1,791)	
Sales	550	550	550	550	6,500	7,350	22,550
Capital	–	–	–	–	–	–	12,000
Total: Cash receipts	550	550	550	550	6,500	7,350	34,550
Raw materials	760	760	870	870	870	760	7,060
Outworkers	700	700	800	800	800	700	6,500
Capital equipment	–	–	–	–	–	–	950
Stationery/labels	200	–	200	–	200	–	1,200
Heating/lighting	–	–	400	–	–	400	1,080
Telephone	–	300	–	–	300	–	1,200
Bank	5	21	47	61	47	34	215
Rent and rates	50	50	1,500	50	50	1,500	4,700
Assistant	400	400	400	400	400	400	2,400
Car expenses	80	50	50	50	50	50	930
Drawings	600	600	600	600	600	600	7,200
Total: Cash payments	2,795	2,881	4,867	2,831	3,317	4,444	33,435
Closing balance	3,955	1,624	(2,693)	(4,974)	(1,791)	1,115	

Profit and loss forecast

(for 1 January 2012 to 31 December 2012)

	Jan.	Feb.	Mar.	Apr.	May	Jun.
Sales	1,900	1,900	1,350	1,350	550	550
less *Direct costs*						
Raw materials	380	270	270	110	760	760
Labour	350	350	250	250	100	700
Total direct costs	730	620	520	360	860	1,460
Gross profit	1,170	1,280	830	990	(310)	(910)
less *Overheads*						
Rent and rates	–	–	–	–	–	671
Heating/lighting	56	56	56	56	56	56
Telephone	100	100	100	100	100	100
Stationery/labels	100	100	100	100	100	100
Administrative staff	–	–	–	–	–	–
Bank	–	–	–	–	–	–
Depreciation	68	68	68	68	68	73
Car expenses	78	78	78	78	78	78
Total overheads	402	402	402	402	402	1,078
Net profit	768	878	428	588	(712)	(1,988)

	Jul.	Aug.	Sep.	Oct.	Nov.	Dec.	Totals
Sales	550	550	6,500	7,350	7,350	5,400	35,300
less *Direct costs*							
Raw materials	760	870	870	870	760	940	7,620
Labour	700	700	800	800	800	700	6,500
Total direct costs	1,460	1,570	1,670	1,670	1,560	1,640	14,120
Gross profit	(910)	(1,020)	4,830	5,680	5,790	3,760	21,180
less *Overheads*							
Rent and rates	672	671	672	671	672	671	4,700
Heating/lighting	134	134	134	134	134	134	1,140
Telephone	100	100	100	100	100	100	1,200
Stationery/labels	100	100	100	100	100	100	1,200
Administrative staff	400	400	400	400	400	400	2,400
Bank	5	21	47	61	47	34	215
Depreciation	73	73	73	73	73	73	851
Car expenses	78	78	78	78	78	78	936
Total overheads	1,562	1,577	1,604	1,617	1,604	1,590	12,642
Net profit	(2,472)	(2,597)	3,226	4,063	4,186	2,170	8,538

Balance sheet forecast

(on 31 December 2011)

ASSETS

---

1 Fixed assets

Freehold property	£......	
Leasehold property	£......	
Office equipment	£......	
Vehicles	£......	
Plant/machinery	£......	
Other equipment	£......	
Total fixed assets (A)		£......

2 Current assets

Cash in hand and at bank	£......	
Stock	£......	
Debtors	£......	
Total current assets (B)		£......
Total assets (A) + (B)		£......
Capital and liabilities		

3 Capital

Shareholders'/proprietor's capital	£......	
Profit and loss	£......	
Total capital (C)		£......

4 Medium-term liabilities

Loans	£......	

5 Current liabilities

Overdraft	£......	
Tax payable	£......	
Creditors	£......	
Total liabilities (D)		£......
Total capital and liabilities (C) + (D)	£......	

Summary

1 Forecasts are very important if you make commitments on the basis that the figures are reasonably accurate.
2 Make the forecasts conservative.
3 A cash flow forecast is not the same as a profit and loss forecast.
4 If you find it difficult to produce the forecasts, ask for help, for example from a Business Link (or equivalent organization) or an accountant.
5 The treatment of VAT and depreciation need special attention.
6 Once you have the forecasts, use them to assess how viable your business will be and whether you will be able to make a living from it.

Other chapters to read

6 The business plan (p. 66); 25 Raising the money (p. 316); 29 Keeping the record straight (p. 370).

25

Raising the money

Raising money needs careful planning, like a military campaign. You should regard it as the biggest sale you are ever likely to make. You need to get your act together to present your case. You need to know how much money you want, who to approach, how long you want the money for, and what security you can offer backers. You also need to know the business plan, the financial figures and the marketplace inside out.

But that is not all. You should expect indifference, lack of interest, disbelief and doubt. You have to convince, persuade and excite sober, serious business people about the prospects for your business. This cannot be achieved by overstatement or rash predictions about success. Demonstrations of competence and skill are what is required.

Of course, a few strike lucky. There may be the odd story about bank managers agreeing overdrafts over the telephone, or someone being able to pick and choose from a variety of backers who all want to put up the funds. But for most it is a hard, hard job – and never more so than in the current climate. Following the global financial crisis, banks seem to have retrenched. They are concerned to restore the strength of their own balance sheets and appear very cautious about lending to small and medium-sized businesses. To help the economy get back to normal growth levels, the government has carved out a deal with the five largest UK banks called Project Merlin. It requires the banks to meet targets for lending to business. So far, lending has fallen short of these targets. The banks claim that this is not their fault: they have made the lending available but there is a lack of demand from businesses. The Federation of Small Businesses does not disagree but claims that the high cost of bank lending is putting small firms off and that greater competition is needed in the banking sector. The government has threatened to impose tax sanctions on the big banks if they do not lend more, so possibly there may be some easing of lending conditions and costs as 2011 progresses.

What is in this chapter?

This chapter looks at:

■ *money*: it explains how much you should consider raising (see below), what it is for (p. 319) and what type you want, for example loans or shares or both (p. 319).

■ *lenders and investors*: it considers how much you and your family can provide (p. 322), what the government, local authorities, charities and so on can do (p. 324), what banks offer (p. 327), what can be obtained from private investors (p. 329) and what venture capital funds do (p. 329).

■ *the presentation*: how to do it (p. 331).

The money

How much money? What should you ask for?

Only when you have drawn up your business plan and done your cash flow and profit forecasts will you know how much money, if any, you need to raise. Take a few deep breaths before you rush round to make an appointment with your bank manager to see if you can get the overdraft you need. First, your bank is not always your first port of call, as you can see from later pages in this chapter. Second, you should take a further, closer, more critical look at the amount of money you think you will need.

Being optimistic, as anyone starting a business must be, you naturally believe you are going to make the sales you have projected on the timescale you estimated and keep the costs down to your forecast figures. But supposing things do not work quite as you hope. Going back to your lender and asking for more money within a short space of time does not inspire confidence, and you may find your second request rejected, if it is not part of your plan. And there you are with a new business to which you have committed time and money, which is now short of cash, and you are unlikely to find any way of raising more.

There is a body of opinion that says when you first approach your lender or investor, ask for twice as much money as you think you will need. At any rate, be very conservative and go for more money than you think you are going to use. Obviously, the business plans that you present need to tie up with your request for cash, so adjust them if need be, incorporating more conservative figures.

There are drawbacks. First, if your figures are too conservative, it may make your business proposition unviable altogether; if this happens, you do not need to worry about being forced to go back for more, your business will not even get off the ground in the first place, because you will not get the initial backing. The second obstacle to this approach is that it is the natural inclination of any investor to try to make you manage with less money than you say you need.

The sensible advice is to steer a middle course: be pessimistic, while retaining a sensible business proposal.

At this stage, you know more than ever before about your proposed business and are likely to be very committed to it. But if the business does not look right, do not be afraid of ditching this plan and looking for a better one. You probably have only one chance of raising money for a business proposal, so do not choose a failure because it was your first idea.

For many people, this is the first point at which you are really learning what makes a business tick. One sign of a successful entrepreneur is that you can learn from your information and experience and can adapt. You want to go for calculated, but good, risks. If you have already started trading, your business course is set.

Large sums of money

There is another odd fact about raising money: different sums of money can be harder or easier to find, depending simply on their size. Surprisingly, it is sometimes said to be much easier to find very large sums of money for your business (£2 million plus) than sums in the £20,000 to £1 million range (these figures are an indication only; there are always exceptions). This quirk of business funding is of no interest to the vast bulk of people who want to become self-employed or start a business in a small way but, if your plans are on a larger scale, think about being bigger still.

This oddity occurs because there appear to be more people around who are willing to invest in either small businesses that are past the start-up stage (that is, not brand new) and into a big expansion phase or in new businesses that look capable of very fast growth in profits. To achieve either of these objectives, the amount of money invested needs to be substantial to stand any chance of success. Other preconditions for success, apart from large funds, are a very strong management team and a sound market. If you cannot demonstrate that both of these apply to you and your business, your chances of raising very large sums of money are virtually nil.

The money: what is it for?

From your forecasts, you should have an indication of when your need for extra cash arises, how long it lasts for and when you would be able to pay it back or give a good return on it. When starting up, you need money for:

■ the 'once-in-a-business-lifetime' expenses of setting up. These include what you have to spend on your premises, on IT equipment and furniture, on legal and professional costs, and on initial marketing expenditure.

■ working capital. This is what you need to keep yourself going in the time gap between paying out cash for raw materials or stocks and getting in cash from the people you sell to. All businesses need working capital; the amount varies depending on the type of business, the credit terms you can negotiate from suppliers and the credit you extend to customers.

The longer you can get your suppliers to wait for their payment and the shorter the period you allow your customers to pay, the less working capital you need. Your working capital requirements will also be less if you do not need to hold big stocks of goods.

In practice, all these things are easier said than done and you need to work out a strategy for controlling your business that meets your need to keep down the money tied up with working capital, coupled with keeping your suppliers and customers happy. This is covered in more detail in Chapter 26, 'Staying afloat'.

If your business is up and running, you may need funds simply because it is growing and hence the amount of working capital necessary has gone up. Or you may have some specific expansion in mind.

The money: what type do you want?

Overdrafts

If your need for the money is likely to be fairly short-term, an overdraft or some sort of short-term loan is your likeliest bet. Your need for finance in the short term could be to cover a temporary shortage of cash, or it could cover your start-up requirements if these are fairly small.

An overdraft is quick to arrange and relatively cheap, but there will be an upper limit above which you are not to go without the permission of the bank manager. The serious drawback with an overdraft is that the bank can demand instant repayment. While this does not happen very often, you can bet that if the bank does demand repayment or reduction of the overdraft, this will occur when you cannot do so.

If there are no assets, such as debtors, to be taken as security for the overdraft, it is likely that your bank manager will require that you give some personal assets or, less likely, a personal guarantee as security even if you have formed a limited company. One benefit of getting substantial funding is that as a result of the strong balance sheet, personal guarantees, although asked for, can sometimes be avoided.

As a self-employed person you are personally liable anyway, so no further guarantees are needed. In the extreme, this means that if you cannot repay an overdraft, your bank could take you personally to court to recover its money and your personal as well as business assets could be seized.

Note that banks may be wary of taking stocks as security for an overdraft. The manager may insist on property or debtors as the only acceptable security. Always negotiate about the level of security needed; it is in your interests to give up as little as possible.

Coping with a difficult economy – financing schemes

The global banking crisis, subsequent recession and continuing economic difficulties have caused a shortage of bank lending to UK businesses. To tackle this, the government has introduced a number of schemes, including:

- *Enterprise Finance Guarantee.* The government will guarantee 75 per cent of loans by participating banks to viable businesses with turnover of less than £25 million. It covers loans between £1,000 and £1 million. This scheme is due to run until 2014–15. Contact your bank.

- *Export Credits Guarantee Department Letters of Credit Scheme.* The government will share risks with banks providing short-term letters of credit to facilitate export trading. Contact your bank.

To find out about these and other funding schemes, contact Business Link* (England) or the equivalent organizations in other parts of the UK.

Business Link also offers a Financial Intermediary Service that can help if you have been turned down for a bank loan. The service can help you review your case for funding and look at ways to strengthen your relationship with your bank.

Longer-term loans

If you know at the outset that you are unlikely to be able to repay the money you want to raise in the short term, a longer-term source of finance might be the answer (p. 329).

Selling shares

If you have formed a limited company, you may be willing to sell some of the shares in return for an investment in the business. If you do this, it means you will lose some of the potential gains you might get as a result of the shares increasing in value as the profits of the business grow. This is what an outside investor is looking for. The aim is generally to get a good return on the money invested through the shares increasing in value, rather than a stream of income from the business in the form of dividends.

An outside investor, such as a venture capital fund, will at some stage want to sell the shares to realize the profits. If you are hoping to raise money in this way, put in your plan that you intend to have your company floated on the stock market, the Alternative Investment Market (AIM) or PLUS Markets*, say, or that you would like to sell the company, as most venture capital funds want to be invested in a business for a fairly short period, typically three to seven years. Other potential outside investors include 'business angels' – many of these are people who have made money from their own businesses and are looking to invest both finance and expertise in other new or small businesses.

The value you can obtain for your shares, if you are a new company, is a very vexed question. Frankly, they are not worth very much yet, so you might find that you are having to sell a bigger proportion of the shares than you would like to raise the money you need. This can lead to problems about voting control. What the value of the shares is can lead to a lot of haggling.

Opting for this route to raise money needs professional help; you need, perhaps, accountants*, solicitors* and financial advisers*. Ask for references from these professionals to help you to steer clear of rank unprofessionals.

Taking partners

If you have started out as a sole trader but need to raise additional capital, you could do this by taking a partner. What share of the profits each partner gets in return for the capital put in is a subject to be negotiated. There also needs to be clarity about the management role each partner will have. For your own sake, you should do this before you form the partnership. A written partnership agreement is a must (p. 49). A limited liability partnership (p. 49) allows you to work out how you want to divide rewards without making it public, while giving the protection of limited liability.

Lenders and investors

You and your family

The first fact you must come to terms with is that if you do not invest in your business idea, you cannot expect anyone else to do so. As a rough rule of thumb, the absolute most you will probably be able to raise from outsiders is five times as much money as you are putting in yourself, but, needless to say, there are always exceptions. If you are planning a substantial business and looking to raise £1 million or more, say, you may find that investors will put up ten or 20 times as much as you. But normally, you can expect someone to match your own investment, or put up two or three times as much as you do as a maximum. But in the worst case, it could be nothing.

Example

> Winston Carpenter has £10,000 to invest in his business. He works out from his forecasts and his business plan that he needs to raise more money. He is unlikely to be able to raise an extra £50,000 or more, but with a good presentation of his idea, he may persuade someone to lend or invest £20,000, say.

The rationale behind this insistence on how much you must invest yourself is that lenders, such as banks, and investors, such as venture capital funds, want you to be committed to your business, to make you work very hard and with great determination to be successful. If you have not risked the proportion of capital they would like, they may doubt your commitment. However, if you can point to the fact that even though it is a low proportion of the total invested in your business, the sum of money you are investing is still a sizeable proportion of your own personal assets, you could be convincing.

Where are you going to get your share of the money?

If you have money tucked away somewhere, or if you have a lump sum as a result of being made redundant, this is a relatively easy question to answer.

Another common source of the money for your stake is to be given or lent it by someone in your family. But being financed by your family can lead to heartache if things start to go wrong. So do not enter on this course lightheartedly. Conversely, you are more likely to convince your family than anyone else.

Another possible way of raising your share of the funds is to use your personal assets to act as security (for example, a second mortgage on your home) or by giving a personal guarantee. The drawback with this is that if your business fails, you have to find the money to carry on making your repayments, or you have to sell your home. You must give careful consideration before giving personal guarantees or using your home to raise money in this way for your business, and the bank may insist that you first take legal advice.

It would make sense to have some sort of agreed family plan for what would happen if your business failed. For example, you should discuss openly whether you are ready to sell your house and move to a smaller one should the security be called upon to repay your loan. If you cannot have some sort of strategy in your domestic life that is acceptable in return for the prospect of going it alone, you are likely to have family problems when the inevitable pressures mount on the business.

You can get tax relief on these loans. If you are a sole trader or partner, any interest you pay on a loan for business purposes is allowable as a deduction against tax in working out your taxable profits. If you take on a loan to invest or lend money to a close company (most family companies are) you can get tax relief at your highest rate of tax on the interest you pay. To be eligible for this tax relief, you must either own more than 5 per cent of the shares or own some shares and work for the greater part of your time for the company.

When should you put in your money?

The best advice is not necessarily to start your business straight away, investing your money and subsequently approaching other investors later when you need it. The wisest course may be to prepare your forecasts and your business plans and to approach possible sources of finance before you start your business and before you actually need the extra money. To plan ahead and get a commitment in advance can be crucial.

The reason why this could be the best approach is that investors have a couple of infuriating habits. The first is to ask what money you are going to put in when they put in their share. You may be able to point out that you invested £10,000, say, six months ago and since then have worked without drawing any salary, but investors are likely to be unimpressed. That is water under the bridge and may count for nothing as far as they are concerned. The second is for them to adopt an attitude of 'wait and see' how the business develops, while the cash is running out and you are under great pressure to raise more. In this way better deals can be struck for the investor. So do not necessarily rush out and use up your money, if you know you will need extra funds in due course; get your financial backing in advance.

Government, local authorities, charities, CDFIs

You may be able to get grants, allowances, cheap loans or prizes from a variety of sources, including central government or the local authority for the area in which you are based or wish to locate, charities, such as The Prince's Trust* (see p. 37) and, to stimulate regeneration in deprived areas, community development finance institutions (CDFIs). Grants and other funding are often targeted at:

- *specific types of spending*: for example, research and development, property renovation or purchase of equipment.
- *specific areas*: particularly deprived rural or urban areas – see Chapter 17, 'Choosing your workplace'.
- *particular types of business*: say, farming or post offices. In areas of high unemployment, funding may be targeted at encouraging micro-businesses (very small firms, such as one-man plumbers or decorators) to start up.
- *particular types of business person*: for example, young people, women, people from ethnic minorities, the unemployed, older people.

All funding bodies receive far more requests than they can meet, so it is essential that you tailor each application to show how your project will meet the specified aims of the particular body.

Business Link*, Business Gateway*, Highlands and Islands Enterprise*, Business Wales*, Invest NI* and LEAs* have funding direc-tories you can search to find out what grants and other sources are available in your area for your type of business and project. They can also help you to apply.

From April 2011, government support for business in England has been rationalized and now focuses on 13 schemes, collectively called Solutions for Business. Information about all these schemes and how to apply is available through Business Link and, where applicable, through the web sites listed below. In brief, they are:

■ Collaboration Research and Development. Grants between £10,000 and £100 million to fund up to half of projects that bring together industry and researchers.

■ Designing Demand. Ten days' mentoring over six to 18 months on design and innovation. The scheme is aimed at small and medium-sized enterprises (SMEs) with high growth potential. Some parts of the package are free; with others, you would be expected to make a contribution.

■ Finance for Business. Loans of up to £250,000 or finance up to £2 million in return for an equity stake for SMEs that have tried and failed to get commercial finance. Aimed at new and fast-growing businesses that lack a track record.

■ Grant for Research and Development. Grants of £10,000 to £500,000 to test and advance technologically innovative products and processes. Grants cover 35 to 60 per cent of the project costs. Aimed at pre-start and start-up SMEs. Visit *www.innovateuk.org.*

■ Helping Your Business Grow Internationally. Advice from an experienced international trade adviser to help you start or improve exporting, either free or at a subsidized rate. Also the possibility of grants for market research, overseas trade visits, participating in trade fairs and so on. See *www.ukti.gov.uk.*

■ High Growth Coaching. Ten days' business coaching over six to 18 months to assess an SME's potential for growth and develop plans and actions to achieve it. Free or subsidized.

■ Improving Your Resource Efficiency. Package of tools, advice, on-site support, loans and grants to spread best practice in energy and resource efficiency. Some elements of the package are free, others low-cost. You would typically need to provide matched funding for any grants.

■ Knowledge Transfer Partnerships. Aim to help SMEs access knowledge and skills from experts in universities, research organizations and further education institutions. One or more experts join each partnership which typically lasts one to three years. SME contributes one-third of the cost of the expert and a grant covers the rest. See *www.ktponline.org.uk.*

- Manufacturing Advisory Service. Specialist support on processes used in manufacturing. Much of this is free. Longer-term help is available to SMEs at a discounted rate. Visit *www.mas.bis.gov.uk*.

- Networking for Innovation. Access to national networks covering technology and business to stimulate knowledge transfer. To join, go to *https://ktn.innovateuk.org/web/guest/home*.

- Rural Development Programme for England*. Business support for farmers, foresters, landowners and other rural businesses. Cost is determined on a case-by-case basis. See *www.rdpenetwork.org.uk*.

- Understanding Finance for Business. Free specialist advice on the options for funding a start up or growing your business.

- Work Place Training (including Apprenticeships*). Partial or full funding to train apprentices, increase literacy and numeracy skills of employees, or help SMEs to develop management and leadership skills. For information about the apprenticeship scheme, go to *www.apprenticeships.org.uk*.

Similar types of government support exist in Scotland and Northern Ireland, for example:

- **Scotland**. Scottish Enterprise* administers government finance and grant schemes to promote business. There are several strands with a variety of schemes within each strand. For example, a key scheme within the innovation, research and development strand is SMART: SCOTLAND. This can provide up to three-quarters of the cost (to a maximum £70,000) of feasibility studies and up to 35 per cent of the cost (up to £600,000) of developing prototypes. The Scottish Investment Bank supports a number of private-sector schemes for lending to business, including the Scottish Seed Fund which can provide grants between £20,000 and £100,000 for start ups and young businesses that are launching new products, entering new markets or expanding employment. There is also funding available for premises construction, plant and machinery, marketing and so on, if you operate within specified sectors, such as construction, energy, food and drink, forest and timber, life sciences or tourism.

- **Northern Ireland**. Government support is provided through the government agency, Invest NI*. Financial assistance is focused primarily on businesses that aim to sell outside Northern Ireland, are actively pursuing growth and can show that they will contribute to productivity and innovation in Northern Ireland. Start ups may be eligible for financial help with the costs of marketing, consultancy, employment and working capital. To help businesses grow, Invest NI has, for example, programmes aimed at skills development (which can include funding to develop skills projects, hire trainers, and cover materials and trainees' expenses), business and marketing strategies (which can include funding to scope and develop a business plan and employ non-executives who can contribute to the strategy), and capital expenditure. Other schemes foster networking, knowledge exchange and working collaboratively in order to promote research and development and joint ventures. Contact Invest NI for information and application forms.

The situation if your business is located in Wales is rather different. In mid-2010, the Welsh Assembly Government published a new strategy for its economy. This included shifting the focus of its business support to technology and innovation and concentrating resources on six specific sectors: information and communications technology, energy and environment, advanced materials and manufacturing, creative industries, life sciences, and financial and professional services. Moreover, the Welsh Government has decided to move away from providing direct grants to business. Instead it will focus on creating the infrastructure that businesses need and ensuring access to private-sector commercial funding. At the individual business level, it offers holistic support based on advice, collaboration, and fostering networks between business and universities and other research organizations. In general, any funding the Welsh Government does provide will be refundable rather than in the form of outright grants.

Banks

Your bank manager is an obvious port of call, but not always the best or the one you should make first of all. Following the 'credit crunch' and the onset of recession, banks have been less than cooperative about extending or renewing finance to small businesses – a classic case of taking away the brolly when it starts to rain. The government has introduced a number of schemes (see p. 320) to kick-start banks into lending again. Assuming your bank is willing to lend generally, in more normal times, the advantage of going straight there is that if you have been a creditworthy customer with a good record, your manager should favour your application. And this is what should happen to the vast bulk of people with a good business proposition that is well presented and well researched.

But there are a couple of reasons why you should not head straight there or why you might expect not to secure the money you want. In the first place, your presentation of your plan will improve with the number of times you give it. If your bank manager really is your best possibility and you have not practised your presentation, you might blow the opportunity. It could pay you to approach another bank, simply to practise what you are going to say and be prepared for the questions that will be asked.

The second disadvantage may occur if you are looking to your bank to provide substantial funds. Each branch bank manager has a different discretionary lending limit; above the limit your application may need to be processed elsewhere, so you may lose part of the personal touch on which you were relying for a sympathetic hearing of your case.

The moral is shop around. Do not be put off by being turned down; try another bank or another branch that you think may be more used to business deals. Following a government review of business banking, banks must now make it much easier for you to carry your credit history from one bank to another, making it simpler for you to prove your creditworthiness. Banks must also 'unbundle' their products, so you can get a loan from a bank without being forced to move your current account to that bank. When shopping around, remember to ask what rate you will be charged; compare this with what other banks would charge. Banks can offer money in two ways:

1 Overdrafts (p. 319).
2 Loans.

Loans can be very flexible, and the exact terms vary from bank to bank. You can borrow money for periods of between two and 30 years. The rate of interest can be fixed, variable – a number of percentage points over the bank base rate – or in some cases at a monthly managed rate. Sometimes for larger loans (for example, £15,000 plus) you can negotiate a repayment holiday from repaying the capital you borrow. So for, say, one or two years, you pay only interest. You may also be able to arrange stepped repayments. The amount you can borrow can vary from £1,000 to £1 million. The type of loan you can get depends on the viability of your plan.

You can get a list of members that offer business loans from the Finance and Leasing Association*. The Internet can be a useful tool to help you to compare loans and see what's on offer, because some web sites – for example, *www.moneysupermarket.com* – have comparative tables of loans. Alternatively, use a broker to help you, but stick to members of the National Association of Commercial Finance Brokers*, who must follow a code of practice and have proper complaints procedures.

Private investors

There is a growing body of private investors, often called 'high-net-worth individuals', who are prepared to back business ventures. Sometimes, these people are called 'angels', that is they provide money for risky ventures.

The enterprise investment scheme and capital gains tax reinvestment relief give tax concessions to make it more attractive for private individuals to invest in unquoted companies. With deferral relief, it is possible to put off paying capital gains tax if a private investor sells some shares but reinvests the proceeds in the new shares of a private company.

British Business Angels' Association

The British Business Angels' Association* (BBAA) is a trade body for business angel networks, which are organizations able to back entrepreneurs. The BBAA web site contains a list of members.

Small advertisement sections

There are often ads in newspapers with business-to-business sections, such as the *Guardian*, *The Times*, the *Financial Times* and *The Sunday Times*, from people wanting to invest in new enterprises. Alternatively, you could advertise for funds in the same way, although you have to watch out for various legal restrictions.

Venture capital funds

With a venture capital fund money is put up by pension funds, insurance companies, banks, investment trusts, industrial corporations, regional development agencies and private individuals. Some venture capital funds are set up as venture capital trusts (VCTs), which offer tax concessions to investors and invest the fund in growing companies. Not all of the funds will provide money for people who are starting up; most only provide funds for businesses that are expanding. You can get information about VCTs from the British Private Equity and Venture Capital Association (BVCA)*.

Venture capital funds are looking for companies with very good management, operating in a market that is either very large or is growing fast. The funds want to invest in companies that could reach significant profits within three to four years. Many, but not all, want to be able to sell their investment in three to seven years and hope that the company will have grown enough in that time to be floated on the stock market or be sold to another company. This would allow the funds to sell their shares and turn their gains into cash.

If you approach a venture capital fund, the things to look out for are:

- *quantity of shares*: the fund will normally want ordinary shares in return for the investment, as well as loan capital or preference shares, although there are exceptions. The percentage of shares varies from fund to fund; a few may want over 50 per cent, but it is unusual for a fund to want a majority stake in the company. The percentage of shares is not always affected by the amount of money you want to raise or by the voting structure.

- *board director*: the fund will usually want to have one or two directors on your board, and you will have to bear the cost of this. You will normally be able to approve the choice of director. The fees for a non-executive director can be in the £15,000 to £25,000 range.

- *due diligence*: this is the term for the investigation that a venture capital fund will want to undertake before investing in your company. This can include visiting your offices and other work locations, taking up references from customers, potential customers and past employers, studying your accounts and selling systems, and having your product checked technically. The fund will want you to pay for this investigation; you can negotiate on this. How successful your negotiation will be depends on the level of interest shown by other funds.

- *legal and professional fees*: there are yours and theirs. You will have to pay the legal costs for the funds on top of all your costs for raising finance. You will have legal and accounting fees, running into several thousands, plus the fee paid to a financial adviser, often based on a percentage of the money raised. In total, your share of the costs could run up to 10 per cent or more of the money you raise.

- *syndication*: if you are trying to raise a very large sum of money, a venture capital fund may want a partner or two to provide the funds you wish. This may be because providing the amount of money you want could take up a fairly hefty chunk of the total money it has to invest, or it may just want to spread the risk. You may have to do a lot of the work yourself to bring together funds into a consortium to provide the money. This can prove very tricky and adds considerably to the amount of time it can take you to raise the money.

See p. 320 for an outline of government-backed funding schemes; for information contact Business Link* (England) or the equivalent organizations in other parts of the UK.

Other companies

The corporate venturing scheme was introduced to encourage established companies to invest in small, higher-risk trading companies. The investing company gets 20 per cent corporation tax relief on its investment in ordinary shares of the trading company, provided it holds on to the shares for at least three years. Deferral relief is given on gains where they are used to invest in another trading company under the scheme. And losses can be set against the investing company's income.

For your company to be eligible as the target investment, it must be unquoted at the time the investment is made (and with no firm intention to become listed). If, later on, you do become listed, your company does not cease to qualify. The investing company can take no more than a 30 per cent stake in your business.

The presentation: how to do it

There are a lot of useful tips on how to present your plan scattered through this chapter and Chapter 6, 'The business plan'. The step-by-step guide below draws all these tips together.

1 First impressions are all-important. The first thing prospective lenders and investors will see is your business plan. It must be well presented. It should look comprehensive without being over-detailed (if necessary, information can be put in appendices).
2 Practise your presentation of your plan. Do this by getting a colleague or friend to role-play or see if a counsellor at an enterprise agency will take you through it. If necessary, approach a source of finance that you regard as very low-chance and use it to perfect your technique for those opportunities of which you are very hopeful.
3 The next step will be a face-to-face encounter. Look conventional; the people who have money to lend are middle-of-the-road types, so do not endanger your chances of getting the money by dressing in an odd way.
4 Get the facts at your fingertips. Your plan may look good, but if you sound unsure or muddled about the details, doubts about your management ability may be raised.

5 Be clear in your own mind what is interesting or exciting about your proposal. Do not get so bogged down by the details that you cannot bring out the really important points of your business idea.

6 Find out the names and positions of those who can invest. Try to get the real decision-makers, not their advisers or subordinates.

7 Listen carefully to the questions and make sure you answer what you have been asked.

8 If you are asked for further information, make sure it is as well researched and well presented as the rest of your plan and provide it quickly.

9 Do not be too defensive about your idea; assume beforehand that it will be critically assessed.

Summary

1 Treat negotiating for money with the same planning and thought as making a sale.

2 Be very certain that you ask for the right amount of money; it is very difficult to go round a second time to ask for more.

3 It can be difficult to raise less than £1 million.

4 Overdrafts are for the shorter term; long-term finance is provided by loans or selling shares, if you have a company.

5 As a rule of thumb, you will need to invest as much as an outside investor or perhaps half as much. Rare exceptions have managed to put in a much smaller proportion than an outside investor and still retain control.

6 Securing loans on your house or giving personal guarantees is a major step. Do not take it lightly or without discussing it with your family.

7 Money can be raised from banks, private individuals and companies, venture capital funds, charities or local authorities.

8 Make your presentation carefully. Follow the tips on pp. 331–2.

Other chapters to read

6 The business plan (p. 66); 9 Off the peg (p. 83); 24 Forecasting (p. 295); 27 Moving ahead (p. 351).

26

Staying afloat

You are launched. You have premises, even if it is your own home. You have started selling and now must produce the goods. You may have raised money to help to finance the business. So what next? Staying afloat is the name of the game. Learning to live within the income your sales bring is a hard task, but one that has to be learned. A survey by Dun & Bradstreet found that the most common problem areas contributing towards failure are taking on contracts at too low a price, delays in receiving payments and being caught up in the cash flow problems of a larger company.

For some, it is easy: this could apply to you if your sort of business is consultancy, or design, or some other type of work where the overheads can be contained, at least until the time comes for expansion. For others, there is this point to strive towards before your business is truly afloat. This is known as the break-even point and is the point at which the contribution your sales bring is large enough to cover the overheads of your business, for example rent, rates, telephone and some employee costs.

When you see explanations of the break-even point in textbooks, it seems straightforward. Your business struggles towards the level of sales you find from the laid-down formula and once you have reached there, your business is ticking along nicely. In reality, break-even point is not like that at all. It has a most disconcerting habit of moving; as sales increase, so inevitably do the pressures on the business to get the job done. One way to ease the pressure is to increase the overheads and so the cycle continues. Trying to hit a moving target is notoriously difficult; and so is struggling to break even.

To stay afloat in the longer term requires more than being permanently at break-even; you need profits. These can be used to develop new products and markets as existing ones mature and decline.

These are the problems. What about the solution? Clearly, increasing the quantity and value of the sales are top priorities, as well as containing costs. But these take time. The business needs a breathing space to allow sales to develop. To allow yourself that leeway, you must control the business. And cash control assumes the major role in this. Your business will stay afloat (in the short term) if the money goes around; you hope you can keep it going long enough for sales to reach that moving target and get to break-even. You cannot do it for ever; at some stage, it will be clear that your business must raise more money or it will fail. If you are unable to get more funds, you do not want to reach the point of trading illegally, and you do not want your crash to take other small businesses with you. You have to recognize the warning signs (p. 365).

Any well-run business should be interested in cash control, whether struggling to break even or already well into profit. Making the cash go round more efficiently helps to increase your profits. Controlling cash is essentially a question of controlling debtors (that is, people who owe you money), creditors (that is, people to whom you owe money) and stock (including work in progress).

What is in this chapter?

- break-even point (p. 334).
- the plan to control the business (p. 338).
- cash (p. 339).
- your customers (p. 342).
- your suppliers (p. 347).

Break-even point

One management technique you should get to grips with is break-even point. This assumes extreme importance for the sort of business that makes losses initially; possibly, you may raise money to cover that loss-making period or find it yourself. What you are working towards is the point at which the contribution (strictly, gross margin) that you make from sales is sufficient to cover the overheads (also called indirect or fixed costs).

Overheads are the cost of setting up the structure of your business. For example, the cost of your premises does not rise and fall with the quantity of sales you are making. In the long run, you could move to cheaper premises, but this is a major upheaval. In the meantime, this overhead cost is fixed. The value of your sales needs to be built up to the level that contributes to the expense of the premises.

Other examples of overheads are insurance, the cost of equipment – such as cars and computers – heating and lighting, and the telephone. One vexed problem is whether employees are a fixed cost or not. For most businesses, they will be, certainly for a few months (see p. 239 for more about the cost effect of employing people).

How to work out your break-even point

To do this you need to know:

■ gross profit margin.

■ total cost of overheads.

If your product or service is the same item sold many times, you can work out the gross profit (or contribution) on each item sold. The gross profit on each item is the selling price less the direct cost of each item. Direct costs are those items that you only have to pay for because you make a product or provide a service, for example raw materials.

However, if the product can vary, work out the gross profit for one month's sales, say, and use this to find your gross profit margin.

The formula for break-even point of sales is:

$$\frac{\text{Overheads}}{\text{Price of product} - \text{direct cost of product}}$$

This gives you the number of items you must sell to cover the overhead costs, see Example 1 below.

or

$$\frac{\text{Overheads}}{\text{Gross profit margin}} \times 100$$

Gross profit margin is the gross profit divided by the value of sales times 100. This formula gives you the value of sales you must make to cover the overhead costs; see Example 2.

Example 1

Robert Atherton sells quantities of paper cleaning cloths. He buys them in large rolls, cuts them and distributes them as duster-size (12 to each packet). He has worked out the direct cost of each packet of 12 as 10p and sells them for 26p. Thus, gross profit on each packet of 12 is 16p. His overheads are £6,000 in the year, £500 a month. His break-even sales of packets of 12 cloths each month are:

$$\frac{£500}{£0.16} = 3,125 \text{ packets}$$

Example 2

Jane Edwards runs a web design company. Each web site depends on the customer's requirements and the cheapest is likely to be £5,000. For her business plan for the next 12 months, Jane has worked out the number of web sites she is likely to design. For the year, sales are estimated at £300,000 and the direct costs, that is, hardware, software and so on, are forecast to be £120,000.

Gross profit margin is:

$$\frac{£300,000 - £120,000}{£300,000} \times 100 = 60\%$$

The overheads of the business are estimated at £108,000 for the next year, that is, £9,000 a month.

The break-even level of sales for each month is:

$$\frac{£9,000}{60} \times 100 = £15,000$$

Diagrams 26.1 and 26.2 may help you to gain a better understanding of break-even. The level line shows the estimated level of overheads. The dotted line that starts at point O shows the amount of the direct costs for each level of sales. Total costs (line starts at A) are the sum of the direct costs and the overheads.

The continuous sloping line starting at O shows the value of sales at different levels of units sold. X is the break-even point. To the left of X, your business is making a loss; to the right, your business is making a profit.

Diagram 26.1 assumes that the level of overheads stays the same no matter what the level of sales you can make. Frankly, this is difficult to achieve in practice. Once you start doing more business, you may well find that your overheads will go up too. For example, you may find you need more secretarial help, given the increased amount of sales you are making. In Diagram 26.2, you can see the effect on break-even point if there is an increase in overheads for the same business as below. Point X is now further to the right in Diagram 26.2 compared with Diagram 26.1. The break-even sales figure is now higher.

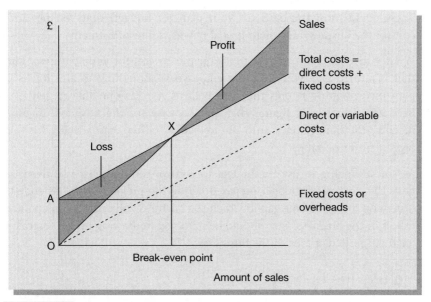

Diagram 26.1 Finding the break-even point of your business

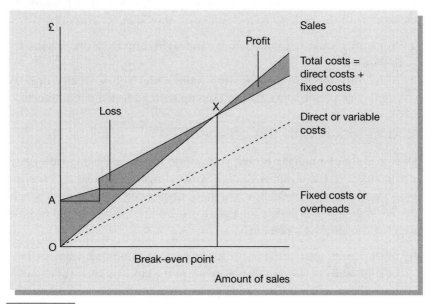

Diagram 26.2 How an increase in fixed costs moves the break-even point upwards

The plan to control the business

When you produced your business plan before you started your business (p. 66), you incorporated some forecasts: profit and loss and cash flow. These could form the basis for your plan (or budget) that you need to control the business, although probably with some adjustments.

What you need for a budget that you use to control your business, but that is also to give you (and any employees) something to aim for, is a plan incorporating figures that you believe you may be able to achieve. Be wary of including figures that are too easy for the business, in case meeting the budget turns into the objective, rather than striving for the biggest profit possible.

As you are going to use the budget to control the business, you need to have the next year's budget prepared before the previous year has ended, otherwise there is a time gap in which the business will drift. If you employ others in the business, they should be involved in drawing up the forecasts for their particular area of the business.

How to use the budget

Every month, as soon as possible after the end of it and not later than a fortnight after, you should have the actual profit, cost and cash figures to compare with the budget. Your comparison should be for two reasons:

1 To identify what has gone wrong, and right, and to derive lessons for the future.
2 To identify problem areas for the future, which may emerge only as your actual performance fails to keep up with budgeted performance.

Keeping in touch with the business

Once you start employing others, you will no longer be dealing with every single aspect of the business yourself. Once others have areas of responsibility, you will need to devise a system of management reporting. There is no one system that is perfect for a particular business, but it should include some of the following elements:

■ *weekly reports*: these could be verbal, for example a meeting. They need to be sufficiently detailed so that everyone in the business knows as a result their objectives for the next week and what is on the critical path to allow sales to be made and products to be purchased or made ready for sale.

▮ *monthly reports*: these should be written by the person responsible, for example salesperson, manager or production staff. They should cover two aspects. First, what has been achieved over the past month, how it compares with budgeted figures and the objectives set in the weekly reports plus any explanations or lessons to be drawn from successes and failures. Second, the reports should consider the outlook for the next month, what should be achieved and what the objectives are.

While management reports allow you to keep informed about the business, they have an important side-effect. They force your employees to concentrate on the objectives of the business, their own performance against budgeted performance, and their own priorities for action in the weeks and months ahead.

Cash

If your cash runs out, your business will fail. It is as simple as that. Your cash can run out for several possible reasons:

▮ you do not sell enough.

▮ your costs are too high for the sales you make.

▮ you do not have enough cash to fund the increased number of debtors and stock quantities that extra business brings.

▮ you fail to collect the debts you are owed.

How to conserve cash

There are three important steps in conserving cash:

1 Knowing how much cash you have and how much you will need.
2 Speeding up the cash inflow from your customers (p. 342).
3 Slowing down the cash outflow to your suppliers (p. 347).

The cash budget

Preparing your business plan (p. 66) will have taken you some way towards knowing how much cash you will need in the business; indeed, the most important purpose of preparing the business plan may have been to raise the cash your forecasts show will be required. Once the business is trading, the cash flow forecasts need to be turned into monthly cash flow budgets.

You can help to conserve cash by paying by instalments as much as possible. For example, consider leasing cars or furniture rather than buying outright (p. 210).

Your aim should be not just to match your budget but to do better than it says. Never despise a penny or a pound that can be saved; very small savings build up over time into very large savings. This penny-pinching attitude applies just as strongly if you have raised money.

Comparing the actual cash performance with the cash budget is an important tool in controlling your cash. It enables you to learn from mistakes and plan your cash requirements in the future.

What else controls cash?

When cash is tight, you will take much more stringent measures than when you are cash-rich. For example, you could consider instituting the following control system:

- daily cash balance.
- weekly or daily bank statement.
- weekly forecast of each individual cash payment in (from customers) and planned cash payment out (to suppliers). This could be set up as a sheet with each named customer and supplier. Each day check what money you have received and tick off on your forecast sheet. Do not pay any cheques until you have received the money you need.

Obviously, when cash is short, you need to put your cash receipts in the bank as quickly as possible; and when you pay people, send the cheque by second-class post. You can say honestly that the cheque has been sent.

Clearly, the system does not work for every business; it is a good control tool for businesses that have a number of large receipts and payments. A retail business would not be able to operate in this way. However, a control sheet for a shop could consist of a weekly forecast of daily takings plus a list of those suppliers you intend to pay that week. Again, the suppliers will not be paid until the forecast cash comes in. For what happens when things are out of control see p. 364.

A cash system like this is a nuisance to operate, so if cash is not particularly short, you could use a variant of:

- weekly cash balance.
- weekly bank statement.

■ monthly payment cycle, that is, set aside one day in each month on which you pay the bills you plan for that month. This means that there is only one day in each month devoted to writing cheques or authorizing payments. If a bill is not paid on that day, it does not get paid until a month later.

Important note: no cash control system can operate if you do not keep proper cash records, for example a cash book. This is explained on p. 372.

Making cash work for you

Your problem may not be shortage of cash; on the contrary, you may have extra cash sitting around. In this case, do not leave it all in the current account. Instead, have sufficient handy to keep the business ticking over and put what you can in a seven-day-notice or call account that earns interest. Remember to give the required notice so that you can transfer what you need to cover your payments in your once-a-month cheque cycle. There are also a few of the high-interest cheque accounts that can be used by small businesses.

Operating your bank account

Most banks have readily available leaflets detailing the charges on your business bank account. If your bank doesn't, ask for the information, so you can work out in advance how much your bank charges are likely to be. Some banks will now tell you in advance what your next month's charges will be based on the current month's account usage. Most banks now make a standard charge for main account services, such as cheques, standing orders, direct debits and cash machine withdrawals. Charges may be lower for Internet banking. One way to economize is to use a credit or charge card for business expenses, as this is paid with a single payment, instead of lots of little ones.

However, it needs careful consideration before a card is given to an employee. Additionally, in the case of companies, use of a credit or charge card is a fringe benefit for employees, which would include you as a director; check how it would affect your individual tax bill.

If your business is on a very small scale, you should consider whether it is possible to run it using a building society account, rather than a bank account, bearing in mind there are limitations, such as no overdraft facility or business advice.

Some banks offer free banking for the first year (or even longer) if a small business opens an account. This can mean with some banks that there are no bank charges even if you have an overdraft.

Going into overdraft

The time to ask for an overdraft (p. 319) is not the day you realize that you will not be able to cover the bills of suppliers who are really pressing you for payment. The bank manager simply will not like it. It is much better for you to present a well-argued case one or two months before you think you will need the facility. This means planning ahead, by using your forecasts or budgets as a proper control tool.

Your customers

Selling is not the end of the story. Any old customer will not do. Making a sale to someone who does not pay their bill at all is worse than no sale at all. The ideal customer is one who pays their bill as soon as your product or service is handed over. Very few businesses are lucky enough to have that type of client. But there are steps you can take to try to ensure that you do get the cash in. First, you can check them out before you hand over the goods to them. Second, you can do everything you can to make them pay up as quickly as possible.

Giving credit to customers, that is, allowing them to become debtors and pay some time after they have received your service or product, costs you money. For example, if a bank charges 10 per cent on an overdraft, an outstanding bill of £1,000 costs you £100 if it is still unpaid after one year. Or, if it is unpaid after three months, the cost to you is £25. The more efficient you are at reducing the amount of time before you receive your payments, the lower the costs.

Investigating potential customers (credit control)

Few businesses can confine their sales to completely 'safe' customers who are guaranteed to pay what they owe and on time; usually, an element of risk is needed to meet your business objectives. But the riskiness or otherwise of customers needs to be assessed so that the risk is known and calculated. Assessment needs information, control and monitoring.

The extent of the investigation must also depend on the amount of the projected sale relative to your total sales. If it is a fairly small sale, the investigation alone may cost as much as the profit from the sale; you should establish a policy of rejecting or accepting such risks as a matter of course. But if the sale would be a significant order for you, further information is needed.

Consider the following steps:

▨ if you are dealing with a large quoted company, check its payment policy. This must be published in its annual report and accounts. Since November 1998, small businesses have by law been able to claim interest for late payments from large businesses and public sector bodies. (This right has been extended under European legislation to businesses of all sizes.) However, surveys suggest that small businesses seldom use this right, possibly because they cannot afford to lose future business from a client as a result of a payment dispute. To find out more about your right to charge interest and the amount you can charge, see The Better Payment Practice Campaign* at web site *www.payontime.co.uk*. An advantage of bidding for government contracts (see p. 17) is that all central government departments have signed up to a prompt payment initiative.

▨ ask the prospective customer for a bank reference (but this will be based only on the bank's experience, so it may indicate relatively little, but it will help in building a general picture).

▨ ask for a couple of trade references. Put a specific question such as 'Up to what level of trade credit is the customer considered a good risk?'

▨ ask a credit reference agency* for a report about this prospective customer. There are three main agencies in the UK (Call Credit*, Equifax* and Experian*), and they keep records of how individuals and businesses manage their existing and past debts.

▨ ask the customer for the latest report and accounts or a balance sheet and profit and loss account. Ask your accountant to analyse them for you.

▨ if you have not already done so, visit the business with a view to meeting the principals or directors. Put any questions that remain unanswered and use this visit to fill in the general picture.

Using the information you have garnered from all these sources, assess how risky you think this customer is and establish a credit limit. A common system is to have five categories of risk, ranging from the top category, who would be considered good for anything, to the bottom category, who you would sell to only on cash terms. You would draw up certain credit limits to apply to each category, for example allowed £1,000 on 30 days' credit. The actual amounts would depend on the size of debts relative to your sales and what is considered normal practice in that industry.

The payment terms you offer (credit terms)

There is a range of possible credit terms you could offer customers. These include:

- cash with order (CWO).
- cash on delivery (COD).
- payment seven days after delivery (net seven).
- payment for goods supplied in one week by a certain day in the next week (weekly credit).
- payment for goods supplied in one month by a certain day in the next month (monthly credit).
- payment due 30 days after delivery (30 days' credit).

You have to choose the best terms you can. This means that you extend credit for as short a time as possible, but obviously industry and competitive practice may to some extent put you in a straitjacket.

There are a couple of ways you can try to encourage early payment of your bills. First, you can offer a cash discount for early payment; for example, payment within seven days of the invoice means the customer can claim a discount of 1 per cent. The problem with this sort of discount is that customers tend to take it (and, if your debtor control is a little sloppy, are allowed the discount) whenever they pay. Introducing a cash discount of this type needs to be accompanied by close monitoring to make it clear to customers that they are entitled to the discount only if they meet the conditions offered.

Sending out invoices

Be very prompt in sending out invoices. This is crucial to any policy of keeping tight credit control. Failure to do this will give the impression to debtors that you do not mind how long you wait for your money, and as we have seen, giving credit costs you money. No matter how busy you are keeping up with the work you do, sending out invoices, as soon as goods are delivered or services supplied, must take precedence.

The records you need for control

There is more detail on how to set up the records you need on p. 370, but the records need to provide you with the following information:

- how much you are owed in total at any time.

■ how long you have been owed the money and by whom; this information is known as an aged analysis of debts.

■ a record of sales and payments including the date made for each customer. This allows you to build up your own picture of the credit-worthiness of individual debtors.

How to chase money you are owed

1 Make sure your credit terms are known to your customer. The best way is to print them clearly on the invoice.
2 As soon as your customer has overstepped the mark and the bill is overdue, ask for the money you are owed. This should be done politely in writing, preferably by e-mail or fax, with a follow-up in the post.
3 If there is no reply within seven days, check that the details of the invoice are correct and that you have quoted all the information the customer needs to identify it, for example the customer's own reference.
4 E-mail or fax again. Follow up with a letter sent by recorded delivery.
5 No reply within seven days? Make a telephone call to find out what the problem is. Do not assume that the customer has no money; there may be queries on the account or other problems. Find out the apparent reason for the non-payment.
6 Use the telephone call to find out if the customer has a weekly or monthly payment run (p. 341) and find out the day this is done.
7 Still no payment? Keep ringing and especially two or three days before the payment run. Try to extract a promise of payment.
8 Keep the pressure up. Do not pester and then drop for a few weeks; all your previous chasing is undone. Keep up a steady and persistent guerrilla warfare.
9 If the customer is always out or in a meeting when you telephone, and you suspect this is due to a desire not to speak to you, try pretending to be someone else who you are sure your customer will want to speak to. If you deal with an accountant or book-keeper, try speaking to the managing director of the customer's business.
10 Try different times of the day and the week: lunchtime is not usually a good time, but first thing Monday morning can be effective.
11 When you eventually manage to speak to the person you want, if he or she says 'I'll chase it up and see what has happened,' say you will keep holding until they do.
12 If the customer says 'The cheque has been posted,' ask for the date this was done, whether it went first- or second-class, how much the

cheque was for and what the cheque number is. Similarly, ask for the date the payment was authorized if it is being paid by automatic transfer. Transfers may take three working days to reach your account, but can be almost instantaneous if covered by the faster payments service. However, coverage of the faster payments service, which is limited to telephone and Internet transactions and standing orders, is patchy. You can check which types of payments and up to what amount are covered by each bank by going to *www.ukpayments.org.uk/ faster_payments_service/value_limits.*

13 If the payment or cheque does not arrive, go to collect the money in person; this is what HMRC does. If paid by cheque, get the cheque cashed as soon as possible, so that it cannot be stopped.

14 Check all the details of any cheque: your name, the amount, the date, the signature.

15 If all the previous steps have failed, send a formal letter, preferably from your solicitor, either threatening to take legal action to recover the debt or to start bankruptcy or winding-up proceedings (p. 366) or threatening to use a debt-collection agency. Keep to the threat.

16 Consider using an agency (see below).

17 Consider issuing a writ for the debt or consider starting bankruptcy proceedings against an individual or winding-up proceedings against a company. Consider using the small claims court. Ask your solicitor's advice.

Using a debt collection agency

Once the money has been overdue for two to three months, you could hand collection over to an agency. They will write and phone and eventually either collect the money, or report that it will only be collected by legal action. The usual charge for an agency is some percentage of the money recovered.

A halfway house to using the full-blown debt collection service is to use an agency to write to overdue customers pointing out that non-payment will be reported to credit reference agencies, which may harm the customer's credit rating. As this is very important to a business, it often has the desired effect. However, payment is made to you not the agency and, so long as this is done, no entry is made on the customer's file at the agency.

Selling your debts to raise cash (factoring)

Essentially, a factor buys your debts in return for an immediate cash payment. Generally speaking, factoring is available for debts from other businesses, rather than individuals. In a full service, the factor takes over your records for debtors and collects the debts. In return, you could receive a payment of up to 80 per cent of the face value of the invoices. The balance of the money will be paid when the debts are collected. Factoring occurs on a continuing basis, not for one individual set of debtors. The factor will often offer insurance against bad debts. There are also less complete services, for example:

■ the factor does not take over your records.

■ the customer does not pay the factor but pays you.

■ invoice discounting, that is, you maintain the records and collect the debts. This means that your use of the service remains confidential and your customers are not aware of it.

While a factoring service seems to be the answer to your cash flow dreams, there are some conditions:

■ if your sales are less than £100,000 a year, you may find it difficult to factor your debtors.

■ the factor will investigate your trading record, bad debt history, credit rating procedure, customers and so on before deciding whether to offer you a factoring service.

■ some factors give automatic protection against bad debts; others do not.

■ you are likely to have to agree to a one year's contract with a lengthy period of notice.

Note that all the separate components of factoring, that is, keeping your debtor records, cash collection, invoice discounting and credit insurance, are available separately from a number of organizations. Compare costs of several factoring services and look at the cost of the individual components.

Your suppliers

Quite a lot of the way you can deal with your suppliers (or creditors when you owe them money) is simply the reverse of what you do with debtors. Taking credit from suppliers is a significant source of finance for most small businesses. However, the other side of the coin is that those suppliers may be short of funds themselves and heavily dependent on getting in the money they are owed as quickly as possible.

When you are short of cash, you may find yourself chasing your customers and cursing them for not paying up while doing exactly the same yourself to other businesses. As a starting point, your first step should be to try to negotiate improved credit terms from your suppliers rather than simply taking unapproved extended credit.

Unfortunately, being open with your suppliers does not always pay off. Saying that you are short of cash this week but you will pay next week can cause panic. Your creditor may issue a writ without delay, and your future credit terms may be affected.

Nevertheless, when the chips are down, one way of seeing yourself through a temporary shortage of cash is to push up the length of time you take to pay your creditors. However, it is a slippery road; what you fervently believe to be a temporary shortage of cash may turn into a permanent shortfall. If you cannot make good the shortfall by raising more permanent funds, you will go to the wall with a lot of unpaid bills. A lot of small businesses like yours will also lose money as a result of your action. Somehow, you have to know where to draw the line (p. 365).

What happens when a supplier investigates you?

Any well-organized supplier will carry out the same screening of you as you do of customers who are going to place largish orders with you. Expect to be asked for:

- permission to approach your bank for a reference.
- two trade references.
- a balance sheet or a set of the latest accounts.
- further information as a result of the supplier's investigation.

The supplier will also probably approach a credit reference agency to see what it has on you and what your credit rating is. However, when you are starting in business, you can provide none of the information mentioned above. You may be forced to pay in cash initially, until you have built up some sort of record. A large supplier may even ask for a personal guarantee. You may be able to avoid this if you can demonstrate that you have sufficient funds raised to get the business through the building-up stage.

The records you need for control

Details of the records you should set up are given on p. 370. But you should be able to derive the following information from them:

- say how much you owe in total at any time.

■ say how long you have owed the money and to whom.

■ a record of what you have paid each supplier and when.

How to delay paying what you owe

Essentially, you can use only a series of excuses, not to say downright lies; there are few honest ways of delaying payment. However, it may be some comfort to know that most successful small businesses at some stage have to delay payment.

The first step to take is not to consider paying any bills until you are asked to.

The second step is to introduce a paying schedule that involves making cheques out only once a month.

Further steps involve simply delaying paying. The sorts of excuse are those mirrored in 'How to chase money you are owed' on p. 345.

Summary

1 The first stage for any new business is to get to the break-even point; after that, building up profits is needed for long-term survival.

2 Watch out for overheads; they have a nasty knack of rising with sales, thus continually pushing up the break-even point.

3 Convert your business plan and forecasts into a budget that gives you, and your employees, something to aim for.

4 Keep control of your business by comparing actual with budget performance; try to draw the appropriate lessons to be learned and plot ahead any changes in your plan that are needed.

5 If you have employees, introduce a system of weekly and monthly reporting and setting of objectives.

6 Controlling cash can keep your business afloat until break-even is reached.

7 Make your cash work for you, that is, if you have spare funds put them in an interest-earning account.

8 Operate your bank account as efficiently as possible.

9 Try to speed up the rate at which your sales are turned into cash. Do this by exercising credit control and investigating potential customers, offering the tightest credit terms you can, sending out invoices promptly and chasing overdue bills. Use 'How to chase money you are owed' on p. 345.

10 Most successful small businesses have to stoop to delaying payment to their suppliers at some time during their development.

Other chapters to read

27 Moving ahead (p. 351); **28** Not waving but drowning (p. 364).

27

Moving ahead

There comes a happy stage for most entrepreneurs when the grinding and grubbing eases off. You're past the break-even stage, you're profitable, and you can start to focus your mind on what else you might achieve.

At its basic level, you might decide that all you want is to provide yourself with a good income and your ambition is limited to maximizing the income, not just in the short term but for the future too. But for others, income maximization is not sufficient. Instead, you can see opportunities to transform yourself from a small business into a larger business. You may even decide that you want to go for growth in a major way, ending up with looking to obtain a quote on one of the stock markets – the growth of the Alternative Investment Market (AIM) has been a huge success for the stock market, and more than 3,000 companies have raised money on it. After all, there are businesses in the FTSE-100 that 20 or 30 years ago were still small. And ironically some of the companies with major stock market values are not huge at all but are valued very highly by investors. Companies may have relatively small revenues, may still be unprofitable but are nevertheless worth millions because of their perceived potential by stock market investors.

Generating large capital values from a business that you start is a roller-coaster, and many businesses lose their founders along the way. Someone else with different management skills may be needed to take up the challenge on your behalf. What you want to achieve is to maximize the value that you can obtain for your efforts.

What is in this chapter?

How to increase profits

The billion-dollar question is: 'How can I increase my profits?' The whole of this book should help you to do so: the sections on how to set up your business in the most efficient manner and those on how to plan and control your business, how to increase your sales and how to manage the workplace properly. All of these can help you to make bigger profits.

However, if you strip running a business down to bare essentials, there are three main ways to make bigger profits. The first two methods are what you would use for the short term; they apply particularly if you are struggling to reach break-even point. But any well-run business should constantly be on the lookout for the sort of improvement you can make. The two methods are cutting costs and increasing prices.

The third way of increasing profits will take longer to achieve the desired result. It is selling more. It will also, very often, involve you in spending more money to carry it out.

The quickest way of selling more is to try to sell more to your existing customers. This implies that your existing customers are happy with your service or product. That is the first step – focusing on and improving the quality of what you do already. Selling more may require greater investments in promotion or selling effort, but obviously your aim should be to make the existing levels of investment work more effectively for you.

You should not overlook the few occasions when you can increase profits by altering your sales mix; it may even mean selling less. This may occur if you have a range of products, one or more of which does not cover its costs. The answer: rationalize your product line. An investigation of your customers may reveal that some of the very small ones do not buy sufficient quantity to cover the cost of selling to them. This may also lead to the conclusion that selling less means higher profits. There may also be the odd occasion when you can alter your sales mix by introducing a product on which there is no profit but that improves your overall profits. For example, a loss leader encourages more purchases of higher-priced products and increases total profits.

In the longer run, there are two more moves that can result in your business showing more profits. You can sell:

1 The same product, but to new markets; or
2 A new product to new or existing markets.

Both of these may involve substantial investment by your business (see Chapter 15, 'Building customer relationships'). If so, you cannot undertake these until you are past the break-even point and generating profits from the existing products and market.

Cutting costs

This is the most effective way in the short term of increasing your profits and the top priority in a recession if your bottom line is being squeezed. You should get into the habit of thinking how many extra sales you have to make to pay for an increase in costs. For example, if your product sells for £100 and your costs for each product are £50, this means that every time you spend an extra £1,000 in your business, you have to sell another 20 of your product to stand still in terms of profit.

The best way of keeping an eye on costs is to have very strict cash control and to carry out regular audits of costs. Do not necessarily assume that because you looked at the costs last month, you will not be able to find room for cutting now. Use the audit checklist starting below to go through all the cost areas. Look at each item afresh and ignore history.

Checklist

■ *raw materials*: are there any alternative suppliers who are cheaper for the same quality and delivery? Can you renegotiate your existing terms from your present supplier? Everything is negotiable and is worth trying.

■ *stocks*: this ties up cash, which means bigger interest charges at the bank. Can you keep lower stocks by organizing yourself more efficiently?

■ *efficient systems*: are all repeated jobs standardized in your business? For example, if you have to do a lot of quotes, is there a standard form that simply needs filling in? Or are you drawing up a fresh form each time you quote? Does this apply in all business areas, financial, production and personnel, as well as selling?

- *the range of products*: is the gross margin you get on each product satisfactory? Does one product require a much greater share of overheads than others? If you stopped selling or manufacturing one of your products, what effect would it have on costs and profit?

- *customers and suppliers*: are your customers taking too long to pay? And are you paying your suppliers too promptly? If you're doing either of these, you are using up cash you do not need to. This means either extra interest charges on your overdraft or less interest because you have less on deposit.

Example 1

Jason Bottomley has a small shop selling jumpers, tops, shirts and so on. He is currently making profits of £15,000, but he does not regard this as sufficient to give him a comfortable living. He wants to increase his profits. His forecast sales and costs look like this:

Sales	£120,000
less direct costs	£60,000
Gross margin	£60,000
less overheads	£45,000
Net profit	£15,000

Jason wants to look at how his profit would be affected if he could cut either his direct costs by 10 per cent or his indirect costs (or overheads) by the same amount. It would look like this:

	Cut direct costs by 10 per cent	Cut indirect costs by 10 per cent
Sales	£120,000	£120,000
less direct costs	£54,000	£60,000
Gross margin	£66,000	£60,000
less overheads	£45,000	£40,500
Net profit	£21,000	£19,500

This shows that if Jason could cut direct costs by 10 per cent, his profit would increase by 40 per cent; if he could cut overheads by 10 per cent, profit would increase by 30 per cent. In fact, he estimates that every time he manages to cut both direct and indirect costs by only 1 per cent he would have more than £1,000 extra income. Quite small cuts can lead to a big jump in income.

- *numbers of employees*: your payroll has the extraordinary ability to mushroom with sales; this includes not only staff directly involved in production or manufacture but also administrative staff, the so-called overheads. The trick is to keep the same number of employees while achieving higher sales. Can you improve their productivity?

■ *payroll costs*: what you pay for staff is not just their salary and benefits. You also have to pay employer's National Insurance. If a pay rise is due, would your employees consider accepting extra contributions to a pension arrangement or childcare vouchers instead? You do not pay National Insurance on this form of 'pay', and it's tax-efficient for the employee too.

■ *the right person for the job*: a lot of time and money is wasted recruiting, training and subsequently dismissing unsuitable staff. Putting a lot of effort into finding the right people in the first place, and not just grabbing what pops up, can be cost-saving.

■ *your own time*: managing your own time better can save money too. Try to sort out some system of priorities in jobs to be done. There are quite a range of time-planning systems available, often based on diaries or very small computers. See if you can find one that suits you.

Increasing prices

There is no automatic link between prices and costs. This means you do not need to feel uncomfortable about raising your prices, even if you have not had an increase in costs. And quite small increases in price can lead to a big jump in profits. There is an example in the box below that demonstrates how effective a price rise can be.

Real life is not as simple as this. Increasing your prices could lead to a fall in sales volume if you are operating in a price-conscious market. This is one of the reasons why you should think carefully about creating some sort of image or impression for your product (see p. 132), such as high quality or good service, so that the sales of your product are not so price-sensitive. To sell on the basis of price alone is a dangerous strategy (see p. 180).

Example 2

Jason looks at the effect of increasing his prices by 5 per cent all round. His new forecast looks like this:

Sales	£126,000
less direct costs	£60,000
Gross margin	£66,000
less overheads	£45,000
Net profit	£21,000

Jason can get an increase of 40 per cent in his profits for a 5 per cent price increase.

Checklist

- *discounts*: try to avoid giving discounts, or if you are giving quantity discounts, make sure you stick to the quantity set. It can be very tempting if you are competing head-on with a competitor to try to win the sale by offering a discount. Keep your nerve and try to emphasize the benefits of your product or service.

- *payment discounts*: do you give a discount for your customers paying by a certain date? Have your customers started to take the discount whether paying by that date or not? Is the discount too big? Do you need it at all, or could you achieve the same effect by better chasing?

- *price discrimination*: can you divide your customers into distinct groups and charge some groups a higher price than others? (See p. 189 for more about price discrimination.)

- *better-quality product:* is there scope to upgrade your product with some improvements? Can you charge a higher price to give a better margin?

- *inflation*: adjust your prices to allow for the effects of inflation.

- *contracts*: try including price escalation clauses in your terms and conditions for any product you are selling.

- *minimum order*: Is it too low? Small orders can take as much time to administer and carry out as large ones, so see if you can set your minimum order at a level that ensures it is at least making a contribution.

Selling more

The third way in which you can increase your profits is to sell more of your products or service – see Example 3 below. This is the most difficult to achieve, and the results will not show up in the short term; however, potentially increasing your sales gives the greatest increase in profits of the three. You are unlikely to be able to double your prices or halve your costs, but you might be able to double the amount you sell.

Your first approach should be to try to sell more of the same products to the same market. You will already have invested time and money in researching this market and refining your product to meet customer needs, so the extra investment needed may be minimal.

You can increase your sales by more effective promotion or better selling. The one method of trying to increase your sales that you should avoid like the plague is cutting your prices. This achieves little except starting a price war because your competitors feel forced to follow suit, and putting pressure on your profit margins and your own profit level.

Cutting prices can increase your profits only if the increase in volume generated is enough to offset the smaller profit you make on each item sold. This could apply only in markets that are very price-sensitive; and in this sort of market, cutting prices is most likely to lead to severe price competition. Think twice before you act.

Example 3

Jason looks at the figures on the assumption that he could increase the amount he sells by 5 per cent, while keeping prices and overheads the same:

Sales	£126,000
less direct costs	£63,000
Gross margin	£63,000
less overheads	£45,000
Net profit	£18,000

Jason finds that a 5 per cent increase in the volume of the sales means a 20 per cent increase in his profits.

Checklist

- *image*: have you thought clearly about how your product is positioned? Can it be differentiated more from your competitors' products?

- *advertising*: are you aiming your message in the right place? Are you getting as much press coverage as you could? Is your advertising consistent with the style of your product?

- *selling*: have you clearly articulated your benefits? Have you prepared a detailed analysis of how your product compares with competitors? Have you developed proper scripts, either for person-to-person selling or telephone selling? Are you following up all leads, pursuing leads to turn them into quotes and converting quotes to orders? Prepare a breakdown of sales statistics, of conversion from leads to quotes to orders and analyse where you are going wrong.

- *remember*: increasing sales means increasing working capital, so your business may need more finance.

Doing all three

In practice, you will try to do all three at the same time: cut costs, increase prices and sell more. It is astonishing the effect that very small across-the-board improvements can have on your profit (see Example 4 below).

Example 4

Jason thinks that he could manage small improvements in all areas by cutting costs by 1 per cent, increasing prices by 1 per cent, and increasing amount of sales by 1 per cent. Doing all three would have this impact on profits:

Sales	£122,412
less direct costs	£59,400
Gross margin	£63,012
less overheads	£44,550
Net profit	£18,462

This means an increase in profits of 23 per cent and gives Jason an extra income of £3,462. The moral is never despise small improvements. They can transform your profit.

Going for growth

Growth businesses are the cream. They make up the top 5 per cent of small companies – and around 20,000 a year are started. There are several subtle differences between the growth companies and the rest. What marks them out?

The definition of a growth company will usually be based upon one of the following measurements: growth in sales, growth in employees and growth in profits. Fast-growing businesses might be aiming for sales of £500,000 in three years from a scratch start or show sales growing at over 60 per cent a year from a base sales figure of say £100,000 or so.

The motivation of the entrepreneur, the team leader, is what drives the business. If you are looking at your business solely to provide you with an income, you're unlikely to have the oomph to push the enterprise into fast growth. The same consideration applies if you have set up your own business because you prefer the lifestyle with its attendant freedom and options to that of being an employee in someone else's company. To make a success of founding a growth business, a driving force is likely to be that you have the ambition of wealth. You want to make yourself financially independent; you want to give yourself that quantity of 'drop dead' money (that is, to know you're financially so secure that you can tell someone to drop dead if you are so minded!).

Without this extra ingredient, the determination to create wealth, there may not be enough motivation to push the business into the highest level of growth. Fast growth is uncomfortable and painful. It creates pressure points and stresses internally. It often requires an unreasonable owner to dragoon unwilling employees to produce the impossible. If your aspiration is simply to create a good lifestyle for yourself, you're unlikely to have the necessary drive to grow a business quickly.

Requirements for a fast-growing business

How do you make your business fast-growing? It's possible to identify a number of key requirements. First, the quality of the management is crucial – and that means you and your team. You need to have the character to lead your team; you need a broad set of business skills, including sales and marketing, often gained through management experience in a large company, and the ambition to grow fast. A good education, often a higher-level qualification, also helps. If you have already run and sold a successful business, this will give you a head start for two reasons: you're more experienced and less likely to make mistakes, and you may have finance available.

Your team needs to be balanced: there needs to be someone who is skilled in finance and accounting, someone in marketing and sales, someone in production and so on. And it makes sense for the team to be offered incentives based on growth, such as share options.

As for the business, it is also possible to identify some factors that contribute to growth. Businesses that select a well-defined market opportunity, frequently a market niche, will find that their salespeople are knocking at a door already ajar. Beware the product that is unique but that as yet has no clearly defined customer base. People must want to buy your product.

It is important to develop a culture within your enterprise that focuses on product quality and customer satisfaction. It can make your whole business much more confident to know that you are selling a product that people hold in high regard and that customers are satisfied. It can be very demoralizing for employees to deal with dissatisfied customers.

Businesses that are technology-based and that are constantly striving to introduce efficiencies through the clever use of technology will also have a head start on the fast-growth route. Innovative businesses, which have a competitive advantage, can also make larger strides than the average company, as long as the product is one the consumer wants to know about. Finally, many fast-growth businesses are also exporters. If you have a product with global demand, the potential market is larger.

Adapting your business

You can look at recruitment and training to improve your management style and team. Analyse your products to improve the quality and look carefully at your current market. Investigate the possibility of raising risk finance to allow you to grow faster. Focus on business planning and improve the systems infrastructure of your business.

Phase 2 money

Going for growth usually means raising more money. Not always. You may have created that elixir of business, a cash-generative model, and be able to fund your own expansion with your own resources.

In most cases, to expand you will need to raise outside money. Chapter 25, 'Raising the money', explains some of the ways you can do this. But Phase 2 money is likely to be different in that it is likely to be substantially more, come from outside sources and be risk capital rather than loans.

However, longer-term loans from your bank could provide the development capital you need for expansion. So revisit your bank manager armed with your essential business plan and forecasts.

But many businesses will be looking to raise risk capital from outside investors in exchange for shares in your company. The size you are now considering may be outside the scope of business angels. So your choices may be to approach a venture capital organization or a venture capital trust to raise development capital. Or to consider a stock market flotation.

The advantage of going to the stock market is that it enables investors to buy and sell their shares. This also means that it allows you the opportunity to expand your business by buying other companies in exchange for shares. Once your shares are publicly traded, your company should be valued higher than it would be if it were still a private company (but this is not always the case).

Which stock market?

There are several stock markets. The main London stock market is probably the least suitable. Unless you would be valued at a reasonable amount, £200 million say, small companies get lost and overlooked in favour of the blue chips. The London Stock Exchange also operates Techmark – a subgroup of companies within the main market. It includes established companies in high-tech industries, such as computers, software, telecommunications and biotechnology. There is also a facility for relatively new, fast-growing companies to join Techmark. Usually, a company needs at least a three-year track record before qualifying for listing, but special rules allow growth companies with a shorter record to join Techmark.

Your choice is probably between two markets suitable for innovative, fast-growing smaller companies. The Alternative Investment Market (AIM) is very suitable for raising sums of money for companies looking for expansion. Unfortunately, floating on the AIM can be very expensive because of the due diligence that needs to be carried out by the advisers. Generally, most of the funds would be raised from institutions rather than private investors, although private investors might buy your shares after the company is listed.

The other option is the PLUS-quoted market. The PLUS markets* are relatively new London-based stock exchanges. There are two markets: PLUS-listed and PLUS-quoted. PLUS-listed is a rival to the London Stock Exchange's main market. PLUS-quoted is a market for small and medium-sized companies. The requirements for floating on PLUS-quoted are less demanding than those for AIM. For example, there is no minimum trading record or minimum market capitalization. The main admission criteria are a corporate adviser to sponsor your float, recent published audited accounts, being able to demonstrate adequate working capital, no restrictions on the transfer of your shares, and the shares must be acceptable for electronic settlement.

There are disadvantages in taking money from the public and becoming a quoted company. You have to meet the rules and regulations, which can be quite onerous, and accept that you have an additional layer of responsibility to your shareholders. Your business is no longer a private company, able to do what it wants with the profits and, in particular, your own rewards.

Managing change

Fast expansion gives you growing pains. Your tightly knit team becomes more loosely knit; the personal element is diluted. You will cease to know personally every bit of information, every customer, every supplier, because growth means delegation.

Managing the next stage of growth means you have to focus on four elements: people, organization structure, processes or working procedures, and technology.

Employees are scared of change. So even if it is very positive, because your business is growing fast, you have to watch out for the developing resistance to changed responsibilities, changed hierarchies of responsibility and changed chemistry for developing teams.

The structure of your organization needs to be flexible to allow for growth, but you will find it creaking at regular intervals. And one of the absorbing tasks of management is how to adapt a structure to ensure that you meet your requirements over the next phase of business growth.

Working procedures need to be documented and updated regularly. Instead of you explaining jobs to new members of staff, existing employees will be explaining them. Unless procedures are written, you can end up losing control over the efficiency of your staff.

Finally, technology plays an important role in growth. Use of technology can improve the efficiency of your workforce and enable more jobs to be done by fewer people. Constantly be on the lookout for ways that tasks can be streamlined and aided by technology.

Growing companies might consider setting up an internal web site, which could be for company data, such as price lists, purchasing details, policies, sales presentations and so on. Company knowledge is captured in this way, doesn't walk out of the door in the head of a leaving employee and is accessible by all employees from their computers at work, at home or away on a sales trip.

Summary

1 There are three ways you can increase profits: you can cut costs, increase prices or sell more.

2 The quickest way of boosting profits is to cut costs and increase prices; but the greatest long-term potential comes from increasing your sales.

3 Do not dismiss any improvement that can be made because it is too insignificant. A series of tiny changes in the right direction can lead to much bigger profits.

4 Growth can be achieved by focusing on certain key requirements, such as a balanced team, a broad skill set, a well-defined market opportunity, a focus on product quality and customer satisfaction, and an emphasis on the clever use of technology.

5 Raising Phase 2 money to fund expansion may mean risk capital from outside investors.

6 Managing change needs careful planning of employees, organizational structure, working procedures and technology.

Other chapters to read

28

Not waving but drowning

If you put this book's guidelines into operation at the right time, fewer of you should need this chapter than the average small business. Nevertheless, there are those who will. Some businesses will go to the wall.

Few people can appreciate before the event how traumatic the slide into failure can be. Gradually hemmed in with fewer and fewer avenues of escape, you have to come to terms with the crushing of your hopes and expectations. For natural optimists, such as entrepreneurs, it is appallingly difficult to do. At what point do you realize that your business is not going to survive? When do you accept that to carry on is to put other businesses in jeopardy and to impose the same pressures on them as on you? At what point does it become illegal to carry on?

That point may be easy to recognize for an outsider, who is calm and rational. But it is incredibly difficult to recognize when you have been fighting for weeks, or even months, to avoid it. You may find that you slid past the point so gradually that you did not have time to notice. Sometimes, matters are taken out of your hands by an outsider, such as a creditor or a bank, beginning the steps to close your business.

The problem of acceptance is made worse by the usual existence of somewhat schizophrenic behaviour. To avoid rumours and doubts emerging about the future of your business, you may well be putting on a brave face to the outside world. And you are doing this while knowing within yourself that it does not ring true. The title of this chapter is from a poem by Stevie Smith. Two lines from this poem are: 'I was much further out than you thought / And not waving but drowning.' This aptly summarizes the dilemma for someone whose business is in financial difficulties.

Further emotional difficulties are caused by society's harsh attitude towards the failure. Even though thousands of businesses fail during a recession, many of them through no fault of their own, there is often little sympathy for those that do. However, since 1 April 2004, if you do go bankrupt, you will normally be discharged after just one year (instead of three as previously). For more information, contact the Insolvency Service*.

This chapter tries to help you to recognize the point at which you have to say: 'Enough is enough.'

What is in this chapter?

- the warning signs of failure (p. 365).
- the final process if you operate as a limited company (p. 366), sole trader (p. 368) or partnership (p. 368).
- what happens afterwards? (p. 369).

The warning signs of failure

Chapter 26, 'Staying afloat', describes how to control your cash to avoid an ignominious end to your business. At some point, you may unfortunately find:

- you only pay a supplier when a writ is issued, and your suppliers are refusing to sell you any more goods.
- you are near or above your overdraft limit at the bank.
- you are unable to raise any more money.
- your liabilities are greater than your assets.

Once your business has reached the point that liabilities (what you owe) are more than assets (what you own), the business is insolvent. It may become insolvent at an earlier stage, when current liabilities are greater than current assets: in other words, when the amount you have in cash and debtors is less than the amount you owe to creditors. This may occur even though you have sufficient fixed assets to cover what you owe. These fixed assets may take too long to sell, at other than a knockdown price, to satisfy your creditors.

As well as insolvency occurring as a result of sales being too low or costs too high, outside events can force it on you. For example, you may be owed a large sum of money by a customer who is slow in paying and may even be unable to pay. A common complaint for small businesses is that some large companies are prone to do just that – be very slow payers – and this can start the vicious circle ending in failure.

Earlier warning signs can be detected that identify businesses that are at a high risk of failure. Studies pinpoint, among other things, these faults – not all of them relevant for the self-employed and small businesses:

- the boss takes no advice.
- the managing director and chairperson is the same person.
- the board of directors does not take an active interest.
- the skills of the business are unbalanced.
- there is no strong financial person.
- there is no budget, cash flow plan or costing system.
- the business is failing to respond to change.

If your business displays some of these characteristics, while not yet being in the advanced stage of failure, get advice now, either from your professional advisers (p. 212) or through Business Link* or equivalent organization (p. 32).

The final process

There are two constructive steps you can take: consider whether you could negotiate with creditors to pay off what you owe in instalments or to pay a smaller sum that they will accept in full settlement. Or you can enter into what is known as a formal voluntary arrangement. This is a procedure whereby you offer to pay a dividend to creditors in full settlement of your debts. You need to contact an authorized insolvency practitioner, who will require fees in advance to carry out the work. Voluntary arrangements are a formal legal procedure and have proved very effective as a means of avoiding liquidation or bankruptcy.

Limited company

You can seek to wind up your company on a voluntary basis, or you may have it imposed on you by the court or under the supervision of the court. And under the 1986 Insolvency Act there are the options of administration and voluntary arrangements. Voluntary winding-up can occur if 75 per cent of the members vote for it. The resolution for voluntary winding-up must be published in the *London Gazette*. If the directors make a statutory declaration, having investigated the company's affairs, that in their opinion the company will be able to pay its debts within 12 months, the winding-up carries on as a members' voluntary winding-up. However, if the company is not solvent, the winding-up is a creditors' voluntary winding-up. The difference between the two is that if it is a members' voluntary winding-up, the members appoint the liquidator. Otherwise, the creditors appoint the liquidator.

The liquidators will normally pay debts in the following order:

1 Loans and debts that have been secured on a fixed asset.
2 The costs of the winding-up.
3 Local authority and water rates, contributions to occupational pension schemes, wages and salaries.
4 Loans and debts that have been secured with a floating charge on the assets, that is, secured on assets in general, not a specific one (though part of the assets may be set aside for unsecured creditors).
5 Ordinary trade creditors.
6 Tax owed to HM Revenue & Customs.
7 Shareholders.

If you do not start proceedings to wind up the company on a voluntary basis, you may find it forced on you if a creditor applies to the court for a compulsory winding-up because you cannot pay your debts. However, following a change in the law, you can no longer normally be forced down this route by a single creditor such as a bank. If you do face compulsory winding-up, the court will appoint a liquidator, who is usually the Official Receiver. The Official Receiver is an officer of the Department for Business, Innovation and Skills*.

The secretary or director of the company must provide the Official Receiver with a statement verified by affidavit, listing the assets or liabilities of the company. The Official Receiver will call a creditors' meeting to decide whether to appoint a liquidator or whether the Official Receiver will carry on in that role. The liquidator will pay off the company's debts in the same order as that outlined for the voluntary winding-up.

The 1986 Insolvency Act strengthened the responsibilities of directors. One of the provisions could mean that a director is made personally liable for a company's creditors. This could occur if the director has allowed the company to go on trading even though there is no way it can avoid insolvent liquidation (that is, the assets of the business cannot be sold to provide a sufficient sum of money to pay all the creditors).

An alternative to winding-up may be to seek a Company Voluntary Arrangement (CVA) – this is a structured agreement with your creditors to repay at least some of your debts gradually over a specified period. It can be used to give a viable company a breathing space in which to recover and return to solvency. New money lent to a company in CVA has priority status (thus removing a disincentive for lenders).

Sole trader

A creditor may force bankruptcy on you by beginning proceedings for payment of a debt. It is very easy for a creditor to make you bankrupt. If you owe someone more than £750 they can bankrupt you quickly. And, even if you pay the debt demanded, if the court thinks you have other debts you cannot pay, you may well still be made bankrupt. Contact the Bankruptcy Association* for more information.

A possible alternative to bankruptcy could be an individual voluntary arrangement (IVA). All or the majority of your creditors must agree to the IVA and typically you pay off a percentage of what you owe over a period of five years. At the end of that time, the remaining debts are written off. The main advantage of an IVA is that it may enable you to retain major assets, such as your home, which would almost certainly be lost through bankruptcy. But, increasingly, creditors are seeking a large final settlement payment towards the end of the IVA period which is likely to necessitate borrowing against or selling your home.

As soon as you realize your debts are no longer manageable, get help from an independent debt advice agency, such as Business Debtline*, Citizens Advice*, National Debtline*, the Consumer Credit Counselling Service* or PayPlan*.

Partnership

With a conventional partnership you have an added problem to that of a sole trader. Each partner is responsible for all the liabilities of the partnership, regardless of what the profit-sharing arrangements are in your partnership agreement. If you have more personal assets than your partner, it is you and your family who will suffer the most.

With a limited liability partnership, the options open to the management or to creditors are much the same as for a limited company.

What happens afterwards?

While you are an undischarged bankrupt, restrictions apply that make your chances of starting another business limited. These restrictions now normally last just a year but can be extended and last up to 15 years if you are found to have acted dishonestly. Be aware that, even though you are likely to be discharged after just one year, a note of your bankruptcy will stay on your credit record for longer – usually six years – and this will make it harder and/or more expensive for you to borrow in future. A voluntary arrangement also stays on your credit file for six years after it comes to an end.

If you are a director of a company that is wound up, you can usually be a director of another company unless you are subject to a disqualification order, bankruptcy restrictions order or undertaking.

Summary

1 Watch out for the warning signs.
2 See if your creditors will agree to your paying off what you owe by instalments or see if they will accept smaller payments in settlement.

Other chapter to read

26 Staying afloat (p. 333).

29

Keeping the record straight

Fate decrees that one of the least interesting business activities is also one of the most crucial for its continued success. Keeping records must rank fairly low in an entrepreneur's satisfaction rating. It is much more gripping to go chasing sales or to carry out a negotiation with a supplier that will lower your costs. But a complete 'seat-of-the-pants' approach to business will only keep you afloat in the short term.

If you hope to avert the dangers of sliding into failure, one thing you should try to achieve is not to allow yourself to be buried in a quagmire of bills, invoices and tax demands. Failure to organize your records from day one may mean just that. However, it is never too late to start; so if you have been pushing aside that task, now is the time to tackle it.

Allowing yourself to drift into paper chaos is understandable. Discovering a system for organizing records that is suitable for your business can be difficult. Too simple a system for your particular business may mean that you cannot derive the information from it that you need. Too complicated a system may mean that you have to spend too much time keeping it up to date. There is no one system that will apply to all businesses. You may find that you need to adjust yours with the benefit of experience until you have developed one that fits what you want.

What is in this chapter?

■ why you need records (p. 371).

■ which records? (p. 371).

■ a very simple system (see p. 372).

■ when the business is more complicated (p. 377).

Why you need records

Good accurate records are needed for two extremely important reasons. First, records are needed to substantiate what is in the accounts.

If you are self-employed or a small company (see p. 42), your accounts do not need to be audited, but they are still required for tax purposes. You do not necessarily have to send accounts in to your tax office, but you must nevertheless still have them and be prepared to produce them if asked. There are hefty fines if you can't.

From 1 April 2009 onwards, you can be asked to provide a tax officer with any information and documents reasonably required for the purpose of checking your tax position. This is an extremely wide power that can mean virtually any type of information or document and can relate to past, present or future tax liabilities. Reinforcing this power above, from 1 April 2009 onwards, the Revenue can enter business premises to inspect the premises themselves, together with business assets and business documents kept there. The Revenue also has new powers to specify exactly which records you must keep, but, at the time of writing, had not yet drawn up any such lists. HMRC has announced that it intends to carry out checks on the record-keeping of up to 50,000 small and medium-sized businesses a year, starting from mid-2011. HMRC will impose fines when it finds significant breaches. It estimates that four out of ten such businesses (around 5 million in total) do not keep adequate records and that up to 2 million small and medium-sized businesses are paying less tax than they should.

The second reason why accurate records are needed is to help you to know what is going on in your business. This, in turn, means you can keep better control and you can plan for the future. It is impossible to make realistic estimates and projections if the basic data are patchy and inaccurate.

Which records?

The first and most important record you need is for cash. You need some way of keeping information about payments into and out of your bank account and also any petty cash that you keep on the premises. The aim of your cash records is so you know at any moment how much cash you have.

For those businesses that do not sell all their goods for cash, your records will need to cope with keeping tabs on what people owe you and how long they have owed it. This allows you to forecast what money you will be getting in during the months ahead and enable you to chase debts.

Most businesses will buy goods, services and raw materials from others. Unless you are forced to pay cash for all your supplies, you will need to organize the bills that you have to pay. Following on from this, if you keep stocks of raw materials or stocks of finished goods, you need to have a tally of what there is: what has come into the business, what is currently held by the business and what has gone out.

Once you start employing people, your employee records need to be meticulous; in particular, records relating to your role as tax collector for the government (p. 257) need to be well organized and up to date.

Finally, information about fixed assets, such as cars, equipment or property, needs to be recorded.

A very simple system

If your business has only a few transactions, for example it is very small, you sell only large items or you sell your time as a consultant, the system you introduce can really be very simple. It would indeed be a mistake to get bogged down in very complicated record keeping, because it would take up a lot of time without improving the accuracy of your system. Complexities such as double-entry book-keeping can be put aside. A couple of simple accounts books may well be sufficient. Being methodical is far more important than sophistication.

Cash

You will need a cash book. This should show the cash payments you receive and make. It gives a way of recording what you have paid into the bank and what you take out of it and your petty cash position.

Diagram 29.1 on p. 374 gives an example of a way of setting up the cash book. As you can see there are two sections: one for recording cash receipts and one for recording cash payments. The cash receipts section has five columns and the cash payments section six columns.

For cash receipts, the columns are from left to right:

- the date you received the payment.

■ your invoice number that has been paid.

■ the name of the person who made the payment.

■ the amount of the payment.

■ the value of what you have paid into the bank.

If you offer discounts for prompt settlement, you will need to have an additional column to show the amount of the discount that was taken.

For cash payments, the columns are from left to right:

■ the date you made the payment.

■ the cheque number.

■ the reference number you put on the supplier's invoice on receipt.

■ the name of the person or business who has been paid.

■ what you have cashed from the bank for petty cash purposes.

■ the amount of the payment.

If it is normal business practice to be offered a discount, you need another column to record the amount taken. When you start paying wages, you will need a further column to record what you have cashed from the bank for this purpose. You might also find it helpful to add a 'miscellaneous' column.

Using the cash book, you should be able to work out how much cash you have and whether cash receipts are exceeding cash payments or vice versa. When you get a bank statement, which should be monthly (and when your business gets more complicated ask for a statement more than once a month), you can check that the two cash balances agree. If they do not, you should be able to identify why, that is, cheques you have sent that have not yet been cashed or cheques you have paid in that have not yet been cleared. This is called a bank reconciliation. It is useful to write your reconciliation down.

Keep all cheque books, paying-in books and bank statements.

Petty cash

You can deal with petty cash items in a number of ways. You could write a voucher or piece of paper each time you use petty cash and keep the voucher in the petty cash box. If you get a receipt for money you spend, staple this to the back of the voucher. Once a month, you could tot these up and put them in your purchases record (see p. 375).

Cash receipts

Date received	Invoice number	Customer	Amount £	Paid into bank £

Cash payments

Date paid	Cheque number	Reference number	Supplier/ payee	Petty cash	Amount of payment

Diagram 29.1 Cash

Another approach is to carry a little notebook with you and jot down the expenses as they occur. A further alternative is to keep a sheet of paper in your office and write down the amounts spent at the end of each day, again stapling any receipts to it.

Finally, you could set up a recording system in your cash book, using perhaps the back half of the book.

Whichever way you record petty cash items, you need to record the date the cash was spent, how much it was and what it was for.

If you are registered for VAT, when you make an entry for your petty cash payments in your purchases record, you will need to know which items include the standard rate of VAT (p. 419) and to work out the amount of VAT you will be claiming.

Sales

Every time you make a sale, you should produce an invoice (or, if you are selling for cash, a receipt). The invoices should be numbered and filed in numerical order. If there are a fair number of invoices, it might be sensible to have one file for unpaid invoices and another for paid invoices. As every invoice is paid, any documentation that comes with the payment should be stapled to it. It should then be transferred to the paid file. A separate file should be kept for every accounting period.

The next step is to write down in your accounts book a record of every sale. For every sale there should be four columns, six if you are registered for VAT. Diagram 29.2 below shows what it should look like. The columns are:

■ the date of the invoice.

■ the name of the customer.

■ the number of the invoice.

■ the amount of the sale, including VAT.

If you are registered for VAT, there should be two further columns:

■ the amount of the VAT.

■ the amount of the sale, excluding VAT.

You could have a further column for the payment date of your invoice.

Example 1

Peter Brown is entering the details of one of his invoices (see Diagram 29.2). The invoice number is 344 and the invoice is to Arnold Warehouses. Peter has charged £1,500, but VAT has to be charged. This comes to £300 and the total, including VAT, is £1,800. When the invoice is paid, Peter will enter the details in the cash book.

Date of invoice	Description: Name of customer	Number of invoice	Amount of sale (incl. VAT)	VAT	Amount of sale (excl. VAT)
12.6.11	Arnold Warehouses	344	1,800.00	300.00	1,500.00

Diagram 29.2 Sales

Purchases

If your business is simple, you can record the details of purchases in the same accounts or analysis book as your sales, perhaps using the second half of it. As every invoice comes in for goods or services that you have bought (or a receipt for items that you pay cash for), it should be numbered and filed in numerical order.

When it comes to recording purchases, a more detailed analysis than for sales can be useful for producing the accounts that you need for tax purposes. If your business is simple, your records may need to be updated only once a month.

You will probably find you use all the columns of your analysis book. The columns should read from left to right (see Diagram 29.3):

■ the date the invoice is received.

■ the name of the supplier.

■ whether the invoice is paid or not, for example a tick if paid.

■ the number you put on the invoice.

■ the amount of the invoice, including VAT.

If you are registered for VAT, you will need two further columns:

■ the amount of the VAT.

■ the amount of the invoice, excluding VAT.

The remaining columns of the book should be devoted to showing the nature of the items purchased. The exact headings you put on the columns will depend on the type of the business. Some examples could be stationery, fares, petrol, postage, heating and lighting. The amount of every invoice, excluding VAT if you are registered, should be entered in the appropriate column.

Example 2

Peter Brown has received an invoice for the telephone. He numbers the invoice 222 and enters the details in the analysis book – see Diagram 29.3. He puts the date he received it, the supplier and the amount of the invoice, including VAT, £252.34.

As he is registered for VAT, he now works out the amount of VAT, that is £252.34 less £252.34 divided by 1.20. This gives £252.34 − £210.28 = £42.06. He enters this in the VAT column and puts £210.28 in the column for the amount, excluding VAT. He puts the amount of the invoice without VAT in the appropriate detailed-breakdown column (in this case 'Telephone').

When he paid the invoice, he ticked the appropriate column and also entered details in the cash book.

Date invoice received	Name of supplier	Paid	Number of invoice	Amount (incl. VAT)	VAT
12.6.11	British Telecom	✓	222	252.34	42.06

Amount (excl. VAT)	Supplies	Car expenses	Stationery	Postage	Telephone	Heating/ lighting
210.28					210.28	

Diagram 29.3 Purchases

Fixed assets

If your business is a limited company, you are obliged by law to keep a record of fixed assets. If your business is fairly simple, a list in a notebook will suffice. This should show the cost of the asset and depreciation.

VAT

You are required to keep separate VAT accounts if you are registered for VAT (see Chapter 31, 'VAT'). You can put these in your analysis book if there is sufficient room. Unless you are using the flat-rate scheme (see p. 429), this should show for each month:

- the amount of the sales, including VAT.
- the amount of VAT charged.
- the amount of the purchases, including VAT.
- the amount of the VAT paid.

When the business is more complicated

There will be many businesses for which the simple system described above will not be sufficient. This will apply to you if you make many sales or purchases each month and keep a lot of stock on the premises. An increasing number of documents and records will be needed. Your business may need to set up a system for recording information which includes some or all of the following records. And it may well be appropriate to introduce a computerized accounting system.

Purchase orders

This could be a formal document that has the name and address of the supplier plus the goods ordered and the details necessary for that. A copy of your letter may suffice, as long as it is numbered and kept in a file. This document will be needed to ensure that what the supplier sends you is actually what you ordered.

A record of what goods are received in the business

As your business grows, you will no longer know yourself exactly what has come in; there may well be employees who do this for you. The only way to keep track of what has been received is to have a formal way of recording it. This could be a specially prepared form to fill in and match against the purchase order. Or it could be a book in which you write down the details. The details are needed before a supplier invoice is passed for payment.

What have you got in stock?

You need to know at any time what raw materials or finished goods you have got in stock. Going to have a look is not the best way of doing this. Written records are the answer, because they are the best way to control and plan your business, and they will protect against staff pilfering.

If you have lots of different items that you keep in stock, stock cards may be the most suitable way of recording what there is. With fewer items, a stock book may suffice.

Sales invoices

This could be a printed form or it could be typed on business stationery and a copy kept.

Employee time sheets

For certain sorts of business, for example manufacturing or assembly, records of how many hours employees work are important and are the basis for paying wages. You could keep a time book with a simple record of when the employee started work and when the employee finished for the day. You also need to keep records for the working time regulations (see p. 260).

Petty cash vouchers

As the business gets bigger with more employees, a proper petty cash voucher will become a necessity. This should show the date, the employee who received the petty cash and what it was for. Any voucher should be signed by an appropriate responsible person with the authority to do so. Wherever possible, a receipt should be attached to the petty cash voucher.

Wages record

You have certain legal duties towards your employees (see Chapter 21, 'Your rights and duties as an employer'). These include giving an itemized pay statement and deducting tax and National Insurance contributions from salaries and wages. Proper records need to be kept, and HMRC* will send you forms to complete. You must keep the following information for all employees:

■ name and address.

■ National Insurance number.

■ PAYE reference number.

■ pay.

■ pension deductions.

■ any other deductions authorized by the employee.

The actual wages record needs to show the payments made:

■ gross pay, with a breakdown of how this is made up, for example bonuses and commission, as well as basic wage.

■ pension contributions.

■ total pay this period.

■ total pay to date.

■ tax-free pay to date (see tables from HMRC).

■ taxable pay to date.

■ tax due to date (see tables from HMRC).

■ tax paid to date.

■ tax due on earnings for this period.

■ employee's National Insurance contributions this period.

■ other deductions.

■ net pay.

■ employer's National Insurance contribution.

This is also information that needs to be set out on an employee's pay slip. You also need to keep records on statutory sick pay, statutory maternity pay, statutory paternity pay and statutory adoption pay and to keep records to show that you are meeting the requirements on the minimum wage and working time regulations.

Rather than deal with wages records and administration yourself, you could outsource this task to a payroll agency. Many accountants* offer a payroll service or alternatively you could use a specialist firm. A search on the Internet will throw up many agencies. Your local chamber of commerce* or business contacts may be able to recommend a good one.

Summary

1 You need records to back up what is in your accounts for tax purposes.
2 Planning the business and controlling it cannot be achieved if records are inadequate.
3 Keeping your records in a methodical way is more important than installing very sophisticated systems for a very small business.
4 As your business grows, you need to create control procedures to ensure that you know what has been ordered, what has been received and the supplier invoice agrees with your purchase order form.
5 You need to know who owes you what amount of money at any time so that you can chase slow or late payers.
6 As your business grows replace your accounting books with a computerized accounts package.

Other chapters to read

18 Information technology – and other equipment (p. 204); **21** Your rights and duties as an employer (p. 244); **24** Forecasting (p. 295); **26** Staying afloat (p. 333); **31** VAT (p. 419).

30

Tax

You have a choice when sorting out tax on your business: enlist a professional or do it yourself. If you operate as a company, it makes sense to use an accountant*. If you are a sole trader or partner, it can be helpful to use a professional to present your accounts and tax calculations but, provided your business is fairly simple and you have the time, you should be able to do this yourself, and the self-assessment tax system is designed to be workable by non-experts.

The starting point for working out your tax is the profit and loss accounts for your business. Whether you are a company, self-employed or a partnership, your accounts must be drawn up in accordance with Generally Accepted Accounting Practice (GAAP) for the UK. These GAAP rules are drawn up by accountancy bodies and change from time to time. As a layperson, it may be hard for you to keep abreast of the changes and this is one reason why most companies are better off relying on an accountant rather than trying to draw up their own accounts. However, small businesses (whether companies or not) can opt to use a short version of the accounting standards called Financial Reporting Standards for Smaller Entities (FRSSE). If you do decide to draw up your accounts yourself, make sure you comply with FRSSE and any relevant updates to it. You can download a free copy of FRSSE and check for updates at the Accounting Standards Board* web site (*www.frc.org.uk/asb/technical/frsse.cfm*).

If you do use a professional, make sure you choose someone who is suitably qualified, normally an accountant and preferably also a member of the Chartered Institute of Taxation (CIOT)* or Association of Taxation Technicians*. Anyone can set themselves up as a tax adviser, and unfortunately there are some with no qualifications or just not up to the job. Even if you use a professional, you are still ultimately responsible for making the correct declarations and paying the correct tax. If your adviser gets it wrong, you will be the one facing investigations, fines and interest – although you might be able to sue the adviser if they had acted negligently or fraudulently. You may also find that, although professionals will do the paperwork for you, they will not necessarily suggest ways you can save tax unless you specifically ask for their opinion on a particular measure.

Under the self-assessment tax system which you must use if you are self-employed or in a partnership, you can submit your tax return and rely on HM Revenue & Customs* (HMRC) to calculate your tax bill for you. Even then, you are still responsible for the accuracy of your bill and expected to make reasonable checks to see that HMRC have got the figure right. You can be fined if you fail to spot an HMRC error.

To keep your tax bill to a minimum and guard yourself against advisers who are no good or HMRC errors, it pays to know a bit yourself about the tax system.

What is in this chapter?

This chapter concentrates mainly on tax if you are a sole trader or partner. It will not answer every question you may have about how your income tax bill is calculated. But you should be able to gain a working knowledge of the system so you know the key moves to make in dealing with your tax inspector. For a more detailed guide, including filling in returns and ideas on saving tax, you could get a specialist tax guide, such as the *FT Guide to Personal Tax*, which is updated every year as the tax rules change. The chapter includes sections on:

- when you pay income tax (p. 383).
- working out your income tax bill (p. 388).
- business expenses (p. 388) and tax relief for capital expenditure (p. 393).
- losses for the self-employed (p. 398).
- National Insurance contributions (p. 400), capital gains tax (p. 400) and business rates (p. 402).
- you and your tax office (p. 405).
- partners (p. 409).
- drawing money out of your company (see p. 411).
- spare-time earnings (p. 413) and property income (p. 415).
- the black economy (p. 417).

When you pay income tax

If you have been an employee, you'll have been used to having income tax deducted from your pay before you get it. If you are a sole trader or partner (see pp. 408–9), you'll have to get used to setting aside part of your profits to pay tax as it falls due.

Everything to do with income tax is worked out by reference to tax years. A tax year runs from 6 April one year to the following 5 April. You pay tax for a particular tax year in three chunks: two interim payments on 31 January falling within the tax year and 31 July following the end of the tax year. These interim payments are estimates. On the following 31 January you make a final payment if the interim instalments come to less than your actual tax bill or receive a refund if you have overpaid.

The interim payments are estimated by initially setting each one equal to half your tax bill for the previous year. If you know your income will be less this year, you can ask for the interim payments to be reduced. If your profits are rising, your interim payments will come to less than you owe. This means, on 31 January, you will have a final payment to scoop up the shortfall and an increased interim payment for the coming year. For example, suppose you have paid two interim payments of £3,000 the tax year just ended (£6,000 in total) but your final tax bill is £8,000. By 31 January, you'll have to pay a £2,000 final payment plus £4,000 as a first interim payment for the current tax year – in other words, £6,000. Make sure you set aside enough to cover the jump in the interim payment as well as the final payment.

Provided you are registered to make your tax declarations online (see pp. 386, 431), you can arrange voluntarily to pay tax weekly or monthly by direct debit (called a Budget Payment Plan). These are still estimated payments and you may still have a final balancing payment to make on 31 January following the end of the tax year. However, you can adjust the amount you pay at any time, for example, increasing the amount if your profits look as if they will be higher than you had initially expected. A Budget Payment Plan may help you to set aside enough to meet your tax bills. You can find details of how to set up a plan on the HM Revenue & Customs* web site.

Which profits are taxed?

Although tax relates to tax years, profits relate to accounting years, which do not necessarily coincide with tax years. You are usually taxed on a 'current year basis', which means that your bill for a tax year is based on profits for the accounting year ending during that tax year. For example, if your accounting year ends on 30 April, your bill for the tax year to 5 April 2012 will be based on your accounts for the year to 30 April 2011. But special rules apply in the first years of your business (see below), unless you opt for 'fiscal accounting'.

With 'fiscal accounting', your accounting year is the same as the tax year (i.e. both end on 5 April). In practice, your accounting year does not have to be exactly the same – for example, a year end of 31 March also counts.

Starting a business

If you have opted for fiscal accounting – that is, your accounting year is the same as (or nearly the same as) the tax year – there are no special rules applying to the opening years of your business. Right from the word go, you are simply taxed on the profits you make each tax year.

If you have some other year end, different rules apply for the first one, two or sometimes three tax years of your business. To find out which rules apply, follow these steps:

- *step one*: find the first tax year in which an accounting date falls that is 12 months or more after the date you started in business. Tax for that year is based on profits for the 12 months up to that accounting date. The normal current year basis applies to subsequent years.

- *step two*: there will be one or maybe two tax years before that covered in step one. In the first tax year, you are taxed on the actual profits you make in that tax year. If there is a second tax year and no accounting date falls in it, you are taxed on the actual profits for that year as well.

To decide what profits you have made in a 12-month period or your actual profits for a tax year, you take a proportion of the profits for the relevant accounting period. You do this using either days or months. For example, if your first accounting period lasts 14 months and two months fall within the first tax year, in the first tax year you are taxed on $\frac{2}{14} \times$ profits for the 14-month period.

You cannot do these sums until you have reached the end of the relevant accounting period and have the final accounts. But that does not mean you can put off paying your tax bill. Initially, you will have to estimate what your profits are likely to be and pay tax based on these provisional figures.

You then correct the figures and your tax bill as soon as you have the actual profit data.

Overlap profits

Under the opening year rules for a new business, some profits are taxed more than once. In the example below, David is taxed on $\frac{2}{16} + \frac{12}{16} + \frac{12}{16} = \frac{26}{16}$ of the profits for his first accounting period – that is £13,000 instead of the actual £8,000 for the period. The excess £13,000 − £8,000 = £5,000 is his overlap profit. You normally do not get tax relief on overlap profits until your business finally ceases. In the meantime, overlap profits are not increased in line with inflation, so the tax relief might not be worth much in real terms by the time you finally get it.

Example 1: Working out profit to be taxed at the start of a business

David Weston started his business on 1 February 2011 but decides to end his accounting year on 31 May each year. To avoid a very short first period, he lets his first accounting 'year' last for 16 months. His profits are as follows:

Accounting year 1/2/11 to 31/5/12	£8,000
Accounting year 1/6/12 to 31/5/13	£12,000
Accounting year 1/6/13 to 31/5/14	£17,000

Step one: the first tax year in which there is an accounting date falling at least 12 months after the start of trading is 2012–13.

Step two: opening year rules apply to the tax years 2010–11 and 2011–12.

David's profits will be taxed as follows:

2010–11: $\frac{2}{16}$ × £8,000	£1,000
2011–12: $\frac{12}{16}$ × £8,000	£6,000
2012–13: $\frac{12}{16}$ × £8,000	£6,000
2013–14: current year basis	£12,000
2014–15: current year basis	£17,000

Choosing when to end your accounting year

You will need to weigh up a number of factors when deciding the best date on which to end your accounting year:

■ fiscal accounting – that is, ending your year on or about 5 April or 31 March – makes your tax affairs very simple but will give you the least time to draw up your accounts to meet the self-assessment deadlines (see below).

- a year-end early in the tax year maximizes the delay between earning your profits and paying tax on them. This is good for cash flow if your profits are rising. You also have plenty of time in which to draw up your accounts. On the other hand, a year-end early in the tax year will involve higher overlap profits. You probably won't get tax relief on these for many years and in the meantime inflation will have eroded its value.

If your business is already established, you can choose to alter your year end. In that case, you might be able to claim some or all of your overlap relief early, but whether overall the change works to your advantage depends on the pattern of profits for your particular business. Get advice from your accountant.

The self-assessment timetable

Under self-assessment, you are required to send HMRC a tax return each year and to pay your tax bill by the due dates.

You are responsible for working out how much tax to pay, though you can ask your tax office to do the sums provided you get your return back early enough. Alternatively, if you send in your return via the Internet, your tax bill is automatically worked out for you. If you send back your return late, there are automatic penalties. Similarly, if you pay your tax late, you will be charged interest and possibly fines too. Key dates for your 2011–12 tax bill are:

The year 2012

- *31 January* First instalment (called a 'payment on account') of your tax bill for 2011–12 is due. It is usually set at half your tax bill for the previous year (2010–11).
- *5 April* End of 2011–12 tax year.
- *April* Receive 2011–12 tax return for the tax year just ended or notice to file a return if you normally do this by Internet.
- *31 July* Second payment on account for 2011–12 tax bill. This is usually set at half your tax bill for the previous tax year (2010–11).
- *31 October* Deadline for sending in your 2011–12 tax return if you are using the paper version. If you miss it, you will either have to file

online instead or face a late filing penalty if you stick with the paper return.

■ *30 December* Latest date for filing your return online if you owe less than £2,000 tax and want it to be collected through PAYE (where you are also getting earnings from a job or a pension) throughout 2013–14 instead of as a single lump sum by 31 January 2013.

The year 2013

■ *31 January* Last date for filing your 2011–12 tax return online. If your two payments on account come to less than the final bill, you must send in your payment for the remaining tax by this date.

The year 2014

■ *31 January* Your 2011–12 tax return becomes final 12 months after the date you filed it, so this is the latest date on which your return should become final. The significance is that, if HMRC is going to open an enquiry into your return, it should tell you by the date your return becomes final. However, HMRC can still investigate your tax affairs for other reasons – for example, suspected fraud. And, if your tax return contained any estimated valuations (of, say, property or unquoted shares) which were not fully explained in the return, HMRC can still open an enquiry into that aspect of your return.

The year 2016

■ *6 April.* Since 1 April 2010, the normal time limit for you or the Revenue to go back and review or reopen a past year's tax return is four years from the end of the relevant tax year (previously five years from 31 January following the end of the tax year). However, the Revenue can go back up to six years if it thinks you have failed to take reasonable care and 20 years if it suspects fraud. You should keep your records for at least six years.

Coping with a difficult economy – extra time to pay

As part of measures to help businesses through the recession and subsequent difficult economic climate, HM Revenue & Customs operates a Business Payment Support Service to consider requests for extra time to pay taxes. Normal penalties will not apply to tax paid late – although interest will. Provided your business is viable, the Revenue may agree to spread your payments.

Working out your income tax bill

For sole traders and partners, you first turn your profits from your accounts into taxable profits (see Example 2 below):

1 If you have taken any items out of stock for your own use, include these in your sales figure at the normal selling price (not cost).

2 Deduct from your profits any business expenses that are normally allowable against tax but that you have not included.

3 Add back to your profits any business expenses that are not allowable for tax purposes (p. 392).

4 Deduct the following items, which are allowable for tax purposes: annual investment allowance (see p. 394), any first-year capital allowances (see p. 395), writing-down allowances (see p. 396), any balancing allowances (see p. 397) and loss relief (see p. 398).

5 Add back any balancing charges from the sale of assets (see p. 398).

6 Deduct any income that is not part of your trading income and on which tax is paid separately, for example bank interest.

Example 2: Working out taxable profits

Patty Woodward, who started her business five years ago and has a year end of 31 July, adjusts the profits from her 2010–11 accounts to provide a figure on which her 2011–12 tax bill will be based. Her profits according to the accounts are £7,500.

1 She has not used any stock for her own use, so no adjustment needed here.

2 She checks carefully against the list of business expenses that are normally allowed for tax purposes (see below). She realizes she has forgotten to include bank charges, which for the year total £48. The adjusted profit figure is now £7,452.

3 However, her accounting profit includes a figure for depreciation of her van of £1,000. She adds this back; her adjusted profits are now £8,452.

4 Patty now claims the allowances she can. She takes the full writing-down allowance on her van. For this year, it comes to £709. She has no losses on which to claim relief. This gives taxable profits of £7,743.

5 She has not sold any assets this year.

6 She has no business investment income. Her taxable profits are £7,743.

Business expenses

What business expenses are allowed?

You can claim, and be allowed, an item as a business expense for tax purposes if it is incurred 'wholly and exclusively' for the business. The golden rule with expenses is that if you are in any doubt as to whether an expense is allowable, claim it.

An expense incurred partly for business and partly for private reasons, for example a trip in your car to a customer, is strictly not allowed if you dropped in to see a friend on the way. However, where the business part can be clearly identified or apportioned, you are allowed to make a claim. For example, you can claim part of the cost of running a car for both business and private reasons based on records you keep of your total and business mileage. Similarly, you may be able to claim some of the expenses of using your home for business based on, say, the proportion of floor area devoted to the business and the proportion of time that space is used for business. Typical allowable home expenses will be part of the costs of heating, lighting, cleaning, telephone, insurance and security. You can also treat fixed costs, such as mortgage interest, rent, council tax, home insurance, water rates and general repairs as being partly for business if part of the home is set aside solely for business. Be aware that if part of your home is used exclusively for business, there could be capital gains tax (CGT) to pay on that proportion when you come to sell your home. HMRC* makes a distinction between using part of the home 'solely' for business and 'exclusively' for business. For example:

■ you use your office solely for business from 9am to 5pm but then for other activities after 5pm. If the office represents 10 per cent of the floor space of the home, you would first work out 10 per cent of your fixed costs on the basis of floor area, then take $\frac{8}{24}$ of the result (the proportion of time the room is used for business) to find the amount you can claim. In this example, the office is used solely for the business part of the time, but not exclusively for business, so there would be no CGT when you sell.

■ you use your office solely for business and no other purpose. If it represents 10 per cent of the floor space of the home, you can claim 10 per cent of the fixed costs. In this case, the office is used exclusively for business and so there could be CGT when you sell the home.

However, you may be able to reduce or eliminate any bill by claiming entrepreneurs' relief (see p. 401), roll-over relief (see p. 401) or your normal annual CGT allowance (see p. 401).

Checklist of expenses you can normally claim

1. General expenses

Claim the expenses of making your product and running your premises:

- cost of goods you sell or use in your product.

- selling costs, such as advertising, sales discounts, gifts costing up to £50 a year (if gift advertises your business or product and is not food, drink or tobacco).

- office/factory expenses, such as heating, lighting, cleaning, business rates, rent, telephone, postage, printing, security, stationery, normal repairs and maintenance.

- proportion of home expenses, if used for work.

- cost of computer software, if its useful life is less than two years. If the useful life is longer, it may be treated as capital expenditure (see p. 393).

- other expenses, such as relevant books and magazines, professional fees, subscriptions to professional and trade organizations, replacing small tools, travel expenses (but not between home and work or, usually, lunches).

- running costs of a car, delivery charges, charge for hiring capital equipment, leasing payment; but special rules apply to some cars. For cars you buy from 6 April 2009, you can claim the full leasing payment for cars with CO_2 emissions up to 160 g/km but only 85 per cent of the payments for cars with higher emissions. However, there will be no restriction if the car is available to you for a period of no more than 45 consecutive days. Spending on leases that started before 6 April 2009 will continue to be subject to the old rules until the end of the lease. Under the old rules, if you lease a car that cost over £12,000 when new, the allowable expense you can claim is limited to $(£12,000 + P)/2P$, where P is the price of the car when new. For example, if the car cost £20,000 when new, you would be able to claim only $£32,000/£40,000 = ⅘$ of the leasing payment.

If you are not registered for VAT, include the cost of VAT in what you claim, as it is a business expense that you cannot get back through the VAT system. If you are registered for VAT, do not include it, unless it is impossible for you to claim it back from the VAT inspector because, for example, it is included in what you have purchased for part of your business that is exempt for VAT purposes.

If you have opted to use the VAT flat-rate scheme (see p. 429), you have a choice. Under the scheme, you pay VAT as a percentage of your VAT-inclusive turnover instead of working out the VAT you have charged less the VAT you can claim back. The VAT you actually hand over to HMRC may be more or less than the VAT you would otherwise have paid. Either:

■ you can work out your accounts excluding VAT from both your revenue and your expenses, in which case you record any profit from using the flat-rate scheme as extra revenue or any loss as an additional expense, or

■ you can work out your accounts including VAT in both your revenue and expense figures and record the VAT you actually hand over as an expense. This is the simpler method to use.

2. Staff costs

Claim the normal costs of employing people:

■ wages, salaries, bonuses, redundancy and leaving payments, pensions to former employees and dependants (but not your salary or your partner's salary), training costs, council tax paid on behalf of an employee, if a genuine part of remuneration package subject to PAYE. This includes the cost of employing family members – such as your husband or wife – provided you can show that the work is actually done and that the wage is the going market rate.

■ pension contributions made on employees' behalf. Cost of providing life, health and sick pay insurance for employees (but not yourself).

■ employer's National Insurance contributions (but not your own, see p. 400).

■ entertaining staff, for example Christmas party.

■ gifts, subscriptions and contributions for benefits for staff, but these could be regarded as employees' emoluments.

3. Financial expenses

■ bank charges on business accounts.

■ accountancy and audit fees, additional accountancy expenses needed as a result of HMRC 'in-depth' investigation but not if the investigation reveals that profits have been understated.

■ interest on loans and overdrafts for your business, and cost of arranging them (but not interest paid to a partner for capital put into the business, or interest on overdue tax).

- charge part of hire purchase payments (that is, the interest plus additional costs).
- business insurance.
- bad debts that you specifically claim (but not a general reserve for bad or doubtful debts).
- incidental cost of obtaining loan finance, but not stamp duty, foreign exchange losses, issue discounts or repayment premiums.

4. Legal and other expenses

- legal charges such as debt collection, preparing trading contracts, employee service contracts, settling trading disputes and renewing a short lease (that is, 50 years or less).
- legal costs of defending yourself against disciplinary action by a body that regulates your profession (but not any fines imposed as a result of that action).
- premium for grant of lease, but limited to the amount assessed on the landlord as extra rent spread over the term as the lease is paid.
- fees paid to register trade mark or design, or to obtain a patent.

What is not normally allowed as a business expense

1 Your own income and living expenses, ordinary clothes, medical expenses, your NI contributions (p. 400), income tax, capital gains tax, inheritance tax, fines and other penalties for breaking the law (but you could pay a parking fine for an employee), VAT surcharge.

2 Depreciation or initial costs of capital equipment, buying a patent, vehicles, computer hardware or software if treated as a capital item (see below), permanent advertising signs, buildings and the cost of additions or improvements to these (but see the 'Annual investment allowance' and 'Capital allowances' sections below). An initial lump sum paid for a franchise is not normally allowable (but should qualify for the annual investment allowance and capital allowances), but any part paid for, say, trading stock or staff training (but not your own training) is normally allowable.

3 Legal expenses on forming a company, drawing up a partnership agreement, and acquiring assets such as long leases.

4 Business entertaining expenses, cost of partners' meals at regular lunch-time meetings, gifts to customers (but see p. 390), normally charitable subscriptions and donations, and donations to political parties.

5 Reserves or provisions for expected payments, such as repairs and general reserve for bad and doubtful debts (but see p. 390).

6 Wages to employees that remain unpaid 18 months after the accounting date.

Tax relief for capital expenditure

The tax rules make a distinction between revenue spending and capital spending. In general, revenue spending is on items that you use up straight away in producing your goods and services or running your business and you can claim these as allowable expenses (see previous section). Capital spending is on items that are durable and that you will use over a period of years. This does not count as an allowable expense and there are different rules for how you claim tax relief on the cost of these items.

The rules for tax relief on capital spending changed markedly on 6 April 2008. There is now an annual investment allowance, in addition to first-year capital allowances and writing-down allowances. The rates of writing-down allowances have changed and some are being phased out. New arrangements for spending on cars were introduced on 6 April 2009.

To qualify for relief, capital spending must be 'wholly and exclusively' for the business. But this does not mean you cannot claim relief for some item that you use in your private life as well as your business. For example, if you use a car half for business and half for private purposes, you treat the car as if it is made up of two separate assets and claim allowances just for the half that counts as a business asset.

If you bring into your business something you already owned privately, you can claim tax relief based on the market value of the item at the time you brought it into the business.

The way in which you pay for equipment does not affect the annual investment allowance or capital allowances you can claim. But you do not claim these allowances for the interest on a loan or overdraft to buy equipment – this is an allowable expense (see p. 391) not part of the cost of the asset. If you buy on hire purchase, the hire charge part is also a business expense and, with leased equipment, you claim the rental as an expense (see p. 392) not a capital cost.

The rules described here apply to sole traders and partnerships. Companies may in addition qualify for relief on spending on research and development and, since 1 April 2008, loss-making companies that spend on environmentally sustainable investment may qualify for capital allowances that produce a cash refund (unlike other capital allowances which can only be paid as a reduction in tax). Your accountant* can give you details.

Annual investment allowance

You can claim 100 per cent tax relief for spending on or after 6 April 2008 on plant and machinery, excluding cars, up to the amount of your annual investment allowance (AIA).

The full rate of the allowance is £50,000 for the tax year 2011–12, but is due to fall to £25,000 from 2012–13. If the accounting period on which your tax bill is based is more or less than 12 months, the allowance is increased or reduced *pro rata*. If you had an accounting period that strad-dles an April when the amount of the allowance changes, you get just a proportion of the AIA for that year. For example, if your accounting year started on 1 January 2012 and ended on 31 December 2012, only 270 of the 366 days will fall on or after 6 April 2012, so your AIA for your 2012 accounting year will be $96/366 \times £50,000 + 270/366 \times £25,000 = £31,558$ in total (rounded up to the nearest pound). However, based on the rules that have applied in the case of previous changes, spending that falls on or after 6 April 2012 will be capped at £25,000, so you would need to have spent at least £6,558 before then to get the full £31,558 allowance for the year.

Every business, whether sole trader, partnership or company, has an AIA. There are anti-avoidance rules to prevent you claiming extra AIA by artifi-cially splitting your business into more than one entity.

If you spend more than your AIA, you can carry the excess forward and get tax relief on it in future years by claiming writing-down allowances (see p. 396), unless the spending qualifies for a first-year allowance (see p. 395) – this is on top of your annual investment allowance.

The AIA is not given automatically. You must claim it and you do this through the self-employment supplement of your tax return. You choose whether to claim and how much (up to the maximum for which you are eligible). Unused AIA cannot be carried forward. You also choose which expenditure to set your AIA against, which may be important if you have to carry some spending forward and different writing-down allowances would apply to different capital items (see p. 396).

Capital allowances

In your accounts, you gradually write off the cost of a capital item as depreciation. But depreciation is not an allowable expense for tax purposes: you have to add it back but can claim capital allowances instead on any spending that is not covered by your annual investment allowance. Capital allowances are basically a standardized measure of depreciation.

The main capital allowance is writing-down allowance (WDA). This writes off your spending at a fixed rate year after year (see below). However, to encourage certain types of spending, you can in some cases claim a higher capital allowance for the year in which you spend the money. This higher allowance is called a first-year allowance. So, if you are buying a capital item, to work out what relief you can claim, work through the following sequence:

1 *Can you claim a first-year allowance?* If so, this gives you immediate 100 per cent relief for the item, whatever its cost, with no balance to carry forward and without using up any of your AIA (see above).
2 *Do you have any unused AIA for the year?* If so, you get immediate 100 per cent relief up to the unused AIA for the year. On any excess over the AIA, you get relief by claiming WDAs.
3 *Claim WDAs* for any other capital spending.

First-year capital allowances

First-year allowances are available alongside the AIA. Currently they are all 100 per cent allowances, which means you write off the full cost of the item in the accounting year in which you buy it. You can claim these allowances for spending on:

■ Eligible new environmentally friendly equipment. For example, energy-saving boilers, refrigeration equipment and water meters. Get details from the Enhanced Capital Allowances* web site at *www.eca.gov.uk*.

■ Low-emission cars with CO_2 emissions of no more than 110 g/km (reduced from 120 g/km which applied before 1 April 2008). Details from *www.eca.gov.uk*.

■ Renovating or converting residential space over shop or other commercial premises into flats for rent.

■ Renovating commercial premises in assisted areas (see p. 194) which have been vacant for at least a year.

Writing-down allowances

Capital spending that you cannot fully write off in the first year is put into a capital pool and you gradually get relief by claiming WDAs. There are two principal capital pools:

- *Main pool*. This covers spending on most items (but see p. 397 for cars) and anything that goes into the special rate pool. The WDA is currently 20 per cent but is due to be cut to 18 per cent from 6 April 2012.

- *Special rate pool*. This covers spending on long-life assets (items expected to have an economic life of at least 25 years) and the integral features of your business premises. Integral features include, for example, electrical systems, cold water systems, space or water heating systems, ventilation or air purification systems, lifts and escalators. The WDA for items in this pool is currently 10 per cent but is due to be cut to 8 per cent from 6 April 2012.

To work out the WDA for each pool, you take the value of the pool at the start of the accounting period plus any new items that do not qualify for the AIA or first-year allowances and multiply the total by the appropriate rate. Deducting the WDA from the value of the pool gives you the value of the pool at the start of the next period. See Example 3 below.

You do not have to claim the maximum WDA. You might want to claim less if, for example, claiming the full amount would waste other reliefs or allowances. Claiming a lower WDA means you carry forward a larger pool which increases the maximum WDA you can claim next year.

If you have an accounting period that straddles an April when the WDA rates change, the WDA for the year is a weighted average of the rates that applied before and after 6 April.

Before 6 April 2008, you could claim a 4 per cent WDA each year for spending on the purchase of industrial and agricultural buildings (but not other types of business premises). These allowances were first reduced, and then abolished from 6 April 2011.

Example 3: What allowances can be claimed?

Adam Horsfield's accounting year ends on 31 December. In May 2011, he spends £50,000 on heating and ventilation systems to update his premises, which completely use up his AIA for the year. In September 2011, he buys a van costing £10,000. The van does not qualify for AIA but Adam can claim a 20 per cent WDA, leaving £8,000 of the cost to go into his main pool and, each subsequent year, he will be able to claim a further WDA on the remaining cost at 18 per cent.

He already has £5,000 in his main pool brought forward from last year, on which he can claim WDA of 20% × £5,000 = £1,000. This means the total capital allowances he can claim for his 2011 accounting year (2010 tax year) are £50,000 + £2,000 + £1,000 = £53,000. The value of his main pool at the start of his new accounting year on 1 January 2012 is £5,000 − £1,000 + £8,000 = £12,000.

Note that Adam could choose whether to set his AIA against the work on the premises or the cost of the van. The van qualifies for a higher rate of WDA (20 per cent in 2011–12 rather than 10 per cent for the work on the premises which count as integral features). So Adam maximizes his allowances for the year by setting the AIA against the items which qualify for the lowest WDA.

When it comes to selling an asset on which you have claimed capital allowances, you have to reduce the value of your pool by the lower of the sale proceeds or the original cost. Do this before working out the amount of the allowance you can claim for the accounting year in which you sell the asset. If the sale proceeds are more than the value of the pool, the difference (the balancing charge) will be taxable as if it were extra profit for the year. Note that this also applies to an asset that has formed its own separate pool (see below). If the sale proceeds come to less than the pool value of an asset you sell, you can't normally get any tax relief on the residue, unless it was a short-life asset (see below). However, when your business stops trading for good, if the proceeds from getting rid of all the assets in the pool come to less than the value of the pool, you can claim the difference as a balancing allowance that will reduce your tax bill for that year.

Since 6 April 2008, there is another way in which you might be able to fully write off the residual cost of an asset (whether you still own it or not). If the value of your main pool or your special rate pool falls to £1,000 or less, you can claim a WDA equal to the amount remaining in the pool. This applies separately to the main pool and special rate pool so you can claim extra WDAs to a maximum of £2,000 in one year. You can claim less than the maximum if you want to.

Spending on cars

Where you buy a car for your business on or after 6 April 2009, the cost goes into your main pool if its CO_2 emissions are 160 g/km or less and into your special pool if its emissions are higher. In this way, larger, gas-guzzling cars qualify for the lower 10 per cent WDA.

For cars you purchased before 6 April 2009, old rules continue to apply for a transitional period of around five years. Under the old rules a car costing more than £12,000 has its own separate capital pool and the maximum you can write off in WDA each year is capped at £3,000.

Motorcycles and vans do not count as cars and come under the ordinary rules described above.

What is not included in the main pool or special rate pool

These items have separate pools of expenditure:

- if you choose, any piece of plant and machinery (but not cars) that you expect to sell or scrap within five years of buying. With these short-life assets, for example tools or a computer, you have to choose to put it in a separate pool within two years of buying it. If, when you sell the equipment, you sell it for less than its value after deducting the capital allowances you have claimed on it, you will be able to write off the difference in that year. If you sell it for more than the value, the difference will be taxable as if it were extra profit. If you do not sell it within eight years (was four years for items bought before April 2011) of the fourth anniversary of the end of the accounting year in which you bought the item, its value will be added to your main pool as if it had never been treated separately.

- items that you use both privately and for business. You can claim capital allowances only for the part that corresponds to the business proportion of your use.

Losses for the self-employed

If you have made a loss in your business, you normally claim tax relief on it by deducting it from other income or a capital gains, or by carrying the loss forward and deducting it from future trading profits from your business.

Deducting the loss from other income and capital gains

You can either deduct your trading loss from any other income or capital gains that you have in the tax year in which your loss-making accounting year ends, or you can carry the loss back and set it against other income or gains for the previous tax year. Other income could be, for example, dividends from shares or earnings from a job.

You must claim this relief within 12 months of the 31 January following the end of the tax year to which the loss relates. For example, suppose you have been in business for some time, your accounting year ends on 31 July and you made a loss in your 2010–11 accounting year. These accounts form the basis of your tax bill for the 2011–12 tax year. Your tax return and final tax settlement for 2011–12 are due on 31 January 2013. You then have a further 12 months – in other words, until 31 January 2014 – to elect to deduct your losses from other income and gains for 2011–12 or for 2010–11.

If you have other deductions that will reduce the tax bill on your other income and gains to nil in one of the tax years, opt to deduct the loss in the other year. If after setting the loss against income and gains for one or both years, there is still some loss left over, you can carry the excess forward to set against future profits (see below).

Deducting the loss from future trading profits

If you make this choice, you carry forward the loss and set it against the next future profits from the same trade. If you have any losses left over, you carry them forward against future profits *ad infinitum*, until they are used up. If you are going to use your loss in this way, you have to use the whole of the loss before you can use any other deductions, such as outgoings or allowances, that you may have. The main disadvantage of making this choice to use up your loss relief is that it takes a while to turn it into cash.

To use this option, you must tell your tax office within four years of the end of the tax year to which the loss relates. For example, if the loss was made in the accounts being assessed for the 2011–12 tax year, you have until 5 April 2016 to make your claim.

If you are starting a new business

If you spend money before your business actually starts, it may count as pre-trading expenditure. It will be set against the earnings of your business in its first year and, if it creates a loss, you can get loss relief. You can get tax relief on expenditure going back seven years.

There is special tax treatment for any losses you make in the first four tax years of a new business (as long as your inspector believes it was reasonable to plan for profits during that period). You can get a tax refund by setting the loss against any other income (for example, wages from a job) that you had in the three years before the loss. Set the loss off against the earliest year of income first, then the next earliest and so on.

If you want to set off your loss in this way, you need to tell your tax office in writing within 12 months of the 31 January following the end of the tax year to which the loss relates.

Other taxes you might pay

National Insurance contributions

If you are self-employed, you normally have to pay Class 2 National Insurance contributions. If your earnings from self-employment are expected to be less than a certain amount, £5,315 in 2011–12, you can claim exemption from payment, but this is seldom worth doing given the value of the state benefits you lose. Class 2 NI is paid at a flat rate of £2.50 a week in 2011–12, which you can pay monthly by direct debit or you will be sent a bill each quarter. Paying Class 2 contributions means you may be able to claim incapacity benefit, basic maternity allowance and basic retirement pension, and your spouse or civil partner might get bereavement benefits in the event of your death.

If your earnings from your business are above a certain amount, £7,225 in 2011–12, you will have to pay Class 4 contributions. These are earnings-related, collected along with income tax and are 9 per cent of your profits between the lower limit up to a specified maximum, £42,475 in 2011–12, and 2 per cent of all earnings above the upper profit limit.

Example 4: Class 4 National Insurance

Carolyn Harbury has profits of £45,000 for her accounting year ending in 2011–12. Class 4 National Insurance contributions are payable at 9 per cent on profits between £7,225 and £42,475 plus 2 per cent of £45,000 − £42,475 = £2,525. For Carolyn, this means paying contributions of (£42,475 − £7,225) × 9% + £2,525 × 2% = £3,223.

Capital gains tax

You do not normally pay capital gains tax (CGT) on business stock you sell, but you might have to pay it when you dispose of land and buildings, plant and machinery or goodwill, or shares in your business if you operate as a company. Disposing includes selling, giving away, exchanging or losing.

From 6 April 2008 onwards, there were major changes to the CGT rules applying to individuals. Although the changes do not apply to companies (which pay corporation tax on capital gains) they do affect you if you as an individual sell shares in a business you own. They also affect you if you are a sole trader or partner selling your business or assets used in the business. The main rules are:

- since 22 June 2010, capital gains tax is charged at two rates, of 18 per cent and 28 per cent. To find out which applies, you add your chargeable gains to your income for the year. Any part of the gains falling in the basic tax rate band or below is taxed at 18 per cent. Any part that falls into the higher-rate tax band or above is taxed at 28 per cent.

- you have a yearly CGT tax-free allowance, which means you can make up to £10,600 of otherwise taxable gains in 2011–12 without having to pay any tax.

- you can claim entrepreneurs' relief when you dispose of part or all of your business. This limits the tax rate to 10 per cent on the first slice of business assets that you sell during your lifetime. This slice is set at £10 million for disposals in 2011–12 onwards. There is no minimum age limit for claiming this relief. To qualify, the business must be a trading business and you must have held it for at least one year. If it is a company, you must be an employee or director who owns at least 5 per cent of the shares and voting rights.

If you sell or otherwise dispose of assets from your business, and make a gain, you could pay capital gains tax on the gain. But if you replace the assets in the three years after the sale or one year before the sale of the old one, you can claim roll-over relief and defer paying capital gains tax. You can also claim relief if you do not replace but use the proceeds to buy another qualifying business asset. You usually get the relief by deducting the gain from the old asset from the acquisition cost for the new one. So when you sell the new one, the gain on it has been increased by the size of the gain on the old one. However, if you replace again, you can claim further roll-over relief. And so on. Capital gains tax will not have to be paid (under current legislation) until you fail to replace the business asset.

Not every business asset qualifies for the relief. But if it is land or a building used by the business, goodwill, fixed plant or machinery, for example, it will qualify for roll-over relief.

If you work from home, think carefully about the space you use for your business:

- if you use part of your home exclusively for business, you maximize the amount you can claim in allowable business expenses (see p. 389) but a proportion of your home becomes liable for CGT. There may be no CGT to pay if the gain comes to less than your annual allowance or you are able to claim roll-over relief (because you will also be using part of a new home for the business). If there is a CGT bill, it may be reduced if you can claim entrepreneurs' relief.

■ if you do not use any part of the home exclusively for business (for example, you work in a room from 9am to 5pm but it becomes a family room out of office hours), there will be no CGT when you sell the home. However, non-exclusive use reduces the proportion of the home-related costs that you can claim as allowable business expenses (see p. 389).

For more information about capital gains tax, contact HM Revenue & Customs*.

Business rates

If you occupy business premises, you must normally pay business rates (non-domestic rates). These apply wherever in the UK your business is situated, although the way the rates are set and the relief available vary from one country to another. However, the basic principle is the same across all the countries of the UK: your bill is worked out by multiplying the rateable value of your property – an estimate of what it could generate in rent each year – by an appropriate multiplier (sometimes called 'poundage'). Rates are levied on an annual basis with the year running from 1 April to the following 31 March.

In each country, business rates are collected by your local authority or local council. In general, they are pooled in a central pot for the country as a whole and then redistributed to local areas.

The rateable value of properties is updated every few years – usually five, but less frequently in Northern Ireland. This is to keep the values in line with commercial rents. The latest revaluation in England, Scotland and Wales came into effect from April 2010, while Northern Ireland rates are still based on values that came into effect in April 2003. Potentially a revaluation could mean a big jump in your rates bill, if commercial rents have been increasing. However, in England transitional relief spreads the increase over five years. In Scotland and Wales, the multiplier was adjusted to offset the change in rateable values and so limit the size of the increase.

If your property is partly for business and partly for private use – for example a shop with a flat above – business rates are payable on the business part of the property and council tax (domestic rates in Northern Ireland) on the rest. The same treatment may apply when you use part of

your home for business purposes, though each case is considered individually. In 2003, an English tribunal case (*Tully* v. *Jorgensen*) set out some useful
principles. It ruled that, where home-based work involves using furniture
and equipment normally found in a home and residential use is not com-
promised, business rates might not be due. But business rates are likely to
be chargeable if you make structural alterations to your home, hire staff,
use specialist equipment or have customers visit your home.

The sections below outline the business rating system in each country of
the UK and the table on pp. 404–5 summarizes the relief available that may
reduce or eliminate your bill.

England

For the year from 1 April 2011, the multiplier is usually 43.3p. However,
this is reduced to 42.6p if you qualify for small business rate relief (see table
on pp. 404–5). A small business is one whose premises have a rateable value
below £18,000, or £25,500 in London.

Example 5: Small business rates in England

Arif Patel works from a small workshop with a rateable value of £3,000 a year. This is
small enough to qualify for small business rate relief (see pp. 404–5) which reduces
his rates bill in two ways. Firstly, he can use the lower multiplier of 42.6p rather than
43.3p. Therefore, his basic bill for 2011–12 is £3,000 × 42.6p = £1,278. But he also
qualifies for small business rate relief of 100 per cent for the whole period 1 April 2011
to 31 March 2012, meaning he does not pay any business rates at all.

In the following year (assuming the increase in the small business rate relief is not
extended further), he will get 100 per cent relief for the period 1 April 2012 to 30
September 2012 and then 50 per cent relief from 1 October 2012 to 31 March 2013.
Based on the 2011 rateable value (since the increase for 2012 is not yet known), this
would give a business rates bill of (0% × $^{6}\!/_{12}$ × £1,278) + (50% × $^{6}\!/_{12}$ × £1,278) =
£319.50.

Scotland

Scotland has set its standard poundage (multiplier) at 42.6p for 2011–12.
However, for premises valued at more than £35,000, there is a 0.7p sup-
plement. In other words, although the terminology is different, Scotland's
multipliers are very similar to those for England. In fact, the Scottish
Parliament has committed that its poundage will not exceed the equivalent
English rate for the lifetime of the Parliament.

Wales

In Wales, there is a single multiplier with no reduction or increase for size of business. In 2011–12, the multiplier is 42.8p. The multiplier is usually increased each year in line with inflation (the annual change in the Retail Prices Index) up to the previous September. The Welsh Assembly has legislated that business rates may not be increased by more than inflation.

Northern Ireland

Business rates in Northern Ireland are more complex than for the rest of the UK because the multiplier has two parts: a regional rate set by the Northern Ireland Executive and a district rate set by each local council. In 2011–12, the regional rate is 31.46p. The district rate ranges from 16.7748p in Castlereagh (giving a total multiplier of 48.2348p) to 29.5002p in Armagh (giving a total multiplier of 60.9602p). Although these multipliers look high compared with the rest of the UK, we must bear in mind that Northern Ireland is using more historic rateable values, so the total rates bill for comparable properties in other parts of the UK is not necessarily so very different.

Main rate reliefs[1]	
Transitional Relief (following 2010 revaluation)	**England**: Caps the yearly increase in your rates bill. For small businesses, the maximum is 7.5% in 2011–12; 10% in 2013–14; 15% in 2014–15.
	Scotland and Wales: Not available
	Northern Ireland: Not applicable
Small Business Rate Relief[2]	**England**: Reduction in rateable value: 50% if rateable value less than £6,000; between 50% and 0% for rateable values up to £12,000. Temporary increase: 1 October 2010 to 30 September 2012. Reduction in rateable value: 100% if rateable value less than £6,000; between 100% and 0% for rateable values up to £12,000.
	Scotland: Reduction in rateable value in 2011–12: 100% if combined rateable value of all premises up to £10,000; 50% up to £12,000; 25% up to £18,000; 25% up to £25,000 for properties with individual rateable value not exceeding £18,000.
	Wales: Reduction in rateable value: 50% if rateable value up to £2,400; 25% for rateable values up to £7,800. Post offices: 100% if rateable value up to £9,000; 50% up to £12,000. Temporary increase: 1 October 2010 to 30 September 2012. Reduction in rateable value: 100% if rateable value less than £6,000; between 100% and 0% for rateable values up to

£12,000. Temporary increases to March 2012 for childcare premises with rateable value up to £12,000 and retail premises with rateable value up to £11,000.

Northern Ireland: Reduction in rateable value: 50% if rateable value up to £2,000; 25% for rateable values up to £5,000. Post offices: 100% if rateable value up to £9,000; 50% up to £12,000.

Rural villages	**England**: 50% reduction if: only village store or post office and rateable value under £8,500; only village pub or petrol station and rateable value under £12,500; other rural business and rateable value under £16,500.
	Scotland: 50% reduction if: only village store or post office and rateable value under £8,500; only village pub or petrol station and rateable value under £12,750; other rural business and rateable value under £17,000.
	Wales and Northern Ireland: not rural-specific, but see Small Business Rate Relief above for post offices and retail premises.
Empty premises	**England**: First three months: 100% reduction. Next three months: 100% reduction if industrial premises.
	Scotland: First three months: 100% reduction. Next three months: 50% reduction. 100% relief without time limit for industrial premises and properties with rateable value up to £17,000.
	Wales: First three months: 100% reduction. Next three months: 100% reduction if industrial premises. 100% relief without time limit for properties with rateable value up to £2,600.
	Northern Ireland: Properties with rateable value of £2,000 or more: first three months: 100% reduction; 50% after that without time limit. 100% relief without time limit for industrial premises.

[1] This is just a broad summary. For details of these and other reliefs (e.g. for listed buildings and charities) and to claim relief, contact your local authority or council.
[2] Usually given automatically, but you must let your local authority or local council know if your circumstances change.

You and your tax office

When you first start in business

When you first start working for yourself, you need to inform your local tax office, which is your contact point for both income tax and National Insurance contributions. You must normally do this as soon as possible, otherwise you could face a fine linked to any tax paid late or unpaid. Fill in form CWF1, which is available from HMRC*. You can also register over the Internet or by telephone. Your tax office will pass details to the VAT section of HMRC, which will then contact you to find out whether you need or want to register for VAT (see Chapter 31, 'VAT'). By autumn 2011, the Business Link* web site is due to include a new area for business start ups. This start-up 'hub' will include an HMRC tax registration 'wizard' that will let you register for all your business taxes and payment arrangements using a single online form.

If you have finished a job as an employee, you will have form P45, which should be sent to your tax inspector so that the amount of your personal allowances and the amount of tax to be paid for that tax year can be sorted out. If you start self-employment part way through the tax year, having been an employee before, you can ask for a refund of part or all of the tax paid under PAYE if you can show that you will otherwise pay too much tax. This can help with the cash flow problems of starting the business.

Once you have started a business

When you first start in business, there are no interim payments of tax for the first year or so, because there is no track record from a previous year on which to base any payments. You'll be sent a tax return in the April following start up and, as usual, you have until the following 31 January to send in your return and to pay the tax due. For example, you might start in business in, say, June 2011. You'll get a tax return in April 2012, and your first tax payments must be made by 31 January 2013. At that time, you'll pay all the tax due for the 2011–12 tax year plus the first interim payment for 2012–13 which will be set at half the amount due for 2011–12. By the end of 2012, the HMRC web site is due to offer an online facility for small and medium-sized businesses that will give you a single view of your tax position for all the main taxes you have to pay.

Your tax return

If your business is very small and the rest of your tax affairs uncomplicated, you may receive a short four-page tax return. HMRC will have selected you for the short return on the basis of your previous years' affairs, but it is up to you to make sure that you are eligible to use the form. If not, you need to contact HMRC to get the full tax return (or alternatively use the online tax return service). Anyone with more complicated business affairs will in any case be sent the full return.

The full tax return includes supplementary pages for self-employment, which ask for name, address and description of your business, the period on which your tax bill is based and details of the business's income, expenditure and profits. You must also fill in the details required in the main section of the tax return and fill in the supplement 'Self-employment'. There is a short version of the supplement for businesses with a turnover of less than the VAT threshold (see p. 421). Exceptionally, you might not have all the information you need to complete the return on time – for example, if you have not yet made up your first set of accounts. In this case, you should estimate what your profits will be and enter provisional figures on the supplementary pages. These should be as realistic as possible, taking into account all the information you have to date. Your tax office wants to know why figures are not yet available and when you think they will be.

Normally, if your tax return is incomplete, you will be treated as having missed the deadline and will face a penalty if tax is paid late as a result. However, HMRC says that a return containing provisional figures will not be treated as incomplete, provided you have taken all reasonable steps to obtain the final figures and you make sure you send final figures to your tax office as soon as they become available. There will be interest to pay if the finalized figures show that more tax was due than the provisional figures indicated.

Being investigated

During the 12 months after you have sent in your tax return together with your self-assessment (if you are working out your own tax), HMRC can choose to audit your return and assessment. After the 12 months have passed, HMRC can still investigate you, but only if it suspects fraud or discovers an error.

If you have been selected for audit or investigation, HMRC must by law write to you telling you that this is the case. It does not have to tell you why you are being investigated, but it must say whether your whole return is being investigated or just some aspect of it, for example how you calculated your capital allowances. The tax officer has wide-reaching powers to ask for any relevant documents, and the self-employed are required, by law, to keep documents for five years after 31 January following the end of the tax year to which they relate. If you fail to produce the documents asked for, you will be fined.

The tax officer may request an interview, the purpose of which will probably be to establish:

- why your business, and hence profits, are different from other similar businesses.
- whether you have correctly calculated adjustments for tax purposes.
- if you have assessed your own tax bill, whether you have made any errors or omissions.
- if the amount shown for what you have taken out of the business seems adequate to support your lifestyle. You may need to work out an estimate for your living expenses, for example general household expenses, as well as leisure expenditure and so on.

If the tax officer is satisfied with your records and explanation, there will probably be a fairly minor, or even no, adjustment to your accounts. However, if a more serious view is taken, you may find that your figures for profit for this and previous years are increased.

Either following or during the investigation, you will be sent an assessment if extra tax is deemed to be due. You will have to pay interest on the tax, and there may also be penalties.

Do you count as self-employed?

It may be obvious that you are self-employed, but sometimes it is not clear-cut. You cannot simply declare yourself self-employed; you will have to convince your tax inspector that you are. And recently, HMRC has been taking a closer look at those claiming to be self-employed, particularly sub-contractors working in the construction industry, and people ceasing to be employees but returning to the same work as consultants, and reclassifying them as employees. The sort of points that will help you to establish self-employment are:

1 Working for more than one customer.
2 Showing that you control what you do, whether you do it, how you do it and when and where you do it.
3 Providing the major items of equipment you need to do your job.
4 Being free to hire other people, on terms of your own choice, to do the work that you have agreed to undertake.
5 Correcting unsatisfactory work in your own time and at your own expense.

If you do the above, there will probably be little difficulty in persuading an inspector that you are self-employed. You can check whether you are likely to be classified as employed or self-employed, by using the HMRC online employment status indicator tool at *www.hmrc.gov.uk/calcs/esi.htm*.

Partners

If you decide to take a partner, your tax treatment becomes a bit more complex because, as well as individual tax returns for each partner, you have to complete a partnership tax return.

What is the taxable income?

The taxable income for your partnership is worked out in much the same way as if you were working on your own and taxed as a sole trader. From your sales figure, you can deduct business expenses that are allowable for tax purposes (p. 388). Your partnership can get tax relief on capital expenditure (annual investment allowance and capital allowances, see p. 393) and losses (p. 398). Each partner can set their allowances against their share of the profits.

If your partnership has any non-trading income, such as interest, this will not be included in the taxable profits of the partnership but taxed as investment income. In practice, partnership investment income is normally allocated in the same ratio as the profit share, and each individual partner is given a tax bill for the investment income. Any capital gains of the partnership will be subject to capital gains tax.

If a partner has other income or gains that do not come as a result of the partnership, the partner will be taxed on these as an individual in the normal way.

Who pays what tax?

- profits are normally taxed on a current year basis (see p. 383). For example, the tax bill for 2011–12 will be based on profits for the partnership accounting year ending in 2011–12.

- profits are divided between the partners according to their profit-sharing agreement for the accounting year being taxed – that is, there is no mismatch between your share of the profits and the tax bill.

- tax is worked out for each partner individually based on each share of the profits as if each of you were running your own separate business. If the partnership is new or you have newly joined an existing partnership, opening-year rules (see p. 384) apply to you personally.

- tax on investment income is also worked out for each partner individually. For this purpose, untaxed investment income is allocated to each partner as if it were income from a second business but based on the same accounting period as the partnership's mainstream business. Taxed investment income is allocated to each partner but on the basis of the amount received in each tax year.

■ each partner is responsible only for their own tax bill on their own share of the profits. You can't be asked to stump up the money if other partners don't pay their tax bills.

Tax returns

In April each year, both the partners and the partnership as a whole receive a tax return. The partnership tax return is completed on behalf of the partnership as a whole and shows the income, expenses and so on for the partnership. The partnership return must be returned to the tax office by the normal deadline of 31 January following the end of the tax year but, in practice, it will need to be ready much earlier than that.

Each partner has his or her own tax return to complete and return to the tax office by the deadlines described on p. 386 (31 October 2011 or 31 January 2012 for the 2011–12 tax return). The partner's tax return includes supplementary pages relating to his or her partnership income. The details that must be included are based on information contained in a 'partnership statement'. The partnership statement is a copy of information given in the partnership return.

Therefore, the partnership return must be completed early enough for partners to complete their own paperwork in good time. Timing could be very tight if the partnership has an accounting date late in the tax year. An early accounting date gives the maximum time for getting the accounts prepared ready for early completion of the partnership return.

Changing partners

Each partner is treated as if they were running their own business, so normal opening-year rules (see p. 384) apply to you personally when you join a partnership. Similarly, there are closing-year rules, which are applied individually to you if you leave a partnership.

Losses for partners

Losses can be treated in much the same way as if you were a sole trader (p. 398). You and your partners share the losses on the same basis as you would share any profits; the losses are apportioned on the basis applying in the year in which they arise.

You can each treat your losses as you want. One of you can set them off against other income, while the other can carry them forward and set them off against future partnership profits.

However, if you are a non-active partner who does not spend much time running the business, the amount of losses for which you can claim relief by setting them against other income and gains (see p. 398) or setting them against income for earlier years (see p. 398) is limited to the amount you have contributed to the partnership. And, for investments you make from 2 March 2007 onwards, this 'sideways loss relief' is further restricted to the lower of the eligible amount as described above and £25,000. You will count as a non-active partner if you devote on average less than ten hours a week to the business. There is an exception: the £25,000 limit will not apply where you are investing in a partnership carrying on a film-related trade. You can still claim relief without any restriction by carrying losses forward to set against future profits from the same business.

Drawing money out of your company

If you operate your business as a company, you are strongly advised to get the help of a professional in drawing up your accounts and handling your tax affairs. The aim of this section is not to explain how companies are taxed but to highlight the main points to consider when thinking about how to draw money out of the company for your private use.

Your company has a separate legal identity from you and is subject to its own tax regime – corporation tax. The profits the company makes belong to its shareholders and not directly to you, so you have two main ways in which you can transfer money from the company to yourself:

1 *Salary and fringe benefits*: as a director of the company, you count as an employee. You are subject to income tax and employee's Class 1 National Insurance contributions on any salary (but not fringe benefits) in the normal way. In addition, your company has to pay employer's National Insurance on your salary and many types of fringe benefit. Your company will have to collect these taxes by operating the PAYE system.
2 *Dividends*: you can receive these if you are a shareholder in the company. Dividends are normally subject to income tax but not National Insurance contributions. But see below for various ways in which the HMRC* might challenge your dividend payments.

There is no income tax or National Insurance on salary up to what is called the primary threshold (£7,225 in 2011–12). But, provided you receive an amount at least equal to the lower earnings limit (£5,304 in 2011–12), you will be building up entitlement to certain state benefits such as state basic and additional retirement pensions. So it is worth paying yourself a salary of at least £7,225. Provided your pay is not excessive for the work you do, the company should be able to claim your pay as an allowable expense when working out the level of profit on which corporation tax will be due.

On some fringe benefits, neither you nor the company pay any tax or National Insurance. In particular, this applies to pension scheme contributions. So, if your company pays into a pension scheme for you, that can be a very tax-efficient form of pay. Once again, your company is able to claim corporation tax relief on the amount it pays into the pension scheme for you, but only if the contributions are 'wholly and exclusively' for the purpose of the business. In practice this means that your whole remuneration package, including salary and pension, must be in proportion to the value of the work you do for the company. If you would prefer to take a large proportion of your remuneration in the form of pension contributions rather than pay, you could arrange a 'salary sacrifice' where you formally give up part of your pay in return for pension benefits.

Often you will save tax by putting the rest of your 'pay' in the form of dividends, but get advice from your accountant* or other tax adviser*, especially if you provide your personal services to clients, for example, as an IT contractor. Under legislation referred to as 'IR35', HMRC may argue that despite your personal services company you are in effect an employee of your client(s). In that case, HMRC can charge tax and National Insurance on a notional salary you are deemed to receive even if in fact your company pays you in dividends. Similar rules apply if you are deemed to be providing your services through a managed service company. This situation may arise where you provide services to end-customers through a company, set up and run by someone else, of which you are a shareholder.

Following a change in the law in respect of shares you started to own from 2 December 2004 onwards, where you are an owner/manager of your own company and pay yourself mainly in the form of dividends, HMRC might seek to tax the dividends as if they are earnings if it can show that the main purpose of your mode of payment is to avoid paying tax or National Insurance.

It is common for companies to be owned jointly by a husband and wife. Paying dividends to both spouses can save National Insurance and, especially where one spouse is a higher-rate taxpayer and the other not, income tax too. HMRC has pursued a long campaign against this type of arrangement if only one of the spouses generates the main income of the company. However, a test case (*Jones* v. *Garnett*, also known as Arctic Systems), which went all the way to the House of Lords, was won by the taxpayers. HMRC subsequently issued draft legislation proposing to change the law from April 2009 onwards. However, amid criticisms that the proposals (which were very widely drawn and went well beyond husband and wife situations) were unworkable, the draft legislation was withdrawn. The government has stated that it will 'keep this issue under review'.

Spare-time earnings

There is no quick answer to the question of how you will be taxed if you have spare-time earnings. It will depend mainly on whether your income counts as starting a business. You might find yourself in a dilemma as to how your spare-time earnings will be taxed if:

▪ you are still employed but earning some extra money in your spare time. You might be doing this either because you have started your business in a small way to see how it goes before you take the plunge and hand in your notice; or because you are doing the occasional bit of freelance work to boost your income.

▪ you are not employed, but you are starting your business on a part-time basis. This could be the case if you are at home looking after young children, for example. Some people who earn extra income in this way hope that they will be able to keep it out of the clutches of the HMRC*. Very often they ask for payment in cash. In the section 'The black economy' (p. 417), you will see how HMRC can catch you and what the penalties are if you are caught.

What you must do

By law, you must notify your tax office when you get income from a new source. You have to do this within six months of the end of the tax year in which the income first arose. The onus is on you to tell your tax office, and you cannot plead as an excuse that you did not receive a tax return. Nor does it make any difference whether you are making a profit or a loss; what matters is that you are receiving payments from a new source that your inspector does not know about. If you do not tell your tax office about a new source of income, not only will you have to pay the tax due on that income but you will usually have to pay a penalty on top (linked to the amount of tax you owe and how cooperative you are) plus interest on any tax paid late.

Bear in mind that, if the new source of income amounts to business income, you must in any case tell your tax office that you have started in business as soon as possible (see p. 48).

You need to convince the inspector that your activities amount to a business, rather than just casual earnings. So follow this checklist.

1 Describe your activities as a business or profession.
2 Do not describe your income as 'occasional' or 'casual'.
3 Let your tax inspector know that you believe your sales will repeat and grow.
4 Register for VAT, even if you don't have to, if you consider it appropriate and it won't cost you money (see Chapter 31, 'VAT' (p. 419), for more details). You may have to persuade the VAT people to let you do this.
5 Get headed notepaper for your correspondence.
6 Be careful if your business is writing or consultancy. Explain to your tax office why you regard it as a business – for example, because your work covers other aspects such as research and collation of information or because you carry out your profession or vocation on a regular basis.
7 Keep your accounting records carefully and on a businesslike basis. This is not just good business sense. It is a legal requirement that you keep records and documents used as a basis for working out your tax bill for five years and ten months after the end of the tax year to which the records relate. If you do not keep these records, or fail to produce them on request, you can be fined.

Casual income

If you don't succeed in convincing the tax office, your income could be treated as casual. Casual income will generally be taxed on an actual basis – that is, tax for any tax year will be based on the actual income you have from that source during the tax year. This contrasts with self-employment, where tax is based on the profits for an accounting period ending during the tax year. Self-employment gives you more scope for building in a time lag between making the profits and paying tax on them.

A disadvantage if your income counts as casual is that the treatment of losses is less favourable than if you are taxed as being self-employed. If you make a loss, it can only be deducted from profits taxed in the same way, made either in the same tax year or in the future. It cannot be deducted from any other income you have, for example from your job if you have one.

Property income

The tax treatment of property income is generally outside the scope of this book. However, if you run a hotel or guest house, your income will normally count as earnings from self-employment and be taxed as described on p. 388 or as earnings of your company, if your business is incorporated.

Income from other types of letting is not business income but is treated in a similar way. However many properties you rent out, the income is pooled and treated as a single source of income for tax purposes. You are taxed on the amount of this type of income you get during the tax year. In working out how much income you pay tax on, you use normal accounting rules and can deduct expenses – including interest on a loan to buy the property – in the same way as if you were running a business – see p. 388. However, you can't normally claim the annual investment allowance or capital allowances for equipment and furnishings you provide. Instead, you can claim an allowance for wear and tear. This is based either on items you have actually replaced during the year – called the renewals basis – or on a proportion (usually 10 per cent) of the rents you get less council tax and water rates. You choose which basis to use. See pp. 394–5 for the annual investment allowance and capital allowances you can claim.

Although your income from letting property is treated in a similar way to earnings from a business, it counts as investment income. This means, for example, that you can't use this income for making tax-efficient payments to a pension plan (see p. 433).

If you let furnished holiday accommodation

If the property (including caravans) is let as furnished holiday accommodation for part of the year, the income is treated as earned income, subject to certain conditions. This means, for example, that you are able to get tax relief on these earnings for pension payments (p. 433), and capital allowances for what you spend on equipment and furnishings you buy and use in your letting (p. 395).

If you let out a furnished holiday home anywhere in the European Economic Area (see table below), it is now deemed to qualify for the special tax treatment applicable to UK furnished holiday lettings. This treatment is backdated to the latest of the date the property was first used as a furnished holiday letting, the date the country joined the EEA and 1 January 1994. Check the advantages described below to see if you can now claim a reduction in your tax bill for previous years, for example by claiming capital allowances, loss relief or, for 2007–8 and earlier years, capital gains tax taper relief.

To be treated as earned income, from April 2011 onwards the property must be available for letting to the general public at a commercial rent for at least 210 days in any 12-month period. It must also be let out as living accommodation for at least 105 of those days and not normally occupied by the same tenant for more than 31 days at a stretch during a seven-month period.

Prior to April 2011, if you made a loss renting out properties, you could (among other options) set that loss off against income you had from other sources, such as earnings from a job. From April 2011, the ability to set off losses in this way has been abolished.

European Economic Area (EEA) countries

Austria	Liechtenstein
Belgium	Latvia (since May 2004)
Bulgaria (since January 2007)	Lithuania (since May 2004)
Cyprus (since May 2004)	Luxembourg
Czech Republic (since May 2004)	Malta (since May 2004)
Denmark	Netherlands
Estonia (since May 2004)	Norway
Finland	Poland (since May 2004)
France	Portugal
Germany	Romania (since January 2007)
Greece	Slovakia (since May 2004)
Hungary (since May 2004)	Slovenia (since May 2004)
Iceland	Spain
Ireland	Sweden
Italy	United Kingdom

The black economy

It is illegal to try to conceal any earnings from your tax office. The tax officer has various ways of discovering that you are earning money. Employers who make use of freelance staff, such as consultants, writers and caterers, can be made to give details to HMRC* of the payments made. There is also a department in HMRC that keeps an eye on advertisements in the press to make sure that any source of income has been declared. And if you annoy any neighbours, acquaintances or customers who suspect what you are doing, you also run the risk that they might inform on you to your tax office.

Once your tax office has started an inquiry into your affairs, you will find it very time-consuming. You may find you end up paying interest on unpaid tax from the day it was due until the date of payment; the current rate of interest is 3 per cent. On top of that, the tax officer can slap on penalties, for example for:

■ failure to tell your tax office about taxable income or gains within six months of the end of the tax year, with the penalty geared to the tax you owe and how cooperative you are.

■ failing to send in your tax return by 31 January following the end of the tax year. New and much stiffer penalties have been introduced from 6 April 2011 onwards. If your return is even one day late, there is an automatic penalty of £100 (even if you do not owe any tax). If you still have not delivered your return three months after the deadline, you can be charged £10 a day up to a maximum penalty of £900. If your return is still outstanding after six months, you face a further penalty of £300 or 5 per cent of the tax you owe if this is greater. And after 12 months, there is another fine of £300 or 5 per cent of the tax you owe, except that if your case is deemed serious, the penalty can be increased to 100 per cent of the tax you owe. Keep in mind that these are all penalties for failing to get your tax return in and are additional to the tax you must pay and any fines and interest for paying the tax late.

■ fraudulently or negligently sending in an incorrect return, with the penalty geared to the tax you owe, how the mistake came about and the degree to which you cooperate with HMRC to put it right.

■ failure to produce documents requested by HMRC – initial penalty of £50 plus further penalties up to £30 a day if the failure continues.

■ failure to retain and preserve records – a penalty of up to £3,000.

Summary

1 Consider an accounting year end that will give the greatest delay between earning the profits and paying the tax if you expect profits to rise year by year. Choose fiscal accounting to keep your tax affairs simple.

2 Remember to claim all your business expenses. Where possible, get invoices and receipts to back up your claims.

3 If you use your car partly for business, you can claim part of your car expenses (and capital allowances). If you work from home, you can claim part of the running expenses, but watch out for CGT.

4 Try to cut down the risk of being investigated by your tax office. For example, do not omit items from your tax return, such as bank interest. If you know your profit margin is lower than others in the same business, or if you make a loss, explain why.

5 To avoid fines, keep an eye on the various tax deadlines: 31 October if you are filing a paper 2011–12 return, 31 January if you file online, and pay any outstanding tax by 31 January following the end of the tax year.

6 You must by law keep documents relating to your tax return and assessment for nearly six years. You'll be fined if you can't produce the necessary documents when asked.

7 Tell your tax office about any new source of earnings within six months of the end of the tax year in which the earnings first arose or within three months of starting up if the new income is from self-employment.

31

VAT

One subject that is guaranteed to raise ire among small businesses is VAT. Essentially, the VAT system is operated by businesses acting as tax collectors for the government. As far as the consumer is concerned, it is what is called an indirect tax. It is only paid by the consumer when something is bought, but the amount of VAT cannot be claimed back by a consumer. As far as you the business person is concerned, you pay tax when you buy goods from someone else and charge the tax when you sell them on. Broadly speaking, you hand over to HM Revenue & Customs* (HMRC) the difference between the amount of tax you charge your customers and the amount of tax you have paid your suppliers.

What is in this chapter?

- how the VAT system works (p. 420).
- who has to register? (p. 420).
- what rate of tax? (p. 423).
- voluntary registration (p. 424).
- how is the tax worked out? (p. 425).
- the records you need (p. 427).
- paying the tax (p. 430).
- compulsory online filing (p. 431).

VAT is a complex tax, and this chapter can only outline the principles. The examples given are deliberately simplified. You are advised to ask for professional help with VAT if your affairs are at all complicated.

How the VAT system works

The principle of the system is that tax is paid on the value added at each stage of the business process.

Example 1

Jason King grows timber. He sells £1,000 of oak to A. J. Furniture, which will turn the oak into hand-crafted timber. He charges £1,000 for the timber and adds on 20 per cent to the invoice for VAT. The total A. J. Furniture pays to him is £1,000 plus £200 VAT, £1,200 in all. Jason pays the £200 tax collected (called output tax) to HMRC*.

A. J. Furniture makes the oak into ten tables. These are sold on to a furniture shop run by Doris Bates. Doris is charged £250 for each table plus VAT. On the invoice, this is shown as £2,500 plus £500 VAT. A. J. Furniture claims back the VAT charged by Jason King (called input tax), that is, £200, and hands over the VAT Doris pays to them, £500 (called output tax). This means a net payment of £500 − £200 = £300 to HMRC.

Doris sells the tables in her shop at a price of £500 plus VAT. She receives in total for the tables, £5,000 plus VAT of £1,000. When she makes her VAT return, she claims back the £500 VAT (called input tax) she paid to A. J. Furniture, while handing over the £1,000 VAT paid by the customers (called output tax), a net payment of £1,000 − £500 = £500.

The customers cannot claim back the VAT they have paid on the tables, but all the businesses are registered for VAT and can do so.

VAT is charged on what is called taxable supplies. In Example 1, Jason King makes taxable supplies (the timber) of £1,000, A. J. Furniture makes taxable supplies (the tables) of £2,500 and Doris makes taxable supplies of £5,000 (the tables). Not all goods supplied to businesses are taxable; some are known as exempt, and VAT is not charged on those (see p. 421).

In VAT terms, the VAT that you charge on what you sell is called your 'output tax'. If registered for VAT, the business to which you sell claims back the VAT that it pays you as its 'input tax'. This is done when it makes its VAT return to HMRC.

Who has to register?

It is the person, not the business, who is registered for VAT. Each registration covers all the business activities of the registered person. For VAT purposes, a company is treated as a person. There are a number of reasons why you might not have to register. These include:

- your sales (strictly, the amount of your taxable supplies, see below) are too low, but you might still wish to register for VAT purposes and charge it on your sales (see below).
- your business operates outside the VAT area (see below).
- you make only exempt supplies (see below).
- you carry out non-business activities (but you would still charge VAT on what counts as your business activities) (see p. 422).

If you fail to register when you should do so – and you have 30 days' grace – HMRC* can impose financial penalties. The penalty is 5 per cent of the tax due if registration is up to nine months overdue, 10 per cent if registration is more than nine but not more than 18 months overdue and 15 per cent if registration is more than 18 months late. The minimum penalty is £50.

Your level of sales

You must register your business for VAT if your sales are above a certain limit (strictly, the limit is for the value of your taxable supplies, see below, rather than sales). The limit increases each year in line with the rate of inflation. From 1 April 2011, you must register if:

- your sales in the previous 12 months were more than £73,000.
- in the next 30 days, the 12-month running total of your sales may exceed £73,000.

But you may be excused registration if you can show that exceeding the VAT threshold is temporary and your sales in future will be less. If you are already registered, should your sales fall below the limit above, you can ask to have your registration cancelled. You would have to establish that your sales, excluding VAT, will be £71,000 or less for the next 12 months.

The area for VAT

VAT applies to England, Scotland, Wales, Northern Ireland and the Isle of Man. It does not apply to the Channel Islands. If you have customers or suppliers there, the goods you buy or sell will be treated as imports or exports.

What are taxable supplies and what are exempt?

Broadly speaking, if you supply goods and services in your business (including anything you take for your own use or sell to your staff), these will be taxable unless the government has specifically laid down that they are not. If they are not taxable, they are called exempt.

If all the goods or services that you supply are exempt, you cannot normally be registered for VAT. What this means for you is that you cannot claim back the VAT on any of the things you have bought for your business.

On the other hand, with a business composed of some taxable and some exempt supplies, you will still have to comply with the registration limits for the value of your taxable supplies. You will be able to claim back the VAT you have paid for the whole of your business if the value of your exempt input tax (that is, input tax relating wholly or partly to your exempt supplies) is not more than £625 per month on average and comes to no more than half your total input tax.

The main items that are exempt as far as VAT is concerned are, broadly speaking:

- most sales, leases and lettings of land and buildings (but not lettings of garages, parking spaces or hotel and holiday accommodation). Landlords of non-domestic buildings will be able to charge VAT on rent if they choose to do so.
- providing credit.
- insurance.
- certain education and training.
- most healthcare.
- postal services (but the VAT exemption for Royal Mail's non-statutory postal services, such as Parcelforce Worldwide, was removed from 31 January 2011).
- most betting, gaming and lotteries.
- certain supplies by undertakers.
- membership benefits provided by trade unions and professional bodies.

What is business and what is non-business?

As far as the VAT system is concerned, business is supplying goods or services to someone else in return for something that could be regarded as payment; it does not need to be money. You must be supplying the goods on a continuing basis to be a business activity.

If you are carrying out only non-business activities, you cannot be registered for VAT; if you have some non-business activities, the VAT you can reclaim is reduced.

When is your registration cancelled?

Apart from you requesting it to be cancelled (see p. 421), your registration will be cancelled if:

■ the business is closed down.

■ the business is sold.

■ you take a partner or become a sole trader rather than a partner.

■ as a sole trader or partner, you change the business into a company and vice versa.

What rate of tax?

For taxable supplies, there are three rates of tax:

■ the standard rate, which, at the time of writing, is 20 per cent.

■ a special 5 per cent rate applying to domestic fuel, installation of energy-saving materials in homes and women's sanitary products.

■ the zero rate.

The standard rate is charged unless the government specifies otherwise.

These are the main supplies that are zero-rated at present:

■ most food and drink, but not if supplied for catering, or certain items like chocolate, crisps and so on, which are regarded as 'non-essential', or 'hot food' to be taken away.

■ books and newspapers.

■ young children's clothing and footwear.

■ public transport, but not taxis, hire cars or 'fun' transport, such as steam railways.

■ exports.

■ sales of, and the construction of, new domestic buildings only.

■ dispensing prescriptions.

■ mobile homes and houseboats.

Do not confuse exempt and zero-rated. The effect of the two categories is quite different. Neither charges VAT on what they sell, but the exempt category cannot claim VAT back on what they have paid, while the zero-rated category can. Costs for the exempt category are likely to be up to 20 per cent higher than the costs for the zero-rated category.

Voluntary registration

You can apply to register even if the value of your taxable supplies is below the limit. You have to satisfy HMRC* that you are making taxable supplies in your business. There are two reasons why you might apply to register even if your sales are likely to be below the limit (p. 421). In both cases, registration will mean lower costs.

The first instance would be if you sell to businesses that can claim back VAT, so charging the 20 per cent on your sales will not mean you lose business. If this is the case with you, consider applying to register. You may still decide not to if the administrative set-up is too difficult, for example if you sell a large number of low-value items. But if you register, your costs could be as much as 20 per cent lower than they otherwise would be. See Example 2 below.

Example 2

Susan Hammond runs a car hire service. Her main customers are businesses. She considers whether she should apply to register for VAT, although her present sales of £50,000 are below the limit. Her costs are £20,000 including VAT of £2,000 (she is not charged VAT on all the goods and services she purchases).

If she registers, she will have to charge VAT of £10,000 on her sales of £50,000, but her customers can claim this back. She can claim back the £2,000 of VAT (input tax) she has paid on her purchases. The net result is that she receives £50,000 from her sales, claims back £2,000 VAT and pays £20,000 to her suppliers. Her income goes up from £30,000, before registering, to £32,000, after registering.

An alternative would be to lower her prices as her costs are now lower, but this does not seem necessary as she is not losing sales because of the price she charges.

The second instance of registering being beneficial is if your sales are zero-rated but you are paying VAT on the goods you buy in. See Example 3.

Example 3

> Barbara Croft runs a business making bibs and similar items for babies. Consumers cannot claim VAT back, but clothing for children is zero-rated, so she does not charge VAT. Her sales are £15,000 and her costs are £5,000, including VAT of £500. If she did not register, her income would be £15,000 − £5,000 = £10,000. This would be increased by £500 to £10,500 if she can register voluntarily.

How is the tax worked out?

What do you charge VAT on?

You charge VAT on the taxable sales you make; this is known as output tax. The amount of VAT is worked out on the price for the goods or services you are supplying. Occasional sales of second-hand goods are treated in the same way as new goods but, if your business involves buying and selling second-hand, you'll usually be covered by a special scheme.

You cannot escape charging VAT if you decide to take other goods, for example, rather than money in full payment or in part exchange. In this case, you have to work out the VAT to add on the basis of the open-market value of the goods or services you are supplying.

With discounts, the treatment varies depending on the type of discount. If the discount is unconditional, the VAT is charged on the discounted amount. This is also what applies if the discount is for prompt payment. Whether the customer pays promptly or not, VAT is worked out on the discounted amount. If the discount you offer is dependent on something happening later, for example the customer buying more, VAT is worked out on the full amount for the first payment. If the discount is subsequently taken, the VAT is adjusted at that time. Packaging is treated as part of what you are selling, so there will normally be no extra VAT to pay; and if the thing you are selling is zero-rated, that also applies to the packaging. With delivery, if you charge extra for it, VAT is due on that extra amount. But if the delivery is included in the selling price, no extra VAT is due.

Exports of goods are normally zero-rated, and this also applies to many exports of services, although some are standard-rated.

What you can claim VAT back on

You can claim back VAT on the goods and services you use in your business; these include imports and goods you remove from bonded warehouses. However, there are some supplies on which you cannot claim back the VAT. These include:

- motor cars (but private taxi and self-drive hire firms and driving schools can recover the VAT they pay on cars purchased for their businesses; however, they will have to pay VAT on any private use. And businesses that lease cars to them can claim back the VAT on cars they buy. In both cases, VAT has to be paid on the ultimate sale of the car).
- business entertainment expenses.
- if you are a builder, on certain things you install in buildings.
- on some imports if you do not wholly own them.
- on assets of a business transferred to you as a going concern (because you should not have been charged VAT if the going concern conditions have been met).
- on goods that are zero-rated or are exempt supplies (because you have not been charged VAT).

Working out the amount of input tax you have paid

In Chapter 29, 'Keeping the record straight' (p. 370), you can see how to organize your records to obtain the information you need for VAT purposes. There are also guidelines below on some of the records you need. Basically, if your business is very simple, you can work out the input tax like this:

1 Get all your purchase invoices in date order.
2 In your records (p. 376), you will have some way of showing the VAT you have paid on each invoice.
3 You cannot claim back VAT on exempt or zero-rated supplies.
4 Some invoices show the amount of VAT you are charged, so these are quite straightforward. Enter the amount in the column marked VAT.
5 Other invoices are not so detailed and you will have to work out the amount of VAT yourself. See Example 4 below for how to do this.
6 Remember you can claim back only the proportion of VAT for goods that you use partially in your business. For example, if you run your business from your home, you could claim back the VAT only on the part of your telephone bill that was due to your business.

Example 4

Peter Taylor is working out what VAT he can claim back on some stationery he has purchased for his business. The amount of the VAT is not shown on the receipt he has from the shop. The stationery cost him £4.75. He needs to know the amount of the VAT and the net cost of the stationery.

He divides £4.75 by 1.2 or he does this sum: £4.75 × 1,000/1,200.

Both calculations give the same figure, £3.96, which is the net cost; the amount of VAT he can claim back is £4.75 − £3.96 = £0.79.

The records you need

These are the main additional records you need for VAT purposes, and these must be kept for six years:

■ the tax invoice.

■ a VAT account showing the results for each tax period.

■ the returns to HMRC* showing the VAT payable or repayable.

If you fail to keep your records properly, you can be charged a financial penalty. VAT inspectors will come to see you every so often to check that your records are satisfactory. Although you are still required by law to keep your records for six years, in the normal way, HMRC can go back only three years to review the amount of VAT you should have paid. However, in cases of fraud, HMRC can go back 20 years.

There are special rules about petrol used for your private motoring – check with your VAT inspector. But, broadly speaking, you must keep detailed records of your business and private mileage to support claims that the cost of your private mileage is not included in the business accounts.

Tax invoice

When you supply goods, you should send a tax invoice and keep a copy of it. Your ordinary invoice will do, as long as it includes the following details:

■ invoice number.

■ tax point (see p. 428).

■ your name and address.

- your VAT registration number.
- your customer's name and address.
- a description of the goods or services you have supplied. This should include the quantity supplied, the charge without VAT, the rate of VAT, the rate of any cash discount and the total VAT charged.
- the unit price of the goods or services.

If you are supplying goods and services direct to the public, for example as a shop, you don't need to give a tax invoice unless you are asked for one. And you do not need to provide such detailed invoices for items that are £100 or less, including the VAT. Nor do you need to keep copies of these. There are a number of special schemes for retailers, as it would be very time-consuming to keep records of every single sale, although the use of these schemes is being restricted in the light of new technologies that do now enable shop-keepers to work out the precise amount of VAT due on their sales.

A tax point is nothing more than the date on which you are liable to account for the VAT to HMRC; this is the date on which you provide the goods or services. However, if you issue a tax invoice or receive a payment earlier than this, the tax point is the date you issue the invoice or receive the payment, whichever happens first. If you issue a tax invoice up to 14 days after supplying the goods or services, and no earlier tax point has been created by a previous invoice or payment (as above), the date when you issue the invoice becomes the tax point. Finally, if you want to invoice monthly, you can use a monthly tax point, but you must have written approval from HMRC first.

VAT account

The results for each VAT period need to be summarized separately in your accounting records. This should show the totals of input tax and output tax and the difference between the two, either a repayment to you or the amount due to HMRC.

VAT return

This is the form which you need to fill in at the end of each VAT period, normally every three months, although if you are constantly claiming a repayment, for example because you are zero-rated, you can arrange monthly returns. In the return, you show the information you put in your VAT account; see above. You also enter any bad debts you may have. As a check for HMRC, you have to enter the figures for your total purchases and total sales for the period.

Since April 2010 all companies and self-employed businesses with annual turnover exceeding £100,000 and all newly registering businesses (regardless of size) have to file VAT returns online and pay the VAT due electronically (see p. 430). From April 2012, online filing and electronic payment will be mandatory for all businesses registered for VAT with no exceptions at all.

The VAT period can be arranged to coincide with your accounting year end, which can make keeping your records much more convenient. And to simplify it even more, you can go over to a system of annual accounting for VAT – see below.

There is a misdeclaration penalty that can be imposed. If you make an error in your VAT return of 30 per cent of the gross tax (output and input tax) or £1 million, the penalty charged could be 15 per cent of the VAT due. However, you will not normally have to pay this unless the net tax you have under-declared or over-claimed is more than £2,000 in the period and you have made a voluntary disclosure. However, you will have to pay interest on under-declared VAT.

VAT flat-rate scheme

Businesses with a taxable turnover up to £150,000 can opt to join a flat-rate VAT scheme. This can cut the administration involved. Instead of keeping a record of your inputs and outputs and calculating the VAT due to be paid or reclaimed, under the flat-rate scheme you simply pay VAT as a percentage of your tax-inclusive turnover (including all reduced, zero-rated and exempt income). In most cases, the only VAT records you will need to keep are the relevant turnover figures and the flat percentage rate being used. However, you will still have to send out VAT invoices, and you might want to continue calculating your VAT in full to keep an eye on whether you are paying more or less VAT under the flat-rate scheme. If you find you are persistently paying extra, consider opting back out of the scheme.

The flat rate to be used is set by HMRC and depends on the type of business you are in and varies from 4 per cent for food retailers up to 14.5 per cent for building labourers, lawyers, accountants, IT consultants and architects, although there is a 1 per cent reduction for newly VAT-registered businesses during their first year. The rates are designed to reflect the average VAT payable by firms in the particular sector. Whether you'll pay more or less VAT if you join the scheme depends on whether your VAT payments are usually more or less than the average for your particular industry. For more information, see HMRC leaflet 733 *VAT flat rate scheme for small businesses.*

Annual accounting

Instead of filling in a VAT return every three months, relatively small businesses can instead switch to annual accounting. This offers three advantages:

1 More predictable cash flow because you make regular payments on account throughout the year.
2 A possible cash flow advantage, especially if your turnover is tending to increase each year.
3 Less paperwork – and lower fees if you use an accountant – because you send in just one VAT return a year.

Annual accounting is open to your business if you have a yearly taxable turnover of no more than £1,350,000. You can continue in the scheme until your taxable turnover reaches £1,600,000 a year.

The basic scheme works as follows: you and the VAT office agree an estimate of your likely VAT for the forthcoming year – usually this will be based on what you paid last year. You pay ¹⁄₁₀ of this amount by direct debit from the fourth month through to the 12th month of your VAT year. Within two months of the end of the year, you send in your annual VAT return, making a final balancing payment if further VAT is due or claiming a repayment if the instalments came to more than the total for the year.

If you prefer, you can opt to pay by three larger interim instalments plus a final balancing payment.

Whichever system of annual accounting applies, both you and the VAT office can adjust the interim payments during the year if new information suggests they are no longer appropriate – for example, if your turnover is well below the previous year, you might request that the interim payments be reduced. You can withdraw from an annual accounting scheme at any time by writing to your VAT office.

Paying the tax

Any VAT that is due to HMRC* is payable within one month of the end of the quarterly accounting period or within two months of the end of an annual period. This is regardless of whether you have actually yet received the money from your customers for the VAT due.

If you fail to pay your VAT on time, you are given a warning and could face surcharges. However, penalties are not automatically applied if yours is a small business (with a turnover up to £150,000). Instead, HMRC will initially offer you help and advice to remedy your late payment problem.

Small businesses can pay VAT on a cash accounting basis. With this you pay VAT due only when you have been paid by your customer and claim it back only when you have paid your supplier. You don't have to pay VAT on bad debts. You can opt to use this scheme if your taxable turnover is £1,350,000 or less, you don't owe any VAT (or, if you do, you have made arrangements with your VAT office for its payment), your VAT returns are up to date, and you haven't been convicted of a VAT offence or assessed for dishonest conduct. You can remain in the scheme until your taxable turnover reaches £1,600,000.

You can claim relief from VAT for bad debts that are six months old and that you have written off in your accounts. You can go back three years to claim bad debt relief. However, if you adopt the cash accounting scheme, you automatically get relief from bad debts by never having to pay VAT on them at all.

If you have paid too much VAT as a result of an HMRC error, you have the right to ask for interest on the amount of the incorrect payment. You can go back three years to claim back overpaid VAT.

Compulsory online filing

Since April 2010, all companies and self-employed businesses with annual turnover exceeding £100,000 and all newly registering businesses (regardless of size) have to file VAT returns online. This will be extended to all businesses from April 2012.

If you file your VAT returns online, you must pay the VAT due electronically. For example, you can set up a direct debit arrangement and initiate the payment online at the same time as you file the return. Alternatively, you can instruct your bank when each payment is due to make the transfer by BACS.

Summary

1 You do not need to register if the value of your sales is too low, but it could still be worthwhile to apply to do so if you sell to businesses that can claim back the VAT or if you are zero-rated.

2 Do not confuse zero-rated with exempt supplies. If you supply only exempt goods, you cannot claim back VAT on goods you purchase.

3 If the level of your sales falls below a certain limit (£71,000 from 1 April 2011) you can ask to have the registration cancelled.

4 You may save on administration and may also save tax if you switch to the VAT flat-rate scheme. You do not have to stay in the scheme if you find it results in your paying extra tax.

5 You can save on administration and may benefit from cash flow advantages if you opt for the annual accounting scheme.

Other chapter to read

29 Keeping the record straight (p. 370).

32

Pensions and retirement

No doubt all your thoughts and energies are devoted to making your business successful, but spare a thought for what will happen when you retire. Your business might be the sort that you will be able to sell when it comes to retirement. This means you could have a lump sum that you can invest to give yourself an income to live on.

But with lots of self-employed people this is not so; if they retire, the business retires too, because their skills are essential to the success of their enterprise. Even if you hope that you will be able to sell your business on retirement, there is no certainty of this, and you should show some caution in relying on it. You may be forced to retire earlier than you had intended because of ill health, and this might coincide with a bad patch in your business fortunes. Or you may simply not be successful in building your business sufficiently to be able to sell for the sort of sum of money you need. The prudent course is to make separate arrangements to provide yourself with a pension.

This chapter looks at how to build up a pension during your working life. It also looks briefly at what happens from a tax point of view if you sell or give away your business on retirement.

What you get from the state

If you are self-employed, you will pay Class 2 National Insurance contributions. If you have set up a limited company and count as an employee of the company, you will pay Class 1 contributions (and the company will pay employer's contributions), assuming you are paid a salary of more than a given amount. Both these contributions will entitle you to the basic state pension, assuming you have paid sufficient contributions during your lifetime. The Class 4 contributions you make as a self-employed person do not increase your pension.

If you count as an employee of your company, even if you are a director, you may be building up an entitlement under a state additional pension scheme. Formerly this was the State Earnings Related Pension Scheme (SERPS) but was replaced from April 2002 onwards with the state second pension (S2P). Both you as an employee and your company as an employer will pay additional National Insurance contributions. This is known as being 'not contracted-out'. If you contract out, the contributions are either reduced or partially rebated and instead of building up S2P, you build up a pension in either an occupational pension scheme or your own personal plan. However, contracting out through personal plans and some types of occupational schemes is being abolished from 6 April 2012 onwards. If you are affected by this change, you will automatically become contracted into the state scheme again.

S2P is currently an earnings-related pension. It is much more generous than its predecessor, SERPS, for some groups of people: employees earning at least £5,304 but less than £14,400 in 2011–12; many people caring for young children or, say, an elderly relative, and some people who are long-term sick or have a disability. All these groups build up S2P as if they have earnings equal to £14,400 in 2011–12.

Following an important review of pension provision in the UK, the government is introducing a package of measures to contain the cost of future pension provision and increase future retirement incomes. The first tranche of the required changes was made in the Pensions Act 2007. Measures include:

- *raising the state pension age:* overall, people are tending to live longer. Therefore, with an unchanged pension age, they would spend longer in retirement and so their pensions would cost more. To contain the cost, state pension age is being increased in stages. These increases have been accelerated compared with the original measures and are now as follows:

    - women's state pension age (which was 60 before 6 April 2010) is being increased month by month to match men's current pension age of 65 by November 2018.

    - between December 2018 and April 2020, both men's and women's state pension age will rise to 66.

- – the government has proposed that an independent commission may be set up to review state pension age periodically and to recommend further increases if evidence shows that the trend towards people living longer is continuing.

■ *making it easier to build up the full state basic pension:* with a state pension age of 65, you used to need 44 years of National Insurance contributions and/or credits to qualify for the full basic pension. The Pensions Act 2007 has reduced this to just 30 years for anyone reaching state pension age on or after 6 April 2010. It also simplifies and extends the system of giving credits to people who are caring for children or dependent adults. These measures will help women in particular to achieve higher state pensions.

■ *increasing the basic state pension in line with earnings once it starts to be paid*: since 1979, state pensions have been increased only in line with price inflation. This means that, although the pension retains the same buying power year after year, pensioners have not shared in the growing prosperity of the economy. While people in work have enjoyed above-inflation increases in their wages, pensioners dependent purely on the state have become poorer relative to the working population. To address this, since April 2011, the basic state pension is now increased each year in line with the highest of price inflation, earnings inflation and 2.5 per cent. Other elements of the state pension, such as the state second pension, continue to be increased in line with price inflation. Controversially, the price index to which state pensions are linked has been changed to the Consumer Price Index (CPI), which tends to increase at a lower rate than the Retail Prices Index (RPI), which has been standard in the past.

The original package of measures also included a plan to turn the state second pension into a flat-rate scheme (and steps to make this gradually happen are already in action). However, it looks as if this plan may be overtaken by a new proposal to merge the basic pension and second pension to form a single, new flat-rate state pension of around £140 a week in today's prices. It is intended that this would be enough to take pensioners above the poverty line and so reduce the number of older people reliant on means-tested state benefits. In turn, this would remove the disincentive to save for retirement that is inherent in a system where any gain through savings is perceived to be balanced by a loss of benefits.

If you are self-employed

The simplest way of increasing your pension is to start paying money into a personal pension. Because you can get tax relief on what you pay and your money is put into a largely tax-free fund, doing this may be the best way of saving for retirement. Stakeholder pension schemes are personal pensions that meet certain conditions on low costs and flexibility:

- *low charges*: charges must total no more than 1 per cent a year of the value of your pension fund where you started the scheme before 6 April 2005. For schemes started on or after that date, the maximum charge is 1.5 per cent a year for the first ten years and 1 per cent thereafter.
- *flexibility*: the minimum contribution can be no more than £20. You decide when or how often to pay.
- *portability*: you can transfer out of a stakeholder scheme without penalty. Stakeholder schemes must accept transfers from other pension schemes and plans.
- *simplicity*: the scheme must include a default investment option, if you don't want to choose an investment fund for yourself.
- *information*: you must get a statement at least once a year showing you the value of your scheme. If charges alter, you must be informed within one month of the change.

A personal pension will pay out an income; the size depends on how long and how much you have saved, although there are limits imposed on how much you can save (see pp. 437–8). It also depends on how well the investments in the pension fund have done and the level of annuity rates when you retire. You can choose when you want to start receiving the benefits from the plan, provided this is no earlier than age 55.

Former rules that required most people to start drawing a pension by age 75 have now been scrapped.

Under the government's package of measures aimed at increasing future retirement incomes, it is establishing a new system of low-cost personal pension accounts from 2012 (see pp. 259–60). Employees will be automatically enrolled into this system (but can opt out) and both they and their employer will contribute to their accounts. Self-employed people will not be automatically enrolled and there will be no compulsory contributions for them, but they can choose to join the system if they want to.

Personal pensions

Personal pensions can be very flexible, provided you choose the right plan.

For example:

- you can invest a lump sum when you want or save on a regular basis.
- you can alter the premium from time to time.
- the pension can be level or start off lower but increase each year.
- you can choose a smaller joint-life pension, which will be paid as long as either of two people is alive.
- they must offer an 'open-market option', which allows you to shop around to see if you can use the sum of money you have built up with one company to get a higher pension from another company.
- you can normally choose to take a lower amount of pension and have a tax-free lump sum as well.
- some schemes let you put off buying a pension (an 'annuity') at the time you want to retire and draw an income direct from your pension fund instead. This is useful if annuity rates are poor at the time you retire, but it is an option only suitable for large pension funds of £250,000 or more, say, or other stable sources of income.
- generally, you can use your pension scheme to back up a mortgage in much the same way as an endowment mortgage.
- most of the plans have loanback facilities, which allow you to use your pension to get a loan.
- self-invested personal pensions (SIPPs) give you wide freedom to choose how your pension fund is invested, including investment in commercial property, which opens the way for your pension fund to own your business premises and lease them back to you.

Getting tax relief

Personal pensions are generally efficient ways to save for retirement because they have the benefit of several tax advantages. You get tax relief on what you pay in, your investment builds up largely tax-free, and you can take part of the proceeds at retirement as a tax-free lump sum.

Because of these tax breaks, the government limits the amount you can invest. But, for most people, the limits are fairly generous. The main limits

– which apply to the total of your savings through any number and types of pension scheme – are as follows:

■ *annual limit for tax relief*: you can pay as much as you like into a pension scheme but the maximum contributions on which you can get tax relief are the greater of £3,600 a year and 100 per cent of your UK earnings. Included in your UK earnings are profits from self-employment or working in a partnership and the salary (but not dividends) you pay yourself if you operate as a company. Anything paid into your pension scheme(s) by an employer (say, your company) does not count towards this limit.

■ *annual allowance*: this is a cap on the increase over a year in the total value of your pension savings and is set at £50,000 for 2011–12. Prior to 6 April 2011, the annual allowance was much higher (£255,000) but had become surrounded by some very complicated rules designed to limit the amount of tax relief that people on high incomes could get. The complex rules have been abolished but the allowance reduced in order to contain the amount of tax relief that a person can claim each year. Since you can normally get tax relief on contributions up to 100 per cent of your UK earnings, this £50,000 cap is relevant only to people earning more than £50,000 a year. If they, say, paid £60,000 into a pension scheme – in other words, £10,000 more than the annual allowance – they would face a tax charge to claw back the tax relief on the excess contributions. There are two exceptions to the cap. First, if you have not used up the full £50,000 allowance in any of the past three years, you can carry the unused part forward and so make a one-off contribution as high as £200,000 in one year without a tax charge. Secondly, the annual allowance does not apply in the tax year in which you start to draw your pension, giving scope for a large, last-minute contribution – following the sale of your business perhaps.

■ *lifetime allowance*: the total of your pension savings should not exceed this limit, which is set at £1.8 million in 2011–12 and reducing to £1.5 million from 2012–13. Savings in excess of the lifetime limit are subject to tax at 55 per cent at the time they are drawn out of the scheme as a lump sum or 25 per cent if drawn out as taxable income.

If you are paying into a company pension scheme, your contributions are deducted from your pay before tax is worked out, so you automatically get income tax relief up to your highest rate on the contributions you make. There is no National Insurance relief on the contributions.

If you are paying into most other types of scheme, including personal pensions and stakeholder schemes, you get tax relief at the basic rate at source by handing over an amount from which you have already deducted the basic rate tax relief – see the Example below. The pension scheme provider then claims the amount of basic rate relief from HMRC* and adds it to your scheme. You get this basic rate tax relief even if you are a non-taxpayer or pay tax only at the starting rate. If you are a higher-rate taxpayer or additional-rate taxpayer, you can claim extra tax relief through your tax return.

If you have a retirement annuity contract (a type of personal pension started before 1 July 1988), you may have to pay gross contributions of the full amount and then claim all the tax relief due through your tax return.

Example

Daniel Patterson is considering putting money aside for retirement. His self-employment earnings in 2011–12 are £60,000. This means the maximum he can pay into one or more pension schemes this year without incurring a tax charge is £50,000. In fact, he needs some of his earnings to live on and decides he can afford to pay £8,000 into a personal pension.

The £8,000 is treated as a net contribution from which tax relief at the basic rate of 20 per cent has already been deducted. The pension provider claims £2,000 from HMRC and adds this to Daniel's scheme. This means that a gross contribution of £8,000 + £2,000 = £10,000 goes into the scheme.

Daniel pays tax at the higher rate of 40 per cent on at least £10,000 of his 2011–12 earnings, so he can claim further tax relief through his tax return. Tax relief at 40 per cent on the £10,000 contribution comes to £4,000. But Daniel has already had basic rate relief of £2,000. So he gets further relief of £4,000 − £2,000 = £2,000.

A total of £10,000 has gone into Daniel's pension scheme at a cost to him of £8,000 − £2,000 = £6,000.

Choosing a personal pension

Many schemes are available, and it is very difficult to choose which is the right personal pension. An independent financial adviser (IFA)* can help, but they have differing levels of expertise, so you should shop around in the same way as you do for your business insurance.

You can choose between a pension plan from, say, an insurance company, bank, building society, unit trust manager, fund supermarket or discount broker. There are different types of personal pensions, including:

■ *with-profits*: the insurance company invests your money as it thinks fit, often in bonds, shares and property. The company will guarantee a minimum pension or lump sum of money you will get, but this will be fairly low. However, you stand the prospect of receiving a higher pension in the end, because the company adds bonuses to your pension, depending on the profits it makes on its investments. The company aims to smooth the bonuses by holding back some profits from good years to hold up the bonus rate in lean years, but there is no guarantee that a bonus will be paid every year. Usually, annual bonuses once added to your plan can't be taken away, but you might lose some of these bonuses if you transfer your plan to another company.

- *unit-linked*: with this type of policy, you have some choice as to how your money is invested. Commonly, you can choose for the money to be invested in property, shares, fixed-interest investments such as gilts, cash investments such as bank deposit accounts or you can choose to invest in a mixture of all these. With a unit-linked plan, the value of your pension is directly linked to the value of the investments, so it can fluctuate. This could be a problem if values happen to be low when it comes to retirement.

- *deposit-administration schemes*: these give a safe, if unexciting, return similar to a bank or building society account.

- *self-invested*: you build your own portfolio of investments. These might be individual shareholdings, some unit trust holdings, gilts, corporate bonds – you choose. Charges for self-invested plans are often higher than for fund-based plans.

Nearly all personal pensions expose you to investment risk. In the current economic climate, you'll need no reminder that the value of your pension fund – and so the pension you can buy with it – can fall if share prices or other investments tumble. Bear in mind that a pension is a long-term investment, so a short-term slide in the stock market need not necessarily concern you (and could in fact be a good opportunity to pay extra into your pension). However, a fall in share prices shortly before retirement could be disastrous, so in the ten years or so before retirement, you should aim progressively to shift your pension fund away from shares and into safer investments, such as bonds and deposits.

If you are the director of a company

If you are a director of a small company, you can take out a personal pension in the same way as if you were self-employed.

The company could set up a special sort of occupational pension scheme (called a small self-administered scheme or SSAS) for you and other employees of the business. But, since 6 April 2006, when a single uniform set of rules started to apply to all types of pension scheme, there is little to choose between an SSAS and a self-invested personal pension (SIPP). With both:

■ *you can choose how the pension scheme invests its fund*: this can include, for example, buying commercial property or other assets to be used by the company.

■ *the scheme can make a loan up to half the value of its assets to your business*: the loan must be secured, interest must be charged at a commercial rate, repayments must be made regularly, and the maximum term is five years.

This area of pensions is very specialized. If you do want to go ahead, consult an independent financial adviser* or other adviser with specialist knowledge, but don't be rushed into decisions by salespeople. Consider straightforward ideas too, like a personal pension.

When you retire or sell

If you retire and sell, give away or dispose of your business you may have to pay capital gains tax. However, the bill will be reduced to an effective tax rate of 10 per cent if you can claim entrepreneurs' relief (see p. 401). This is available for the first £10 million of gains over your lifetime from selling business assets.

If you give away business assets (doesn't need to be at retirement), your gift can be free of inheritance tax. Business relief means that there will be no inheritance tax to pay on business assets such as goodwill, land, buildings, plant, stock and patents. If the business is a company, you can also get 100 per cent business relief on transfers of the shares. Agricultural relief can mean no inheritance tax on owner-occupied farmlands and farm tenancies (including cottages, farm buildings and farm houses). Get advice from an accountant* or other tax adviser*.

Summary

1 Saving for retirement through a pension scheme can be very cost-effective. This is because you can get tax relief up to your highest rate of tax. But the tax relief is effective only on contributions up to £50,000 a year.

2 A self-invested personal pension (SIPP) or small self-administered scheme (SSAS) can give tax-efficient support to your business by, for example, owning its property or lending it money.

3 Entrepreneurs' relief reduces capital gains tax when you dispose of your business or shares, if you meet certain conditions.

4 There may be no inheritance tax to pay on your business when you give it away or leave it on your death.

References

This section provides a handy list of further reading and names and addresses of organizations. The inclusion of any commercial organization in this section is not to be taken as a recommendation. You must rely on the usual precautions, for example taking up references.

Useful web sites

The Internet is a handy source of information, news and advice. Three sites worth investigating are my company's web sites *www.smallbusiness.co.uk, www.growthbusiness.co.uk* and *taxguide.co.uk.* Also have a look at:

www.britishchambers.org.uk
www.businesslink.gov.uk
www.bvca.co.uk (funding)
www.bbaa.org.uk (business angels)
www.companieshouse.gov.uk
www.bis.gov.uk/employment (employment law)
www.hmrc.gov.uk (tax and VAT)
www.frc.org.uk/asb/technical/frsse.cfm (accounting rules for small businesses)
www.statistics.gov.uk (government statistics)
www.data.gov.uk (government data)
www.legislation.gov.uk (UK legislation)
www.contractsfinder.businesslink.gov.uk (government contracts)
www.netregs.gov.uk (environmental regulations)
www.number10.gov.uk/the-coalition/the-government/ (government departments)

Directory web sites

Kellys: *www.kellysearch.co.uk*
Kompass: *http://gb.kompass.com*
Yell: *www.yell.com*
Thomson Directories: *www.thomsonlocal.com*

Search engines

www.thesearchenginelist.com
www.alltheweb.com (part of Yahoo!)
www.bing.com
http://uk.ask.com
www.google.co.uk
www.lycos.co.uk
www.ukdirectory.co.uk
www.webcrawler.com
http://uk.yahoo.com

Web sites with businesses for sale

Business For Sale: *www.businessesforsale.com*
Dalton's Weekly: *www.daltonsbusiness.com*
Nationwide Businesses: *www.nationwidebusinesses.co.uk*
RightBiz: *www.rightbiz.co.uk*

Web sites with information about vacant premises

www.startinbusiness.co.uk

Web sites selling mailing lists

http://marketingfile.com
www.businessmailing.co.uk

Networking sites

www.facebook.com
www.linkedin.com
www.twitter.com

Search engine optimization and social media marketing

www.seomoz.org/learn-seo
www.seop.com/social-media-marketing

Mobile computing

www.pcmag.com

www.which.co.uk/Computer_Reviews
www.which.co.uk/publications/magazines/which-computing

Business support schemes

www.businesslink.gov.uk (England)
http://business.wales.gov.uk (Wales)
www.bgateway.com (Scotland)
www.investni.com (Northern Ireland)
https://ktn.innovateuk.org/web/guest/home (knowledge transfer)
www.innovateuk.org (research and development)
www.ktponline.org.uk (knowledge transfer)
www.mas.bis.gov.uk (manufacturing)
www.ukti.gov.uk (exporting)

Contacts

Access Northern Ireland, PO Box 1085, Belfast BT5 9BD. Tel: 028 9025 9100. *www.dojni.gov.uk/accessni*

Accountant: to find one, look in *Yellow Pages* under 'Accountants'; or for a list of members in your area, see separate entries for Association of Chartered Certified Accountants and the Institute of Chartered Accountants.

Accounting Standards Board, part of the Financial Reporting Council. *www.frc.org.uk/asb*

Advertising Standards Authority (ASA), Mid City Place, 71 High Holborn, London WC1V 6QT. Tel: 020 7492 2222. *www.asa.org.uk*

Advisory, Conciliation and Arbitration Service (ACAS). Helpline (employment queries): 08457 47 47 47. Publications 08702 42 90 90. CP01 Disciplinary and grievance procedures *www.acas.org.uk/index.aspx?articleid=2174*. *www.acas.org.uk*

Apprenticeships. Tel: 08000 150 600. *www.apprenticeships.org.uk*

Association of British Insurers (ABI), 51 Gresham Street, London EC2V 7HQ. Tel: 020 7600 3333. *www.abi.org.uk*

Association of Chartered Certified Accountants, 29 Lincoln's Inn Fields, London WC2A 3EE. Tel: 020 7059 5000. *www.acca.co.uk*

Association of Colleges. Tel: 020 7034 9900. *www.aoc.co.uk/en/about_colleges*

Association of Consulting Actuaries, St Clement's House, 27–28 Clement's Lane, London EC4N 7AE. Tel: 020 3207 9380. *www.aca.org.uk*

Association of Taxation Technicians, 1st Floor, Artillery House, 11–19 Artillery Row, London SW1P 1RT. Tel: 020 7340 0551. *www.att.org.uk*

Audit Bureau of Circulations, Saxon House, 211 High Street, Berkhamsted, Hertfordshire HP4 1AD. Tel: 01442 870800. *www.abc.org.uk*

Bankruptcy Association, FREEPOST LA1118, 4 Johnson Close, Lancaster LA1 5BR. Tel: 01539 469474 (weekdays 10am–12.30pm). *www.theba.org.uk*

Battery Compliance Scheme. *www.environment-agency.gov.uk/business/ regulation/107939.aspx*

Better Payment Practice Campaign. *www.payontime.co.uk*

British Bankers' Association (BBA), Publications Unit, Pinners Hall, 105–108 Old Broad Street, London EC2N 1EX. Tel: 020 7216 8800. *www.bba.org.uk*

British Business Angels' Association (BBAA), 100 Pall Mall, St James, London SW1Y 5NQ. Tel: 020 7321 5669. *www.bbaa.org.uk*

British Chambers of Commerce, Oak Tree Court, Binley Business Park, Harry Weston Road, Coventry CV3 2UN. Tel: 024 7644 6615. *www.britishchambers.org.uk*

British Exporters' Association, Broadway House, Tothill Street, London SW1H 9NQ. Tel: 020 7222 5419. *www.bexa.co.uk*

British Franchise Association (BFA), Centurion Court, 85f Milton Park, Abingdon OX14 4RY. Tel: 01235 820470. *www.thebfa.org*

British Insurance Brokers' Association (BIBA), 8th Floor, John Stow House, 18 Bevis Marks, London EC3A 7JB. Consumer Helpline: 0870 950 1790. *www.biba.org.uk*

British Library Business and Intellectual Property Enquiries, St Pancras, 96 Euston Road, London NW1 2DB. Tel: 020 7412 7676. Document Supply: Customer Services, Boston Spa, Wetherby, West Yorkshire LS23 7BQ. Tel: 01937 546060. *www.bl.uk*

British Private Equity and Venture Capital Association (BVCA), 1st Floor North, Brettenham House, Lancaster Place, London WC2E 7EN. Tel: 020 7420 1800. *www.bvca.co.uk*

British Rate and Data (BRAD). Subscription sales, Tel: 020 7728 4315. *www. bradinsight.com*

British Standards Institute (BSI), 389 Chiswick High Road, London W4 4AL. Tel: 020 8996 9001. *www.bsi-global.com*

Business Debtline. Tel: 0800 197 6026. *www.bdl.org.uk*

Business Gateway. Tel: 0845 609 6611. *www.bgateway.com*

Business in the Community, 137 Shepherdess Walk, London N1 7RQ. Tel: 020 7566 8650. *www.bitc.org.uk*

Business Link (England): local offices are due to be closed by November 2011. Tel: 0845 600 9006. *www.businesslink.gov.uk*

Business Link is the main government small business one-stop shop for England. See separate entries for the equivalent organizations for other parts of the UK:

- Business Gateway (Scotland)
- Business Wales (Wales)
- Invest NI (Northern Ireland).

Business Wales. Tel: 03000 6 03000. *http://business.wales.gov.uk*

BvDEP. Northburgh House, 10 Northburgh Street, London EC1V 0PP. Tel: 020 7549 5000. *www.bvdep.com*. For publications giving information about listed and unlisted companies.

Call Credit (credit reference agency). Tel: 0113 388 4300. *www.callcredit.co.uk*

Chamber of Commerce (or Trade): to find local branch, see *The Phone Book* or contact British Chambers of Commerce (see separate entry).

Chartered Institute of Patent Attorneys, 95 Chancery Lane, London WC2A 1DT. Tel: 020 7405 9450. *www.cipa.org.uk*

Chartered Institute of Taxation (CIOT), First Floor, 11–19 Artillery Row, London SW1P 1RT. Tel: 020 7340 0550 or 0844 579 6700. *www.tax.org.uk*

Chartered Management Institute, Management House, Cottingham Road, Corby, Northamptonshire NN17 1TT. Tel: 01536 204222. *www.managers.org.uk*. CMI runs more than 40 courses a year. It also has a very comprehensive library of management-related data, including electronic databases. Some of its services carry charges.

Citizens Advice. Look in *The Phone Book* under 'Citizens' Advice Bureau'. *www.citizensadvice.org.uk*

Companies House. Tel: 0303 1234 500. *www.companieshouse.gov.uk*

- England and Wales: Crown Way, Maindy, Cardiff CF14 3UZ.

- Scotland: 4th Floor Edinburgh Quay 2, 139 Fountainbridge, Edinburgh EH3 9FF.

- Northern Ireland: Companies House, 2nd Floor, The Linenhall, 32–38 Linenhall Street, Belfast BT2 8BG.

- London: Companies House Executive Agency, 21 Bloomsbury Street, London WC1B 3XD.

Consumer Credit Counselling Service, Wade House, Merrion Centre, Leeds LS2 8NG. Tel: 0800 138 1111. *www.cccs.co.uk*

Co-operatives UK, 1st Floor, Holyoake House, Hanover Street, Manchester M60 0AS. Tel: 0161 246 2900. *www.cooperatives-uk.coop*

Criminal Records Bureau, PO Box 110, Liverpool L69 3EF. Tel: 0870 90 90 811. *www.businesslink.gov.uk/crb*

Department for Business, Innovation and Skills. *www.bis.gov.uk*

- Employment law: *www.bis.gov.uk/employment*

- BIS does not provide services direct to businesses. Instead contact Business Link (see separate entry).

Department for Communities and Local Government, Eland House, Bressenden Place, London SW1E 5DU. Tel: 0303 444 0000. *www.communities.gov.uk*

Department for Enterprise, Trade and Investments (Northern Ireland). *www.detini.gov.uk*

Department for the Environment, Food and Rural Affairs. Tel: 08459 33 55 77. *www.defra.gov.uk*

Department for Work and Pensions. For local office see *The Phone Book* or web site. *www.dwp.gov.uk*. Guide to pension auto-enrolment and workplace pension reform: *www.dwp.gov.uk/docs/auto-enrol-and-wpr-the-facts.pdf*

DirectGov. *www.direct.gov.uk*. This web site is intended to be a one-stop shop for all government information and services. The government is testing an alternative site: *www.alpha.gov.uk*

Direct Marketing Association (DMA), DMA House, 70 Margaret Street, London W1W 8SS. Tel: 020 7291 3300. *www.dma.org.uk*

Disclosure Scotland, PO Box 250, Glasgow G51 1YU. Tel: 0870 609 6006. *www.disclosurescotland.co.uk*

E-mail Preference Service. *www.dmachoice.org*

Employee Ownership Association, CAN Mezzanine, 32–36 Loman Street, London SE1 0EH. Tel: 020 7922 7737. *www.employeeownership.co.uk*

English Heritage, Customer Services Department, The Engine House, Fire Fly Avenue, Swindon SN2 2EH. Tel: 0870 333 1181. *www.english-heritage.org.uk*

Enhanced Capital Allowances. *www.eca.gov.uk*

Environment Agency, PO Box 544, Rotherham S60 1BY. Tel: 08708 506 506. *www.environment-agency.gov.uk*

Environment and Energy Helpline. Tel: 0800 585794. *http://envirowise.wrap. org.uk*

Equality and Human Rights Commission. *www.equalityhumanrights.com*

- England: Freepost RRLL-GHUX-CTRX, Arndale House, Arndale Centre, Manchester M4 3AQ. Helpline: 0845 604 6610.
- Wales: Freepost RRLR-UEYB-UYZL, 3rd Floor, 3 Callaghan Square, Cardiff CF10 5BT. Helpline: 0845 604 8810.
- Scotland: Freepost RRLL-GYLB-UJTA, The Optima Building, 58 Robertson Street, Glasgow G2 8DU. Helpline: 0845 604 5510.

Equifax (credit reference agency). Tel: 0845 603 3000. *www.equifax.co.uk*

Euro Info Centres. To find nearest centre see *www.europe.org.uk*. These centres have been set up by the European Commission. They are designed to help the public and businesses get information on what the EU does.

Experian (credit reference agency). Tel: 0844 481 5870. *www.experian.co.uk*

Export Marketing Research Scheme. Contact British Chambers of Commerce (see separate entry).

Extel cards. Available through LexisNexis subscription services – try your nearest public business library.

Faster Payments Service. *www.ukpayments.org.uk/faster_payments_ service/value_limits*

Fax Preference Service Registration Line. Tel: 0845 070 0702. *www.fps online.org.uk*

Federation of Small Businesses (FSB), Sir Frank Whittle Way, Blackpool Business Park, Blackpool, Lancashire FY4 2FE. Tel: 0808 2020 888. *www.fsb.org.uk*

Finance and Leasing Association, 2nd Floor, Imperial House, 15–19 Kingsway, London WC2B 6UN. Tel: 020 7836 6511. *www.fla.org.uk*

Financial advisers: to find firms that can help you raise finance, ask your local Business Link (England), Business Gateway (Scotland), Business Wales (Wales) or InvestNI (Northern Ireland).

Financial Services Authority (FSA), 25 The North Colonnade, Canary Wharf, London E14 5HS. Tel: 0845 606 1234. *www.fsa.gov.uk*

■ FSA Register: *www.fsa.gov.uk/register/home.do*

■ The FSA's former consumer functions are now handled by: Money Advice Service. Consumer helpline: 0300 500 5000. *www.moneyadviceservice.org.uk*

Forum of Private Business (FPB), Ruskin Chambers, Drury Lane, Knutsford, Cheshire WA16 6HA. Tel: 0845 612 6266. *www.fpb.org*

Franchise directories: *Franchise World Directory* (£20 hardcopy/£9.99 online) published by Franchise World, Highlands House, 165 The Broadway, London SW19 1NE. Tel: 020 8605 2555. *www.franchiseworld.co.uk*. For a constantly updated directory of all franchises available in the UK and Republic of Ireland. *www.franchiseadvice.com*

GLE, 10–12 Queen Elizabeth Street, London SE1 2JN. Tel: 020 7403 0300. *www.gle.co.uk*

Government contracts – tendering for them. *www.contractsfinder.businesslink.gov.uk*

Government legislation. *www.legislation.gov.uk*

Growth Company Investor, Octavia House, 50 Banner Street, London EC1Y 8ST. Tel: 020 7250 7010. For information about the Alternative Investment Market (AIM) and PLUS. *www.growthcompany.co.uk*

Health and Safety Executive (HSE), Rose Court, 2 Southwark Bridge, London SE1 9HS. HSE Infoline: 0845 345 0055. Publications: 01787 881165. *www.hse.gov.uk*

Highlands and Islands Enterprise, Cowan House, Inverness Retail and Business Park, Inverness IV2 7GF. Tel: 01463 234171. *www.hie.co.uk*

HM Revenue & Customs (HMRC). For local tax office, see *The Phone Book*. National Insurance enquiries: 0845 302 1479. Helpline for Newly Self-Employed: 0845 915 4515. New Employer Helpline: 0845 60 70 143. Self-Assessment Helpline: 0845 900 0444. Business Payment Support Service: 0845 302 1435. VAT National Advice Service: 0845 010 9000. Publications Orderline: 0845 9000 404. Online employment status indicator tool *www.hmrc.gov.uk/calcs/esi.htm*. *www.hmrc.gov.uk*

Independent financial adviser (IFA) (to find one):

- IFA Promotion. *www.unbiased.co.uk*
- The Institute of Financial Planning, Whitefriars Centre, Lewins Mead, Bristol BS1 2NT. Tel: 0117 945 2470. *www.financialplanning.org.uk*
- MyLocalAdviser. *www.mylocaladviser.com*
- The Personal Finance Society. *www.findanadviser.org*

Information Commissioner, Wycliffe House, Water Lane, Wilmslow, Cheshire SK9 5AF. Helpline: 0303 123 1113 or 01625 545745. *www.ico.gov.uk*

Insolvency Service. Enquiry line: 0845 602 9848. *www.insolvency.gov.uk*

Institute of Chartered Accountants in England and Wales, Chartered Accountants' Hall, Moorgate Place, London EC2R 6EA. Tel: 020 7920 8100. *www.icaew.co.uk*

Institute of Chartered Accountants in Ireland, Chartered Accountants House, 47–49 Pearse Street, Dublin 2, Republic of Ireland. Tel: (00 353) 1 637 7200. *www.charteredaccountants.ie*

Institute of Chartered Accountants of Scotland, CA House, 21 Haymarket Yards, Edinburgh EH12 5BH. Tel: 0131 347 0100. *www.icas.org.uk*

Institute of Consulting, 4th Floor, 2 Savoy Court, Strand, London WC2R 0EZ. Tel: 020 7497 0580. *www.iconsulting.org.uk*

Institute of Directors, 116 Pall Mall, London SW1Y 5ED. Tel: 020 7766 8866. *www.iod.com*

Institute of Patentees and Inventors, PO Box 39296, London SE3 7WH. Tel: 0871 226 2091. *www.invent.org.uk*

Institute of Trade Mark Attorneys, 5th Floor, Outer Temple, 222–225 Strand, London WC2R 1BA. Tel: 020 7101 6090. *www.itma.org.uk*

Insurance broker (to find one). See *Yellow Pages*. For members of British

Insurance Brokers' Association, see separate entry. To check authorization, see entry for Financial Services Authority.

Intellectual Property Office, Concept House, Cardiff Road, Newport, South Wales NP10 8QQ. Tel: 0300 300 2000. *www.ipo.gov.uk*

International Organization for Standardization (ISO). *www.iso.org, www. standardsinfo.net.* The ISO member for the UK is the British Standards Institute (see separate entry).

Invest Northern Ireland (Invest NI), Bedford Square, Bedford Street, Belfast BT2 7ES. Tel: 0800 181 4422. To find local office, see *The Phone Book* or web site. *www.investni.com*

Jobcentre Plus. For local office, see *The Phone Book* or web site. *www.direct.gov.uk*

Labour Relations Agency, 2–16 Gordon Street, Belfast BT1 2LG. Tel: 028 9032 1442. *www.lra.org.uk*

Law Society of England and Wales, 113 Chancery Lane, London WC2A 1PL. Find a solicitor: 0870 606 2555. *www.lawsociety.org.uk/choosingandusing/findasolicitor.law*

Law Society of Northern Ireland, 96 Victoria Street, Belfast BT1 3GN. Tel: 028 9023 1614. *www.lawsoc-ni.org*

Law Society of Scotland, 26 Drumsheugh Gardens, Edinburgh EH3 7YR. Tel: 0131 226 7411. *www.lawscot.org.uk*

Lawyers for Your Business (England and Wales). For a list of lawyers in your area, e-mail: *lfyb@lawsociety.org.uk. www.lawsociety.org.uk/choosingandusing/helpyourbusiness/foryourbusiness.law*

learndirect. Tel: 0800 100 901. *www.learndirect.co.uk*

Local authority. See *The Phone Book* under the name of your authority or ask at your public library.

Local Enterprise Agency (LEA). To find a local agency, contact the National Federation of Enterprise Agencies or Business Link (see separate entries).

Local Enterprise Partnership. For information: *www.communities.gov.uk/localgovernment/local/localenterprisepartnerships.* To access funding, contact your local authority.

London Stock Exchange, 10 Paternoster Square, London EC4M 7LS. Tel: 020 7797 1000. *www.londonstockexchange.com*

Mail Order Protection Scheme (MOPS). See entry for the Safe Home Ordering Protection Scheme.

Mailing Preference Service, DMA House, 70 Margaret Street, London W1W 8SS. Tel: 020 7291 3310. *www.mpsonline.org.uk*

Market Research Society, 15 Northburgh Street, London EC1V 0JR. Tel: 020 7490 4911. *www.mrs.org.uk*

Mutuals Information Service. Tel: 020 7187 7377. *www.mutuals.org.uk*

National Association of Commercial Finance Brokers, 3 Silverdown Office Park, Fair Oak Close, Exeter, Devon EX5 2UX. Tel: 01392 440040. *www.nacfb.org*

National Business Register, Somerset House, 6070 Birmingham Business Park, Birmingham B37 7BF. Tel: 0800 069 9090. Offers free information, advice and support on setting up a new business, new company, trade mark or brand and domain name. *www.start.biz/home.htm*

National Debtline. Tel: 0808 808 4000 (freephone). *www.national debtline.co.uk*

National Farmers' Retail & Markets Association (FARMA), 12 Southgate Street, Winchester, Hampshire SO23 9EF. Tel: 0845 45 88 420. *www.farma.org.uk*

National Federation of Enterprise Agencies, 12 Stephenson Court, Fraser Road, Priory Business Park, Bedford MK44 3WJ. Tel: 01234 831623. *www.nfea.com*

Natural England, 1 East Parade, Sheffield S1 2ET. Tel: 0845 600 3078. *www.naturalengland.org.uk*

NetRegs. *www.netregs.gov.uk*

Newly Self-Employed Helpline (HM Revenue & Customs). Tel: 0845 915 4515.

NI Business Info. Tel: 0800 027 0639. *www.nibusinessinfo.co.uk*

Nominet UK, Minerva House, Edmund Halley Road, Oxford Science Park, Oxford OX4 4DQ. Tel: 01865 332244. *www.nominet.org.uk*

Northern Ireland Environment Agency. *www.ni-environment.gov.uk*. *www.doeni.gov.uk/niea/waste-home.htm* (waste regulations)

Number 10 (all government departments). *www.number10.gov.uk/the-coalition/the-government*

Office for Harmonization in the Internal Market (OHIM), Avenida de Europa 4, E-03008 Alicante, Spain. Tel: 00 34 96 513 9100. *http://oami. europa.eu*

Office for National Statistics. *www.statistics.gov.uk*

Office of Fair Trading, Fleetbank House, 2–6 Salisbury Square, London EC4Y 8JX. Tel: 08457 22 44 99. Publications: 0800 389 3158. *www.oft.gov.uk*. (But for consumer advice, information on specific consumer rights or to make a consumer complaint against a trader, contact the Consumer Direct advice service on 08454 04 05 06. *www.consumerdirect.gov.uk*)

Patent agent (to find one): consider a member of the Chartered Institute of Patent Attorneys or contact the Institute of Patentees and Inventors (see separate entries).

PayPlan. Tel: 0800 280 2816. *www.payplan.com*

Planning officer: contact the planning department of the local authority (district, borough, unitary or metropolitan) for your area. See *The Phone Book* under the name of your authority.

PLUS Markets, 33 Queen Street, London EC4R 1BR. Tel: 020 7429 7800. *www.plusmarketsgroup.com*

Postcomm, Hercules House, 6 Hercules Road, London SE1 7DB. Tel: 020 7593 2100. *www.psc.gov.uk*

Prince's Initiative for Mature Enterprise (PRIME), Tavis House, 1–6 Tavistock Square, London WC1H 9NA. Helpline: 0800 783 1904. *http://prime.org.uk*

Prince's Trust, The, 18 Park Square East, London NW1 4LH. Tel: 020 7543 1234 or Freephone: 0800 842 842. *www.princes-trust.org.uk*

Professional Contractors' Group, Heathrow Boulevard, 280 Bath Road, West Drayton UB7 0DQ. Tel: 020 8897 9970. *www.pcg.org.uk*

Public Service Mutuals. Tel: 0845 165 5545. *www.co-operative.coop/corporate/ Public-Service-Mutuals-/what-we-do*

Recruitment and Employment Confederation, 15 Welbeck Street, London W1G 9XT. Tel: 020 7009 2100. *www.rec.uk.com*

Regional Development Agency (RDA), England's RDAs are due to be closed by March 2012. In the meantime, contact Business Link or find contact details for your local RDA on this web site: *www.englandsrdas.com*

Royal Institution of Chartered Surveyors (RICS), Contact Centre, Surveyor

Court, Westwood Way, Coventry CV4 8JE. Tel: 0870 333 1600. *www.rics. org*. Find a surveyor: *www.rics.org/findasurveyor*

Royal Mail. To contact your local business sales centre tel: 08457 950950. *www.royalmail.com*

Rural Development Programme for England, Temple Quay House (Zone 2/18), 2 The Square, Bristol BS1 6EB. Tel: 0117 372 3634. *www.rdpenetwork. org.uk*

Safe Home Ordering Protection Scheme (SHOPS) (formerly the Mail Order Protection Scheme), 18a King Street, Maidenhead SL6 1EF. Tel: 01628 641930. *www.shops-uk.org.uk*

Scottish Enterprise. To find local office, see *Phone Book* or tel: 0845 607 8787. *www.scottish-enterprise.com*

Scottish Environment Protection Agency, SEPA Corporate Office, Erskine Court, Castle Business Park, Stirling FK9 4TR. Tel: 01786 457700. *www.sepa.org.uk*

Shell *Live*WIRE, Design Works, William Street, Felling, Gateshead NE10 0JP. Tel: 0845 757 3252. *www.shell-livewire.org*

Small Firms Enterprise Development Initiative (SFEDI), Business Incubation Centre, Durham Way South, Aycliffe Industrial Park, County Durham DL5 6XP. Tel: 0845 467 3218. *www.sfedi.co.uk*. Provides learning and skills support for small and home-based business owners.

Solicitor (to find one): look in *Yellow Pages* or for a list of their members in your area, see separate entries for the Law Societies.

Start-Up Britain. *www.startupbritain.org*

StartUp Saturday. *http://startupsaturday.co.uk/*

Tax adviser (to find one): for tax compliance work consider a member of the Association of Taxation Technicians or Chartered Institute of Taxation (see separate entries). For advice, consider a member of the Chartered Institute of Taxation.

Telephone Preference Service (TPS), DMA House, 70 Margaret Street, London W1W 8SS. TPS Registration line: 0845 070 0707. *www.tpsonline.org.uk*

Trading standards offices: contact your local council.

UK Border Agency. Tel: 0300 123 4699. *www.ukba.homeoffice.gov.uk*

UK Business Incubation, Faraday Wharf, Aston Science Park, Holt Street, Birmingham B7 4BB. Tel: 0121 250 3538. *www.ukbi.co.uk*

UK Science Park Association, Chesterford Research Park, Little Chesterford, Cambridge CB10 1XL. Tel: 01799 532050. *www.ukspa.org.uk*

UK Trade and Invest Information Centre, Europa Building, 450 Argyle Street, Glasgow G2 8LH. Tel: 020 7215 8000. *www.ukti.gov.uk*. This is a government organization that supports businesses trading internationally.

Valuation Office Agency. Tel: 0845 602 2010. *www.voa.gov.uk*. During 2011, business rates information will be moving to the Business Link web site and council tax and rent office information will be moving to DirectGov (see separate entries).

Water UK, 1 Queen Anne's Gate, London SW1H 9BT. Tel: 020 7344 1844. *www.water.org.uk*

Welsh Assembly Government, Cathays Park, Cardiff CF10 3NQ. Tel: 0845 010 3300. *http://wales.gov.uk*

■ Department for Education and Skills. *http://wales.gov.uk/about/ civilservice/directorates/educationandskills/?lang=en*

■ Department for Business, Enterprise, Technology and Science. *http:// wales.gov.uk/about/civilservice/directorates/bets/?lang=en*

Young Enterprise UK, Peterley House, Peterley Road, Oxford OX4 2TZ. Tel: 01865 776 845. *www.young-enterprise.org.uk*

Useful books and literature

As reference books:

Tolley's Capital Gains Tax 2011–12, £111.95 (LexisNexis)

Tolley's Corporation Tax 2011–12, £111.95 (LexisNexis)

Tolley's Value Added Tax 2011, £159.95 (LexisNexis)

Tolley's Employment Handbook, 25th edition, £115.00 (LexisNexis)

Tolley's National Insurance Contributions 2011–12, £109.95 (LexisNexis)

Tolley's Company Law Handbook, 19th edition, £108.00 (LexisNexis)

Business Development Series: Forming a Limited Company by Patricia Clayton, £15.99 (Kogan Page)

The Company Secretary's Desktop Guide by Roger Mason, £18.99 (Thorogood)

The Company Secretary's Handbook by Helen Ashton, £16.99 (Kogan Page)

Business Development Series: Essential Law for Your Business by Patricia Clayton, £15.99 (Kogan Page)

FT Guide to Personal Tax 2011–12 by Sara Williams and John Bloxham, £14.99 (Financial Times Prentice Hall) has a more detailed exposition of tax treatment for the sole trader, capital gains tax and dealing with self-assessment. Copies can be ordered by calling 020 7250 7010 or via the web site *www.taxguide.co.uk/content/buy-tax-guide-now*

Bankruptcy Explained by John McQueen, £14.95 (Bankruptcy Association)

Discipline and Grievances at Work, £4.95 (Advisory, Conciliation & Arbitration Service). Order from *www.acas.org.uk*

How to Market Your Business: A Practical Guide to Advertising, PR, Selling and Direct and Online Marketing by Dave Patten, £12.99 (Kogan Page)

The Business Plan Workbook by Colin Barrow, Paul Barrow and Robert Brown, £19.95 (Kogan Page)

Tolley's Employer's Pay and Benefits Manual, £169 (LexisNexis)

Index